DO NOT REMOVE
CARDS FROM POCKET

A FAUSTIAN BARGAIN

U.S. Intervention in the
Nicaraguan Elections and
American Foreign Policy in the
Post–Cold War Era

William I. Robinson

*with Afterwords by Alejandro Bendaña
and Robert A. Pastor*

Westview Press
BOULDER • SAN FRANCISCO • OXFORD

Copyright © 1992 by Westview Press, Inc.

Published in 1992 in the United States of America by Westview Press, Inc., 5500 Central
Avenue, Boulder, Colorado 80301-2847, and in the United Kingdom by Westview Press, 36
Lonsdale Road, Summertown, Oxford OX2 7EW

Library of Congress Cataloging-in-Publication Data
Robinson, William I.
    A Faustian bargain : U.S. intervention in the Nicaraguan elections
and American foreign policy in the post–Cold War era / William
I. Robinson.
        p.   cm.
    Includes bibliographical references (p.   ) and index.
    ISBN 0-8133-8233-5 — ISBN 0-8133-8234-3 (pbk.)
    1. United States—Foreign relations—Nicaragua.   2. Nicaragua—
Foreign relations—United States.   3. Nicaragua—Politics and
government—1979–   4. Elections—Nicaragua—History—20th century.
I. Title.
E183.8.N5R64   1992
327.7307285—dc20   92-4578
                                                                             CIP

Printed and bound in the United States of America

The paper used in this publication meets the requirements
of the American National Standard for Permanence of Paper
for Printed Library Materials Z39.48-1984.

10   9   8   7   6   5   4   3   2   1

· CONTENTS ·

Democracy in Nicaragua, U.S. Intervention, and
the Electoral Outcome, 151
U.S. Intervention, Authentic Democratization,
and Low-Intensity Democracy, 155

• ACKNOWLEDGMENTS •

This book is the fruit of the labor, sacrifice, and courage of a great many people. For those who must remain anonymous, the most important reward for their efforts, I am sure, is not being mentioned by name in an acknowledgments section, but having the truth see the light of day. Words cannot describe the contribution—to the truths exposed in this work and to the cause of truth and social justice in general—made by these selfless people, who are, all of them, veritable coauthors of this work. I ask these people to judge if, in the pages that follow, I have lived up to the task at hand and the responsibilities that I assumed.

Beyond the anonymous contributors, there are many people whose support and assistance are deeply appreciated. I owe a very special thanks to Kent Norsworthy, who read the manuscript during several phases of its preparation and offered never-ending support, critical advice, editorial assistance, and, above all, friendship. The quarterly magazine *Covert Action Information Bulletin*, an invaluable publication that I recommend to anyone interested in U.S. government actions and policies at home and abroad, provided critical assistance. Its tireless and talented co-editor, Louis Wolf, deserves special recognition for his contributions as well as personal thanks for his support and friendship. I am also indebted to my good friend David MacMichael, who read the manuscript and offered invaluable, chapter-by-chapter editorial recommendations. Nelson Valdés read the manuscript and gave needed encouragement during the writing phase. Malcolm Gordon, Tom Barry, and Beth Sims (the latter two from the Inter-American Hemispheric Resource Center in Albuquerque, New Mexico) also read the manuscript and made critical suggestions. I am grateful for the interest shown by Roger Morris in this project, the encouragement he gave throughout the writing phase, and his special help in securing a publisher. I appreciate the very insightful comments made to me by Noam Chomsky on the final version of the draft manuscript. Special thanks also to Alejandro, Francisco, Genardo, David, and the other *muchachos*. Thanks to Roma Arellano, Barbara Kohl, and the Latin America Data Base of the University of New Mexico for their technical assistance. I enjoyed working with Barbara Ellington, senior acquisitions editor at Westview Press, and with Martha Leggett, project editor, and thank them both for their diligence in working with me on the manuscript and the various stages of production. Financial assistance provided by the Latin American Institute at the University of New Mexico for a portion of the research is also gratefully acknowledged. The content of this book is, of course, my sole responsibility.

x ▪ ACKNOWLEDGMENTS

There is no doubt that I could not have written this book if it were not for the encouragement, patience, and love provided by my wife, Gioconda; son, Amaru; and daughter, Tamara.

Beyond individual contributions, I want to stress that this book is an undertaking of the Center for International Studies (CEI). The CEI was established in Nicaragua in April 1990 to carry out comparative research and documentation in the field of international relations, with special attention to the possibility of peaceful political transformation in the Third World and the impact of global changes on these processes. The center was formed by a group of foreign policy experts in conjunction with the Central American University in Managua. The CEI provided the institutional sponsorship for this project as well as financial assistance and documentation. Its team, including directors Alejandro Bendaña and Víctor Hugo Tinoco, and Niurka Passafacqua Olivera and Ana Clemencia Teller, among others, contributed to the effort that produced this book.

This book is truly a collective product of the Nicaraguan people, who made a unique, humane, and profoundly inspiring revolution and who have defended their dignity in the face of an unjust war and endless hardships. It is to the Nicaraguan people, and especially to all those who gave their lives struggling for a better future for Nicaragua, that this book is dedicated.

William I. Robinson

The International Significance of Nicaragua

"As President of the Nicaraguan people and as a Sandinista leader, I take pride—and all Sandinista militants can take pride—in the greatest victory," declared Daniel Ortega. It was 6:00 A.M., February 26, 1990. The day before, Nicaraguans had gone to the polls, and by dawn enough tallies were in from the country's voting booths for the Supreme Electoral Council (SEC) to announce that the opposition had won the elections by a margin of some 54 to 42 percent. Ortega was giving his concession speech, and the eyes of the world were riveted on Nicaragua. "Today, February 26, opens a new path for Nicaragua, like that which we opened on July 19, 1979," he said. "In this new path the war and the contras will disappear, and national interests will prevail over interventionist policies."[1]

The election results shocked almost everyone. In Nicaragua they stunned both the Sandinista National Liberation Front (FSLN), which had come to power a decade earlier at the helm of a popular revolution, and the National Opposition Union (UNO), the U.S.-backed anti-Sandinista coalition. In the United States, although the opposition victory surprised even the Bush administration, U.S. policymakers gloated over the results, hailing them as a "victory for democracy."

The Nicaraguan elections were the most observed in world history and have stood out as a historic precedent in Latin America for the peaceful transfer of power by a revolutionary movement that came to power by armed struggle. U.S. involvement in those elections has been seen by some as a laudable effort that succeeded in bringing about the democratization of Nicaragua and that should therefore set a pattern in U.S. foreign policy. But behind that involvement lay newly evolving and more intricate modes of U.S. intervention in sovereign nations. The U.S. role in the Nicaraguan electoral process, both public and private, covert and overt, in fact constituted one of the most sophisticated and extensive foreign operations launched in the first year of the Bush administration. Much of that foreign policy initiative, how-

1

ever, has remained shrouded in secrecy. As the demise of the cold war opens new possibilities for the attainment of democracy in the Third World outside of superpower relations, the international experience of Nicaragua in the past decade merits the deepest reflection. I hope that this book will contribute to such reflection by bringing to light dimensions of U.S. involvement in the Nicaraguan elections heretofore unknown to the public.

Before I proceed, I must offer several caveats. U.S. involvement deeply influenced the electoral process, but to what extent it determined the outcome itself is open to question. The Sandinistas entered the electoral process in a situation of major disadvantage. Throughout the 1980s, Nicaragua was under relentless external pressures—military, economic, political, diplomatic—that took a heavy toll on the incumbent party. In the final years of their rule, the Sandinistas presided over a desperate economic crisis marked by hyperinflation and a tumultuous drop in living standards. Nicaragua faced increasing international isolation and, given the breakup of the socialist bloc, dim prospects for international assistance without a reconciliation of relations with the United States. Nicaraguans were thirsty for a change, and it should not have come as a surprise that the electorate voted for change. What is remarkable is not that the Sandinistas were voted out of power but that, given the enormous international mobilization of resources by the United States following on the heels of a decade of U.S. warfare, the FSLN received 42 percent of the vote.

In assessing how U.S. involvement affected the outcome of the elections, we must not strip Nicaraguan actors of their own historical and social relevance. The outcome of the voting was a product of Nicaragua's history, including the thought and policies of the Sandinistas, who were influential autonomous actors. Endogenous factors were not a by-product of U.S. intervention. Nevertheless, whether the outcome would have been different had the United States not intervened in the Nicaraguan elections is less important than that the results were determined, not on election day, but in the ten years of conflict with the United States that preceded the elections.

The Nicaraguan electoral process grew simultaneously out of the internal dynamic of Nicaraguan society and the Sandinista Revolution and the external dynamic of the U.S.-imposed war. Insofar as much of Nicaraguan history has been a struggle for national identity in the face of foreign domination, we would be hard-pressed to separate the external dimensions of the Nicaraguan election process from the domestic ones. Therefore, an analysis of the elections requires critically examining the revolutionary process, the Sandinista programs, and the Sandinistas' electoral strategy, and it requires recognizing that the revolutionary process was inextricably tied up with the conditions that the prolonged warfare and conflict with the United States imposed on the internal political system. For instance, with the 1979 triumph over the Somoza dictatorship, the FSLN emerged for the first time from guerrilla clandestinity. But it never got the chance to shed the structures of internal organization that grew out of clandestinity and to make the transition to a modern political party operating under normal conditions of civic or electoral struggle because in early 1981 the Reagan administration declared war on Nicaragua. The Sandinistas were forced to organize and lead a national defense effort that was conducive to maintaining a centralization of powers, command-oriented political behavior, and the stifling of internal party democracy. Only in the framework of wartime conditions can the FSLN's political deficiencies be analyzed. These same conditions shaped and propelled the electoral process. The locus of analysis in this book is neither external nor internal factors but rather how these factors are *interwoven*.

This book does not attempt to provide an overall analysis of the Nicaraguan elections. Rather, it is about U.S. intervention in those elections. The concluding chapter does refer to the FSLN electoral strategy and to other powerful factors in the outcome of the vote. But, again, asking if U.S. intervention was the determinant of the outcome phrases the issue in the wrong manner. From the U.S. perspective, the elections were optimally being held at a time of great duress for the FSLN leadership, and electoral intervention was simply the continuation of ten years of war strategy. From the Nicaraguan perspective, the factors that guided the electorate in making its decision were heavily influenced by events in the years preceding the electoral process.

This book exposes and analyzes U.S. involvement in the elections, which included large-scale support for the anti-Sandinista opposition. But as we shall see, the U.S. role went far beyond official U.S. funding for the opposition. U.S. involvement included covert tactics and secret transactions, international networks, propaganda campaigns, military aggression, and multidimensional political and psychological operations. At the same time, the FSLN enjoyed the support of external forces, an issue that could well be the subject of another book. In several of the chapters I make mention of this support and its relevance to the theme of this book—U.S. involvement in the elections.

The crux of the issue, however, is not the external support that was provided to one or another political group in Nicaragua. Rather, the issue is *external intervention in the electoral process*. This intervention was solely and wholly an undertaking of the United States—the hegemonic, intervening foreign power. To delve into a quantitative examination of which group in Nicaragua received more monetary contributions or material donations from abroad (although I do address this in several chapters) is to confuse external linkages of nationally based political forces with external intervention in the affairs of a sovereign nation. Moreover, such an examination obscures a phenomenon clearly demonstrated in this book: The Nicaraguan elections were a contest, not between the Sandinistas and their domestic political opposition, but between the Nicaraguan Revolution and the United States.

* * *

This book is put together on the basis of three types of sources. The first type is public documentation, whether government documents, press reports, or other materials in the public domain and in the reach of investigators. The second type comprises documentation prepared for private use, which I obtained through the course of the study, such as internal memorandums.

The third type is direct interviews with representatives of the different actors: the U.S. government and "private U.S. organizations" (including sources from the State Department, the White House, the National Endowment for Democracy [NED], the private groups that worked with the U.S. government, and intelligence organs), the international observers, the Nicaraguan opposition, and the Sandinistas. Many of these sources provided information over the course of a three-year period (1988–1990) on the condition of anonymity, with the understanding that they were speaking on background or off the record and in full confidence that their positions would not be compromised. It is not only out of adherence to the journalistic ethic but also out of respect for these sources that I generally limit reference to information from them to a mention of which of the four categories of protagonist they fit.

This work is not intended to be an exhaustive study of the U.S. role in the Nicaraguan electoral process. That role was, at best, surreptitious, and there are still many gaps shrouded in secrets and classified files. To wait for all of these details to become declassified, or revealed through extended investigation, could take decades. I have not included information provided by confidential sources when it could not be cross-checked or supported by other available evidence. I hope that future investigators will uncover enough evidence to make these details public. The extensive use of footnotes will point investigators and researchers in the right direction.

*   *   *

In presenting a detailed reconstruction of U.S. intervention in the elections, this book might appear to be painting a conspiratorial picture. Webster's dictionary defines the word *conspiracy* as "a combination of persons for an evil purpose; a plot." Whether the U.S. intervention in the Nicaraguan electoral process was for an "evil purpose" is a matter of value judgment, and those making the judgment will do so on the basis of personal, social, or historical identification with one or another of the groups involved. But there is no doubt that U.S. involvement in the electoral process was *not* a coincidental convergence of the independent decisions and programs of U.S. governmental and private agencies and the resources they brought to bear on the electoral process. This involvement was a calculated "combination of persons" and resources. There were clearly defined goals and methodologies that brought protagonists and their resources into conscious coordination. The term I have chosen to use in this book to make reference to this coordinated campaign is the *U.S. electoral intervention project*.

I do not wish to imply, however, that this combination of persons and resources in a coordinated campaign meant that the United States acted harmoniously. To the contrary, the U.S. intervention was replete with all of the endless "turf" fights, bureaucratic infighting, interagency disputes, and individual rivalries and conflicts characteristic of U.S. foreign policy operations. In addition, different aspects of the electoral intervention project were clearly carried out by different individuals and institutions acting autonomously from others. But just as the whole is greater than the sum of the parts, so, too, the intervention project was qualitatively superior overall to its component aspects. I do make reference to differences and disputes among the U.S. agents where they are relevant to the reconstruction of the intervention project. But, again, this book has limited boundaries, outside of which falls the dynamic of rivalries and competing positions internal to the community of U.S. actors. Moreover, the point here is that despite internal rivalries, contradictions, and weaknesses, the United States successfully carried through the operation because it managed to mobilize vastly superior resources in the campaign against Nicaragua.

Another comment on language: I frequently use the term *agent*, or *operative*, to describe different U.S. individuals or groups involved in the intervention operation. Given the changes in U.S. foreign policy, and in particular the shift from "covert" to "overt" in the form of U.S. intervention (as analyzed in Chapter 1), I use this term in a context larger than that of an employee of one of the U.S. intelligence agencies carrying out a clandestine mission. Although these kinds of "classical" agents were very much involved in the electoral intervention project, I have broadened the term to mean representatives of U.S. institutions who consciously represented these institutions in pursuit of clearly defined intervention objectives. In other words, "operative" (or "agent") refers to those individuals consciously acting as part of the U.S. foreign policy operation and representing one or another institution charged with executing aspects of that operation, regardless of whether these institutions were intelligence organs or these individuals were classic undercover agents.

The Nicaraguan opposition during the electoral process is treated in this book within the context of its relation to the U.S. foreign policy operation. The opposition was composed of diverse groups and individuals with different interests and distinguishing political projects. The point here is that there was a convergence between the anti-Sandinista Nicaraguan opposition and U.S. foreign policy operations. But this was not a convergence between equals or among independent actors. Rather, it was between a senior partner and a junior partner that took on the character of a subordinate. If as a result the opposition assumes the profile of a marionette in this book, that is because it did behave as a marionette of U.S. policy (during the electoral campaign as well as during the U.S. war against Nicaragua).

I have divided the book into eight chapters. In Chapter 1 I analyze the origins, characteristics, and development of U.S. foreign policy as they relate to the Nicaraguan case, focusing particularly on the introduction of political operations, the emergence of the NED and its "promotion of democracy" as a novel component of foreign policy, and the new electoral intervention. Chapter 2 presents the events that characterized U.S.-Nicaraguan relations in the 1980s, including the development of U.S. policy toward Nicaragua, the transitions from the Carter to the Reagan to the Bush administrations, Sandinista policies and strategies in the face of U.S. hostilities, and the Central American peace negotiations. Chapters 3 through 7, the core of the study, examine the functional aspects of the U.S. role, the nuts and bolts of electoral intervention. Here I name the protagonists, reveal hitherto unpublished materials, and expose and reconstruct the actions of those involved in the U.S. project. In Chapter 8 I explore the impact the U.S. role might have had on the outcome of the elections and on democracy in Nicaragua as well as the precedent-setting implications for U.S. foreign policy, among other issues addressed by way of conclusion. As the book's subtitle indicates, however, my objective is less to draw conclusions than to document the untold story of U.S. involvement in the Nicaraguan elections. This documentation speaks for itself.

Following the text are two guest commentaries, one by Alejandro Bendaña, secretary general of the Nicaraguan Foreign Ministry under the Sandinista government and now director of the Center for International Studies in Managua, and the other by Robert A. Pastor, the Carter administration's director of Latin American and Caribbean affairs of the National Security Council and now professor of political science at Emory University. Both of these men played important roles in the Nicaraguan elections, Bendaña as a member of the FSLN National Campaign Committee and Pastor as executive secretary of the Council of Freely Elected Heads of Government, which sent a team to observe the electoral process, under the chairmanship of Jimmy Carter. Anticipating that this book would generate controversy, I invited Bendaña and Pastor to provide critical commentary from two different perspectives. I expect that the combination of the main text and the guest commentaries will set broad parameters for debate on the scholarly and political issues raised in this book.

• ONE •

The New Intervention

The beginning of wisdom is calling things by their right names.

—Confucius

We, of America, have discovered that we, too, possess the supreme governing capacity, capacity not merely to govern ourselves at home, but that great power that in all ages has made the difference between the great and the small nations, the capacity to govern men wherever they are found.

—Elihu Root[1]

"If the issue can be democracy, then we can win this battle."[2] The "issue" being referred to was how to package U.S. foreign policy toward Nicaragua in 1989 for the public. And the "battle" was the decade-long campaign the United States had waged against the Sandinista government in Nicaragua. The words were as fitting for U.S.-Nicaraguan relations as the 1980s came to a close as they were for the person from whose office they came, Carl Gershman, the president of the NED.

Ten years earlier, most U.S. citizens had not known where, or even what, Nicaragua was. But that tiny Central American country of 3.5 million people was catapulted in the 1980s to the front page of U.S. newspapers. The Reagan administration had chosen Central America as its experimental theater of operations for the new cold war, and Nicaragua was the "test case." "If we cannot defend ourselves there [in Central America]," said Ronald Reagan in his watershed speech to a joint session of Congress in 1983, "then we cannot expect to prevail elsewhere. Our credibility would collapse, our alliances would crumble, and the safety of our homeland would be put at jeopardy."[3] The watchword was "national security," and the threat was from the "evil empire," from "communist expansionism" seeking a beachhead in the U.S. backyard. The Sandinistas, according to Reagan, would "export subversion" all the way to Harlington, Texas.

So the United States launched a multifaceted campaign against Nicaragua that would eventually become the major foreign policy debacle of the 1980s.

7

The United States created the "contras," a fifteen thousand–strong army that became notorious for its brutal human rights violations, and guided it in pillaging Nicaragua. The United States provided the contras with assassination manuals, mined Nicaragua's harbors, bombed its airports, and ceaselessly threatened to launch a full-scale invasion. Despite attempts to justify these actions, the United States failed to gain the moral high ground. In 1986, the U.N. International Court of Justice found the United States guilty, on multiple counts, of violating international law in its policy toward Nicaragua. Much of the world community as well as the U.S. public condemned U.S. policy as not only illegal but also profoundly immoral.

By the time Reagan left office in 1989, the "evil empire" was fully engaged in *perestroika* and *glasnost*. A new détente set in, and the cold war faded out. Central America and other regional "hot spots" were receding as theaters for superpower confrontation. Nonetheless, anti-*Sandinismo* did not recede in concert with anticommunism in the late 1980s. Washington's goal remained the destruction of the Sandinistas. But the rhetoric and the means changed: It was now not the defeat of a communist-Soviet-totalitarian threat to national security that the United States was after in Nicaragua; it was the establishment of democracy. Ronald Reagan departed from the White House and George Bush moved in; exit the cold warriors and procontra fanatics, and enter the gentlemen from Washington promoting that benevolent and universal value, democracy.

The cold warriors gave way to the political operatives of the "democracy network," who launched their global "democracy offensive." Now the goal of policy was democracy in the Philippines. Where the United States in the name of anticommunism had propped up the Marcos dictatorship for fifteen years, it now facilitated the electoral victory of the "democratic" Corazon Aquino. In Chile, where the Central Intelligence Agency (CIA) had staged a bloody military coup against Salvador Allende's democratically elected socialist government in 1973 and had installed the Pinochet military dictatorship, the United States now promoted a "democratic" alternative to its own creation. In Panama, longtime CIA asset Manuel Noriega had to be removed to "restore democracy."

Everyone claims to support democracy. And the person who succeeds in wearing its banner carries the moral high ground. But what does it mean when the language of democracy bears no relation to actual practice or promotion of democracy? And when the rhetoric of democracy becomes an ideological smokescreen for antidemocratic policies and practices and for secret, illegal intervention abroad? We can argue endlessly about the concept of democracy in the abstract, but of more importance is what U.S. foreign policy does, not what it claims to be. Such policy undertakings are the subject of this book.

U.S. involvement in the 1990 Nicaraguan elections was advertised and sold to the public as a benevolent and impartial contribution that helped the Nicaraguan people exercise their right to choose their political destiny through the ballot. But the U.S. role was in fact blatantly interventionist in nature and was perhaps the most extensive, complex, and sophisticated foreign policy operation the Bush administration undertook in its first year in office. Far from being a departure from U.S. foreign policy in recent decades, the U.S. electoral intervention project in Nicaragua evolved out of that policy. It constituted a shift in focus, from the "contra" phase to the electoral phase, of a single, evolving policy. To understand how this came about, let me sketch the development of recent U.S. foreign policy and in particular the conceptual/ strategic framework in which policy toward Nicaragua developed.

WAR AS POLITICS
AND POLITICS AS WAR

Politics is the marshaling of human beings to support or oppose causes. Political warfare is the marshaling of human support, or opposition, in order to achieve victory in war or in unbloody conflicts as serious as war. . . . *Such marshaling must be the objective of all international action, from the delivery of public speeches to the dropping of bombs. Whether it does so overtly or covertly, political warfare must provide to foreigners true, concrete reasons why they ought to consider themselves on "our side," and concrete inducements for them to significantly enhance our side's chances.*
—Angelo M. Codevilla[4]

Despite the myth of a peaceful, isolationist past, U.S. history is one of continued conquest of other peoples and nations. In its two centuries as an independent nation, the United States has waged some 175 declared and undeclared wars around the world and has sent troops across other countries' borders on an average of once a year.[5] U.S. expansion westward involved the invasion and annexation of half of Mexico. The modern history of Central America and the Caribbean is an account of continual U.S. armed intervention and of the annexation of territories—Puerto Rico, the Canal Zone, Guatemala. In the Pacific, the conquest of Hawaii was an incident of the Spanish-American War, and the seizure of the Philippines was an aftereffect of that same war. After World War II, the United States, under the rationale of "defending the Free World," unabashedly filled the vacuum left by the collapse of the old colonial empires to deploy its military forces and political agents around the globe. That deployment has involved the use of military force more than two hundred times.[6]

Although the United States had emerged from World War II as the dominant world power, its hegemony was shaken in the 1960s and 1970s by nationalist revolutions in the Third World, culminating in the U.S. defeat in Vietnam and the subsequent collapse of the client regime of the shah in Iran. For a period after the defeat in Indochina, the Ford and Carter administrations experimented with global power-sharing with the other Western nations (Trilateralism) and with the détente with the Soviet Union begun under Richard Nixon by Henry Kissinger.

For the U.S. right wing, wedded to the post–World War II concept of "the American Century," this deterioration of global hegemony, the Pax Americana, was heresy. In control of the Reagan administration, resurgent hegemonists launched a worldwide counteroffensive against liberation movements and nationalist Third World governments, against the "evil empire," against all things un-"American." This Reagan Doctrine, an aggressive global campaign to recover U.S. influence where it had been lost in the preceding two decades, was backed by the biggest peacetime military buildup in U.S. history and by a redeployment of U.S. military, paramilitary, intelligence, and political forces around the globe. *Low-intensity conflict* entered the U.S. foreign policy vocabulary in the 1980s as a term for new modalities of engagement against nationalist and revolutionary movements and governments.[7] The United States fomented and directed counterrevolutionary insurgencies in Nicaragua, Afghanistan, Angola, and elsewhere to "roll back" nationalist and revolutionary movements and governments that sought to establish independence from Washington.

The oft-cited Santa Fe document, drafted in the summer of 1980 by conservative Republican officials as a blueprint for the new U.S. foreign policy, sounded the bell: "War, not peace, is the norm in international affairs. Containment of the Soviet Union is not enough. Detente is dead. Survival demands a new U.S. foreign policy. America must seize the initiative or perish. An integrated global foreign policy is essential. . . . A worldwide counterprojection of American power is in the offing."[8]

As U.S. strategists revamped foreign policy, they carried out systematic analyses of why the United States had lost in Vietnam and developed new political and military doctrines for the "counterprojection of American power." They argued that although the United States had concentrated on preparing for conventional or nuclear war with the Soviet Union in Europe, the vast majority of the conflicts in which the United States had engaged since World War II were unconventional encounters with "Soviet proxies" in the Third World. In conventional warfare, superior firepower predominates. But in unconventional conflicts, superior firepower in itself is not the deciding factor. Strategists concluded, therefore, that the United States had failed because it had not recognized that unconventional (i.e., revolutionary) war is often more a political than a military undertaking.

In Vietnam the United States enjoyed vast conventional military superiority, won most of the battles, but lost the war precisely because the outcome of the war was determined by imperfectly understood political variables. Conventional military supremacy did alter those variables, but the military apparatus was still only a means to achieve political ends. U.S. strategists rediscovered, as they do periodically, the famed nineteenth-century Prussian military theorist Karl von Clausewitz and his axiom that "war is the extension of politics by other means." They studied modern insurgent and counterinsurgent experiences, ranging from British and French attempts at suppression of nationalist uprisings in their colonies to the revolutionary campaigns of Mao Zedong, Vo Nguyen Giap, and Ché Guevara.

The strategists drew several essential conclusions regarding future U.S. participation in unconventional war and then applied these conclusions to Third World conflict situations, including Nicaragua. First, the target of such

U.S. campaigns must be the population itself, the minds of the people rather than the enemy's military forces. Second, in this undertaking U.S. policymakers have to take into account the specific culture, sensibilities, and history of the target population as well as the capabilities of the revolutionary forces. Campaigns against other countries are to be tailor-made to suit the particular circumstances of each foreign policy operation. Third, it is not enough to try destroying revolutionary forces; a counterrevolutionary movement has to be created, legitimized, and presented to the target population as a viable alternative to the government to be overthrown or to the movement to be defeated. Fourth, new forms of political and military organization have to be developed. (This conclusion helped lead to the formation of the NED, among other organizations.) Fifth, interventionist projects can be sustained only if there are strong U.S. constituencies that support the effort. These constituencies, too, have to be garnered and the effort legitimized in their eyes.

These "lessons" of Vietnam led to a simple, yet fundamental premise: The ultimate objective of unconventional engagements is to achieve the political, not merely the military, defeat of the enemy. "Low-intensity conflict is revolutionary and counterrevolutionary warfare" is the frequently quoted characterization made by Colonel John Waghelstein, former head of U.S. military advisers in El Salvador. "It is *total war* at the grassroots level—one that uses *all* of the weapons of total war, including political, economic and psychological warfare, the military aspect being a distant fourth in many cases."[9]

This conceptualization confused analysts on both sides during the U.S. campaign against Nicaragua in the 1980s, because the proxy military aggression through the contras was the most pronounced, and devastating, feature of the war and because U.S. policy appeared to single-mindedly pursue the military defeat of the Sandinistas. "Low-intensity conflict," as it was introduced during the contra war, also proved a confusing term because for the victims of this type of warfare, such as Nicaraguans, there was nothing "low intensity" about it.[10]

The type of unconventional conflict in which the United States engaged against Nicaragua and other countries demanded heavy doses of political operations and of psychological warfare (known as PSYOPS, or psychological operations). The "failure to identify and assimilate the lessons of the chief defeats the United States has suffered internationally in the post War period [and] above all, the Vietnam War," pointed out a member of the National Security Council (NSC), reflected great U.S. weaknesses "at the psychological-political level of conflict."[11] And because low-intensity conflict is essentially a political battle between contending forces, it provided the logical doctrinal framework for overcoming these weaknesses. Starting in the early 1980s, the United States began reorganizing the apparatus of state and the instruments of foreign policy to enhance the capacity for sustained low-intensity conflict, political operations, and psychological warfare.[12] Central America was foremost in the attention of U.S. strategists. "In low-intensity conflict theaters such as Central America, there is scope for application of the full range of U.S. psychological-political capabilities," explained one of these strategists.[13]

From 1979 until the end of the Reagan administration in 1988, U.S. political and psychological operations against Nicaragua were often eclipsed by the military dimensions of the conflict. Nevertheless, political operations were broadly conducted. These fell into three categories: *political action*, described by U.S. strategists as "a full range of activities including certain kinds of multilateral diplomacy, support for foreign political parties or forces, and support for or work with international associations of various kinds"; *coercive diplomacy*, described as "diplomacy presupposing the use or threatened use of military force to achieve political objectives"; and *covert political warfare*, described as "the covert aspects of active measures, [including] support for insurgencies, operations against enemy alliances, influence operations, and black propaganda."[14] For its part, psychological warfare, as described by one NSC official, is the "handmaid" of political warfare, "the planned use of communications to influence human attitudes and behavior. It consists of political, military, and ideological actions conducted to create in target groups behavior, emotions, and attitudes that support the attainment of national objectives. [PSYOPS] will usually be carried out under the broader umbrella of U.S. national policy."[15]

NICARAGUA: THE WAR OF ATTRITION

If the quick destruction of the enemy is not possible, then one should concentrate on "wastage"—making the war more costly to him through laying waste to the enemy's territory, increasing the enemy's suffering, and wearing the enemy down in order to bring about a gradual exhaustion of his physical and moral position . . . to destroy his will by operations that have direct political repercussions.

—Karl von Clausewitz[16]

The 1980 Republican platform explicitly established the goal of overthrowing the Sandinista government, a goal already being quietly proposed by the Carter administration.[17] The defeat of the Nicaraguan Revolution became the cornerstone of the Reagan Central American policy and the test case for the Reagan Doctrine.

The U.S. strategy toward Nicaragua, from Reagan's virtual declaration of war in 1981 right through to the 1990 elections, was a process of attrition using multiple well-synchronized military, economic, political, diplomatic, psychological, and ideological pressures against the revolution. The contras, initially the remobilized remnants of Somoza's defeated National Guard, were unleashed on the Nicaraguan countryside, and they ground away at economic and social infrastructures and terrorized the rural population. Nicaragua was denied access to its established U.S. markets and eventually had all of its U.S. trade embargoed, while Washington used its influence in international lending agencies to cut Managua off from its normal sources of financing. U.S. diplomatic pressures, especially on European allies and Latin American nations, hampered Nicaragua's efforts to develop new markets and sources of credits. The constant threat of a direct U.S. invasion was used effectively to force Nicaragua to maintain high levels of defense mobilization and expenditure, to impose a war psychosis on the population, and to modify the behavior of different actors—the Nicaraguan government and population, the international community, the U.S. public—in ways conducive to the continuation of the attrition process.[18]

Washington expected that under the tremendous pressures on all fronts, the Sandinista government would eventually collapse or surrender—"Say uncle," as Reagan put it. The aim was to isolate, delegitimize, and suffocate the revolution to the point where it was no longer considered a viable political option in the eyes of the population or of other populations that might take inspiration from it. "Properly articulated, the failure [of the Nicaraguan Revolution]" to fulfill promised social changes "could serve as a powerful political message in other Latin American societies facing revolutionary warfare," said one architect of Reagan policy. "Of course, pointing out promises not fulfilled cannot stand alone. It must be part of a comprehensive and integrated political-military strategy."[19] It was necessary to defeat "the threat of a good example."

One of the striking features of the war of attrition was the way in which it adroitly exploited mistakes made by the Sandinista government and weaknesses in the revolution, manipulated raised expectations, and capitalized on legitimate grievances. One CIA manual prepared for use by the contras instructed anti-Sandinista forces to carefully determine "the needs and frustrations of the target groups" and to channel these into "generalized anti-government hostility." The population had to be led to identify the Sandinistas as "the cause of their frustration," and only through their elimination would there be respite from these frustrations and fulfillment of needs.[20] In this way, U.S. strategists sought to turn the revolution against itself, to warp its logic and undercut its internal cohesion. To paraphrase Régis Debray's 1960s comment on Latin American political struggles, the effort was to create a "*counter*revolution *within* the revolution."[21]

The attrition process sought to undermine the Sandinistas' broad social base and generate a social base for anti-Sandinista forces. It is not that the United States created all of the problems that the revolution faced (although it *did* create many of them). Rather, U.S. strategists demonstrated an uncanny ability to exploit problems and limitations stemming from objective conditions, and from Sandinista mistakes, to generate and mobilize anti-Sandinista constituencies. As the 1990 elections approached, the goal was to "harvest" ten years of attrition into an anti-Sandinista vote. The process of attrition laid the groundwork for the electoral intervention project, which was itself a complex and multidimensional undertaking in political warfare. The seeds of the Sandinistas' electoral defeat were planted, watered, and fertilized during a period of prolonged counterrevolutionary warfare. Electoral intervention was the harvest. The Sandinista government committed numerous mistakes during its tenure and adopted policies that contributed to its own electoral defeat, but these should be interpreted in the context of the dynamic of U.S. political warfare.

FROM THE CIA TO THE NED

The creation of the National Endowment for Democracy was part and parcel of the resurgence of intervention abroad and the development of low-intensity conflict doctrines. Those involved in the NED's creation were the same people who were developing overall U.S. foreign policy and who argued that an aggressive worldwide campaign should greatly expand the role of specialized political and psychological operations in foreign policy. They maintained that the CIA was ill-equipped to carry out the type of specialized political intervention required for the post-Vietnam recovery and expansion of U.S. influence.

The Truman administration created the CIA in the wake of World War II as a covert branch of the U.S. state in the cold war.[22] Since its inception, the CIA has carried out thousands of covert operations, overthrown countless governments, and killed hundreds of thousands of people, and millions more indirectly, as a result of its actions.[23] CIA political operations involved the creation and covert funding of allied political groups and individuals in target countries—media, political parties, trade unions, businesses, and associations.

At the height of the cold war in the 1950s and 1960s, despite occasional scandals and failures like the Bay of Pigs, the CIA enjoyed the respect of much of the U.S. public, and the full extent of its activities remained hidden from the international community. But during the 1970s, as many of its seamy covert operations became public, the CIA fell into disrepute. In 1974–1975, congressional investigations revealed the sordid underworld of CIA covert activity at home and abroad. Top-level CIA officers defected and exposed the history of overseas intrigues, and investigative journalists uncovered unsavory details of U.S. secret activities.[24] These revelations gave the lie to the high-minded sentiments that righteous U.S. leaders uttered about democracy, justice, and the rule of law. By the late 1970s, following the U.S. defeat in Indochina and the delegitimization of foreign intervention, the CIA had been badly discredited. In the United States, bipartisan and constituent support crumbled. In target countries abroad, association with CIA programs meant instant repudiation.

In addition to the stigma, there were other problems with CIA activities abroad. The CIA had proved adept at staging coups, conducting assassinations, and installing dictators. It achieved this stated goal in 1973 in Chile, for instance, when it orchestrated the military overthrow of the democratically elected government of Salvador Allende. In Guatemala, it was impeccably efficient in organizing the removal of the elected government of Jacobo Arbenz. The CIA showed similar proficiency in operations in Brazil, Iran, the Congo, the Philippines, Iraq, and dozens of other countries.[25]

Yet there was something clumsy about these operations. The political aftermath of covert operations seemed to create new, more complex, long-term problems for the United States. The CIA could destabilize quite well, but, its detractors argued, it could not create stability. Nearly four decades after the CIA overthrew the Arbenz government, Guatemala remained a cauldron of guerrilla insurgency, gross human rights violations, and social instability. The Pinochet regime lasted sixteen years but was an international pariah. Iran's nationalist prime minister, Mohammed Mossadegh, was ousted in the CIA-led coup of 1954 that installed the shah and recovered Iranian oil fields for Western petroleum companies. But despite twenty years on the throne, the Western-oriented shah was unable to sustain himself in the face of a rising Islamic fundamentalist movement, which rejected the nontraditional values for which he stood, and of popular struggles against his policies. CIA operations seemingly lacked sophistication and long-term vision. The CIA was not able to create stable governments or to mold structures in civil society itself that could provide long-term protection for a U.S.-dominated market economy and a pro-U.S. political program. Here, the capable hands of a political surgeon were needed, not the heavy hands of a paramilitary assassin.

The new, post-Vietnam breed of political professionals lobbied for the establishment of a new institution that would use sophisticated techniques, including elections, to achieve lasting results.[26] Thus, while CIA intervention continued, a more specialized, sophisticated entity with a focus on political operations and on a long-term vision of U.S. interests came into existence with the creation of the National Endowment for Democracy in 1983. This new entity would not only play the role of skillful political surgeon; it would also overcome the taint associated with the covert political operations that the CIA had been carrying out abroad. Specifically, the NED would take over much of the funding and political guidance for political parties, trade unions, business groups, news media, and civic organizations that the CIA had traditionally supplied.[27]

The idea was to create a further division of labor within the organs of U.S. foreign policy. The NED would not replace the CIA but would specialize in the overt development of political and civic formations, supplementing CIA covert activities and synchronizing with overall U.S. policy toward the country or region in question. Moreover, the seemingly public nature of the NED would allow the use of public relations techniques to an extent unprecedented in U.S. foreign policy. The NED, with its ideological underpinning of "promoting democracy," would be well equipped for rebuilding U.S. domestic consensus for political operations abroad.

PROJECT DEMOCRACY

The proposed campaign for democracy must be conceived in the broadest terms and must weave together a wide range of superficially disparate aspects of U.S. foreign policy, including the efforts of private groups. A democracy campaign should become an increasingly important and highly cost-effective component of . . . the defense effort of the United States and its allies.

—Raymond Gastil[28]

The NED initiative dates back to 1979, when a group of government officials, academicians, trade unionists, business leaders, and politicians connected to the U.S. foreign policy apparatus created the American Political Foundation (APF)[29] with funding from the United States Information Agency

(USIA) and from several private foundations.[30] Although New Right conservatives figured prominently in this effort, the APF brought together representatives from all of the dominant sectors of U.S. society, including both parties and leaders from labor and business.[31] The APF recommended in 1981 that a presidential commission examine "how the United States could promote democracy overseas."[32] The result was White House approval for Project Democracy.[33] The State Department then provided the APF with several grants, and the White House also gave funds out of a special presidential fund handled through the National Security Council.[34]

At its onset, Project Democracy was attached to the NSC and was supervised by Walter Raymond, Jr., a high-ranking CIA propaganda specialist who worked closely with Oliver North on covert projects, particularly anti-Sandinista propaganda campaigns.[35] Raymond had been assigned to the NSC in 1982 by CIA director William Casey as chief of the NSC Intelligence Directorate. In 1983, Raymond became director of the Office of International Communications and Public Diplomacy at the NSC, where he took direct control of the NED project.[36] "Overt political action," explained Raymond, could help achieve foreign policy objectives by providing "support to various institutions [and] . . . the development of networks and personal relationships with key people."[37]

In a memorandum to national security adviser William Clark, Raymond explained that the creation of the NED as a "vehicle for quasi-public/private funds" would fill a "key gap" in U.S. foreign policy—it would be a "new art form."[38] Raymond and his staff at the NSC worked closely with conservative Democratic congressman Dante Fascell of Florida. Fascell, a founding member of the APF and later an NED board member, chaired the House Foreign Affairs Committee, which would draft the legislation creating the NED, and organized support for the project within Congress.[39]

In June 1982, Ronald Reagan, in a speech before the British Parliament, announced that the United States would pursue a major new program to help "foster the infrastructure of democracy around the world." Shortly thereafter, Reagan signed National Security Decision Directive 77 (NSDD 77), which laid out a comprehensive framework for employing political operations and psychological warfare in U.S. foreign policy. NSDD 77 focused on three aspects of Project Democracy.[40] One was dubbed "public diplomacy"—psychological operations aimed at winning support for U.S. foreign policy among the U.S. public and the international community. The directive defined "public diplomacy" as "those actions of the U.S. Government designed to generate support for our national security objectives." An office of public diplomacy (OPD) operating out of the White House was established.[41] The General Accounting Office (GAO) ruled OPD an illegal domestic propaganda operation in 1988, and the Iran-contra investigations revealed a number of serious violations of law by the office.[42]

A second aspect laid out in the NSC directive was an expansion of covert operations, and a third was the creation of a "quasi-governmental institute" to ensure that the NED's activities would be directed at "support [for] United

States policies and interests relative to national security."[43] This led to the formal incorporation of the NED by Congress in November 1983.[44] Constitutive documents describe the NED as an "independent" and "private" organization. Close scrutiny, however, reveals that structurally and functionally it operates as a specialized branch of the U.S. government. The NED is wholly funded by Congress with funds channeled through the USIA and the Agency for International Development (AID), both entities of the Department of State.[45] All NED grants are submitted to the State Department for approval, and U.S. embassies abroad frequently handle logistics for and coordination of NED programs. The State Department and other executive agencies regularly appoint personnel to participate in NED programs.[46]

One Project Democracy participant described its goals and methods as follows: "Such a worldwide effort [a "crusade for democracy"] directly or indirectly must strive to achieve three goals: the preservation of democracies from internal subversion by either the Right or the Left; the establishment of new democracies where feasible; and keeping open the democratic alternative for all nondemocracies. To achieve each of these goals we must struggle militarily, economically, politically and ideologically."[47]

The countries in which the NED became most involved in the 1980s were precisely those set as priorities for U.S. foreign policy, top among them Nicaragua. In countries designated as hostile and under Soviet influence, such as Nicaragua and Afghanistan, the United States organized "freedom fighters" (antigovernment insurgencies), while the NED introduced complementary political programs.[48] Those countries designated for transition from right-wing military or civilian dictatorships to stable "democratic" governments inside the U.S. orbit, including Chile, Haiti, Paraguay, and the Philippines, received special attention. The NED also prepared for future campaigns in Cuba, Vietnam, and other countries on Washington's enemy list.

Even though the NED was originally a creation of the Reagan anticommunist crusade, it made an easy transition to the post–cold war era. As the rubric of anticommunism and national security became outdated, the rhetoric of "promoting democracy" took on even greater significance. *Perestroika* and *glasnost* have highlighted the issue of democratization as an authentic aspiration of many peoples. But U.S. strategists have seen in the collapse of the Soviet system an opportunity for accelerating political intervention under the cover of promoting democracy. In this context, "democracy" and "democratization" have nothing to do with meeting the authentic aspirations of repressed and marginalized majorities for political participation and for greater socioeconomic justice. Waving the banner of "democracy" does, however, provide a powerful ideological rationale for U.S. foreign policy operations.

MODUS OPERANDI OF
THE NEW POLITICAL INTERVENTION

On paper at least, the NED is supposed to operate overtly, providing assistance in other countries to groups and individuals serving U.S. interests.

In this way, political intervention by the United States can be described, not as "CIA bribes," "covert payoffs," or "secret intervention," but as "democratic, nonpartisan assistance." The semantics of intervention have changed. It is easier and more ideologically satisfying to sell intervention as promotion of democracy than as pursuit of national security. Transferring political intervention from the covert to the overt realm does not change the character of such intervention, but it does enable policymakers to more easily build domestic and international support for this action. This shift from covert to overt intervention also provides U.S. policymakers with greater flexibility in pursuing their country-specific objectives. Indeed, a bipartisan consensus in Washington for promotion of democracy was easily secured in the 1980s and facilitated electoral intervention in Nicaragua.

Despite its officially overt character, the NED also engages in extensive covert operations. In fact, overtness appears to be more an aspect of the "democracy" rhetoric than of actual NED policy. NED activities are often shrouded in secrecy, and NED officials operate more often in the shadows than in the open. Although this situation appears contradictory, the NED's secret activities have their exact counterparts in the clandestine, under-the-table dealings that are a traditional part of the U.S. political system and that are far from alien to U.S. political professionals who carry out NED operations.

The NED functions through a complex system of intermediaries in which operative aspects, control relationships, and funding trails are nearly impossible to follow and final recipients are difficult to identify. Most moneys originating from the NED are first channeled through U.S. organizations, which in turn pass them on to foreign counterparts that are themselves often pass-throughs for final recipients. Dozens of U.S. organizations have acted as conduits for NED funds. As a result, financial accounting becomes nearly impossible, thereby facilitating all sorts of secret funding, laundering operations, and bookkeeping cover-ups that allow for unscrutinized transactions. Because of the multitiered structure of go-betweens, it is difficult to establish the links between U.S. government operations, on the one hand, and seemingly independent political activities in other countries, on the other hand. In this Alice's Wonderland of political intervention, things are not what they seem, at first blush, to be.

The NED, as a congressionally chartered organization, is made up of "core groups." These groups, which handle the appropriated NED funds and programs, are the National Democratic Institute for International Affairs (NDI) and its counterpart, the National Republican Institute for International Affairs (NRI), which are the "international wings" of the Democratic and Republican parties; the Center for International Private Enterprise (CIPE), a branch of the U.S. Chamber of Commerce; and the Free Trade Union Institute (FTUI), an international branch of the American Federation of Labor and Congress of Industrial Organizations (AFL-CIO). These core groups carry out programs in target countries with those sectors considered strategic pillars of society: labor (FTUI), business (CIPE), and political parties and organizations (NDI and NRI). A host of other U.S. "private" organizations enmeshed with foreign policy, such as the right-wing Freedom House and the Council on the Americas, handle programs for "civic" sectors. The concept behind this sectorial specialization in political intervention is the creation of a societywide network of political, social, cultural, business, and civic organizations in the target country that are dependent on and responsive to U.S. direction or at least sympathetic to U.S. concerns.

A striking feature of the NED structure is the system of interlocking directorates. The boards of the NDI, the NRI, the CIPE, the FTUI, Freedom House, and so on, heavily overlap with the government and private organization officials who promoted Project Democracy and who sit on the NED board itself.[49] Nevertheless, the "democracy gang," as one observer called this interlocked core group of political warfare specialists, does not constitute a unified group in terms of domestic U.S. politics or affiliation. It does not represent a specific sector or ideological strain in mainstream U.S. politics. Instead it includes right-wing Republicans and moderate Republicans; liberal Democrats, conservative Democrats, and even social Democrats; representatives of labor and representatives of business; and so forth. This underscores that the new political intervention is less a creature of the right-wing Reagan presidency than it is a product of the evolution of U.S. foreign policy in the broadest context.

Another characteristic of the NED is its fusion of the public and the private domains in its operations. The blurring of "public" and "private" in U.S. foreign policy was exposed during investigations into the Iran-contra dealings. This was mistakenly seen as an aberration limited to that scandal. It is actually a structural feature of foreign policy in the post–Vietnam War (and post–cold war) period, in which the U.S. government facilitates the flow of private resources in society toward foreign policy objectives.[50] This means tapping the technological, intellectual, and organizational expertise of those not formally in the government. In this process, not only does the distinction between state activity and private activity disappear, but also diverse interests are merged into singular campaigns.

In this framework, the NED operates as a clearinghouse for a complex network of private groups and government agencies that intervene in foreign political affairs under the rubric of promoting democracy. U.S. intervention in the Nicaraguan elections involved the coordinated actions of the White House, the National Security Council, the CIA, the Department of State, the Pentagon, the USIA, the AID, Congress, the Democratic and Republican parties, the AFL-CIO, the U.S. Chamber of Commerce, and dozens of private groups, ranging from Freedom House and the Cuban American National Foundation to the National Association of Broadcasters (NAB) and sectors of the U.S. Catholic Bishops' Conference. The NED played a centripetal role in mobilizing resources for political and electoral aspects of intervention and acted in synchronization with the executive branch, which coordinated overall strategy and national policies.

When the rhetoric of democracy is put aside, the NED is a specialized U.S. government tool for penetrating civil society in other countries down to the grass-roots level. "Psychological-political penetration and subversion of foreign states and of international organizations and movements remains a distinguishing feature of the contemporary strategic environment," noted two advisers to the National Security Council in arguing that the creation of the NED was "just what the doctor ordered" for U.S. foreign policy.[51]

ELECTORAL PROCESSES AND ELECTORAL ASSISTANCE

Intervention in the electoral processes of other countries is not a new feature in the foreign policy of the United States or other great powers. Traditionally, this has been a two-way street. Great power embassies, quietly and sometimes not so quietly, support and encourage favorable local political leaders and movements. Local politicians, for reasons ranging from the venal to the patriotic, secretly accept or openly solicit the support of one great power or another. Since World War II, the United States has intervened in elections in dozens of countries around the world, from Italy and Greece to the Congo, Vietnam, Guatemala, Chile, and Jamaica, in support of U.S. foreign policy goals in the target countries or regions.

The United States, in conjunction with local allies, has grown adroit at staging electoral farces as a mechanism for installing groups Washington deems favorable to its interests or for legitimizing internal social orders and U.S. policies through a "free" vote.[52] This was the case in Vietnam in the 1960s and El Salvador in the 1980s, among other instances. The flip side has been intervention in elections to prevent "adverse" groups from coming to power through the vote. Thus, the CIA gave clandestine funding to centrist parties in the Italian elections of 1948, and in the same period it began working to destroy the political Left in Greece. When "adversaries" did come to power through elections despite U.S. efforts, the United States turned to clandestine destabilization campaigns to remove constitutionally elected governments, as in Chile and Guatemala, or to outright invasions, as in the Dominican Republic in 1965.

Nicaragua is familiar with both U.S. military and electoral intervention. The U.S. military invaded Nicaragua four times in the nineteenth century and then returned in 1912 and stayed on intermittently through the next twenty years. In 1928, the U.S. occupation force organized "elections," supervised by the U.S. envoy, Henry Stimson, who personally chaired the Nicaraguan electoral commission. U.S. Marines staffed polling booths, and U.S. Marine officers counted the votes. It was under these "free elections" and their aftermath that the United States proceeded to create the National Guard, which became the power base for Anastasio Somoza García, founder of the Somoza family dynasty, whose intelligence and support for the United States favorably impressed the dim-witted Stimson. Somoza's coup in 1934, despite its violation of the electoral process established by the United States, raised few objections in Good Neighbor Washington. The Somoza regime was recognized by President Franklin Roosevelt and continued to rule for forty-five years, with U.S. support, until it was overthrown in 1979 by the Sandinista movement.

The new electoral intervention is more sophisticated. In the post–cold war era, the role of the electoral processes in U.S. foreign policy has changed. The process tends to be less a crude product exported from Washington than a careful blend of indigenous political factors with U.S. policies. Washington became encouraged by the prospects for such a convergence after repressive military regimes in several Latin American countries turned over power to elected civilian governments.[53] In subsequent electoral processes, such as in the Philippines and Chile, sectors of the local elite joined forces with the United States as a mechanism for transition from military dictatorships to more stable, ostensibly civil, and "democratic" arrangements that would preserve elements of the status quo (and U.S. domination) while also restoring minimal political and civil liberties.[54]

Rather than crudely imposing elections, the United States increasingly penetrates foreign electoral processes in operations that are many times more elaborate and extensive than before. As part of Project Democracy, U.S. involvement in electoral processes abroad expanded dramatically in the 1980s. In 1984, the State Department established the Office of Democratic Initiatives, attached to the AID, "to support and strengthen democratic institutions." Between 1984 and 1987, the AID spent more than $25 million through the office for electoral processes abroad, mostly in Latin America.[55] After 1987, the NED assumed many of these operations, and its programs began to home in on electoral processes.

Electoral processes, if effectively penetrated, offer the United States a staging ground from which to gain key points of leverage over target societies, to steer the intervened societies down the roads the United States sees fit. Moreover, control over electoral processes provides the United States with the opportunity to permeate the institutions of civil society and the political structures of the target country and to try from that vantage point to bring about long-term stability around free-market economies and social orders tied to U.S. interests.[56]

Electoral democracy in the new political intervention is more than mere public relations. Formal electoral processes allow for transplanting viable political systems into intervened societies—that is, stable, electorally legitimized institutions that at least resemble U.S. or Western analogies and that are apparently national but are susceptible to U.S. direction and control. In the U.S. construct, these should be the characteristics that define (and circumscribe) all, or almost all, of the competing groups in a pluralist political system ("Tweedledum, Tweedledee, and Tweedledip, ad infinitum," sardonically commented one observer).[57] This undertaking does require the development of more formal democratic structures in which the sharpest social tensions may be diffused and sufficient internal social bases incorporated to sustain stable environments. Often social grievances and mass aspirations for democratization are channeled into controlled electoral processes with manageable and nonthreatening outcomes. The trappings of democratic procedure, however, do not mean that the lives of those in the intervened nations become filled with authentic or meaningful democratic content, much less that social justice or greater economic equality is achieved. The latter are, at best, seen as hopeful by-products, not the goals, of U.S. foreign policy.

To undertake this new form of electoral intervention, the United States has created an elaborate machinery for "electoral assistance": "get out the vote" drives, ballot box watching, poll taking, parallel vote counts, civic training, and so forth. In this new elections industry, the United States dispatches specialized teams to carry out everything from "party-building seminars" to "civic training" and "international monitoring" and employs the tools of mass psychological manipulation and the new means of communications developed during the past fifty years. In these campaigns, the U.S. teams attempt to shape and manage (and, in certain circumstances, hijack) indigenous political processes. (The extent to which the outside political professionals actually control or even understand the system and the local political figures with whom they deal is often questionable. Outsider accounts are often self-serving and deluded. Nevertheless, as part of the new techniques, the U.S. teams employ local operatives to provide a more accurate reading of indigenous conditions.)

The substitution of the NED for the CIA and the introduction of overt "political aid" in U.S. foreign policy operations have helped Washington legitimize electoral assistance. Said one Project Democracy counselor, "In most countries, foreign financing of campaign activities is viewed as an extreme form of interference in internal affairs. Neither the donors nor the recipient groups want the existence of the funding known. Typically, the funds flow through the intelligence agencies of foreign governments. . . . Ironically, it is often more politically effective to provide the money openly. The most obvious advantage to overt transactions is that if one is not hiding anything, one is not subject to exposure. . . . Procedural secrecy [is] maintained only to protect recipients working clandestinely."[58]

THE PHILIPPINES, CHILE, PANAMA: PRELUDES TO NICARAGUA

Before being applied to Nicaragua, the machinery of electoral intervention was tested out by the United States in three "success stories"—the Philippines, Chile, and Panama. In both the Philippines and Chile, the goal was to remove U.S. allies, brought to or maintained in power by earlier U.S. interventions, whose continuation in office no longer served U.S. interests. The U.S. effort in these two countries intersected with indigenous and broadly based movements against dictatorial governments. In the case of Panama, the aim was to legitimize an opposition created by the United States after the existing regime fell out of favor with Washington and to build an international consensus in favor of military aggression. In Nicaragua, the goal was to remove a designated enemy.

In the Philippines, the United States had propped up Ferdinand Marcos for many years. But, by the mid-1980s, the Marcos dictatorship had spawned a mass protest movement as well as an armed insurgency. It became clear that Marcos's days were numbered, with or without U.S. support. Despite differences among U.S. policymakers, Washington turned to facilitating his removal in circumstances it could control.[59] Between 1984 and 1987, Philippine organizations received $6 million from the NED. In the eleventh hour of a popular uprising, after Marcos attempted electoral fraud in the 1986 voting, the United States convinced the dictator to step down. The United States then recognized the NED-supported candidate, Corazon Aquino, as winner of the elections. Aquino, a member of the Philippine traditional elite, also enjoyed genuine popularity as an anti-Marcos symbol.[60] In backing her, the United States latched onto her popularity and posited itself as the firm champion of a new "democratic" government.

Although the United States claimed for itself a pivotal role in organizing the Aquino victory, it is difficult in the general context of Philippine politics and the special circumstances attending the removal of an aging and enfeebled political boss (Marcos died soon after the election) to identify to what extent U.S. intervention in the Philippine election caused the campaign or its result (in terms of voter behavior) to be different than they would have been without outside interference. Nevertheless, U.S. pressure on Marcos was essential in getting him to step down and go into exile. More importantly, the United States gained important experience in the new electoral intervention, particularly in giving the character of a plebiscite to elections in which political forces are polarized into two camps, a "democratic opposition" (which U.S. aid and advisers ensure will be dominated by moderate, pro-U.S. elites) versus a dictatorship. As we shall see, this tactic was adroitly applied to the Nicaraguan vote.

These "Philippine techniques" were further developed in Chile. The United States had spent millions of dollars in the 1960s in Chile in covert electoral intervention to bolster favored parties and marginalize the Left,[61] but the United States was unable to prevent the election of Allende. After helping to overthrow Allende, the United States provided consistent support for the military dictatorship of Augusto Pinochet. In 1985, given the demise of military regimes in other Southern Cone countries and mounting unrest inside Chile, the Reagan administration concluded it was time to phase out the Pinochet regime. Between 1985 and 1988, the United States shifted its support from the dictatorship to the elite opposition. As in the Philippines, this was no "democratic awakening" in Washington. It was a strategic shift in policy based on a recognition that these old-style dictatorships were no longer capable of defending U.S. interests and that they threatened to engender mass opposition beyond the control of the United States and local allies.[62]

The United States spent approximately $3 million through the AID and the NED to organize and guide the coalition that ran against Pinochet in the 1988 plebiscite.[63] U.S. advisers designed the coalition's campaign and even produced its media advertisements, exporting U.S. campaign techniques, particularly new communications technology and the use of television. "In Chile, we went in very early," said one consultant sent down by the NED. "We literally organized Chile as we organize elections in precincts anywhere in the United States."[64] This intervention, combined with strong pressures from ubiquitous U.S. advisers, helped strengthen the moderate opposition and marginalize leftist oppositions, which from 1983 until then had taken the lead in mobilizing mass opposition to the dictatorship. U.S. assistance was made conditional on the unity of the sixteen opposition parties. Funding was then provided to the more moderate among them, especially the Christian Democratic Party, which in the 1960s was the main recipient of covert CIA support; the party's leader, Patricio Aylwin, went on to win the 1989 presidential elections with more NED support. And as in the Philippines, U.S. pressures on Pinochet were crucial in assuring the dictator would respect the outcome of the elections.

Nevertheless, the Chileans were experienced and skilled political actors, and the anti-Pinochet forces were already well organized. There was a convergence among popular sectors, the Chilean Left, the elite opposition, and U.S. interests in getting rid of Pinochet. Therefore, the extent to which U.S. support determined the outcome is open to question. As one observer put it, through intervention the United States was able to put the icing on what was a Chilean cake.[65] The same techniques developed and refined during the U.S. electoral intervention in Chile were later applied in Nicaragua. There, however, the United States both baked the cake and iced it.

The relationship between electoral and other forms of U.S. intervention, including military forms, crystallized in Panama. In 1984, the United States supported the candidate backed by the Panamanian Defense Force, Nicolás Ardito Barletta, over the opposition, Arnulfo Arias. Although Noriega's candidate won by fraud, he was immediately recognized by Washington. In the following three years, however, U.S. policy toward Panama turned, for strategic geopolitical reasons, against the Noriega regime.[66] Washington launched a broad destabilization campaign that included economic sanctions, coercive diplomacy, psychological operations (especially, the "demonization" of Noriega in U.S. public opinion), and, reportedly, a $10 million covert CIA operation. It was in this context that the United States set its sights on the 1989 elections.

After Aquino's victory in the Philippines, the State Department sent John Maisto, a diplomat at the embassy in Manila who had overseen the transition in the Philippines, to the U.S. Embassy in Panama. With NED funding, Maisto sent Yeyo Barria, president of the Panamanian Chamber of Commerce, to the Philippines in 1988 to study Cory Aquino's political campaign.[67] Barria passed through Washington on the way back to map out strategy with the NED and the State Department and then returned to Panama to help organize the Civic Crusade (a loose anti-Noriega coalition of conservative Panamanian political and business groups) among the disparate elite business community and right-wing politicians, with the aid of U.S. advisers and NED funding.[68]

As in the Philippines and Chile, the U.S. program turned the May 1989 vote into a plebiscite between a "democratic opposition" (the Civic Crusade) and a dictatorship (Noriega). The elections allowed the United States to legitimize the opposition it had created and directed and, when the regime committed irregularities and then nullified the vote, to mobilize the international community in favor of further U.S. intervention.

On the eve of the Nicaraguan electoral process, one of President Bush's national security advisers observed, "Since Manila, the United States has gotten into this; we have been brandishing this new tool of giving support to electoral processes. The Plebiscite in Chile was analogous, where we saw we could shake an entrenched regime by [getting involved in] elections. Panama has been a success from the point of view of shining the spotlight and producing an unambiguous international perception of the outcome. We are learning these techniques, and they should be applied to Nicaragua."[69]

TWO

Nicaragua from Carter to Reagan to Bush

We will now see a repeat of the effort (originally undertaken under the Carter adminis-
tration) to create an internal front opposed to the Revolution. They'll do it through every
imaginable institution they can manipulate or establish—trade unions, political parties,
media, religious groups, women's groups, youths, professionals . . . you name it. These
are tried and true methods through which the CIA will try to develop an internal
opposition. They've done this continuously around the world. One new area to watch is
NED activity. NED will be used to send millions of dollars to Nicaragua, in conjunction
with CIA operatives from behind-the-scenes. This is now the new stage in the battle to
destroy the revolutionary project in Nicaragua.

—Philip Agee[1]

In 1987 and 1988, with the signing of Esquipulas II and the Sapoá agreements, the
Government of Nicaragua committed itself to holding free and fair elections and to
allowing greater freedom of the press, association and expression. . . . The democratic
opposition groups must continue their efforts to create the social and political conditions
necessary to achieve a meaningful democratic opening and promote the participation of
Nicaraguan citizens in the political, social and economic life of their embattled country.
In recognition of the importance of supporting [these] efforts . . . the National Endowment
for Democracy proposes a series of new programs.

—NED Nicaragua "Fact Sheet"[2]

THE MYTH OF A DEMOCRATIC OPPOSITION

In Washington's language, the opposition forces that ran against the Sandinistas in the elections were the "democratic" and "independent" opposition.
But in essence the opposition was neither: It was a right-wing grouping drawn
from the Nicaraguan elite classes, and it had been carefully cultivated over
the years as an instrument in the U.S. effort to destroy the Sandinistas.[3]
Employing the terms *democratic* and *independent* made it easier to label the

27

government "totalitarian," but much of the opposition was willing to invoke nondemocratic and extralegal means to promote its struggle. One editor of the anti-Sandinista newspaper *La Prensa*, Jaime Chamorro (brother-in-law of Violeta), explained the division of labor between the contras and the internal opposition: "The armed resistance is fundamental to stopping the [Sandinista] imposition. The contras are fighting with arms, and we are fighting in another way, together with the political parties and private enterprise."[4] The opposition perpetually turned to the United States, first to displace Somoza and then to remove the Sandinistas. Rarely did opposition leaders address the people themselves; like the United States, they rejected the concept of any government or social movement they could not control.

Covert CIA support for the internal opposition started under Jimmy Carter's administration and continued through to George Bush's. U.S. strategy during the war of liberation against the Somoza dictatorship was to try to replace Somoza with representatives from the conservative opposition and to preserve the National Guard as an institution so as to prevent a popular Sandinista victory—in short, to create a *"Somocismo sin Somoza."*[5] The CIA began covert assistance to conservative anti-Somoza opposition elements in 1978. Six months after the Sandinista triumph in July 1979, Carter signed a top-secret finding authorizing an expansion of this covert funding, including funds for Violeta Chamorro's newspaper, *La Prensa*. At least $1 million was channeled to these groups, "intended to build ties for the agency [CIA] . . . to keep an opposition alive and insure that the agency would have contacts and friends among the leaders of a new [post-Sandinista] government."[6] Central to the Carter policy was an effort to bolster the conservative political opposition in the hopes of minimizing the FSLN's influence on Nicaraguan political life and thus reroute the revolutionary project onto a mildly reformist path.

The Reagan administration, allegedly more concerned with controlling the Sandinistas' supposed "export" of their revolution, shifted the U.S. focus to external aggressions (behind this was a shift in strategy from trying to co-opt to trying to overthrow the Sandinistas). But the administration also continued covert and other forms of assistance to the internal opposition, piecing together an alliance of the most right-wing elements.[7] This became the Coordinadora Democrática Nicaraguense (CDN), which comprised four conservative political parties, two trade unions groupings affiliated with the AFL-CIO and the Christian Democratic International, and the Superior Council of Private Enterprise (COSEP). The latter was described by the U.S. ambassador as "the bellwether of our policy here."[8] The COSEP was a grouping of hard-line right-wing industrialists, agribusinesspeople, and financiers who went on to constitute the heart of the internal opposition during the years of the contra war, providing a major focus of political leadership to the anti-Sandinista forces inside the country.

In 1981, the AID donated $1 million to the COSEP as "a symbol of political and moral support for Nicaraguans discontented with the Sandinista regime."[9] The U.S. Army's 1979 publication *Guide for the Planning of Counterinsurgency* detailed the function of the AID in counterrevolutionary wars, emphasizing its role in the formation of "American groups" to assist in achieving the objectives of the U.S. program.[10]

Although the American groups are under the direct supervision of the U.S. ambassador, their members are usually nationals of the target country. In official AID terminology, these groups are referred to as "private voluntary organizations" (PVOs). An enormous increase in AID assistance to Nicaragua took place after 1979; in fact, in 1980 more AID funds were channeled to "indigenous PVOs" in Nicaragua than to those in any other Latin American nation.[11] The recipients of these funds were the COSEP, other groups from the CDN, and elements of the Roman Catholic church hierarchy. This early activity was important because, although the AID program in Nicaragua was terminated by the Reagan administration in 1981, the AID returned later in the decade to work with these same PVOs and to become involved in the elections.

In September 1983, President Reagan signed a secret finding authorizing an expansion of the CIA program against Nicaragua. The thrust of the program was increased military assistance for the contras. At the same time, in a section on "political action" the finding included a significant increase in support for the internal opposition. It stated that "financial and material support will be provided to Nicaraguan opposition leaders and organizations to enable them to deal with the Sandinistas from a position of political strength." Under the heading "propaganda and civic action," the finding stated that "guidance and media assistance will be provided to Nicaraguan opposition elements. . . . Propaganda will be used to promote pluralism, human rights, freedom of the press, free elections and democratic processes inside Nicaragua and through-out the region." The amounts in the program were $19 million in authorized funds, plus up to $14 million in contingency funds. According to congressional sources that studied the documents, the $19 million was for the military and paramilitary (contra) operations, and the $14 million was for the political (internal opposition) operations.[12]

Although specific names of opposition leaders and groups are censored out of the document, analysts widely assume that "guidance and media assistance" refers to covert aid for *La Prensa* and for several opposition radio programs, particularly Radio Corporación and Radio Católica inside Nicaragua and Radio Impacto in Costa Rica. Other recipients were assumed to be the CDN political parties and the right-wing Permanent Commission of Human Rights. These are the groups that later received millions of dollars in assistance from the NED.

The 1983 authorization remained in effect on a year-to-year basis, and because these were contingency funds, the administration was not required to report details to Congress.[13] These funds ran at least $10 million a year between 1983 and 1988. Even during the eleven-month period (December 1984 to October 1985) when the Boland amendment prohibited funding for the contras, the CIA was authorized to continue this contingency funding for the internal opposition. In closed testimony before the Iran-contra committees, Donald Gregg, the CIA officer and former national security adviser for George

Bush who became embroiled in the Iran-contra affair, explained that during that eleven-month period, the CIA spent $13 million on the internal opposition.[14] As will be seen later, the CIA spent another $11 million dollars during the April 1989–February 1990 electoral process.

Simple arithmetic indicates that as much as $100 million was spent on secret CIA assistance to the internal opposition elements in the ten years preceding the 1990 elections. Given that these are secret funds whose existence has become public, it is reasonable to assume that further CIA programs and funding conduits remain undisclosed. This U.S. patronage in the years preceding the elections allowed the internal groups to remain viable until the time of the elections, when they were called on to come together, fuse with the contra external anti-Sandinista front, and mobilize associated constituencies for the voting and beyond.[15]

THE 1984 ELECTIONS

As far back as 1969, the FSLN had stated as part of its program the goal of institutionalizing authentic, democratic elections in Nicaragua. The Fundamental Statute, approved in August 1979 as a provisional constitution in the wake of the disintegration of the *Somocista* state, said that elections would take place "as soon as the conditions for national reconstruction might permit." The Sandinista leadership gave some thought to holding elections within the first few months of the revolutionary victory, when the FSLN was at the peak of its popularity. But the notion was opposed by the conservative members of the governing coalition, among them Violeta Chamorro and Alfonso Robelo, who feared a sweep for the Sandinistas.

The government announced instead in 1980 that elections would be held in 1985 and then in November 1983 moved the date up to November 1984. The FSLN had several objectives for these elections. One was to meet its commitment to the Nicaraguan people to create and institutionalize an authentic democracy in the framework of political pluralism and a mixed economy. In this context, the Sandinistas hoped that the elections could help diminish internal tensions by laying a foundation for political consensus. Beyond this, the Sandinistas saw the popular ratification of their government through a free vote as a means of ideologically disarming the U.S. aggressors. The war was escalating, and the Sandinista army was on the defensive. The Sandinistas thought a free election could isolate U.S. policy internationally and head off the growing fusion of the contras and the internal opposition.

Until then, the United States had helped justify its war policy with the argument that the Sandinistas had refused to hold elections. Now Washington was faced with having a Sandinista government legitimized by popular ballot and thereby having U.S. aggressions seen as even more illicit. Washington therefore mounted a two-pronged strategy of organizing a boycott of the 1984 elections among the internal Nicaraguan opposition and trying in advance to discredit the elections among the international community as a "Soviet-style sham."[16]

To head the abstentionist plan, the administration sent to Managua Arturo Cruz, a banker and Conservative Party leader who had been living in Washington since 1968 as an employee of the Inter-American Development Bank. Named a member of the original post-Somoza transitional government, he went back to Washington in 1981 as Nicaragua's ambassador. Intimidated by the disapproval of powerful U.S. political figures, particularly House Majority Leader Jim Wright (D-Tex.), with whom he developed close relations, Cruz resigned in 1981 and remained in the United States, from where he participated in several contra initiatives. Cruz, who in 1984 was receiving a monthly salary of $6,000 from the CIA,[17] declared before ever setting foot in Managua that he had no intention of actually running.[18] Cruz went through the motions of being named the presidential candidate of the CDN and then of entering into discussions with the government on the terms of participation in the voting. This allowed the United States and the opposition to give the appearance of desiring to participate, if only the process were fair. The "decision by Nicaragua's main opposition alliance to boycott the elections," reported the Washington Post, "represented a deliberate effort to embarrass the ruling Sandinistas, even at the cost of sabotaging the opposition's own goal of encouraging the growth of democratic pluralism."[19] The article continued, "Opposition leaders admitted in interviews that they never seriously considered running, but debated only whether to campaign for two months and then withdraw from the race on the grounds that the Sandinistas had stacked the electoral deck against them" so as "to help the U.S. government assert that the elections will be a sham in the absence of the main opposition." After the electoral episode, Cruz returned to the United States, and in 1985 became a member of the contras' Political Directorate.

Although the CDN went along with the U.S. boycott, several other parties did participate.[20] These parties, including a faction of the Conservatives and the Independent Liberal Party (PLI) of Virgilio Godoy, were allegedly bribed and pressured by Washington to withdraw their candidates. For instance, a U.S. Embassy official offered $300,000 to the Conservative Party and $50,000 each to four of its leaders if they would withdraw.[21] One Conservative leader who turned down this bribe recalled, "Two weeks before the election, a U.S. Embassy official visited my campaign manager and promised to help him with money to succeed me as party leader if he withdrew from my campaign."[22] Similarly, Ambassador Harry Bergold met with presidential candidate Virgilio Godoy and insisted that he withdraw his candidacy.[23] Godoy did so the following day, although a majority of PLI members decided to keep the party in the race for legislative seats.

Despite the U.S. boycott, the 1984 elections were held under the intense international scrutiny provided by 504 officially registered observers and some 2,000 journalists. The elections were held to be free and fair by international standards,[24] especially given the wartime conditions. In fact, in comparison with U.S.-directed elections in neighboring El Salvador and in other countries where the United States stage-managed "demonstration elections" as part of counterinsurgency programs, the 1984 Nicaraguan voting was a model of democratic exercise and a free and fair vote.[25] British Liberal Party's Lord Chitnis, a veteran electoral observer, compared Nicaragua's elections with El Salvador's, which the United States had touted as marvelous proof of democracy in that country: "In every major respect that I can think of the election in Nicaragua was superior to the elections held in El Salvador in 1982 and 1984. . . . The Nicaraguan elections were almost a model."[26]

The 1984 elections were a test of the democratic vocation of *Sandinismo*. Although voting was not compulsory, of the approximately 1.5 million voters who registered, 1.1 million, or some 75 percent, went to the polls. The FSLN captured 67 percent of the votes. Of the remainder, those factions of the Conservatives, Liberals, and Social Christians that participated pooled 29 percent (the remaining 4 percent went to three leftist parties).[27] Because representation in the National Assembly was proportional, every one of the contending opposition parties got at least one seat. Additionally, every presidential candidate who ran also got an assembly seat, thus assuring more than proportional minority representation.

Although the FSLN won the elections, a careful analysis of the results indicates the extent to which the attrition strategy had succeeded in eroding the Sandinistas.[28] Electoral authorities estimated that some 20 percent of those abstaining were from war zones and were unable to vote because of contra activity, added to 6 percent of total ballots declared null because of one or another technicality. If the remaining abstainers are counted as votes for the opposition, and if this number is added to those who cast ballots for participating anti-Sandinista parties, the FSLN comes out with the support of some 55–60 percent of the voting-age population.[29] Importantly, the 1984 election results reveal that the attrition process against the Sandinistas had not yet reached levels significant enough to defeat the FSLN. Seen from the logic of U.S. war strategy as it stood in the mid-1980s, Washington made a wise decision in opting for a boycott.[30]

The boycott of the elections, however, undermined the possibility that the United States would play a meaningful role in internal reconciliation. In addition, with its campaign to discredit the voting, the United States gave notice that with or without ideological justification the aggression would continue. Within hours of the Nicaraguan vote, and when U.S. voters were still going to the polls in their own presidential elections, the Reagan administration mounted an artificial "MiGs crisis." In a special "news" broadcast, the White House announced that "intelligence sources" had detected Soviet freighters carrying advanced MiG-21 jet fighters to Nicaragua. Of course, there was no such MiG delivery, as the White House later admitted. This psychological operation was intended to upstage coverage of the Nicaraguan electoral results and to turn attention away from the popular mandate that the Sandinista government had just attained, which statistically was about twice as great as that of the Reagan administration.[31]

The lesson for the Sandinistas was that in the world of realpolitik international relations, winning a free election was not the same as securing international approval. The observers were there, the mechanisms were all in order, the vote tally was impeccable, and the majority of votes pooled by the FSLN was an authentic popular mandate for the Sandinista government. But the battle was lost internationally. This lesson bore heavily on decisions made in the 1990 elections.

A few days after the November 4 voting, Ambassador Bergold called a Nicaraguan Foreign Ministry official to his office. "From now on you have to understand that everything will center on the contras," he told the official. "That is our main instrument."[32]

IRAN-CONTRA SCANDAL: FROM MILITARY TO POLITICAL FOCUS

In the interlude from the 1984 elections to the signing of Esquipulas, the war intensified and the attrition process pushed on. The seeds of the next round were germinating. Two closely related developments, the Iran-contra scandal that erupted in the fall of 1986 and the Central American peace process that came to fruition with the signing of the Esquipulas peace plan in August 1987, would profoundly transform the nature of the U.S.-Nicaraguan conflict.

Reagan policy toward Nicaragua required an ongoing investment of political capital. But unless this investment could show tangible dividends in the short term, it would generate high political costs for Washington. Indeed, throughout the 1980s the policy engendered not only opposition in the U.S. population at large but also bitter tactical and strategic debates among policymakers about how best to confront the "Sandinista menace." Although the public was concerned with issues of morality in foreign policy, policymakers had always defined the Nicaraguan Revolution as the adversary. The majority of these critics, Democrats and Republicans alike, considered military aggression and covert interventions to be legitimate and necessary instruments of U.S. foreign policy. Differences with the Reagan administration were over the circumstances in which these instruments were to be viably used.

Reagan had focused on externally based military aggression spearheaded by the contras. Many objected to the contra strategy precisely because they saw it as a high-risk option that, even if it could undermine the Sandinistas, would entail unacceptable political costs at home and abroad. These opponents also saw Reagan's behavior toward Nicaragua, particularly in the glaring disregard for international law and world opinion, as so reckless that the policy threatened to backfire and endanger broader U.S. interests.

The mounting political costs from a policy that could not win domestic or international support (and was having an embarrassing lack of success in the field as well) eventually "imploded" in the form of the Iran-contra crisis. The capture of U.S. mercenary Eugene Hasenfus in southern Nicaragua in October 1986 opened a Pandora's box of revelations on the actual conduct of Reagan policy, including the secret sale of weapons to Iran and diversion of profits to the contras, among other schemes for sustaining the anti-Sandinista campaign. These revelations, while they produced the most serious U.S. political crisis of the Reagan administration, by no means brought an end to the anti-Sandinista policy. By demonstrating the counterproductive nature of the Reagan contra crusade, the Contragate scandal exacerbated existing strategic differences among U.S. policymakers. The scandal gave impetus to those arguing that the focus of the anti-Sandinista campaign should shift from military aggression to internal political intervention.

The public debate among policymakers was expressed as a partisan, Democratic-Republican split over Nicaragua policy. Key Democratic leaders in Congress, including Speaker of the House Jim Wright and Senator Christopher Dodd (D-Conn.) from the Foreign Affairs Committee, were highly visible among the opposition to Reagan. Although the partisan character of the debate was important, it led some to lose sight of the general consensus that united those who differed, not over ends, but over means. In the wake of Contragate, opposition to Reagan's strategy also spread within the Republican Party and within "nonpartisan" centers of foreign policy influence, including influential groups such as the Carnegie Endowment for Peace, Freedom House, and the Center for Strategic and International Studies. Anti-Sandinista strategists in Congress, the State Department, the NED and its core groups, and the think tanks who did not agree with Reagan policy began to coalesce around the idea of promoting the "civic" opposition inside Nicaragua.

NICARAGUA'S PEACE GAMBIT

For us [Nicaragua] defense is a political *process. It is only military in that we are forced to take up arms in order to defend ourselves, but for us the process of defense is essentially political—political conviction, political motivation, political organization.*

—Sergio Ramírez[33]

Many policymakers rejected Reagan administration policy precisely because Nicaragua's prolonged and tenacious resistance to it showed policymakers that tangible results would be difficult. In the face of Washington's "total war," the Sandinistas designed a strategy of "total defense," mobilizing the nation to withstand U.S. aggressions.[34] Nicaraguan resistance meant that the cost of Reagan policy would continue to mount, making that policy inviable or workable only at unacceptably high costs.

In the military sphere, the FSLN drew on its pre-1979 guerrilla experience to reorganize the country's army and popular defense structures (civilian militia, rural self-defense communities, etc.) to face the unconventional warfare of the contras and, if necessary, a direct invasion by the United States. Between 1980 and 1984, because of the threat of a direct invasion, the Sandinistas worked at developing a regular, conventional army—the Sandinista People's Army (EPS). The EPS was an important deterrent to a U.S. invasion, but it was ill-equipped to face the contras' irregular warfare, and poorly trained and armed militia units bore the brunt of contra attacks.

Between 1984 and 1985, the Sandinistas upgraded the training and the military hardware of both the regular army and the popular defense structures so as to provide them with an offensive and a preemptive/pursuit-oriented capacity. This included the introduction of more sophisticated Soviet-bloc armaments, especially assault helicopters, vehicles for troop mobilization, artillery, antiaircraft batteries, communications and reconnaissance systems, and Cuban assistance in higher staff development. (The Sandinistas had originally appealed to Western countries for military assistance, but the United States pressured these countries to withhold supplies, thereby forcing Nicaragua into singular dependence on the socialist countries for its defense needs.)[35] Also, the Sandinistas instituted a military draft in late 1983, which allowed for integrated national defense planning. Under the guidance of officer and support service cadres from the EPS, conscripts were organized into irregular warfare battalions and other specialized units.

All of this totally changed the character of the war in its military aspects and gave Nicaragua the ability to confront the irregular warfare of the contras and go on the offensive. In 1983 and 1984, the contras had seized the initiative, spread throughout the countryside, and posed a real danger. The tide turned between 1985 and 1987. The EPS launched successive campaigns that inflicted heavy losses on the contras, flushed them from many zones, and sent many of their troops into Honduran base camps. These national defense mobilizations succeeded in altering the strategic military-political correlation of forces. This was called the "strategic defeat" of the contras; it undermined their ability to pose a strategic threat to the country and was a key turning point in the war.

In the diplomatic sphere, Nicaragua appealed to the world community to contain U.S. aggressions. The government sustained an extraordinarily dynamic foreign policy based on the position that international law must dictate relations among nations and based on the moral rightness of its case. Despite incessant anti-Sandinista propaganda cranked out of the White House, which inculcated an anti-Sandinista prejudice in a portion of the U.S. public, Nicaragua largely succeeded in gaining the moral high ground in the international community. Washington found its policy increasingly isolated and condemned. The "Nicaraguan issue" became a headache for U.S. representatives wherever they turned in the world.

Years before the United States and the USSR set about to negotiate an end to regional conflicts, the Sandinistas were advocating negotiations and compromise as an alternative. In 1983, Nicaragua appealed to the Mexican and Venezuelan governments to help avert what it feared was an impending war with Honduras springing from tensions over the contras' presence in that nation's territory. This initiative led to the formation of the Contadora Group of Latin nations to mediate officially between Nicaragua and its neighbors and unofficially between Nicaragua and the United States. Both within the Contadora framework and in unilateral initiatives, Managua presented numerous proposals to the United States and to the other Central American countries for peace and for normalization of relations. These proposals addressed each and every concern that the United States had raised publicly.[36] Although Nicaragua's overtures fell on deaf ears in Washington, the existence of this alternative made it more costly for Reagan to push war.

Despite the Sandinistas' diplomatic successes and battlefield victories over the contras, the U.S. war exacted enormous costs on Nicaragua. The strategic defeat of the contras, for example, improved the prospects for peace but hardly meant that the war was over. Washington could employ its resources indefinitely to keep the contras alive as a proxy instrument of military aggression, even if this meant sustaining small, terrorist groups scattered around the country. This would mean a permanent diversion of the country's resources from social welfare and economic development toward defense, an endless hemorrhage on society.

In 1985, the same year as the mass campaigns to inflict the strategic defeat on contras were launched, the defense effort consumed 60 percent of the budget, 40 percent of material output, and 25 percent of the gross national product (GNP). These outlays forced reductions in the educational and social programs that had been the proudest accomplishments of the revolution. Three years later, a report issued by the United Nations Economic Commission on Latin America (ECLA) noted, "The chief factor behind hyperinflation, which had become the key visible indicator of the crisis, was the rapid growth in the emission of new currency to finance the public sector debt, whose reduction continues to be made difficult by the inelasticity in fiscal expenditures due to defense needs."[37]

The U.S. siege shattered the economy and tore the social fabric, imposing a nationwide war psychosis and producing pain and suffering for tens of thousands of families. Years of low-intensity warfare had left $12 billion in economic damages in a society with barely 3.5 million people and with an annual GNP of some $2 billion. Proportionally equivalent figures for U.S. society would be approximately 5 million casualties and economic losses of $25 trillion.[38]

At the same time, the Soviet Union and Eastern European countries were undergoing momentous changes. Managua had turned to these countries in the early and mid-1980s for economic assistance not so much to replace Western aid as to create multiple worldwide sources of assistance—the "diversification of dependence." And these countries supported Nicaragua's defense of its sovereignty and right to self-determination before the world community. But U.S. economic sanctions (combined with the 1980s world economic crisis) and efforts to isolate Nicaragua from international economic intercourse eventually drove Managua into a more singular dependence on Soviet and Eastern European aid for economic survival. The Sandinistas, who had never looked to Eastern Europe as a model, saw the changes internal to those countries as healthy and overdue. But those changes also meant by the late 1980s that alternative sources of international assistance were drying up, and countries like Nicaragua were left in a dangerous state of political isolation and dwindling options.

Achieving peace had become imperative. By 1987, the Nicaraguan government had recognized that it would have to take bold new initiatives to accelerate the struggle for regional peace and coexistence with the United States. Real limitations on the options for achieving self-determination were becoming apparent, and sights were set on attainable goals. Moreover, by mid-1987 the Sandinistas were breathing a little easier not only because of Reagan's turmoil but also because the contras were now in check. Managua launched a political-diplomatic offensive whose purpose was (1) to persuade the United States to forgo military aggression as an instrument of policy toward Nicaragua and (2) to transfer from the military to the political terrain contradictions internal to Nicaraguan society. After much internal discussion, the FSLN leadership decided the time was ripe for a peace gambit.

ESQUIPULAS

On August 7, 1987, the presidents of the five Central American republics, meeting in the Guatemalan town of Esquipulas, signed the historic Esquipulas Agreement (also known as the Esquipulas Accords).[39] The accords laid out a comprehensive framework for restoring peace to Central America. They stressed respect for human rights, for political liberties, and for the construction of authentic democracies. They called for an end to armed struggle by irregular forces in the region. Governments and irregular forces were to negotiate cease-fires, and these forces were called on to lay down their arms and join political processes. Esquipulas committed each signatory to take a series of measures to promote democratization and reconciliation inside their respective countries. These measures included granting amnesties to irregular forces and providing them with the opportunity, and the guarantees necessary, to transfer their struggles from the military to the political terrain through electoral processes observed by the United Nations and the Organization of American States (OAS). The accords stated that these electoral processes as well as all of the other measures would be carried out in accordance with the constitutional order in each country.

The accords were essentially the product of a series of pressures that had been building in the region for several years in favor of a political alternative to Reagan's military-dominated approach. As the 1980s progressed, the war against Nicaragua increasingly destabilized the entire Central American region. By its very nature, the war could not be contained within Nicaraguan borders, and its internationalization was proving almost as costly for U.S. allies as for Nicaragua.[40] The other Central American governments came to recognize that a strategy of trying to destroy the Sandinistas through an armed counterrevolution was a tenuous proposition with few possibilities of success. Certainly, they came to understand that it would not be the promising and relatively painless process in which they had agreed to participate in 1981.

Nicaragua's Central American neighbors had been caught between the contrary paths of collaborating with the United States or seeking regional peace and cooperation. Peace, meaning accommodation with the Nicaraguan Revolution, was the indispensable condition for economic growth, domestic stability, and healthy international relations. Nevertheless, local elites feared the winds of social revolution blowing out of Nicaragua. And economically dependent on the United States, they came under strong U.S. pressures to submit to U.S. policy dictates. The Honduran, Salvadoran, Guatemalan, and Costa Rican governments all ruled over societies marked by extreme inequalities in the distribution of wealth and power and by highly restricted space for democratic participation. These political and economic elites saw the Nicaraguan Revolution as inimical to their interests, both because the revolution's social reforms and popular programs set a "subversive" example and because they feared the Sandinistas would support leftist movements in these countries. But they also came to see regional conflagration spawned by U.S. policy as potentially even more dangerous.

Since the early 1980s, Honduras and Costa Rica in particular had been drawn through a combination of incentives and pressures into providing bases and facilities for the contras and political-diplomatic support for White House policy. Honduras was chosen for its location as the principal springboard for the contras. Participation in the anti-Sandinista campaign meant millions of dollars pouring into the pockets of Honduran military officers, businessmen and women, and politicians. But over time, and with their strategic defeat inside Nicaragua, the contras became an increasingly uncontrollable occupation force in large areas of Honduran territory. Their presence caused social and political unrest.[41] Against this backdrop, Contragate chilled the atmosphere in Honduras. "The contras are no longer a profitable business," said one Honduran political leader at the time. "Everyone now fears public implication in the Contragate scandal, and wants to keep his nose clean; no one wants to continue with an enterprise clearly doomed for failure."[42]

Unlike Honduras, important sectors in Costa Rica were opposed to involvement in the contra project from the beginning and pushed for a position of effective neutrality. Costa Rica's political stability in the post–World War II period and its democratic image within the international community meant that the country had much to lose and little to gain from involvement in the Reagan strategy. With Contragate, the risks involved became glaringly apparent; numerous embarrassing revelations surfaced in the international press on CIA and State Department manipulation of the Costa Rican government of President Luis Alberto Monge.[43]

The more astute political protagonists in these countries—among them President Oscar Arias of Costa Rica, elected in late 1986—saw Reagan's policy as a threat to their own interests. These Central American actors became public opponents—sometimes quite vociferously—of the contra policy. As with Reagan's anti-Sandinista, anti-contra opposition in Washington, they did not advocate replacement of the policy with nonintervention; rather, they favored a shift from the military to the political track—or to the "containment" of the Nicaraguan revolution.[44]

At about this time, Congress also commissioned the GAO to evaluate the impact of U.S. policy in Central America. Regarding Nicaragua, the GAO report concluded, "The United States never clearly defined its objectives nor sought a consensus to achieve its goals. It invested too heavily in the military option and did not follow through, or largely ignored other tactics, such as a more active support of the civic opposition."[45]

The emergence in the United States of the new option of democratization and promotion of the civic opposition gave the Central Americans an alternative power base in Washington with which to ally themselves. In this way, Arias assumed a prominent position. He correctly gauged U.S. and international political winds, and his proposals coincided with those of Senator Dodd and others from the Democratic leadership in Congress.

The Esquipulas Agreement represented a necessary adjustment in regional political-diplomatic relationships to the real changes that had taken place during 1984–1986 in the correlation of forces between revolution and counterrevolution. These changes were the result of Nicaragua's strategy of total defense, the strategic defeat of the contras, the isolation of the contra policy internationally, and the Contragate crisis, all of which were disarticulating the Reagan strategy. Once the agreement was signed, the Esquipulas process took on a remarkable dynamic.

Esquipulas gave Nicaragua's peace gambit a real chance to succeed. From the Sandinistas' point of view, several developments had enhanced its prospects. First was the impending political-military defeat of the Reagan strategy as a result of Contragate and the strategic defeat of the contras. Second was the overwhelming international support enjoyed by the Central American peace process. Third was the changing international environment of the late 1980s, characterized by the resolution of regional conflicts in southern Africa and elsewhere.

It was precisely the confluence of these three factors that favored a transfer from the military to the political terrain as the acceptable form of conflict.[46] The international consensus emerged at first as a counterweight to the unilateralist Reagan policy. In Washington, this counterweight eventually grew into a new working consensus for policy, which was adopted by the incoming Bush administration and laid the groundwork for the electoral intervention project.

The Esquipulas Agreement implied contradictions for Nicaragua and constituted a profound setback for U.S. war policy. The peace process, frantically opposed by the Reagan administration and its right-wing members, such as Assistant Secretary of State for Inter-American Affairs Elliot Abrams, who had made heavy political investments in the contra policy, threw Washington off balance. It would take nearly two years for the administration to adjust its policy accordingly. By signing the agreement, neighboring governments accepted in writing the legitimacy of the constitutional government of Daniel Ortega. The accords called for the demilitarization of the Nicaraguan counterrevolution and thereby delegitimized the armed contras as an instrument for combatting the Sandinista Revolution.

But this demilitarization involved trade-offs. It opened up Nicaraguan society to U.S. political penetration. In defense against the siege by a foreign aggressor, the Nicaraguan government had taken a series of restrictive measures, including a state of emergency that limited civil liberties. These measures were far less severe than similar ones in neighboring countries, such as El Salvador, where a state of siege was in effect for much of the 1980s, and were consistent with emergency measures taken by the United States and other Western countries during times of war. In any event, these were restrictions on civil rights, not human rights—a critical distinction given the gross violation of human rights in neighboring countries supported by the United States. The restriction of liberties, however, was seen, not as normal, but as exceptional and temporary under wartime conditions. The government made the decision—and then ratified that decision by signing Esquipulas—to go ahead and lift all restrictions in spite of U.S. efforts to continue prosecuting the war. Thus the Nicaraguan government put itself in a position of greater political vulnerability. It did so in the interests of accelerating the momentum toward peace for the Nicaraguan nation, even if this meant weakening *Sandinismo* as a political force.

Nicaragua took sweeping steps in compliance with the Esquipulas Agreement. The Sandinistas lifted the state of emergency, freed most imprisoned Somoza National Guardsmen and contras, enacted an amnesty law, set up a national reconciliation commission, and opened a national dialogue. Nicaragua sustained and deepened the process even as in neighboring countries internal reconciliation efforts faltered and gave way to noncompliance and ineffectual government commitments. The Sandinistas calculated that these steps would further weaken U.S. war policy and isolate the contras.

Peace became "contagious" in the war-torn countryside. Local priests and community leaders headed citizen peace commissions that tried to get the contras to put down their arms under the amnesty program. The struggle was now essentially political, resting on a military balance favorable to the Sandinistas and giving them flexibility in pursuing avenues for the disarming of the contras. In November 1987, the government agreed to negotiate directly with the contras over their reintegration into civilian life to force them to occupy the democratic space opening up.

But the contras balked. After having pulled back when Esquipulas was first signed, they renewed military harassment in late 1987, with the encouragement of the Reagan administration. In early March 1988, the Sandinista army launched one of the largest offensives in the history of the war, Operation Danto. The offensive left more than one thousand contra casualties. Under this military pressure and under political pressure to negotiate, the contras and their U.S. backers agreed to talks. On March 21, the day after the offensive ended, the contras and the government sat down to dialogue in the southern Nicaraguan town of Sapoá. Despite sharp internal divisions over the phasing out of the anti-Sandinista military strategy, the contras signed the historic Sapoá Accord—a cease-fire that marked the beginning of the end for them. Although there would be more fighting later, the cease-fire brought relative peace for the first time in seven years to numerous Nicaraguan communities.

All of this had consequences in Washington. With the Iran-contra scandal, the consequent dissolution of the Central American policy, and the approaching presidential elections, the Reagan administration lost control of events in the region. The Esquipulas Agreement and Nicaragua's subsequent implementation of it strengthened the hand of those in Washington who had been arguing for the civic track and created new regional and international conditions for the U.S. anti-Sandinista campaign at the political level. The signing of the agreement signaled the fundamental turning point in the Nicaraguan-U.S. contradiction, nailed the lid on the coffin of Reagan's contra policy, and ushered in the subsequent strategy of internal political intervention that would culminate with the electoral intervention project.

FROM ESQUIPULAS TO NANDAIME

Even before Esquipulas was signed, the Reagan administration set about on a two-track approach of trying to both subvert and manipulate the agreement. The White House declared it "fatally flawed" and tried to rehabilitate the contra project. It also tried to redefine and modify the Esquipulas Agreement into an anti-Sandinista instrument, taking advantage of the space opened up inside Nicaragua. U.S. actions were not yet focused specifically on elections. In accordance with the Nicaraguan constitution, voting was scheduled for November 1990, still a long way off. The U.S. focus was on sending opposition leaders back into Nicaragua, weaving together an international network of support for them, and opening up lines of communication and patronage from Washington.[47]

"We are in a completely new political game and we have to change our strategy to meet it," explained Alfredo César, a member of the contra Political Directorate. "We are in a period when we have to test the Sandinistas to the limit—a contest between their capacity to maneuver and our capacity to maneuver."[48] A year later, César would quit the contras, return to Nicaragua to help run the UNO campaign, and then go on after the elections to become a key insider in the Chamorro government.

Some referred to this period in U.S. strategy as the "Chileanization" phase, a reference to the CIA campaign against the Chilean government of Salvador Allende that centered on organizing internal right-wing forces to destabilize the elected government.[49] According to this view, opposition forces would incite violent confrontations with the government that would result in international scandals over "Sandinista crackdowns" and would spiral into escalating civil disorder and instability.[50] In this way, Washington would "test the waters" of the Esquipulas opening and try boxing the Sandinista government into a perennial catch-22 in which it would either have to grant free rein to a foreign aggressor to organize internal destabilization within its sovereign borders or suppress such activity. If the Sandinistas chose the former, external intervention in the political process would continue apace. If they responded with the latter, "brutal Sandinista repression" could be denounced. In either case, attrition would proceed under more favorable conditions in this interim period in which U.S. policy was being redefined.

A key goal became to promote unity between the contras—who continued to play a central role in U.S. strategy right up until the Chamorro government was inaugurated in April 1990—and the internal civic opposition. Until then, leaders of the opposition claimed they had no ties with the contras and in fact deliberately downplayed any connections as part of their tactic of presenting themselves to the Nicaraguan people and the world as the "democratic center," the civic alternative to the military counterrevolution. Now the Reagan administration changed its rhetoric. The contras were no longer "freedom fighters" who would overthrow the Sandinista totalitarians but rather were a pressure mechanism that would open up internal political space for the civic opposition, a guarantee against Sandinista reneging. The contras announced a few weeks after Esquipulas that in the new period they would "coordinate actions and policies with the remnants of the internal opposition parties and trade unions inside Nicaragua."[51]

The Nicaraguan Interior Ministry charged that the CIA had drawn up Plan Oliver to bring about this unification.[52] Although the Interior Ministry did not document these charges, the internal opposition did in fact send a twelve-member delegation to Guatemala City in early 1988 to meet with the Directorate of the Nicaraguan Resistance (the contra umbrella group), for the expressed purpose of drawing up joint plans. On their return to Managua, right-wing leaders told local reporters that two U.S. citizens whom they presumed to be CIA agents were present during the meeting and pressured them to merge with the contras.[53] CIA and State Department officials admitted that $10–12 million was spent out of the CIA's "political" account for the opposition in the period between the signing of Esquipulas and August 1988.[54]

Washington sent in a new ambassador, Richard Melton, who, according to one State Department official, was "the brainchild" of Chileanization tactics.[55] Melton replaced Harry Bergold, a moderate career diplomat who had fallen out with Elliot Abrams.[56] Melton, a close collaborator of Abrams, was well seasoned in covert operations.[57] Before arriving in Managua, the fifty-two-year-old Melton was Elliot Abrams's right-hand man and head of the Central America Desk at State, from which he played a key role in Oliver North's operations out of the National Security Council.[58]

Before departing for Managua, Melton declared, "I want to make it crystal clear what America stands for and the values of democracy and how the Sandinistas don't meet even the minimal standards."[59] No sooner had he arrived in Managua than he announced that his mission was to "go all out" to bolster the "democratic opposition."[60] From his arrival in April to his expulsion in July 1988, Melton and his team shuffled in and out of opposition offices and meetings, consulting over U.S. funding channels and political strategies.[61] In May, Congress took up a bill to provide the NED with a special appropriation (the first of several such appropriations for the Nicaraguan opposition) of $1 million "for U.S. backing of internal opposition groups."[62] Shortly afterward, NED president Carl Gershman arrived in Managua and was escorted around the country by Melton.

In June, Melton addressed a COSEP meeting in Estelí. At this meeting, the opposition called for the dissolution of the Nicaraguan government and its replacement by a "government of national salvation." (A year later, the UNO published its electoral platform, which stated that if it won the elections, it would form a "government of national salvation.") The right-wing and fiercely anti-Sandinista *Washington Times* reported that "the Embassy has channeled money to a number of opposition parties and organizations."[63] "Three of the expelled embassy staffers—economic officers John Day and David Nolan and political officer John Creamer—were renowned for their wide contacts among Nicaragua's political opposition," noted the report.

The joint embassy-opposition organizing activity culminated in July with an opposition rally of ten thousand anti-Sandinista protesters in the town of Nandaime. It ended in a violent confrontation between police and rioters. Forty-two of the rioters and organizers were arrested and eventually convicted on charges of incitement to riot. The Nicaraguan government charged that the demonstration was organized by the CIA as a deliberate provocation and presented strong circumstantial evidence. Melton and six other embassy officials were expelled from Nicaragua for violating the Vienna protocols on diplomatic relations, which specify that diplomatic personnel may not interfere in the internal political affairs of host countries. In retaliation, the United States sent the Nicaraguan ambassador, Carlos Tunnerman, and six of his staff members back to Managua.

The United States described the Nandaime incident as Sandinista "repression" of civil liberties and as "proof" that Nicaragua did not intend to comply with the Esquipulas Agreement. There was a predictable outpouring of anti-Sandinista propaganda in the U.S. media. Most international news stories focused on a "Sandinista crackdown" of a "burgeoning protest movement" against the government. Although the Nicaraguan government's charges were scoffed at, Speaker of the House Jim Wright confirmed their accuracy several months later. "We have received clear testimony from CIA people," said Wright at a Capitol Hill news conference, "that they had deliberately done things to provoke an overreaction on the part of the Government of Nicaragua" and "to provoke a riot or antagonize [Sandinista] officials."[64]

Newsreels from the Nandaime events establish that the protesters initiated the violence by attacking police.[65] These newsreels reveal that all of those who were seen attacking police had congregated together and were similarly dressed in lightly colored *guayabera* shirts and dark pants, as if in uniform. According to the section on "urban insurrection" in the CIA's *Psychological Operations in Guerrilla Warfare* manual, which had been distributed to the contra forces several years earlier, "shock brigades" engaged in insurrection should dress similarly and participate in political opposition activities so that they can identify one another and situate themselves strategically prior to provoking violence. The CIA manual, intended as a primer for training the contras and their supporters in the techniques of psychological and political operations, dedicated a section to instructions on how to organize urban disturbances. The similarity between the Nandaime events and the guidelines set out in these passages of the manual is remarkable.[66]

The Melton Plan, as it was called, marked a bridge between the crude Chileanization efforts at internal destabilization and the hammering out in Washington and Managua of a more refined democratization strategy that would lead directly in the following months to the electoral intervention project. The right wing called for renewed contra aid in the wake of the Nandaime incident, but Congress instead opted for a special $1 million appropriation for NED activities in Nicaragua, approved in August. The congressional vote demonstrated that the sentiment in Washington had now shifted in favor of the civic alternative to the contras.

FROM ELECTORAL BOYCOTT TO
ELECTORAL INTERVENTION

President-elect George Bush was presented in late 1988 with several proposals for Nicaragua drawn up by influential policymaking think tanks. Most of these proposals recommended carrying through the shift to the internal political track, although they also stressed the importance of preserving the element of military pressure.[67] The most influential of these reports was one drawn up by a "working group on Central America" commissioned by the conservative Freedom House. Titled *Peace Through Democracy*, the report argued for a democratization strategy that involved gradually substituting "political development aid" to the internal opposition for the so-called humanitarian aid that was being provided to the contras, with a view toward challenging the Sandinistas at the ballot box and through other civic actions. Among the members of the working group was Bernard Aronson, whom Bush named assistant secretary of state for inter-American affairs.[68]

In accordance with the Nicaraguan constitution, the next elections were scheduled for November 1990. The Sandinistas eyed these scheduled elections as a new opportunity to try reaching a modus vivendi with the United States and a reconciliation inside Nicaragua, which was now enjoying more favorable conditions than in 1984. Reagan's policy was in its eleventh hour, and the Esquipulas peace process had gained tremendous international support.

Nevertheless, there were jitters in Managua: The economy was still deteriorating, the U.S. handling of the Nandaime incident managed to reverse the positive international praise for Nicaragua's careful compliance with Esquipulas, and despite all the momentum toward peace, the contras were still in existence. As late as 1989, a Pentagon official threatened that even if the contras were moribund, "2,000 hard-core guys could keep the pressure on the Nicaraguan government, force them to use their economic resources for the military, and prevent them from solving their economic problems."[69] The Sandinistas feared that despite all of the positive signs, the change of administrations in Washington did not automatically guarantee a change in policy.

Something dramatic was needed at this delicate stage to give a new, and final, push to the peace process; to guarantee that it could lead down no road other than an end to the conflict with the United States; and to ensure that the incoming Bush administration would have no back door out of an accommodation. In early 1989, the Sandinistas played their last card. Following a month-long meeting of the Sandinista leadership in January, Daniel Ortega proposed in February, at the fourth of a series of follow-up presidential summits to the original Esquipulas conclave, to move the elections up to

February 1990 (see Chapter 7). As the Sandinistas saw it, the game, and all the players therein, would shift to the electoral arena. Shortly afterward, the new U.S. secretary of state, James Baker, reached agreement with the congressional leadership on Nicaragua policy, signing a "bipartisan accord" on March 24. The United States "is united in its goals" and would seek to "translate the bright promises of Esquipulas into concrete realities," stated the accord, which meant the "democratization of Nicaragua."[70] The U.S. government "retains ultimate responsibility to define its national interests and foreign policy."

With the shift in emphasis from the external military to the internal political track in U.S. strategy, policy toward elections in Nicaragua was reversed: In 1984 Washington organized abstention among the opposition; now Washington would organize and direct the opposition's participation in elections. On the one hand, the United States was limited in its choices; in the new circumstances Managua was calling the shots in disarming U.S. policy. On the other hand, U.S. strategists recognized that the attrition process, although still in an early stage in 1984, had matured by the late 1980s to the point where sending the opposition in to participate became a worthwhile gamble so long as the terms of that participation were carefully arranged for maximum advantage through the electoral intervention project.

According to the emerging reasoning in Washington, U.S. policy was indeed in trouble, but just maybe the situation could be turned against the Sandinistas; maybe an electoral coup d'état was possible. Policymakers in the administration and in the foreign policy establishment did not fully agree on exactly what the end goal of such an electoral intervention project should be. There were three different scenarios. If the opposition won, then U.S. policy would have scored a tremendous victory. This outcome was the most preferable. If it lost the elections but gained significant internal space and political leverage, then the anti-Sandinista attrition process—now focusing less on the military and more on economic sanctions and political/ideological combat—would push forward in improved circumstances. Then there was always the third option, the back-door out of claiming post facto fraud and trying to discredit the voting should conditions warrant or permit.

Many in Washington straddled between the second and third options. Placing all bets on an all-out victory ran the risk that the whole thing could backfire if Washington made such a gamble and the Sandinistas then won. The administration decided not to opt for any one scenario; it would proceed step by step. In any case, these scenarios were not mutually exclusive. To the contrary, actions in pursuit of any one of them tended to reinforce the other prevailing options. Coming on the heels of a decade of war and the international circumstances of diminished Soviet and Eastern European support for Nicaragua, the electoral intervention project became a no-lose proposition for the incoming Bush administration.

• THREE •

Creating a
Political Opposition

Agents of influence are allies in the councils of a foreign power. It is misleading to think of agents of influence as mere creatures of a foreign power, mercenaries, or robots carrying out orders. Because such people exercise influence—indeed this is why they are culti- vated—their sympathies cannot be wholly secret (but the degree to which they coordinate their activities with a foreign power is likely to be secret). So for a government to maintain or increase the influence of its agents abroad, it must provide them the "cover" that only a certain ambiguous kind of success can bring.

—Angelo Codevilla[1]

Reagan's policy was to take the political protagonists out of Nicaragua. Ours is to put them back in.

—Bernard Aronson[2]

The internal opponents of the Sandinistas had spent as much time since 1979 squabbling among themselves over petty issues and personal rivalries as they had spent engaged in anti-Sandinista activities.[3] During the years of the contra war much of this opposition operated as a "fifth column" supporting the contra military aggression.[4] The NED's programs with civic and political groups during this period were all directed at activities adjunct to the contra effort. Nicaragua's prominence in U.S. foreign policy gave the opposition groups an international spotlight and access to funds and support from abroad vastly out of proportion to their real size or political influence. The U.S. largess exacerbated divisions because money was now available for any professed opposition group. It became more profitable to set up one's own party, no matter how tiny or noninfluential at home, than to actually organize the population against the Sandinistas. Although stymied at times in its political activities under state-of-emergency restrictions, the opposition did more to hamper its own cause than the Sandinistas did. Believing for years that a contra military victory or a U.S. invasion would oust the Sandinistas, the opposition never bothered to organize at the grass roots or take up serious

47

programmatic development. "It is true that we have never really tried to build up a big membership or tried to show our strength by organizing regular demonstrations," admitted one opposition leader, Luis Rivas, a former president of the Social Democratic Party. "Perhaps it is a mistake, but we prefer to get [foreign] governments to put pressure on the Sandinistas."[5]

These factors resulted in astonishing fragmentation; by 1989 there were no fewer than twenty-one different opposition political parties and several additional factions. These included four or five factions for each of the two traditional political groups—conservatives and liberals—and no fewer than four Christian Democratic groups, one Social Democratic Party, one Socialist Party, and one Communist Party, and two factions of a "Central American unionist" current, among others.[6] "We don't have so many social classes and sectors here to justify the existence of so many parties," said bemused Sandinista Bayardo Arce. "How can we compete with them when they are subdivided and revised so often that we can't even keep track of them?"[7]

U.S. consultants hired by the NED to analyze the potential for electoral organizing among the Nicaraguan opposition had nothing but gloomy assessments. The anti-Sandinista forces were "centrifugal in dynamic, fratricidal in outlook," bemoaned one. Another observed that the opposition was "bureaucratic, static, atomized, with low credibility in the population."[8] In the words of one U.S. consultant, "Unification is the single most important ingredient for success."[9] Above and beyond the problem of fragmentation, the United States needed to provide the opposition with a political definition that went beyond vague anti-Sandinista rhetoric. The framework for the anti-Sandinista strategy would be to create institutions and embody them with political content.

STEP I: LAYING THE GROUNDWORK

After Esquipulas was signed, the National Democratic Institute for International Affairs launched its "democratic development program," to which the National Republican Institute for International Affairs soon signed on.[10] "We have set about to unify the opposition and orient its anti-Sandinista activities," said NDI President Brian Atwood, an assistant secretary of state for legislative affairs under the Carter administration.[11] The initial phase called for formalized and systematic contacts with the opposition. One NDI memo explained:

> The various political parties which are included in the civic opposition have been unable or unwilling to forge an effective coalition due to personal or ideological rivalries. . . .
> NDI and NRI, following conversations in Washington with visiting [Nicaraguan] party representatives and meeting with the other core institutes of the NED, visited Caracas, Panama, and Nicaragua to hold exploratory talks with civic opposition leaders. . . . Follow-up talks have also taken place and FTUI and CIPE have agreed to pursue opportunities for strengthening the civic opposition.[12]

The NDI and the NRI began organizing seminars with opposition leaders in Managua and abroad. These seminars were intended to "generate international support and attention for the opposition leaders, put the Sandinistas on notice, and explore the possibilities for the civic opposition to take major advantage of the Esquipulas opening," explained one NDI official.[13] The seminars, funded with $600,000 of NED moneys,[14] were to "provide training in how to formulate organizational strategy and tactical planning to the civic opposition. . . . [The seminars were] designed around three core themes: party planning and organizational strategies, constituency building, and coalition formation." The training efforts would also stress "recruitment and development of resources," "constituency support, . . . and the development and delivery of a coherent message. These sessions [were to] focus on methods for identifying and expanding a base of support and on communication techniques which are compatible with the political culture."[15] The first workshop was held in Madrid and was followed up by at least ten more over the next year, mostly in Managua.

The two institutes also sent U.S. consultants and "international experts" to Nicaragua to analyze the opposition's strengths, weaknesses, and needs. One NDI team sent to Managua reported:

On the surface, the overall environment for change in Nicaragua appears to favor the opposition. The economy is in shambles. . . . Poverty and despair are evident everywhere. . . . It is hard to know where the Sandinista mismanagement ends and the country being bled white by the contra war begins. This should not be a problem for the democratic opposition; incumbents are almost always blamed for the mess at hand and, to the extent the internal opposition successfully differentiates itself in the public mind from the controversial Contras, it can be reasonably assumed they will not be saddled with the responsibility for the current economic meltdown. . . .

At least 14 party fragments compete for support among the anti-Sandinista forces. If a cohesive democratic base is not constructed now, the chances one will come together for the 1990 presidential elections is even more remote.[16]

This sixteen-page report was meticulous, laying out a concrete, multithematic agenda for the U.S. organizers.[17] It also warned that two separate alliances were coalescing. One was "Center-Right," and the other "Center-Left." The first was grouped around the CDN. The other alliance was grouped around the Popular Social Christians, Liberal Independents, Socialists, and Communists. The tendency toward two alliances would have to be rigorously countered by the building of a unitary formation, the report concluded.

The workshops and inflow of funds and advisers succeeded in bringing together top and midlevel leaders from more than a dozen political parties. Bickering and rivalries continued, but U.S. political tutelage put into motion centripetal forces. By late 1987, seven of the parties began huddling on their own, in between NDI and NRI missions, and started referring to themselves as the Group of Seven. Another alliance became known as the Group of Eight, although the actual numbers of parties and factions in these two groupings shifted by the day. In 1988, the NDI and the NRI encouraged the two groupings to come together as the Group of Fourteen, which would later formally coalesce into the UNO coalition.

But in early 1988, U.S. activities were not yet focused specifically on elections, which were scheduled for November 1990. In the first year after Esquipulas was signed, the goals were to weave together an international network of support for the opposition, consolidate a body of civic leaders, and begin to cohere a national formation—the "national civic front" about which U.S. political operations strategists spoke. With the arrival of Ambassador Richard Melton in Managua, the opposition took to the streets to test its strength, which led to the Nandaime events in July 1988.

A turning point in the project came in midsummer 1988. Tucked away in an air-conditioned meeting room in Washington, D.C., sixteen officials from the State Department, the NED, and its core groups met to evaluate the progress in U.S. policy over the previous year and to map out a more comprehensive course of action. The meeting agenda called for "a more broadranging [sic] strategy" toward Nicaragua and the "development of an internal opposition." The record stated that the meeting would deal with the "definition of a political agenda." The record identified:

- [Organizing] activities inside the country, better than outside [sic] . . .
- Enlisting the support of the Central Americans generally . . .
- In preliminary phases—creat[ing] lines of vertical command . . .
- Continu[ing] to organize seminars and workshops, focusing on imparting group dynamics, styles of leadership, hypothetical situations. . . .
- Encourag[ing] more outside visitors to Nicaragua; visitors can provide moral and political support . . . construct[ing] other like-minded groups, not just U.S. [groups]. . . .
- Try[ing] to establish a permanent [U.S.] presence in the country.[18]

Melton was present at the meeting and argued an unorthodox position. Having spent much of his brief tenure in Managua shuffling from one session to another with the opposition, Melton was acutely aware of the weaknesses in the anti-Sandinista movement and the difficulties the United States would encounter. The opposition suffered from "factionalism and egoism," complained the U.S. diplomat. This "translate[d] into sectarianism," and therefore "opposition unity [was] illusory in Nicaragua." Melton argued for a strategy seeking "unity of action instead of a unified opposition."[19]

Others disagreed. One NED official, Adelina "Chiqui" Reyes Gavilán, a Cuban-born anti-Castro militant who had worked with the Friends of the Democratic Center in Central America (PRODEMCA, an NED-funded group that promoted the contras) and would become NED's Nicaraguan program coordinator, argued that a unity-in-action strategy could be a first step but that a united opposition should be the end goal.[20] The anti-Sandinista forces "need[ed] political and financial support from multiple sources" and "should be encouraged to mobilize and channel popular discontent" inside Nicaragua.

With this approach in mind, she said, the United States should bring its resources and pressures to bear on the opposition so that it unified. Reyes insisted that a majority of the Nicaraguan electorate was undecided. An abstention from this undecided block would favor the FSLN. So U.S. strategy should be to provide would-be abstainers with incentives for casting their lot with the opposition.[21]

Others at the meeting spoke of "overcoming opposition on the Hill," and "co-opting Democrats." It was suggested that Melton as well as former Carter administration ambassador to Barbados Sally Shelton Colby, an NED board member and wife of former CIA director William Colby, be sent to Congress to muster support for, and exchange ideas on, the "broadranging strategy." The participants discussed expanding programs for labor, the communications media, business, women, and youths. One State Department representative explained that the Reagan administration had already consulted with Dante Fascell and other congressional leaders on special congressional supplements for Nicaragua NED programs.

With the injection of fresh NED funds a month after the meeting, new groups were brought in and existing projects expanded. The one that stood to gain the most was Delphi International Group. By 1988, Delphi had become the largest single recipient of NED funds for Nicaragua, and it would now take charge of vastly expanded programs to build up opposition communications media and several civic groups (see Chapter 4 for details). Delphi's president, Paul Von Ward, was a former government official who had held several State Department posts in the United States and overseas between 1966 and 1979.[22] Delphi described itself as a multinational consulting and management firm. Before getting involved in Nicaragua, Delphi had functioned as a large-scale contractor for the USIA and the AID.[23] Starting in 1984, the NED began contracting Delphi out for diverse projects in Latin America, including involvement in the 1988 plebiscite in Chile.

Delphi hired Henry "Hank" R. Quintero in 1987 to run its Nicaragua programs. Quintero was an intelligence community veteran who had served since World War II as an intelligence analyst with the Department of Defense, the Department of State, and the USIA, among other posts. He, together with Richard Miller and Carl "Spitz" Channel, had run the Institute for North-South Issues (INSI), which was exposed in the Iran-contra scandal as an Oliver North front group. The INSI had laundered illegal contra funds while at the same time holding a $493,000 NED contract.[24] Quintero and Von Ward quickly became familiar faces in Managua.

U.S. strategists turned to the CDN as the starting point of the unification effort and the core of a broader coalition. Nonetheless, the CDN, with its narrow base, was itself unsuitable for the electoral campaign. Its extreme right-wing positions could undermine the unity effort by alienating centrist and more moderate rightist forces, especially those working with the NDI. The NED contracted Delphi for a program to merge the CDN into a larger opposition umbrella and see to it that in this process the CDN would put aside ultraright sectarianism in favor of unity. The NED provided $44,000 to

Delphi, in two successive grants, for this process.[25] Delphi's report on the program noted, "The CDN is the principal coordinating group of the democratic civic opposition in Nicaragua. . . . The CDN has been able to implement its principal objective of . . . promoting cooperation and dialogue leading to a broader-based united civic opposition. The general program of the CDN consisted of the role it played in the development of a civic opposition to the Sandinistas during the pre-electoral period. The organization is now involved in getting the 14 political parties and the various private sector organizations to come together and make a set of proposed electoral law changes."[26]

STEP II: UNIFYING THE OPPOSITION— FROM THE GROUP OF FOURTEEN TO THE UNO

In February 1989, the five Central American presidents held their fourth summit, in Costa del Sol, El Salvador. There Daniel Ortega announced that the elections would be moved up from November 1990 to February 1990 (see Chapter 7). Washington interpreted this as the signal to launch the next stage in the anti-Sandinista campaign—the final drive to unification and the formation of an electoral coalition. Just days after the presidents' meeting, an NED team headed by Carl Gershman arrived in Managua to map out an accelerated plan of action. The core of the visit was a strategy session at the U.S. Embassy compound with the chargé d'affaires, John Leonard, and other key embassy personnel, including political officers Valentino Martínez and Christopher McMullen, both of whom had been active in organizing the opposition.

In Nicaragua the electoral clock was now ticking, and in Washington the new Bush administration was keen to go forward on the new track laid out in the Bipartisan Accord. Gershman and Leonard did not mince language in their discussion. They spoke of creating a formal electoral coalition: "What should the procedure be to organize the opposition around a single candidate? It should include as many parties as possible, COSEP and the labor movement, women and youth. The CDN would form the core."[27] The opposition, they agreed, would have to be instructed "to postpone any announcement of a presidential candidate. To do so now would provoke divisions in the fledgling movement. First [we must] successfully negotiate [with the Sandinistas] the conditions for the elections, the rules, and then they can squabble amongst themselves over the candidates."[28]

A flood of visitors raced to Managua from Washington to oversee unity negotiations. These visitors brought one overriding message: "It is essential that the opposition understand that failure to unify jeopardizes external assistance."[29] One top opposition leader confessed, "The pressures on me from the [U.S.] Embassy to join are really intense. They are distributing a lot of cash; it's difficult to resist."[30]

In early May, the NED brought opposition representatives to Washington for consultations with the NED, core group officials, and members of Congress. Another critically important visit to Washington was made in May by Violeta

Chamorro and her daughter Cristiana Chamorro. The former was invited to address the NED's conference "The Democratic Revolution." NED officials capped the visit by arranging an invitation from President Bush to the White House. "Mrs. Chamorro and *La Prensa* have become symbols of freedom of expression and the struggle against tyranny and dictatorship," said President Bush, expressing his "deep regard for Mrs. Chamorro and of her unceasing efforts to carry on the tradition of her assassinated husband over the last ten years in the face of Sandinista harassment and intimidation."[31] It would still be another month before the formation of the UNO coalition and two more until Chamorro was nominated its presidential candidate. But with the Bush-Chamorro meeting, the White House had signaled that it had selected its candidate and had launched the campaign to build her international image.

A week later, Chiqui Reyes arrived in Managua to make the rounds. These included two plenary meetings at the U.S. Embassy compound with the opposition leadership.[32] U.S. organizers were now on third base. In June, the NDI's executive vice president, Ken Wallock, and program officer Mark Feierstein traveled to Managua to hammer out details with opposition leaders for a marathon meeting in July to formally bring the UNO into existence. The meeting was attended by, in addition to the usual NED and U.S. Embassy officials, analysts and consultants whom the NDI and the NRI brought in from throughout the Americas to offer concrete advice on how to mount the electoral campaign.

These "experts," several of whom had previous experience in NED programs, included the NED-funded Panamanian opposition leader Plutarco Arrocha; the coordinator of the anti-Pinochet coalition that the NED had brought together in Chile, Genaro Arriagada; and U.S. Democratic political consultants Glenn Cowan, Willard Dupree, and Larry Garber. Forty-two Nicaraguan representatives from the fourteen parties and from civic and trade union groups attended. Culminating two years of U.S. efforts, the formal promulgation of the UNO at the conference was somewhat anticlimactic.

After the UNO was formed, U.S. officials held a second round of meetings with opposition leaders to arrange support structures, make candidate selections, and launch the electoral campaign itself. In August, Gershman met with UNO leaders in Costa Rica. Wallock and Feierstein also visited Managua again, as did an NRI team and teams from Delphi and the other U.S. groups. The NDI and the NRI brokered the formation of a UNO "secretariat" (which would later become the Political Council) and the opening of a Managua UNO headquarters (see Appendix A, document 6).[33] In anticipation of vastly expanded congressional funding, NRI director Keith Schuette, who had been an assistant to Secretary of State Alexander Haig, wrote to the organization's general counsel, David Norcross. Schuette explained that a program to assist the UNO was being financed temporarily out of "existing funds which have been reprogrammed with NED approval," pending the formal allocation of more funds. "I am certain that you understand the gravity of the needs of UNO as they attempt to unseat a communist totalitarian regime at the ballot box."[34]

STEP III: NEGOTIATING THE RULES

The other pressing U.S. concern now was what Gershman and Leonard had referred to as "negotiating the rules of the game." Between April and July, Washington exerted an inordinate amount of public pressure on Managua to modify the electoral regulations. The NDI had drawn up a "blueprint" on the conditions that would be demanded of the Sandinista government for the elections.[35] "The opposition [needs] to develop a strategy to bargain their own participation in the electoral contest," the blueprint stated. "It is likely that this strategy will require timely, consistent and forceful help from democratic forces outside Nicaragua."

In October 1988, the Nicaraguan National Assembly approved a new electoral law, an updated version of the bill that had guided the 1984 elections. The law provided all of the traditional Western electoral guarantees plus broad incentives and opportunities for opposition groups, such as guaranteed public campaign financing and media space for all parties, no matter how small.

The vote would be secret, voluntary, and universal. Every participating party would be entitled to appoint inspectors at each voting booth and to be present before and during voting and at the time of the count. Electoral registration lists would be publicly posted and available for inspection by any participating party. The law itself left no loopholes for fraud or cheating in the actual voting and tallying. From beginning to end, the process was transparent. The law guaranteed all of the liberties necessary for parties to carry out broad national campaigns without restrictions. The Supreme Electoral Council was an independent power of state, a fourth branch of government established by the constitution whose sole function was to administer the electoral law. Each party would be assigned seats in the National Assembly in accordance with the percentage of votes pooled, thereby making the electoral process more representative than the winner-takes-all system in the United States. Moreover, the government threw the doors open to international observation, inviting the United Nations, the Organization of American States, and Jimmy Carter's Council of Freely Elected Heads of Government to observe the process from beginning to end.

Although the rules of the game were already fair, the government agreed to consider additional opposition demands. President Ortega called a series of meetings with opposition parties in March and April 1990 to take up their proposals. The government convened this dialogue with an eye toward building genuine consensus around the electoral process and toward assuring that the 1984 boycott would not be repeated. A total of seventeen amendments were proposed in these meetings, and fifteen of them were subsequently incorporated into the electoral law.[36] Some of these changes did enhance electoral freedoms and opportunities and help instill confidence in contending political forces. Such changes included reinforcing existing prohibitions on the use of state institutions or government property to proselytize for one or another party, broadening the composition of the SEC, further reducing the minimal requirements for party registration, and eliminating a minimal 5 percent rule for winning seats in the legislature.

Simply ignoring that a Library of Congress study of the Nicaraguan electoral law had praised it as exemplary less than a month earlier,[37] President Bush claimed in a highly publicized statement in May 1989 that even after these reforms were implemented, the electoral legislation would make the voting "a stacked deck." This stacked-deck assertion quickly became the White House buzzword. Syndicated conservative columnists churned out criticisms on a daily basis in newspapers across the United States, and State Department and White House briefings harped each day on the same theme. Congress even voted to condemn Nicaragua's electoral law as "inadequate to assure fair elections." The idea behind the stacked-deck rhetoric was to force critical modifications in the structure of the Nicaraguan elections so as to enhance the overall conditions in which Washington could make its electoral intervention strategy viable and effective. The game was to threaten use of Washington's powerful propaganda machinery to delegitimize the electoral process if Managua did not make the concessions the United States wanted. As Senator Richard Lugar (R-Ind.) put it, "We are in the first innings. The laws have been promulgated in Nicaragua, and Daniel Ortega is trying to sell them. Our politicians, our journalists, must be prepared to put forward our case."[38]

These were psychological operations seeking to cast doubt on the integrity of the elections. Washington was trying to set itself up as the arbiter of Nicaragua's electoral process. "If cannons are the final arguments of kings, political warfare is one of the first arguments," observed one U.S. government specialist. "Political warfare serves [our] purpose well" by applying "the use of words, images, and ideas and associated forms of action to impose one's will on one's opponent."[39] Seen in this light, the campaign to discredit the Sandinistas' electoral behavior provided Washington with a lever for exerting pressures on the Nicaraguans, for influencing media coverage, and for shaping the thinking and behavior of electoral observers and the international community. And in the background was the unspoken threat that the 1984 tactic of having the opposition withdraw could be repeated.

Top among U.S. demands was the free flow of foreign funds to the opposition. Such foreign funding for electoral campaigns is permitted in no other country in the world, including the United States, where it is punishable as a felony.[40] It is a tremendous irony of history that laws in the United States prohibiting any foreign interference in U.S. elections were revamped and strengthened by Congress in 1963 in response to interference in the internal political affairs of the United States by the Somoza regime. The regime had hired the consulting firm of Irving Davidson in 1955 to represent the Nicaraguan government in the United States. Irving Davidson engaged in what the Senate Foreign Affairs Committee found to be illegal lobbying in favor of U.S. government contracts and assistance grants, the purchase by Nicaragua of military equipment, and bribery of U.S. government officials. This bribery included campaign contributions to specific congressional elections in 1960, to both presidential candidates in that year, and to the Republican National Committee for the 1964 congressional elections. The later donations were described as "political gratuity to the Republican Party, . . . a favor from the Government of Nicaragua" to help elect legislators who would curry favor for Nicaragua and to oust those critical of the dictatorship.[41]

The president of the SEC, Mariano Fiallos, explained to U.S. legislators why Nicaragua opposed the demand by quoting Senator Lloyd Bentsen (D-Tex.), the U.S. Democratic vice-presidential candidate in 1988, from a speech he had given in early 1989 regarding foreign funding for U.S. elections: "I do not think foreign nationals have any business in our political campaigns. They cannot vote in our elections, so why should we allow them to finance our elections? Their loyalties lie elsewhere; they lie with their own countries and their own governments."[42]

According to the Bush administration, the United States had to fund the opposition to "level the playing field." The Nicaraguan government eventually succumbed to U.S. insistence (for more on this, including Managua's reasoning in permitting foreign funding, see Chapter 6). It agreed to allow Nicaraguan parties to receive donations from abroad for the elections, provided that 50 percent of direct campaign donations was deposited in a "fund for democracy," managed by the SEC, which would help pay for nonpartisan electoral expenses (ballot cards, tallying computers, etc.).

Another demand was that public campaign funds be divided equally among all participating parties rather than in proportion to the amount of votes each party received in the 1984 elections. This was paired with insistence that all parties fielding candidates, regardless of their national strength or representivity, be given equal time slots and space in the media. Applied to the United States, this would mean that Lyndon LaRouche's Labor Party and the Communist Party USA would receive the same amount of public money as the Democratic and the Republican parties. It would also mean that all four parties would be given equal attention in the U.S. media.[43]

A third demand had to do with the military. Initially, the opposition had called for prohibiting the members of the army from voting, which the Sandinistas steadfastly rejected as an antidemocratic move and a denial of citizens' rights for soldiers. U.S. advisers first backed the opposition position. But when it became clear that the Sandinistas would not budge, U.S. advisers and opposition leaders shifted the demand to the abolition of the military draft. Even though the electoral law already forbade members of the military from running for office or engaging in political proselytizing, these advisers made the argument that the draft was an opportunity for the Sandinistas to indoctrinate youths and to therefore win unfair political advantage.

Regardless of the merits of this argument,[44] the demand was tied to the larger electoral intervention strategy. As I discuss in Chapter 7, contra military activity continued, and the threat of U.S. military force against Nicaragua remained throughout the electoral process. Indeed, contra activity and the implicit threat of U.S. intervention were an integral component of the overall strategy. The Sandinistas were to be pressured into suspending the draft even though the two reasons for implementing it continued to exist.[45] Raising the issue of the draft with such vehemence in a country fully at war was intended, not to enhance the real democratic content of the elections, but to develop the draft issue as a key plank in the UNO electoral platform.[46] Pressures continued until the Sandinistas finally agreed to suspend the draft for the duration of the electoral process. This agreement was reached in August—the same month that thousands of contras began invading Nicaragua from Honduran territory in violation of the Bipartisan Accord (see Chapter 7).

If the Nicaraguan electoral process had been an endogenous exercise unfettered by foreign interference, each demand regarding the "rules of the game" could have been evaluated on its own merit and internal circumstances. But the whole issue of ground rules had less to do with democratic elections than with advancing a war strategy in which ground rules for elections were but the terms under which U.S. intervention could proceed.

STEP IV: SELECTING AN OPPOSITION CANDIDATE—A CORY AQUINO FOR NICARAGUA

By August, the rules had been "successfully negotiated." It was time to select the UNO ticket. According to UNO rules, the fourteen parties would elect candidates for president and vice president through separate rounds of voting in which each candidate would need the approval of at least ten parties. The meeting dragged on for several days. After five rounds of voting, the fourteen parties reached the minimally necessary agreement (ten votes) on Violeta Chamorro, owner of the right-wing newspaper *La Prensa*, as presidential candidate. But selecting a running mate nearly split the fragile alliance. Support for the two contending vice-presidential candidates, COSEP leader Enrique Bolaños and Independent Liberal Party president Virgilio Godoy, was split down the middle by the eighth round of voting; an impasse had been reached.

Although there were strong personal rivalries and personality clashes, the struggle between the two candidates had deep political roots. Bolaños, one of the best-known anti-Sandinista leaders, represented the very heart of the politicized Nicaraguan big business community. He had enjoyed close ties to Washington since well before the Sandinista triumph and had even admitted to having maintained close contacts with the CIA in the 1984 elections, assuring that the COSEP would support a boycott of those elections.[47] The COSEP and the right-wing parties of the CDN believed him to be the natural candidate for president and only reluctantly gave in to Chamorro. Godoy was from the Center-Left camp, and the COSEP accused him of having backed antibusiness labor legislation and of having favored Sandinista unions over locals affiliated with the right-wing parties during his tenure as minister of labor (1979–1983).

As the power broker, Washington had opted for the Chamorro-Godoy ticket out of a strategic consideration, much to the dismay of the COSEP and the Far Right. The PLI, considered by many Nicaraguans as the rightful successor to the traditional Liberal Party that had been captured and perverted by the Somozas, was one of the few parties outside of the Sandinistas that had a nationwide organizational structure and a significant base. Godoy had run as the PLI's presidential candidate in 1984 and had received more than 9 percent of the vote even after he had, under U.S. influence, announced his withdrawal. U.S. organizers reasoned that he could win over centrist and moderate groups that might oppose the UNO coalition if Bolaños's Far Right were to dominate. Washington's ultimate fear was that if Bolaños were elected, a third block of moderate and Center-Left forces might field its own candidates and split the anti-Sandinista vote.

On round nine, four dissident parties still holding out for Bolaños openly threatened to withdraw from the UNO rather than back the Chamorro-Godoy ticket. On September 2, however, the U.S. Embassy broke the impasse. Embassy official Valentino Martínez pulled the four parties into a private meeting that lasted four hours. When they emerged, the four representatives said they had reached agreement to back Godoy.[48] Bolaños kept quiet, but other COSEP leaders were furious. "We'll still get the last word," promised one spokesperson, proposing that the COSEP run Bolaños on an "independent ticket."[49] "They [the four dissident parties] were bought by Martínez with $10,000 each," charged Ramiro Gurdián, head of the powerful agribusiness association Nicaraguan Union of Agricultural Producers.[50] Gurdían gave no proof for his accusation. But on a separate occasion one NED strategist noted, "Through the allocation of the aid resources, the donors [i.e., the U.S. brokers] can obtain some degree of influence. In a close election within the recipient group, that marginal influence could well swing the balance between factions."[51]

The NED provided more funds to Delphi to prolong its program with the CDN and keep the lid on the anger of the COSEP and the Far Right parties. "During this period, the CDN focused its activities on involvement in the process of choosing opposition candidates for president and vice president, and encouraging the factions of the opposition to remain unified behind the final choice," reported Delphi.[52]

With the ticket chosen, packaging of Chamorro for the media and the political jet set as the "Cory Aquino of Nicaragua" began. The sixty-year-old housewife had little personal experience in politics. She had served briefly on the first government junta formed after the overthrow of Somoza but had resigned after eight months, giving health problems as her reason. Yet Washington's choice was logical. She was the widow of the martyr Pedro Joaquin Chamorro, the publisher of *La Prensa*, who was murdered by Somoza cronies in 1978. Chamorro's husband was one of the most esteemed figures in Nicaraguan history. Respect for his memory would maintain opposition unity and win popular support. Violeta Chamorro was chosen to head the UNO ticket as a figurehead, a symbolic candidate. She was thus a "unity candidate," and someone who could attract the votes of would-be abstainers. Chamorro's nomination would "assure that the vote will be not only an election, but also a plebiscite on Sandinista rule," noted Carl Gershman.[53]

Chamorro was politically awkward and not knowledgeable on domestic and international affairs. Her inner circle of advisers kept her closely shielded from the press and the public, developing, as one put it, a Reagan campaign strategy of limited public exposure and carefully controlled statements. The image to be created for this woman from the traditionally Nicaraguan aristocracy, whose own four children were equally split between Sandinistas and counterrevolutionaries, was that of a mother figure above the fray bent on reconciling war-weary Nicaraguans. Chamorro's campaign strategists leaned heavily on psychological images of motherhood, devout Christianity, unity, and the martyr Pedro Joaquin Chamorro, while synchronizing these with the main themes of the UNO campaign.[54] Doña Violeta, as she is called, floated into campaign rallies dressed in white and with arms outstretched, an aristocratic caricature of the suffering Nicaraguan mother yearning for conciliation and peace.

Religious symbolism was particularly important in this devoutly Catholic country. Chamorro had long maintained a close relationship with conservative Catholic leaders, particularly Cardinal Miguel Obando y Bravo, the archbishop of Managua. During the 1980s, Obando y Bravo became the premier anti-Sandinista symbol, receiving millions of dollars in U.S. funds from the AID and from private religious and conservative groups.[55] Although the cardinal did not openly endorse Chamorro, his statements left little doubt as to where he stood. Obando y Bravo or priests close to him frequently shared the platform at UNO meetings.[56] Also, the cardinal's archdiocese received $4.166 million from the AID during the electoral campaign.[57] In *La Prensa*'s last edition before the polls opened on February 25, the newspaper's front page featured a nine-by-thirteen-inch photograph of Obando y Bravo blessing Chamorro and Godoy. Under the banner headline "Cardinal Blesses Violeta and Virgilio," the lead article assured readers that church-state relations would be "excellent" under "the future governors of Nicaragua."[58]

Chamorro was also selected because she could win international support for the opposition. The U.S. strategists propagated a parallel with Cory Aquino of the Philippines. One Washington supporter observed,"Telegenic, Violeta Chamorro is better suited than her defeated rivals for the important war of images abroad. It was with the Aquino analogy in mind that the State Department backed her nomination in none too subtle fashion."[59] Cory Aquino's husband, Benigno Aquino, was also a martyr, having been slain by agents of dictator Ferdinand Marcos. And the NED had actively promoted the Aquino candidacy in its Philippine operation.

When Vice President Dan Quayle visited Manila in mid-1989, he asked Aquino if she could time a planned trip to Washington to coincide with a visit to the U.S. capital by Chamorro. "It would be a great thing for the advancement of democracy in Central America if you could meet and talk with Mrs. Chamorro," Quayle told Aquino.[60] White House press officials arranged all the details: Chamorro and the Philippine leader would pose for a photo opportunity, and that image of the Nicaraguan reconciler would be flashed around the world, including inside Nicaragua. "It's intended to increase recognition throughout the world that she can get things done and Ortega can't," said one U.S. official. "Her association with Aquino is a boost in that direction."[61]

But after the plan became clear, the Philippine Embassy in Washington complained to the White House that it should not manipulate Aquino. Aquino did go through with the breakfast but only on condition that there be no photo opportunities and no cross-statements on Nicaragua and the Philippines.[62]

Creating Chamorro's international image did not stop with the Aquino parallel. Another administration official explained that the United States planned flashy meetings between Chamorro and world leaders, including Pope John Paul II, Prime Minister Margaret Thatcher, and other European leaders.[63] Chamorro made her European tour in November after meeting with Bush. The purpose of these visits, in which photo opportunities were stressed and statements were kept to a minimum, was to have the *image* of Chamorro beside world leaders reverberate in the minds of the Nicaraguan electorate. What was important was that Chamorro be seen as capable of securing the political and economic support of the developed capitalist world. The photos were splashed across La Prensa and repeated each night on the UNO television slots.

STEP V: FUNDING THE OPPOSITION

We are going into this election process [spending] $1 billion dollars. We funded the Contras, we have destroyed [Nicaragua's] economy, we have taken Mrs. Chamorro and we pay for her newspaper to run, we funded her entire operation, and now we are going to provide her the very best election that America can buy.

—George Miller (D-Calif.)[64]

Political unity of the opposition was step one in the U.S. game plan. Step two was providing this unified opposition with the financial and material resources necessary to organize and sustain a nationwide electoral campaign. When the United States was bringing together the opposition, the propaganda line was that the elections would be "rigged." In the next step, Washington conceded that the elections might be "free" at a technical level but that "free elections [did] not mean fair elections."[65] For the elections to be "fair," U.S. resources were needed to "offset the Sandinista advantage" and "level the playing field." In addition to "private" and secret funding, the Bush administration opted to make a massive "overt" investment in the opposition using the NED and the AID as the conduits. In September 1989, the White House submitted a request to Congress for a $9 million electoral appropriation.

The request triggered several weeks of intense debate in Congress on how best to develop and carry through an electoral strategy that could promote U.S. aims.[66] The tumultuous discussion did not examine whether the United States should be intervening in Nicaragua's internal political process or whether such intervention contravened international law. Nor did the discussion ask whether the UNO and its constituent groups were really democratic forces—the same U.S. political system that was intervening in Nicaragua's affairs had long since reached consensus that the Sandinistas were the anti-democratic enemies and that the conservative opposition supportive of U.S. policy was the "democratic" ally. The voices, such as those of Senator Tom Harkin (D-Iowa), who argued that "when we began to interfere in the political process by pouring in massive amounts of funds to candidates for their campaign organizations, to Nicaragua or any other country, we began to seriously erode the very principles of democracy,"[67] could have been counted on one hand.

Extreme Right legislators such as Senator Jesse Helms vehemently opposed any electoral aid to the opposition because, they argued, this would legitimize the Nicaraguan political system and undercut the U.S. war against the country. Another argument was that so much funding for the opposition would actually harm its prospects. "I want to see the opposition to the Sandinistas win that election, make no mistake," said one. "However, I am concerned that the infusion of such a large amount of money in what I consider to be a very inexact manner, will in fact operate to cripple the very people we are trying to help."[68] There was also partisan bickering. Some Democrats expressed concern that the Republicans would somehow use the package for partisan ends. They wanted to assure that the NED would be a bipartisan instrument of U.S. policy.

In lobbying for the package, Gershman told legislators, "We debated the issue for hours and we finally reached the consensus that it is not in our interests [to give direct campaign aid to the UNO] for two reasons: One, it would hurt the opposition itself. And second, it would threaten to damage the bipartisan consensus. We concluded that there was a lot we could do to strengthen the opposition without giving direct aid to its campaign." Gershman added that the NED had brought five UNO representatives to Washington to discuss the aid package. "When they arrived, the first thing they did is ask for direct aid," he said. "But they were persuaded" to change their position. "UNO then realized that the most healthy thing for them would be to help maintain bipartisanship in the United States." Such was the paternalism in the U.S.-UNO relationship (and the cynicism of U.S. policymakers) that Gershman concluded his remarks by saying, "This debate has really been a wonderful exercise in American democracy, and I certainly hope it has been a lesson for our Nicaraguan friends."[69]

In the end, the administration and Congress repeated their March 1989 performance, negotiating a "bipartisan" agreement around the $9 million. The moneys would go to "supporting the electoral infrastructure" in Nicaragua and leveling the playing field by giving infrastructural and institutional support to the UNO, the so-called nonpartisan civic groups (see Chapter 4), and "nonpartisan voter registration." (The U.S. government does not provide a fund for voter registration in the United States, where abstention hovers at around 50 percent.) No money would go directly to the UNO candidates, and no money could be spent directly on the UNO campaign.[70] The bill allocated $5 million for Nicaraguan "political organizations, alliances, independent elements of the media, independent labor unions, and business, civic and professional groups."[71] The bulk of these funds went to the NDI and the NRI to support the UNO parties.[72] Another $2.9 million was set aside for discretionary spending through the NED. An additional $1 million went to observer groups, including Jimmy Carter's group and Allen Weinstein's Center for Democracy (CFD).

The farce of giving millions of dollars to a political group fielding candidates in a country in the midst of an electoral campaign, with the qualifier that these moneys could be used only to strengthen infrastructure and institutions, not to support actual campaign purposes, did not deter U.S. representatives from repeatedly extolling their "neutral" and "nonpartisan" stance toward the elections. This claim that the United States was "not taking sides" when one side had been a target of ten years of U.S. warfare and the other was the creature of U.S. intervention would have been a comical assertion had U.S. officials not made it repeatedly during the electoral process, each time with a straight face. The purpose of this public policy was to project an image among the U.S. public and the international community of benevolent support for democracy in Nicaragua, in contrast to the "mistake" of the contra war and the military strategy. The Iran-contra scandal had to be erased from the public mind if a base of support in the United States was to be established and internal constituencies enlisted in favor of the electoral intervention project.

In addition, the United States disregarded the fact that these were multiparty elections. Seven parties of diverse ideologies fielded candidates independently of the UNO and the FSLN. Washington's single-minded support for the UNO effectively marginalized the rest of the opposition and polarized the elections. One non-UNO opposition leader complained bitterly, "The United States funded only those groups that would go along with what the United States wants for Nicaragua."[73]

In sheer monetary terms, the United States publicly spent $12.5 million through the NED on the elections. If we add covert spending and circuitous spending, the figure approaches $30 million, or about $20 per voter.[74] In contrast, George Bush spent less than $4 per voter in his own 1988 campaign.[75] Such was the level of funding, that Washington bureaucrats erected myriad controls and safeguards on the management of the package. A team of eleven accountants from the U.S. firm Price Waterhouse was dispatched to Nicaragua to conduct concurrent audits, as were separate teams of accountants from the GAO. The NDI and the NRI sent two public project managers to Nicaragua to remain there for the duration of the campaign and publicly supervise the spending. The NDI also appointed Democratic campaign consultant Michael McAdams as a special UNO budget liaison.

Extensive oversight was intended in part to preserve bipartisan consensus in Washington around the project by allaying fears that the administration would use the funds in ways that Congress did not approve. Bureaucrats wrangled over whether or not this or that U.S. purchase was used by the UNO or by a civic group or whether receipts matched actual purchase prices. Lost in the shuffle was the simple fact that the United States was attempting to take over a foreign electoral campaign.

The assertion that U.S. funds were "not supporting a particular candidate" was farcical on other accounts as well. First, apart from the NED moneys, millions of additional dollars were provided for the UNO's electoral campaign through both direct and circuitous U.S. government efforts as well as through covert CIA operations (see Chapters 5 and 6). Second, NED moneys were in fact used for campaign activities either by disguising them or by describing them as "nonpartisan" for technical convenience. For instance, thousands of "verifiers" were organized and paid by the NED supposedly as neutral citizens who would cross-check voter registration lists. Yet the training form given to each verifier instructed that person to introduce himself or herself by saying, "Good day. We are from UNO."[76] Third, without exception, all of the leaders of the independent civic groups receiving NED funds were also national leaders of the political parties that made up the UNO coalition (see Chapter 4).

The distinction between nonpartisan assistance and civic groups, on the one hand, and the UNO political parties coalition, on the other, was nonexistent outside of Congress and AID and NED paperwork. "Very frankly, money that we are providing here is what would be known in American political parlance as 'soft money,'" said Representative David Obey (D-Wisc.). "It is money which is going to parties and Members know very well that a dollar which goes to a party computer or a dollar which goes to a get-out-the-vote campaign helps the candidate every bit as much as it helps the party."[77]

Because the NED charter technically prohibited direct campaign support for the UNO, U.S. strategists decided to set up a conduit for the opposition coalition. This was the Institute for Electoral Promotion and Training (IPCE), which was formally established on October 17, the same day that Congress approved the $9 million. According to the arrangement, instead of providing funds directly to the UNO, the NDI and the NRI would channel them through the IPCE as "nonpartisan" spending. The NED characterized the IPCE as "a multipartisan organization . . . to conduct nonpartisan activities that promote participation in the electoral process rather than UNO candidates."[78] IPCE's five-member board of directors, however, comprised Alfredo César, the UNO presidential candidate's chief campaign adviser; Luis Sánchez, UNO's official spokesperson; Guillermo Potoy, César's "right-hand man" and a leader from the UNO-affiliated Social Democratic Party; Silviano Matamoros, who led a faction of the Conservative Party integrated into the UNO; and Adán Fletes, a leader of the Democratic Party of National Confidence, also a member of the UNO coalition.

In addition to this overlapping leadership, NED documents stipulated that the IPCE was to "share UNO office space" in the different regions of the country and that the IPCE was to "utilize UNO's infrastructure and equipment as long as they [were] used for institute activities." The IPCE was to employ individuals "who are associated with or partisans of UNO."[79] One Price Waterhouse auditor said, "It's really difficult sometimes to differentiate between what's UNO and what's IPCE." Many IPCE personnel were "UNO activists being paid with IPCE money, working out of UNO regional offices, using UNO vehicles, using UNO desks."[80]

The IPCE was conceived entirely in Washington. Carl Gershman wrote to UNO leaders in late August:

We have the honor of extending an invitation to four members of your distinguished organization to visit Washington on the week of September 11. The principal purpose of the visit would be to provide UNO representatives with the opportunity to share with us your ideas and appreciations on the Nicaraguan reality. The members of this delegation will also be able to take advantage of this visit to meet with diverse representatives of the United States Congress. . . .

We will leave the makeup of the delegation to your own criterion; nevertheless, we would like to take advantage of this opportunity to make the following suggestion: Lic. Luis Sánchez, Dr. Silviano Matamoros, Lic. Guillermo Potoy, and Lic. Alfredo César. . . .

As you already know, NED was created to help strengthen democratic institutions throughout the world. . . . We are very interested in the development of democracy in Nicaragua, a country which we consider of prime importance in Central America. For this reason we feel that your visit could significantly advance our objectives.[81]

The UNO leaders "accepted" Gershman's suggestion regarding the composition of the delegation. The NED gave Freedom House, which organized the trip, a grant of $10,900 dollars to bring the UNO group up under the heading "international political and electoral training activities."[82] During their visit, the five signed an agreement with the NRI and the NDI on initial funding using moneys reprogrammed by the two U.S. institutes.[83] "We have come looking for support," said César at a luncheon sponsored by Freedom House. "We hope the Congress will move quickly" to approve the $9 million.[84]

There was another reason for creating the IPCE as an entity separate from the UNO. The Nicaraguan electoral law stipulated that any candidate, party, or coalition receiving campaign donations from abroad had to deposit 50 percent of the donation into the SEC's Fund for Democracy. But if the NED moneys were given to a nonpartisan entity, then there would be no legal requirements for turning over 50 percent of those funds.[85]

A third motivation behind the creation of the IPCE was to strengthen the hand of those factions within the UNO that the United States was most actively supporting. Two centers of power emerged within the coalition out of the internal struggle around candidate selection. One clustered around the UNO Political Council, made up of one representative from each of the fourteen member parties, and the other was represented by Alfredo César, Antonio Lacayo (both in-laws of Violeta Chamorro), and the Chamorro inner circle of advisers. A significant portion of the Political Council had backed Bolaños as the vice presidential candidate, whereas Chamorro's inner circle, headed by César and Lacayo, had teamed up with the U.S. Embassy in pushing for Virgilio Godoy. Creating the IPCE with a board of directors that controlled the funds gave the Chamorro inner circle a power base with which to build up patronage and maintain discipline within the UNO.[86]

At a conceptual level, the IPCE fit into what U.S. strategists referred to as a "national civic front." In this scheme, U.S. programmers set up different functional mechanisms that allowed for each component of the national civic front to function in relation to the other and to the overall coalition. In this respect, the relationship between the UNO and the IPCE was described as a "coalition-center structure" in which the coalition (UNO) was the political core and the center (IPCE), was the "technical and logistical" appendage. Through this coalition-center structure, the IPCE functioned as a mechanism for the effective linkage between the United States and the UNO, or, more precisely, it functioned as an instrument for guiding and controlling the UNO and the disparate political groups therein.[87]

▪ FOUR ▪

Consolidating a "Civic Opposition Front"

Since 1979 civic and democratic groups inside Nicaragua have been fighting a rearguard action against the Sandinistas. The United States [will] bring together the various parties and interest groups. Such multisectoral, national rallying points could allow each group to be a more effective force than it could be in isolation. These nonpartisan, inclusive coalitions, bridging party rivalries and occupational conflicts of interest, could be bulwarks against Marxist revolutionaries or militarists. A U.S. political aid program would be an appropriate source of aid and an encouragement to such umbrella coalitions.
—William A. Douglas and Michael A. Samuels[1]

Unifying and organizing the political parties were the staging points for a broader effort undertaken by the United States to penetrate (or create from scratch) the institutions of Nicaraguan civil society and to influence or orient their activities. U.S. political intervention strategists refer to these efforts as the creation of a "civic opposition front" that brings together political parties, the communications media, trade unions, business associations, civic groups, youths, women, and other groups. Washington had already been supporting the CDN political parties, trade unions, and the COSEP as well as *La Prensa*.

But in the new circumstances posed by Esquipulas and the electoral process, the effort had to be vastly expanded. Political operatives from the State Department, the CIA, and NED groups skillfully assembled the civic opposition front during the eighteen-month period between the arrival of Ambassador Richard Melton in Managua (April 1988) and the opening of the electoral campaign. As with the formation of the UNO, the initial work centered around the CDN. Delphi International Group reported on a meeting its organizers held with the CDN and other opposition leaders in Managua in March 1989:

The topic of the form a united civic opposition should take in the upcoming pre-electoral period received considerable discussion. The idea discussed included a movement that was coordinated by a commission of political party, private sector, and labor union representatives and four nonpartisan notable citizens developed

67

into the preferred option [*sic*]. CDN and COSEP preferred a triangular approach with a coordinating committee composed of political party, private sector organization, and labor representatives. . . . A third option under discussion was that of a movement which would include representatives of the political parties and private sector organizations. It was finally concluded that such a broad based movement should reach beyond the representation considered in the three options listed above. It also was determined that it would be important to have the youth organizations represented, as well as the women's movement.[2]

TAKE I: ORGANIZING LABOR

According to the U.S. strategy, labor was a particularly crucial element because the Sandinistas enjoyed strong support among workers; this had to be eroded. Melton had argued that "organizing labor should be the key concern" and "the rallying point for the opposition."[3] Exploiting economic hardship would be critical to anti-Sandinista organizing. Numerous overt and covert U.S. support programs were mounted to give the opposition unions "a sophisticated knowledge of political tactics; how to run a meeting; how to organize a rally." The anti-Sandinista unions "could help in the building of national coalitions, [in unison] with the Coordinadora Democratica," that could bring workers to vote for the pro-U.S. opposition.[4]

In contrast to the youth and women's sectors, where NED organizers had to start from scratch, the United States had a long history of trying to create a pliant trade union movement in Nicaragua and since 1979 had been actively promoting anti-Sandinista trade unions. The NED channeled support to the opposition trade unions through a "core group," the Free Trade Union Institute, one of two international bodies run by the AFL-CIO for operations in Latin America, and the American Institute for Free Labor Development (AIFLD). In the NED–AFL-CIO structure, the endowment provided grants to the FTUI, which in turn were provided to AIFLD officials to carry out programs.

Much investigation has been done on the CIA's role in creating the AIFLD as a bulwark against militant trade unionism in the Americas. In almost every country in Latin America, the AIFLD has cultivated trade unions that support U.S. foreign policy.[5] From 1984 to the elections, the FTUI received some $3 million in NED moneys alone for Nicaraguan programs.[6] The FTUI has explained its mission in Central America as "organizing public demonstrations" and "identifying and combatting anti-democratic groups."[7] The typical FTUI program includes "democratic education" programs. These "concern the role of the United States, its government, and its people in world affairs," explained one founder of the NED. "Many politically active workers in other nations receive a great deal of false and malicious propaganda designed to discredit the United States and its leading role in the democratic world."[8]

Like its political counterparts, the non-Sandinista trade union movement was splintered into small groups of diverse ideologies. These groups included the Confederation of Trade Union Unity (CUS); two opposing Christian Democratic labor factions—both of whom called themselves the Nicaraguan

Workers' Confederation (CTN); the General Confederation of Labor—Independent; and the Communist Party's Federation of Trade Union Action and Unity. U.S. strategy hinged on unifying these different groups. Of the NED moneys, $477,522 was slated specifically for the category "labor unity and international solidarity" with the opposition unions.[9]

The strongest of these anti-Sandinista federations was the CUS, which the AIFLD had been supporting since Somoza's time. Following the signing of the Esquipulas Accords, the AIFLD funded a meeting in Managua of the CUS and its five analogous federations in Central America under the aegis of the Confederation of Central American Workers (CTCA), the regional affiliate to the International Confederation of Free Trade Unions (ICFTU). The official purpose of the meeting was to "pressure their respective governments to comply with the Esquipulas commitments." In practice, the meeting was dedicated to drawing up a regionwide anti-Sandinista labor strategy. During the meeting, the other federations pledged to mount "solidarity programs" with the CUS in their respective countries.[10]

The idea was to take advantage of international trade union structures and the labor infrastructure that the United States had already created in the area. This triangular U.S.–CUS–Latin American program was to "redirect NED funds toward other trade union movements outside of Nicaragua to assist them in mounting solidarity campaigns on behalf of their Nicaraguan counterparts."[11] One conduit was the Mexico City–based Inter-American Regional Organization of Workers, which, under the aegis of the Alliance for Progress had worked closely with AIFLD nearly three decades earlier.[12] AFL-CIO president Lane Kirkland personally asked the presidents of the ICFTU federations throughout the Americas to provide financial assistance to the opposition trade unions in Nicaragua, with the goal of providing $12,000 monthly in "private" funds. "Please make checks payable to 'AIFLD-Nicaragua Solidarity Fund,'" stated a letter he sent them.[13]

Because of the stigma of being directed by the "gringos" that attached to trade unions and unionists, the FTUI relied on a complex of third-country mechanisms for sending human resources to the opposition unions. The NED and the AFL-CIO created a Nicaraguan labor solidarity office in Costa Rica and funded a group in that country, the Center for Democratic Advice (see next chapter for details), whose tasks included sending Latin union organizers into Nicaragua. In addition, the NED and the AFL-CIO brought in a team of twenty organizers from the AIFLD-funded Venezuelan Federation of Workers (CTV). The CTV also provided several hundred thousand dollars in direct funding.[14]

The AIFLD transferred funds from its other regional and general budgets to finance the anti-Sandinista trade unions. In late 1988, for instance, the AFL-CIO launched a campaign among affiliated Latin American groups, particularly the CTV,[15] the Costa Rican Federation of Democratic Workers, and the National Workers Federation of Costa Rica (both affiliated with the CTCA and funded by the AIFLD), to channel material and financial support toward the Nicaraguan opposition unions. In fact, the CTV printed in Caracas much of the electoral materials for the anti-Sandinista unions and then shipped them to Nicaragua.

With international structures in place, U.S. officials worked feverishly inside Nicaragua for labor unity in the opposition. Second Secretary David Nolan and other officials from the U.S. Embassy in Managua had held a series of meetings with CUS and CTN leaders in the spring of 1988, urging them to work at unifying all the unions so as to confront the government under one banner.[16] The FTUI was given $992,000 in the wake of the Esquipulas Accords to organize the diverse groupings into a single front. Later in 1988, the FTUI sponsored several trade union seminars in Managua, from which emerged the Permanent Congress of Workers (CPT) umbrella organization. By the time the electoral process began, the CPT was working as a homogeneous entity, the trade union corollary to the UNO.

An August 1989 FTUI document expressed satisfaction with the progress achieved in bringing labor into the electoral intervention project. It described plans to spend another $1 million, recently approved as part of special congressional appropriations, for mobilizing workers and their families. The plan involved using a "multiplier" system to organize forty-two hundred activists. After being trained and put on FTUI salary, each activist would operate in one of the forty-two hundred administrative zones in Nicaragua where voting boards were set up. These activists were "to mount an effective nation-wide effort to register workers and their families and then see that they vote." The FTUI had to "motivate these activists for their roles" as well as provide "transport and communications support" for the network, stated the document. Overall FTUI "supervision and direction of the effort" were described as "critical" to its success.[17]

The plan involved using a trained Managua headquarters staff to supervise an elaborate network reaching down to ten-member voter teams in towns and villages. The national headquarters were staffed with Venezuelan and Costa Rican teams and top CPT leaders under the supervision and direction of the FTUI. In the next level down, provincial organizers were sent out to each of the country's sixteen provinces. Directly under their supervision were one hundred district organizers "whose first responsibility was to recruit and train about 400 labor activists for the next level down."[18] And so on. In this way, the NED created and controlled a vertically organized nationwide structure for intervention in the electoral process via the trade union sector.

As part of the FTUI program, the CPT was to "coordinate its electoral activities over the next six months with the civic, political, religious and human rights organizations now becoming active in the campaign," stressed the NED documents.[19] "CUS has developed good working relationships with its allies in the CPT. Despite the diversity in political ideology and outlook, they all share a common goal: to mobilize as much voter activity as possible. They expect to function during the campaign as a single unit in pursuit of that objective."[20] Between August and December, the FTUI held a total of 147 training programs—130 local, 16 departmental, and 1 national—with the NED funds. The newly trained activists were sent around the country with NED salaries and per diems.

During the electoral campaign, the special "task force on Nicaragua" set up in the State Department worked closely with the AFL-CIO and the NED to direct clandestine and third-party support to the unions. Task force official Roger Noriega, who had earlier helped manage the so-called contra humanitarian aid packages, took a lead role in moving AIFLD moneys through the AID.[21]

The AIFLD also set up a private fund-raising drive in the United States to finance some of the six UNO labor candidates, particularly CUS leader Alvin Guthrie, who was running for the National Assembly. Because AIFLD statutes prohibit it from directly financing the electoral campaigns of candidates in its overseas programs, AIFLD official David Jessup, who oversaw the organization's Nicaragua programs, set up a separate bank account under the name "AIFLD-CUS" in early 1989 and sent personal letters out to AFL-CIO unions around the country asking for "private donations" to be "forwarded to Alvin" through AIFLD headquarters in Washington.[22]

Two labor sectors that became special targets of U.S. operations were health workers and teachers. U.S.-sponsored organizing activities focused on trying to form parallel unions among teachers and health workers to counter the National Association of Nicaraguan Educators (ANDEN) and the Federation of Health Workers. The CPT sent out the FTUI-trained organizers to the country's hospitals, health clinics, and schools, and the U.S. Embassy assigned two officials to supervise them, Joel Cassman, "economic and commercial attaché," and Kathleen Barmon, head of "regional labor affairs" at the U.S. Embassy in Tegucigalpa, the Honduran capital.[23]

The strategy was to push bread-and-butter demands for salary increases at a moment of severe austerity and then have the political opposition back this demand. The demand was legitimate. Teachers were among the most severely underpaid, but the government was in no position to grant significant pay raises. The backdrop to the issue was the dramatic expansion since 1979 of educational opportunities. The number of public school teachers had jumped from about twelve thousand under Somoza to thirty-six thousand by 1989. Given the economic crisis, the government faced the choice of paying a few teachers well or providing teachers for everyone at lower wages. By unconditionally backing the teachers' demands, "the opposition looks like [it] cares about the teachers' economic situation and we don't," said a member of ANDEN.[24]

After several weeks of agitation among teachers, CPT organizers called a strike, culminating on May 28 with a march and rally in Chinandega led by leaders from the UNO and from the CPT. Cassman and Barmon were at the rally, where they promised that the United States would provide economic assistance for strikers.[25] The strike was resolved over the next few days when the teachers accepted a government offer of a package of nonmonetary salary supplements. The government expelled the U.S. diplomats for interfering in the domestic political affairs of their host country.[26]

The leader of the strike in Managua was Hortensia Rivas Zeledón, the wife of UNO Political Council member Luis Sánchez and a graduate of the FTUI seminars. Rivas Zeledón was the national organizer for the parallel teachers' union, the Federación Sindical de Maestros de Nicaragua. At the rally in Chinandega, Rivas Zeledón did not mention teachers' salaries but did call on the crowd to vote for the opposition. "We have to unite and overthrow this regime," she said.[27] Shortly after the teachers' strike, Rivas Zeledón met secretly in San José, Costa Rica, with Carl Gershman, who promised that U.S. assistance would be forthcoming. Gershman then contacted David Dorn of the conservative American Federation of Teachers, which is affiliated with the AFL-CIO, to discuss expanding U.S. support for an organizing effort among Nicaraguan teachers. "I hope you can call her at the earliest possible time," Gershman told Dorn, "and call me if you have any questions."[28]

TAKE II: WOMEN, YOUTHS, AND THE VIA CÍVICA—COMPLETING THE CIVIC FRONT

The substantive dimensions of low intensity conflict [must be] directly linked to the political-social milieu of the indigenous area. Effective operations [are] aimed at the political-social system with all its nuances and require skillful political organizers who have penetrated deeply into the fabric of the indigenous system.

—Sam Sarkesian[29]

In designing an electoral intervention, U.S. strategists developed a systematic analysis of Nicaraguan society. "The U.S. needs to modify its terms of reference for each country to which it's going," said one NDI officer. "We need to develop a country specific strategy for Nicaragua."[30] NED strategists identified women and youths as two special constituencies that would have to be organized to complete the "civic formation."

Demographically, Nicaragua is a society of youths. Some 50 percent of the population is younger than thirty, and the voting age is set at sixteen years. Youths were the core of the revolutionary energy that overthrew the Somoza dictatorship. Most Sandinista leaders were young, and the most militant, enthusiastic groups were of the youths, be it at schools, in workplaces, or in neighborhoods. Young men were the backbone of the military defense effort. On the basis of the Nicaraguan experience some social scientists even developed new theories of youths as a third revolutionary sector, after workers and peasants.[31] Thus, the chances for U.S. success were tied to reaching Nicaraguan youths. One NED report observed:

Youth under the age of 30 constitute more than 44 percent of the voting age population. . . . For the past 10 years, the education of Nicaraguan youth has been restricted by a political system that has discouraged and often repressed independent political discussion and activity. The Sandinistas have retained exclusive control over the most formal and informal educational institutions, and youth have been forcibly drafted into the military where they are indoctrinated in the basic tenets of Marxist-Leninist dogma. The result is a youth population with a limited political experience and little or no understanding of democratic institutions.[32]

Delphi was assigned to launch the youth project. The NED gave Delphi $33,000 early in 1988 to create the Centro de Formación Juvenil (CEFOJ)[33] and another $118,000 in 1989 to consolidate this new "civic youth organization."[34] The plan was to hold seminars throughout 1988 for a core group of salaried youth leaders from opposition political parties. This group would form a national leadership and would be paid from NED funds. In turn, the group would select regional leaders who would oversee local activists working in secondary schools, communities, and recreational centers to organize an anti-Sandinista political youth movement.[35]

In a progress report submitted to the NED, Delphi affirmed that the program was successful: The CEFOJ carried out "a series of seminars on political activism and the use of propaganda,"[36] including meetings with opposition political parties, La Prensa and staff from the other opposition news media, and business leaders, to discuss bringing youths into each component of the opposition coalition. The CEFOJ had made important inroads at the high school and university level, where the Sandinista youth organization and prorevolutionary student associations were strong. "More and more young people are joining CEFOJ's efforts to establish a democratic government once and for all," concluded Delphi.

The NRI also pitched in on the youth effort, especially by bringing "youth leaders" that it had developed through its work with the Conservative Party. The Republican organization allocated $45,000 from its general budget for youth work during the electoral campaign. "Planning continues for the second stage of the 'Nicaragua-FY89' program," stated one NRI memo in August 1989. "The second portion of this program is designed to bring together a large scale Seminary/Rally to politicize and educate the Youth elements of the United Opposition forces."[37] Another NRI document affirmed that "youth participation in the civic opposition forces has been seen as a vital, yet untapped resource. [NRI] seminars will bring these elements into the already active and organized opposition."[38]

The NED described the CEFOJ as a "non-partisan civic youth association" dedicated to promoting "nonviolent efforts to strengthen democratic institutions."[39] But a CEFOJ spokesperson was more candid in his description of the group's objectives in the electoral campaign: "If Mrs. Chamorro wins but the Sandinistas continue to exist, for us the situation would be the same as before the elections. . . . Whether the opposition wins or loses, the elections will merely be one more step forward in the intensification of our struggle against communism. . . . After the elections we will proceed to spark a fire that will culminate in the uprising of the people to overthrow the Sandinista communists."[40]

Meanwhile, women were identified as another special sector. Targeting women, the backbone of most Nicaraguan families, would be a way to penetrate the very nucleus of society—the family. The draft of young men was particularly unpopular among mothers, who saw their sons shipped off to war fronts and often returned maimed or dead. Women predominated in the informal market that dotted Managua and other urban centers. The

Sandinistas' economic policies in favor of producers and consumers, rather than traders, had a positive effect on the poor overall, but they antagonized the "market women," who made up sizable constituencies. In addition, many women had become empowered through the revolutionary process, particularly by their participation in mass organizations such as the women's association, neighborhood groups, and trade unions. The U.S. organizers concluded that women as a group needed to be separated from *Sandinismo*, were susceptible to U.S. psychological pressures, and could play a critical role in the electoral intervention project.

Delphi designed a "women's project" that focused on organizing efforts in the marketplace and in households. The NED provided Delphi with a grant to form the Nicaraguan Women's Movement (MMN) in April 1989 by bringing together female leaders from several UNO parties and creating a board of directors.[41] "Nicaragua women have begun to speak of the decisive role they must play in organizing rallies and protests," explained one document, which prescribed "seminars and workshops tailored to train 'multipliers' to train and motivate their peers to participate":[42]

> As in most Latin American countries, women hold a position of special influence in the life of the family and the community and thus constitute an important potential force for encouraging democratic political participation at the grassroots level. . . . This emerging movement is made up of women from across the political spectrum, including trade unionists, professionals, church activists, peasants and market women, nurses, teachers, and housewives. Organizing meetings will be held in Managua and in other cities in the interior of the country, including Granada, Masaya, León, Jinotega, and Rivas. Through meetings, courses and public campaigns, Nicaraguan women will be mobilized to take an active role in the electoral process. . . . Nicaraguan women have begun to recognize their shared responsibility in rebuilding the political, social and economic life of the country, and the decisive role they must play in reaching out to all Nicaraguans with their democratic message.[43]

The system of "multiplier" political training used in the trade union, youth, and women's projects is standard in most NED-funded programs in Nicaragua. This method of political organization developed by U.S. foreign policy experts in political warfare is recommended in CIA, AID, and Department of Defense political operations manuals.[44] In fact, some of the language of the Delphi documents was remarkably similar to that of the CIA's 1984 contra "assassination manual"—*Psychological Operations in Guerrilla Warfare*. There was one major difference, however: The old references to the "freedom fighters' struggle" against the "communist dictatorship" were updated in the post-Esquipulas period to refer to the "civic struggle" for "democratic objectives."

As with the UNO/IPCE spending, the NED claimed that the youth and women's projects were nonpartisan, civic education activities. Funds allocated to them from congressional appropriations could not be used for direct activities in support of any candidate. To conform to such technicalities in designing the CEFOJ and MMN programs, U.S. advisers resorted to the same tactics as NDI/NRI officials used in making IPCE funding nonpartisan (see

Chapter 3). For instance, the MMN produced a poster that began circulating in November 1989 urging women to vote. The actual words selected for the poster did not state, "Vote for the UNO." Yet the colors used were blue and white (the colors of the UNO campaign), and the background of the poster was a hand with the index finger raised to symbolically signify the number "one"—the meaning in Spanish of UNO.

Similarly, Delphi produced a joint MMN-CEFOJ leaflet, also in blue and white, allegedly to explain to the population how to fill out the paper ballots on election day. The leaflet was designed as a sample ballot—that is, a sample of what voters would be handed on election day to fill out and drop in the ballot boxes. In the CEFOJ samples, the column for the UNO was in boldfaced block letters that were larger and darker than the letters used to list the other parties. Moreover, the leaflet listed only four of the ten parties or coalitions that actually ran candidates and appeared on the actual ballots. The FSLN was not included in the four parties listed on the CEFOJ sample ballots.

VIA CÍVICA

By mid-1989, U.S. officials could take satisfaction in their achievements. The machinery of electoral intervention had been mounted and set in motion. Consensus on the strategy had been achieved in Washington. The Nicaraguan government was under pressure to open up in the way Washington saw fit and advantageous for the opposition. The opposition was becoming unified and was developing a profile. NED officials in Washington analyzed overall progress: "There are three main centers of activity in this election. One is the political parties grouped in UNO. Another is the labor group in CPT. Each of these has come together fairly well and there is a good working relationship between them. . . . The third group is a civic group which has yet to solidify. Conceptually, this is a vital part of the democratic process. . . . The civic group needs to be independent and non-partisan, but it should also coordinate with the other two main groups and avoid duplication of effort."[45]

Shortly afterward, the NDI sponsored a seminar in Managua between U.S. organizers and civic opposition representatives. The purpose of the meeting was to set up the structures for the "civic component" and then to "arrive at an agreed-upon division of labor among the three components."[46] Among those attending the Managua meeting was Henry Quintero. This time he was representing yet another organization, the International Federation for Electoral Systems (IFES). This group, formed just months before the beginning of the Nicaraguan electoral process to "support and improve the process and management of free elections in emerging democracies throughout the world," was put in charge of running the Via Cívica program. As could be expected, the IFES board of directors heavily interlocked with other NED groups. Among those on the IFES board was F. Clifton White, the Goldwater Republican who had worked with William Casey and CIA agent Walter Raymond on Project Democracy and on various contra support programs.[47] With his curious hop-skip-and-jump from INSI to Delphi and then to IFES as Nicaraguan projects coordinator,[48] Quintero was able to get the ball rolling on a handful of critical anti-Sandinista programs, including Via Cívica.

At a press conference after the meeting, civic leaders announced the formation of Via Cívica. This new organization, they proclaimed, was "a nonpartisan grouping of notables" who would press their cause "through ballots, not bullets." Via Cívica, without any interest in promoting one or another political position, would merely help register the voting age population and promote civic values. "Just think of it as a League of Women Voters" was how Quintero put it.[49]

All ten directors of this new group were vocal and well-known anti-Sandinista activists. Three were UNO political leaders, five were COSEP leaders, and two represented the CPT unions. Olga María Taboada, named as head of women's affairs for Via Cívica, was a national coordinator of UNO's Nicaraguan Conservative Party.[50] Hortensia Rivas Zeledón was another Via Cívica board member.[51] Via Cívica also formed a youth wing, headed by Fanor Avendaño, director of the CEFOJ youth movement and a leader of the UNO-affiliated Conservative Party. With Via Cívica established, the three separate components of the U.S. program were in place and were expected "to function during the election as a single unit," one NED document concluded.[52]

During the course of 1989, the NED gave the IFES three successive grants totaling $540,000 for Via Cívica. There was other funding as well, channeled through San José, Costa Rica.[53] Jerónimo Sequiera, a Via Cívica board member, and member of COSEP's board, had set up a Nicaraguan company, Construcciones y Proyectos, SA (CYPSA), the local subsidiary of Inversiones Martínez López (IML). In early 1989, IML, which was founded by a one-time Somoza minister of finance who moved to Miami after the overthrow of the dictatorship, opened an office in San José. Then on August 1, Via Cívica president Carlos Quiñonez, also a UNO leader, sent Sequiera to San José to meet with Henry Quintero and IFES president Richard Soudriette. Four weeks later, on August 28, Quintero entered Managua and registered with immigration officials as a "consultant for CYPSA."[54] During the San José and Managua meetings, hundreds of thousands of dollars were provided to Quiñonez and Sequiera by IFES officials.[55]

The U.S. funds for Via Cívica were used to set up offices and pay a full-time staff.[56] In addition, the IFES paid fifteen hundred Via Cívica "volunteers" $1 per day during the course of the electoral campaign.[57] The prevailing exchange rate and internal prices made this $30 per month superior to an average worker's wages. This funding was sustained throughout the campaign and even continued well after the voting.[58]

With so much money floating around, some opposition leaders reached for the cookie jar. Olga María Taboada fell out of favor with her U.S. sponsors after she allegedly embezzled thousands of dollars in NED funds that Delphi had sent down for the MMN. In October 1989, Barbara Haig and Chiqui Reyes Gavilán from the NED met with Taboada and demanded that she account for $9,900 in funds given to her earlier. They asked her to produce the MMN's checkbook, but Taboada refused. Delphi continued the efforts to recover the funds. In January 1990, Delphi head Paul Von Ward made a special trip to Managua with no results. NED's chief financial officer finally wrote to Joe Sullivan, head of the Central America Desk at the State Department and a key member of the Nicaraguan task force: "I think at this point it should be a matter between Delphi and the Women, and Delphi should use every effort to try to recoup the money."[59]

The conceptual framework behind the trade union, women's, youth, and Via Cívica projects was to face the Sandinistas at every level of society where *Sandinismo* held influence. U.S. funds, political training, and guidance were instruments to erode this influence and construct an opposition as the alternative. "Building the institutions of democracy" meant creating or strengthening the institutions of the pro-U.S., anti-Sandinista opposition organizations, achieving vertical and horizontal linkages among them, and qualitatively transforming their political activity. This was not a contest of "democracy versus totalitarianism" but one of the political and organizing skills of the Sandinistas versus the political skills of U.S. experts operating through Nicaraguan proxies.

TAKE III: CREATING COMMUNICATIONS MEDIA FOR THE OPPOSITION

The first requirement for success in a particular country would be a communications program. In order to overcome the sense of isolation of potential opponents, communications should emphasize information on the activities and intentions of those opposed to the regime. It should also facilitate their acquisition of the supplies they need outside the country. [The goal is] the increase of confidence in the population for those opposed to the regime and the decrease of confidence in the ruling elite.

—Raymond D. Gastil[60]

In the early 1980s, when Washington's campaign against the Sandinistas was just beginning, U.S. strategists targeted the communications media as a critical element in the overall strategy. The role of propaganda and communications as ideological aggression against Nicaragua was at the heart of the U.S. war and of the electoral intervention project. This aggression was meant to influence the U.S. public (creating a domestic constituency for the war), the international community (mobilizing the resources of other countries for the war effort and isolating Nicaragua internationally), and the Nicaraguan population (inundating Nicaraguans with a host of messages conducive to the overall objectives of the war). Several U.S. agencies became deeply involved in the communications and propaganda efforts, among them the CIA, the NED, the State Department, the Office of Public Diplomacy, and the USIA.[61]

Covert and psychological operations aimed at influencing the coverage of Nicaragua in the United States and in the international media involved "leaking" information, manipulating and even paying off journalists, planting disinformation and black propaganda, and designing a public relations blitzkrieg out of the Office of Public Diplomacy. The war of images was complex and multidimensional. It sought to "demonize the Sandinista government," as one administration official admitted, in order to "turn it into a real enemy and threat" in the eyes of the U.S. public and international community.[62] Like worn-out records, the themes of a lack of democracy in Nicaragua, political repression, persecution of the church, economic disaster, militarization, the export of revolution, and so forth, were repeated on a daily basis during the course of a decade. Although the Reagan administration never managed to sell the contra project, it did successfully inculcate a negative and undemocratic image of the Sandinista Revolution in the United States.

The flip side of the strategy was to inculcate the image of the contras and of the internal opposition as the democratic alternative. Even though endless public relations programs could not overcome the blood-stained image of the contras, and the Iran-contra scandal reinforced that view, the portrayal of the internal opposition as wholesome civic leaders and democrats proved an effective and crucial aspect of the electoral intervention project.[63] (Inside Nicaragua the messages transmitted by U.S. psychological warfare specialists were of a different character, as we shall see in Chapter 7.)

The propaganda campaign also created communications media for the counterrevolution so that it could spread its messages among the Nicaraguan population. The USIA set up Radio 15 de Septiembre, which was run by the contra military group, the FDN, out of Tegucigalpa for most of the 1980s. In San José, the CIA opened Radio Impacto, which operated as a commercial front station and transmitted into Nicaraguan cities more sophisticated messages than the crude anticommunism of the FDN's outlet.[64] Among those who were associated with Radio Impacto at different times during the 1980s were Alfredo César and Violeta Chamorro's son, Pedro Joaquin, Jr., as well as prominent journalists from La Prensa and from right-wing radio stations inside Nicaragua. Radio Impacto targeted both the Costa Rican population and the Nicaraguans across the border. The USIA also expanded Voice of America transmitters in the Caribbean Basin region so as to inundate Nicaraguan airwaves. In 1986, the USIA set up Radio Liberación to substitute for 15 de Septiembre in the contra northern front based in Honduras. With a powerful A.M. transmitter in Tegucigalpa, the new radio station was soon bathing Nicaraguan airwaves. Modeled after the successful Radio Impacto, Radio Liberación shed the crude anticommunist baggage and ran high-tech programming, including music, "news" programs, and features, shipped in from USIA studios in the United States. The contras also had several shortwave radio stations, including Radio Miskut, which broadcast to Nicaragua's Atlantic coast in the native Miskito langauge, and Radio Monimbó.[65] The contras also published propaganda newsletters and magazines and were assisted in these activities by the USIA and were funded out of general budgets provided by the CIA.

The bulk of U.S. resources and attention went into these externally based outlets. Much of the NED's media activities in the preelectoral period involved financing anti-Sandinista publications published outside of Nicaragua, particularly in Costa Rica and in Washington. Freedom House managed most of these programs, participated in the contras' public relations efforts, and worked with the NSC as a liaison between the Office of Public Diplomacy and private conservative groups.[66] (Freedom House specializes in the preparation and international circulation of information promoting conservative ideology and U.S. foreign policy.) The organization received some $3 million from the NED between 1984 and 1989 for such activities as distributing articles favorable to right-wing causes, organizing press conferences, and funding academic studies. With approximately $1 million in NED funding, Freedom House created a Central American publishing house called Libro Libre (Free Book) that was based in San José and that was administered by the Nicaraguan Xavier Zavala Cuadra.[67] Libro Libre was dedicated to publishing "intellectual" works of prominent anti-Sandinistas from Nicaragua and from other Central American countries, which were promoted commercially and circulated among government, diplomatic, and university circles in the region. The NED also paid Freedom House to create a Central America information and research center (CINCO) in Costa Rica. The CINCO functioned as an anti-Sandinista think tank dedicated to supporting "Nicaraguan democrats who believe that an accurate record of events and careful analysis of internal issues will serve as an intellectual foundation for a democratic future."[68] Roberto Cardenal, a former editor of La Prensa, was appointed to administer the CINCO. Another Costa Rican–based NED project was the publication of an anti-Sandinista quarterly journal, Pensamiento Centroamericano. Through these three outlets, the NED published books and articles by Pedro Joaquin Chamorro, Jr., Jaime Chamorro, Pablo Antonio Cuadra (another La Prensa editor), and other prominent opposition figures.

Despite the emphasis on externally based propaganda, the CIA, the USIA, and the NED maintained a foothold in the internal opposition media outlets throughout the 1980s, the most important of these being La Prensa. Given its prominence for the United States as a leading symbol of the anti-Sandinista campaign, that La Prensa's publisher went on to become the presidential candidate for the UNO coalition should come as no surprise. The United States had to generate an image of La Prensa as a struggling "independent" news outlet defending freedom and democracy in the face of Sandinista repression. One NED document exclaimed, "The history of La Prensa is one of struggle, courage and, at times, tragedy, parallel to that endured by the country and the people of Nicaragua. While La Prensa is by no means the sole key to a political opening in Nicaragua, it is probably true that without La Prensa a meaningful political opening cannot occur."[69] Of course, there was nothing "independent" about La Prensa. It was funded by the United States and functioned as an important outlet inside Nicaragua for the U.S. war and as the unofficial organ of the internal opposition.

La Prensa began to receive covert CIA subsidies (through third-party "cutouts") as early as 1979 to enable it to play a counterrevolutionary role similar to that the CIA had cultivated in other countries where the United States had launched destabilization programs. (A similar role was played, for example, by El Mercurio during the 1970–1973 U.S. operation against the

Allende government in Chile and by the *Daily Gleaner* in Jamaica in 1976–1980 in the CIA's anti-Manley effort.)[70] Tensions over *La Prensa*'s shift to the right and editorial position in favor of the growing U.S. hostility resulted in the resignation of its incorruptible managing editor, Xavier Chamorro, brother of the assassinated Pedro Joaquin Chamorro, along with 80 percent of the staff. They all went on to found *El Nuevo Diario*, which was supportive of the Sandinistas but maintained its independence. Pedro Joaquin Chamorro, Jr., became the new editor of *La Prensa*. Following in the footsteps of other *La Prensa* editors and star reporters who had left Nicaragua in the early 1980s to take up positions as leaders and advisers with the different contra media outlets, Chamorro, Jr., went into self-exile in Costa Rica, where he produced *Nicaragua Hoy*, a weekly contra news supplement financed by the CIA and distributed free of charge to Costa Rican and other major Latin American newspapers.[71] In 1988, he became a member of the contras' Political Directorate, a position he held for approximately one year. In mid-1989, he returned to the country to work on his mother's presidential campaign.

In addition to covert support, the newspaper also received millions of dollars from third sources, including "private" U.S. groups tied in with policy toward Nicaragua such as the Americares Foundation and Oliver North's secret network. The NED began funding the newspaper in 1984, one of its first operations. Between 1984 and 1985, *La Prensa* received $150,000 in NED funds channeled through the Washington-based organization PRODEMCA.[72] In 1986, the NED transferred the *La Prensa* operation to Delphi.

La Prensa's activities are a textbook study in how a psychological warfare organ operates. In this role, *La Prensa* worked closely with U.S. Embassy personnel in Managua and coordinated its editorial policy in unison with overall U.S. strategy and the contra war. When the Sandinistas tried to curb the excesses in *La Prensa*'s openly destabilizing activities through limited censorship, the issue was pounced on as evidence of their "anti-democratic tendencies." When Congress debated the Reagan administration's request for $100 million in military aid to the contras in the spring of 1986, *La Prensa* came out in open and vigorous support for approval of the package.[73] Jaime Chamorro even traveled to Washington to lobby in favor of the package and wrote an editorial in the newspaper asserting that the contras had "every right to seek aid from other countries."[74] This support was then brandished by the White House in its legislative lobbying as proof that "Nicaragua's only independent newspaper" was even supporting the package.[75] After the approval of the package, which led to a major escalation of the war, the government decided to close *La Prensa*, although it was allowed to reopen after the Esquipulas Accords were signed.

Critics of the censorship of *La Prensa* forgot that in times of war, nearly all countries employ censorship. The U.S. government resorted to tight control over information during the invasions of Grenada and Panama, the Gulf War, World War II, and the Civil War, among other limitations on press freedom during times of conflict.[76] Despite the images conjured up by Washington of a "muzzled press," the communications media in Nicaragua were a lively battleground of provocative debates, polemics, and confrontation during the 1980s. A *New York Times* editorial in March 1988 noted, "There's more diversity of published and spoken opinion in Managua than in Guatemala, Honduras and El Salvador."[77]

In the post-Esquipulas shift to the internal political track, Washington turned its attention to bolstering the media outlets of the internal opposition. The NED created a Nicaraguan independent media program and put Delphi in charge of it. This project involved a huge expansion of both funding and direct political guidance for the creation and expansion of the opposition media, including *La Prensa* and several radio stations.[78] *La Prensa* received almost $1 million from the NED from 1987 to the elections for newsprint, salaries, supplies, and wire service contracts.[79] In addition, the NED helped set up clandestine structures and third-party conduits in three offshore centers—San José, Costa Rica; Caracas, Venezuela; and Miami. Of these, the Caracas connection was the most interesting and the most clandestine. It involved four-way coordination among the CIA, *La Prensa*, Venezuelan groups, and the NED, which played the lead role in organizing the overall operation.

Details of this arrangement were worked out in February 1989 when Violeta Chamorro traveled to Caracas to attend the inauguration of Carlos Andrés Pérez. She was accompanied by her daughter Cristiana Chamorro, who had recently returned to Nicaragua from a USIA training course in Washington and had taken over as managing editor of *La Prensa*, and by Pedro Chamorro, Jr. Pérez explained to the Chamorros that he intended to provide support to *La Prensa* but that he did not want money to come officially from either his government or his party. Rather, a private foundation should be created to handle these transactions. He instructed Cristiana Chamorro and Pedro Chamorro, Jr., to get in touch with Eladio Larez, a businessman and president of two Venezuelan media outlets, Radio Caracas and Television RCTV.

On returning to Managua, Cristiana Chamorro wrote to Carl Gershman:

> My mother and I returned Monday from Caracas [where] we met with the people who Carlos Andrés appointed to manage the [National Democratic] Foundation. The man who contacted us [was] Dr. Eladio Larez. The Foundation is going to be run by personalities from the private Venezuelan sector tied to the communications media. Regarding the mechanism for the functioning of the Foundation in conjunction with the National Endowment and the purchases which will be made for La Prensa, Dr. Larez said that he was in agreement with everything we have already arranged. . . . Ona will continue to make purchases and . . . [send] the materials via Miami–Costa Rica or via Venezuela, and that in the event the Venezuelan route runs into complications, they would seek out a Venezuelan company based in Miami, which would then appear as the one handling things. [See Appendix A, document 4.][80]

The letter went on to stress that the National Democratic Foundation would take pains to assure that it appeared to be the source of funds for *La Prensa*. (The foundation's board of directors included leaders from different private media outlets, the Venezuelan Federation of Business Chambers, politicians, and representatives from the CTV.)[81]

Pedro Chamorro, Jr., was instrumental in coordination from Miami. In 1988, he moved from San José to Miami and started producing a local version of *Nicaragua Hoy* in the Spanish-language edition of the *Miami Herald*. He also wrote editorials in *Diario las Américas*, another paper purportedly tied to the CIA.[82]

The NED funding mechanism was also used to support other Nicaraguan organizations besides *La Prensa*. By channeling moneys to Nicaraguan beneficiaries through "legitimate" third-party conduits in other countries, the NED could conceal its support for Nicaraguan groups. Should the operation be uncovered, NED's accounting books would be clean, and responsibility would rest with the conduit.

THE "INDEPENDENT RADIOS PROJECT"

Of the twenty-three radio stations that existed in Nicaragua prior to the Sandinista Revolution, fourteen belonged to the Somoza family or to close associates of the dictatorship. These were nationalized by the Sandinista government and run as public stations. The others remained privately owned by Sandinistas, opposition groups, or independent journalists. The most prominent of the opposition stations were Radio Corporación and Radio Católica. Both radio stations enjoyed constant funding from diverse U.S. and international sources. Conservative sectors within the U.S. Bishops' Conference, together with several prominent contras, set up Friends of Nicaraguan Radio Católica to raise funds for the station.[83] On the honorary board were the right-wing Boston archbishop Bernard Law, who also endorsed private fund-raising activities for the UNO campaign (see Chapter 6); Alejandro Bolaños Geyer, brother of COSEP leader Enrique Bolaños; and several relatives of the overthrown dictator, Anastasio Somoza.

In 1988, Delphi, already in charge of the overall Nicaragua media project, launched its Independent Radios Project with the objective of equipping and advising the opposition radios.[84] The project was begun with initial grants from the NED totaling $150,000. "The months leading up to the elections will be crucial ones for Nicaragua," stated a Delphi summary of the project. "Many Nicaraguans live in isolation from the political life of their country, though their ability to feed and clothe their families and all of their hopes and aspirations for their children depend on what develops in the political arena. With both television stations under government control, radio remains the best means for reaching the masses of Nicaraguans throughout the country."[85]

The program funded four radio stations during the campaign: Radio Corporación, Radio Mundial (in Managua), Radio Darío (in León), and Radio San Cristóbal (in Chinandega). This program included training for radio journalists and programmers. Delphi coordinated its youth and women's projects with the radio program. CEFOJ director Fanor Avendaño, for instance, was the liaison between Delphi and Radio Darío and Radio San Cristóbal.[86]

In August 1989, the Bush administration suspended the USIA-managed Radio Liberación (operated from Honduras by the Nicaraguan Resistance) and redirected these resources toward the creation of Radio Democracia (a new outlet inside Nicaragua) in consonance with the transfer of the campaign from outside to inside Nicaragua. The NED selected lawyer Roger Guevara Mena, a UNO leader, to put together a board of directors for Radio Democracia. In October, Guevara Mena wrote to Gershman affirming that the board was in place. It was composed exclusively of anti-Sandinista opposition leaders from the UNO. Radio Democracia, the letter explained, would serve as an "instrument of democratization and the formation of a civic consciousness, functioning both in the pre- and post-election period, in order to offset the FSLN's instruments for consciousness formation."[87]

TELEVISION, TOO

The print media and radios were easy for U.S. strategists; television presented a more difficult challenge. Before 1979, there were two television stations. One belonged to the Somoza family and the other to several of Somoza's close business associates. Both were nationalized in 1979 and run as public television channels. In October 1987, a group of Nicaraguan businessmen requested a license to open up a private television station in Managua. That petition was followed by another one in 1988 from Pedro Chamorro, Jr., who proposed to open a station with assistance from Venezuela and from supporters in Miami.[88] The government turned down these requests, arguing that television should remain an exclusively public domain accessible to all sectors. (The electoral law already guaranteed airtime to all candidates.) The United States therefore decided to send in experts in video and image propaganda and to guide and fund the UNO's television media strategy.

In early 1989, Don Fisk of the State Department's Nicaragua Desk, who had been acting as State's liaison with the contra offices in the United States, contacted Miami TV reporter Carlos Briceño. Fisk told Briceño that the administration was setting up a television project for the internal opposition and that there would be some money and a role for him. Fisk told Briceño to get in touch with Barbara Haig, who had already been briefed on the project.[89]

The Nicaraguan-born Briceño had lived in the United States for most of his life. He had worked with the *Miami Herald* and with the local NBC affiliate and had won an Emmy award before moving on to become Miami correspondent for the Spanish-language UNIVISION television network. Briceño had developed close relations with contra leaders and with members of the internal opposition as they passed through Miami. Among Briceño's associates was Pedro Joaquin Chamorro, Jr., with whom Briceño had worked on the 1988 project to open a television station in Managua.

Briceño wrote to Haig in March 1989, "Regarding the project which Pedro J. Chamorro and I are working on: Force the Sandinistas to grant us a broadcast licence to open an independent TV in time for next year's elections." "Dan Fisk suggested I give you a ring," said the letter.[90] Attached to the letter was a project proposal for NED funding.

Haig wrote back to Briceño several weeks later, after the government refused to allow a private station, instructing him to revise the proposal to request funding for the installation of a television programming studio in Managua. Briceño's modified proposal, submitted on UNIVISION letter-head,[91] outlined plans to open a fully equipped production facility that would prepare half-hour programs, a "fast-paced, entertaining and aggressive show that could be a hybrid between a regular newscast and a news magazine." The objective of these shows would be to "motivate and encourage Nicara-guans to participate politically again. It could serve as a catalyst for Nicara-guans to begin demonstrating their displeasure with the present state of affairs that has been pent up for the last ten years." "In Nicaragua," the proposal continued, "the impact of 30 minutes a day of independent programming would have a devastating effect on the Sandinistas."[92]

With NED financing, Briceño proposed sending a team of U.S. and inter-national technicians, trainers, and journalists to Nicaragua. "The scant tele-vision technicians that are in Nicaragua are probably working for the Sandi-nista television network. Therefore, the production equipment, reporters, photographers, and technicians will necessarily have to be recruited from outside of Nicaragua, probably in Miami and Central America." The proposal included a budget of $346,338 for equipment and $365,000 for salaries (including $75,000 for himself as "president/executive producer"). Briceño concluded that he was "ideally suited for the position" because he had "excellent contacts inside the country with members of the Opposition and the media."

Haig wrote back to Briceño explaining that before the project could begin, the NED would have to obtain from opposition leaders in Nicaragua a "request" for assistance from Briceño because NED statutes specified that the endowment could not initiate projects but could merely "[respond] to requests from democratic groups abroad." The timing for arranging such a request was perfect. The NED had scheduled a visit to Washington of opposition repre-sentatives for late April. Briceño could meet with them as they passed through Miami and ask that they submit a formal request. On April 30, Briceño presented the opposition group with a letter that he had written in Spanish and had addressed to "Gentlemen of the 'Fourteen Opposition Parties.'" The letter explained that the objective was not only to produce opposition pro-grams aimed at the Nicaraguan electorate but also to prepare English-language transmissions for outside of Nicaragua to "denounce the Sandinista fraud." The letter continued:

The ideal would be for the Sandinista regime to concede a licence for the opening of a new television channel. But in the meantime, and as we continue applying internal and international pressures for this, it is crucial to begin now to take the first steps in making use of the 30 minutes daily of television time [granted to each candidate] for the elections.

This production facility, in addition to producing commercials for the political campaign, will include reports in English and Spanish on the electoral process aimed abroad so as to keep the world informed on the compliance or non-compliance of the Sandinistas. . . .

I want to stress that the united opposition must continue to pressure for a modification of the Media Law, and in particular, for the elimination of Article 11, which relates to the use of satellite transmissions. . . . If you participate in the elections and there are anomalies, the opposition needs to have the capacity to almost instantly transmit an international condemnation of this fraud through the use of satellite signals. . . .

The Nicaraguan opposition will not have to pay for anything on this project, since there are international organizations prepared to finance it so long as the opposition remains united and the programming is done professionally.

It is vital to get this project moving starting right now, for which reason I need the following from the United Opposition: 1. That you endorse the project in a letter stating so; 2. That the equipment necessary can be introduced into Nicaragua under the exemption from customs duties granted to the opposition parties.[93]

Two days later, on May 2, Briceño sent another letter to Haig, again on UNIVISION stationery: "I met with most of the opposition members here in Miami on their way back to Managua. There was incredible support on their part."[94] On their return to Managua, the UNO leaders faxed a one-page letter to Briceño: "We continue to demand that the Sandinista regime grant us a licence for an independent television station. To date, the Sandinistas have refused to concede this license, and for this reason we have agreed to support Mr. Carlos A. Briceño's project." The letter was signed by representatives of all fourteen parties.[95]

Briceño also met with Jeb Bush, son of the president and a close friend of several of the top contra leaders. Briceño requested that Bush lend his support to the project with contacts and with a letter that Briceño could then circulate among potential donors. A few days after the meeting, Bush sent Briceño a letter that strongly endorsed the television project and wished him "every success in generating political and financial support" (see Appendix A, document 2).[96]

In July, Briceño traveled to Nicaragua. On returning, he wrote again to Haig:

I'm back from Nicaragua, but disappointed of the lack of coverage I received from Barricada [the FSLN newspaper]. I guess they were busy trailing Mark Feierstein around. . . . I met with the UNO leaders and its communication's committee, and they are counting on me. . . . According to Luis [Sánchez], I won't have any trouble introducing the equipment. In the worst case I would have to pay a 15 percent import duty on it, which would not be substantial since purchase receipts could be fudged down. [See Appendix A, document 1.][97]

Meanwhile, both Briceño and NED officials continued to look for other sources of support for the project, including European foundations and the same Caracas circles backing La Prensa. At least $100,000 came out of Caracas.[98] In the United States, the NED turned to the National Association of Broadcasters and to sympathetic congressional offices. Briceño met with Bill Haratunian, NAB's international consultant, "who told me about NAB's intention to help in the project. . . . He asked me about the possibility of having the equipment loaned to us; however, that would be the least desirable alternative because the idea is for the equipment to become the basis for the first independent TV in the country if things change. If they don't I plan to take the equipment outside the country and beam a TV signal from a neighboring country" (see Appendix A, document 1).[99]

NED officials also met with several legislative offices, including a group of four senators (Connie Mack [R-Fla.], Bob Graham [D-Fla.], Charles Robb [D-Va.], and John McCain [R-Ariz.]), who in turn agreed to lobby the NAB on behalf of the television project. On July 25, the four sent a letter to NAB president Edward Fritts asking him to assist and asserting that "the promotion of human rights and U.S. national security interests in the region" were at stake.[100] Fritts obliged, sending letters to NAB affiliates around the country. The letters stated:

> We are being asked to donate certain broadcast equipment which would be used to establish a facility to produce TV programming on behalf of groups opposing the Sandinistas in the national elections. . . . I have enclosed a list of equipment needed for an independent production facility in Nicaragua. I ask you to see if you can donate any portion of these items from our equipment inventory for this worthy cause. If you can make a donation of equipment we ask that its title be transferred to "The National Endowment for Democracy," a tax-exempt, 501(c)(3) foundation with whom we are cooperating. They will then tranship it to the proper recipients in Nicaragua. [See Appendix A, document 3.][101]

Briceño's garrulousness and his lack of political savvy left a particularly negative impression with Carl Gershman, who met with Briceño in early August. After the meeting, Gershman sent a fax to Cristiana Chamorro at La Prensa. Gershman asked Chamorro to give her opinion of Briceño and to indicate whether he would be suitable for the assignment. Chamorro wrote back, "With regard to your question on Briceño, I would be able to conclude that he would be excellent with regard to the technical aspects, but he would need a lot of help on political focus, that is, he would need guidance" (see Appendix A, document 5).[102]

In its September 15 board meeting, the NED formally approved the television project and assigned the NRI to supervise it. NED officials also "sanitized" the final, public document, removing all openly partisan, anti-Sandinista references. The production facility was described as "independent." Gone were the references to ten years of displeasure, to "Sandinista fraud," to "winning the minds of the population." Now it was "the development of an effective informational and civic education effort encouraging civic participation." The political objectives of the project did not change; the language was merely professionalized.

The slick UNO television segments and vignettes began airing in September. The segments were highly professional and played heavily on a mixture of sound, image, and core themes sensitive to the Nicaraguan population—religious sentiment, childhood, contrast between misery in the present and hope for the future—which reinforced the psychological content of the U.S. intervention strategy (see Chapter 7). "Psychological and political warfare is about cultural and political symbols, about perceptions and emotions," stated one U.S. expert, "about the behavior of individuals and groups under stress, about the cohesion of organizations and alliances."[103]

Most of the NED groups pitched in to produce the opposition's television and radio ads. Dozens of media consultants were sent to Managua. While the NRI oversaw Briceño's work, the NDI used IPCE funds to send media consultant Peter Fenn to Managua to help with the ads.[104] Fenn designed a TV vignette that showed the Berlin Wall falling and Solidarity head Lech Wałesa. "Now Nicaragua has the opportunity to choose democracy," it concluded. Other television spots juxtaposed scenes of economic and social misery with a bright UNO future, with a backdrop of heavy religious symbolism.

The civic opposition front worked in close conjunction with the UNO-U.S. media strategy. Via Cívica, the CEFOJ, and the MMN placed advertisements in *La Prensa* each day as well as on Radio Corporación and the other NED-funded radios. One IFES report affirmed that Via Cívica had devised a total of sixteen daily thirty-second spots on Radio Noticias, Radio Católica, Radio Mundial, Radio Corporación, and Radio Reloj (all of the opposition). "Provincial radio stations are being checked out, as well as GON [Nicaraguan government] media. Hank [Quintero] encouraged the latter for credibility's sake."[105] Although these advertisements were careful not to endorse the UNO candidates per se, they were aired and published side by side with UNO campaign spots. Because the leadership overlapped almost 100 percent, the same people who spoke publicly for a civic group one minute proselytized for the UNO the next.

THE "WAR OF THE POLLS"

Polls and pollsters have become a methodological and systematic component of political and electoral processes. Surveys on voter behavior and political preferences serve both to guide parties and candidates and to shape public opinion itself. Images of the strengths, weaknesses, and prospects of candidates can be projected and reinforced through the dissemination of survey results. Beyond its own political system, the United States has developed the use of polls as an instrument in its machinery for electoral intervention abroad. The NDI and the NRI, for instance, relied extensively on polling as part of the NED programs in the Panamanian and Chilean elections.

Polls are easily manipulated for the political motives of pollsters and were used by both sides in the Nicaraguan elections as part of broader campaign strategies.[106] Political opinion polling took on enhanced significance in the electoral process because during the long state of emergency in which Nicaragua lived as a result of the war, opinion polling had been essentially prohibited. By the time the restrictions were lifted in 1988 on the eve of the electoral process, there was an almost prurient interest among observers in knowing exactly how much support the Sandinista government retained after all the years of bloodshed and economic decline.

Some dozen Nicaraguan and foreign organizations—pro-Sandinista, pro-UNO, and neutral—conducted voter surveys during the electoral process in what some referred to as the "war of the polls." Independent polls conducted in the final weeks of the campaign—among others, the ABC–Washington Post polls and those conducted by Democratic political consultant Sergio Bendixen and his firm, Bendixen and Schroth, for UNIVISION—showed the Sandinistas winning by a significant majority. Polls conducted by several regional pollsters contracted by the UNO, however, showed the UNO winning by margins similar to the actual voting results.

Given the highly polarized and politicized environment of a country torn by war as well as the methodological difficulties that abounded in Nicaragua, it was no wonder that analysts were often unable to interpret contradictory survey results. There was a peculiar dynamic of polling in Nicaragua that was poorly understood by pollsters and analysts alike during the electoral process. Observers were puzzled over what appeared to be wildly misleading poll results that showed the FSLN to enjoy a substantial lead. Yet the results were not so much *inaccurate* as they were *misread* by analysts, and the value of polls should not be judged by a juxtaposition of poll results and actual electoral results. In Nicaragua, respondents often told different things in different contexts. Responses were highly conditioned by *who* the respondent believed was conducting the poll—that is, if the respondent believed the poll was being conducted by Sandinista, anti-Sandinista, or neutral groups. This, in turn, reflected the dynamic of the electoral process itself, in which voting was less an issue of political preference under conditions of healthy competition than a decision made under conditions of warfare, economic crisis, and foreign intervention (see Chapters 7 and 8). Much could be written on the complex and multidimensional issue of polling in the Nicaraguan election;[107] what concerns us here is specifically the relation between polling and the U.S. electoral intervention project.

Despite the different survey results, polls taken in the pre-campaign period agreed on the existence of a core of FSLN supporters (some 25–30 percent) and a committed anti-Sandinista opposition (some 20–25 percent), with the majority, probably 40 percent or more, undecided and potential abstainers.[108]

Political opinion polling served two essential, yet contrasting, purposes in U.S.-UNO strategy. The first was propagandistic. There was keen awareness among U.S. political operatives of the uses to which polls could be put. The Reagan administration had used polls to demonstrate supposed popular support in Central American countries for Reagan's contra policy to influence votes in Congress.[109] The polls became an important instrument in the international campaign that Washington was organizing to cast doubts on the electoral process, tarnish the Sandinistas' image, and apply pressures on the Nicaraguan government. Polls showing the UNO way ahead and the Sandinistas trailing by wide margins would reinforce arguments that the FSLN could only win through a fraudulent election.

Second, polling became an important medium for assessing the extent to which the attrition process had advanced in the years following the 1984 elections. U.S. strategists used internal polls as a guide in assessing the direction of the undecided majority and the real prospects for converting would-be abstainers into opposition votes. Thus, polling was an instrument to obtain information necessary for U.S. operatives to more effectively and precisely carry out their work among the Nicaraguan electorate.[110]

One polling operation linked to Washington's electoral intervention project was sponsored by the U.S. consulting firm Penn and Schoen Associates, which had organized the polls in Panama as part of the electoral intervention activities in that country. Penn and Schoen had done polling for the electoral campaign of Venezuelan president Carlos Andrés Pérez and had organized its Latin American operations by contracting the Caracas-based consulting group DOXSA. "This proposal details our plan for conducting a polling program in Nicaragua as a means to ensure that NED and the pro-democracy forces have an independent, and reliable, source of statistically-valid data on election trends," wrote Penn and Schoen vice president Robert Green to NED programs director Barbara Haig in October 1989.[111]

According to the NED proposal, "Penn and Schoen polling will tangibly demonstrate the value of the NED's efforts to build democracy in Nicaragua, [for example,] the effectiveness of the communications efforts being made by the pro-democratic forces." The document concluded, "Our polling will be used to provide strategic guidance to the pro-democracy forces about the efficacy of their own efforts. Much as we do in other Latin American countries in which we typically play a partisan role on behalf of one party, our polls could provide feedback on the entire democracy-building program NED and others have designed."[112]

• FIVE •

The International Network

What must be kept secret, if the recipient group must work clandestinely in its country, is information about names of recipients, their location and the channels through which the funds are delivered. . . . Both the propriety and the effectiveness of giving administrative subsidies and/or campaign funds are strengthened if the money is given through multilateral channels. But he who pays the piper can call the tune. If the donor is from a single country, and especially if it is the government of that country, and most especially if that country is a superpower, then the public may have good reason to fear that the recipient group will end up serving merely as a tool of foreign interests. . . . It is much better to be perceived as being under the influence of the democratic world community than as being a paid puppet of the U.S. State Department.
— Ralph M. Goldman[1]

THE VENEZUELAN CONNECTION

A good portion of the electoral intervention project was developed in Washington and executed directly in Managua. But the plan also involved an extensive international apparatus that provided overseas conduits for U.S. political, material, and financial support for the opposition. U.S. strategists took advantage of the vast global network that the Reagan administration had set up in preceding years to sustain the contras. Three key overseas centers took on special importance: Miami, San José, and Caracas. The European allies also had a role in Washington's project.

The setting up of these support structures began in August 1988, when the State Department organized a private meeting in Miami. An "ad-hoc group of Latinamericans" was brought up to discuss how to "bring in Latin American support" for the Nicaraguan opposition. Among those present were NED and AID officials as well as Luigi Enaudi, who at the time was assistant under secretary of state for political planning for Latin America.[2] Bush later appointed Enaudi as ambassador to the Organization of American States.

At the meeting, participants proposed that Cardinal Obando y Bravo act as a liaison with the Venezuelans, whom participants saw as key players. Successive Venezuelan Social Democratic and Christian Democratic governments had a critical role in Central American politics in the late 1970s and the 1980s. The country's twin preoccupations in the Caribbean region—political stability and regional economic integration (particularly, regional markets for Venezuelan oil exports)—led it to develop an activist agenda that included support for the anti-Somoza struggle, participation in the Contadora Group negotiations, and deep involvement in Nicaraguan internal politics.[3] This agenda at times conflicted with Washington's and at other times converged.

Social Democratic leader Carlos Andrés Pérez, who was president in the 1970s and was then reelected at the end of 1988, had been in exile in Costa Rica during the Jiménez dictatorship. There, he developed a close friendship with Pedro Joaquin Chamorro, which gave Pérez an added personal interest in Nicaragua. As Venezuela's president from 1976 to 1980, he developed personal ties with a range of anti-Somoza Nicaraguans, including Archbishop Obando y Bravo, the Chamorro family, and both Sandinista and opposition figures. Pérez's position was similar to that of Arias: Reagan's contra policy was destructive; the Nicaraguan Revolution should be contained instead through the bolstering of the anti-Sandinista civic opposition.

Throughout the electoral process, Bush and Pérez maintained close contact. The CIA decided to reroute through Venezuela at least $200,000 in monthly funds that formerly went to maintaining the U.S. contra offices in Miami.[4] (Another $200,000 monthly was rerouted through San José.) At least two Venezuelan private foundations were used to reroute U.S. funds. One, the National Democratic Foundation, focused on sending money and supplies to *La Prensa* (see Chapter 4). The other, the Romulo Gallegos Foundation, sent campaign materials to the UNO and arranged visits of Nicaraguan opposition leaders to Venezuela. In March 1989, the Romulo Gallegos Foundation organized a visit to Caracas of some two dozen opposition leaders and several contras, among them Pedro Joaquin Chamorro, Jr. At the meeting, Venezuelan officials promised support but also urged the opposition to participate seriously in the electoral process and to abide by the results.[5]

César, who had been present at the Caracas meeting but had not yet made his definitive return to Managua, organized a follow-up meeting in the Venezuelan Embassy in Guatemala with several opposition leaders. Antonio Ibarra was in attendance, as were Donald Lacayo, Guillermo Potoy, and several Venezuelan diplomats. "There will be plenty of money available," César told the participants. "The U.S. intends to help us, but not directly. We're going to do this through Venezuela."[6]

Pérez also met in early 1989 with U.S. officials on the Nicaraguan issue. One NED official drew up an internal summary of these discussions:

CAP [Carlos Andrés Pérez] believes that everything possible should be done to exploit the "cracks" which exist in the system [in Nicaragua]. He believes that the time is right for the international community to do so and that there is hope that the combination of internal and external pressure can force the Sandinistas to compromise. Since La Prensa's situation is urgent, CAP wants to do something immediately which would allow La Prensa to receive U.S. assistance and also pledged to try and come up with some Venezuelan support. He specifically proposed using a Venezuelan institute, which would be comprised of representatives from the media, business, labor and the parties, as a pass-through for NED support. This organization would probably not actually have to serve as a pass-through other than on paper. [See Appendix A, document 7.][7]

Pérez appointed a close aide of his, Beatriz Rangél, whose official title was secretary of the presidency, as his personal representative in some contacts with the Bush administration. Rangél, a Harvard graduate and daughter of Domingo Alberto Rangél, a well-known Venezuelan writer, met with administration officials in Washington several times during the first half of 1989. On at least one occasion, she personally carried a suitcase stuffed with secret funds from Washington and Miami to Caracas for use in Venezuelan-based Nicaraguan operations.[8] In October 1989, Pérez sent Rangél to Managua to head up a three-member "electoral advisory" team to act as a liaison between himself and the Nicaraguan government and opposition. The three registered with the SEC as an observer delegation representing the Venezuelan government. But they worked closely with UNO leaders on financial planning, receipt of supplies from Caracas, and campaign activities.[9]

According to one Venezuelan diplomat, the CIA also called on Tor Halversen.[10] A Venezuelan citizen and former head of the Corporation for Tourism of the first Andrés Pérez administration, Halversen had a long involvement with agency operations in Latin America. In the early 1980s, Halversen played a critical role in funneling money to the contras and in organizing regional anti-Sandinista propaganda campaigns. One former member of the contras' Political Directorate, Edgar Chamorro, recalled that Halversen had sponsored a trip to Caracas of the first contra Directorate in 1981 to launch anti-Sandinista campaigns out of Venezuela. Halversen formed the Committee in Defense of Democracy in Nicaragua following that meeting. "Halversen and his group continued to aid the contras, and took on the task of eroding support for the Sandinistas among Nicaragua's neighbors," recalled Chamorro. "People like him proved very useful in the effort developed to isolate Nicaragua and to build a support system for the contras in neighboring countries. Like us, he could count on the money, contacts, and other support provided by the CIA, and that made him powerful and influential."[11]

THE COSTA RICAN CONNECTION

These regional efforts in Central America were largely coordinated out of San José through an NED conduit, the Center for Democratic Consultation (CAD), which was organized in late 1984.[12] The CAD's purpose was to build up a network of civic forces and political groups in the region that could support U.S. policy. And because the anti-Sandinista campaign was at the heart of that policy, Nicaragua became the chief target of CAD operations.

Between 1984 and early 1988, the CAD received at least $250,000 from the NED for the "training and civic education" of the Nicaraguan opposition.[13]

After Esquipulas, the CAD's role was altered to fit the requirements of internal political intervention. U.S. officials discussed CAD's role and the importance of Central American–based operations: "[Washington needs] to enlist the support of Central America generally, [through] their multisectoral 'CAD Committees/communities.' The civic opposition needs political and financial support from multiple sources so that it can mobilize and channel popular discontent. CAD will set up multi-sectoral committees in all countries of the region as a means of providing political support. The purpose of the CAD program will be to change the philosophy of the opposition, to find their common interests in a unity of action strategy."[14]

The NED initiated a "democratic encounters" program and allocated $247,000 to the CAD to "improve the communications within and among the organizations of the Nicaraguan democratic opposition and promote regional solidarity with the non-violent struggle for democracy in Nicaragua."[15] U.S. officials also made the decision to expand the CAD's liaison operations in other Central American capitals so as to coordinate electoral operations. In 1988, a board of directors was named, comprising representatives from each Central American country noted for their local anti-Sandinista civic and political activities.[16] In San José, Sergio Cambronero, an Argentine, was appointed executive director of the CAD.

With the beginning of the electoral process, U.S. strategists decided to "re-design the original proposal of 'Encuentros Democraticos [Democratic En-counters]' to offer on a short-term basis, substantive contributions to the recently initiated process in Nicaragua," explained one NED document. The plan called for the CAD to deliver both clandestine and overt support to reinforce the already existing programs run by Delphi, the IFES, the FTUI, and other NED groups.[17] For this purpose, the NED allocated another $250,000 to the CAD from special congressional supplements.[18] The U.S. group handling the grant prepared a revised CAD electoral plan: "CAD must become a service unit: to maximize strengths and minimize weaknesses in concrete electoral tasks such as organization, communication, promotion, image and the development of technical electoral assistance. [It must become] a logistic unit: to channel Centralamerican [sic] and international support and to facilitate coordinating procedures among several of the International Organizations with programs in Managua" (see Appendix A, document 8).[19]

Thus, the CAD played a special role in the flow of U.S. money, supplies, and technical and political support to the Nicaraguan opposition, besides serving as a clearinghouse between this support and Latin American and other international structures brought into the U.S. electoral intervention project. Through the CAD, Costa Rica became a key political rearguard. The typical route for the U.S. agents coming from Washington, be they from the IFES, the NRI, Delphi, the NED, or elsewhere, was to pass through San José, meet with CAD agents for money deliveries and planning, and then go on to Managua. Similarly, the CAD became an external meeting exchange for the

Nicaraguan opposition leaders. Using CIA funds allocated for "regional pro-gramming," the CAD also helped provide political training to UNO leaders. And it helped coordinate the activities of the Center for Democracy.[20]

Inside Nicaragua, the role of the CAD was to "increase the effectiveness and support" of the "macro-structure for the 1990 elections" that the United States had brought into being.[21] But unlike the other NED projects in Nica-ragua, very few officials from the U.S. grantee (America's Development Foun-dation) actually traveled to Central America because one of the CAD's purposes was to give a "Latin face" to the U.S. intervention project. Just as it was better to have Venezuelan, rather than gringo, trade unionists on site in Managua advising the opposition's Permanent Council of Workers, so, too, neighboring Costa Ricans and other Latin Americans (among them Argentines and Guatemalans) sent in to Nicaragua from the CAD's San José office would avoid the public appearance of "gringo intervention." The electoral interven-tion project "must be seen as a Nicaraguan initiative; only then can we mobilize regional and Latin American support."[22]

The CAD's role as a "service and logistic unit" facilitating U.S. intervention involved "helping to modernize the democratic civic and political organiza-tions so they may become effective political alternatives" and "assisting the civic opposition to organize the population."[23] Overall, the CAD was to assure that the opposition would be able to "assimilate new skills, develop means of communication and *coordinate ties in order to form a macro-structure for the 1990 elections*" (see Appendix A, document 8).[24]

These goals were to be achieved through different fronts. One, an operation that the NED dubbed "Systems," involved coordination of all of the internal communications of the national civic front so that it could function as a single national unit and effectively utilize the U.S.-funded communications media. In September 1989, the CAD sent a team of communications specialists to Nicaragua. Some supervised the *La Prensa* staff. Others were dispatched to the opposition radios to develop their campaign broadcasting.[25] These com-munications specialists also worked directly with Carlos Briceño on the TV project.[26] In addition to the direct media work, the CAD teams designed and produced the graphic and audio campaign paraphernalia, including posters, billboards, stickers, and radio segments, for the opposition groups, including the opposition youth, women's, and civic groups as well as the CPT opposition trade unions.[27]

Another front was "electoral training." CAD organizers spread throughout Nicaragua and set up opposition structures. These organizers provided logis-tical backup and training to the NED's youth, women's, civic, and trade union groups. From August 1989 to February 1990, the CAD sent in dozens of operatives and organized hundreds of training seminars and meetings in municipalities throughout the country.[28]

In these activities, the CAD did not duplicate the work of the U.S. groups. Rather, it reinforced all of the programs at the technical and the grass-roots levels, within an overall division of labor. For instance, Delphi provided the funds for CEFOJ salaries, office equipment, and seminars. The CAD, in turn, sent in the people who actually carried out the training or who took CEFOJ leaders by the hand and showed them how to operate in the field. Similarly, through the FTUI, Washington provided all of the resources the CPT needed; through the CAD, it sent in the people to apply those resources. Delphi supplied the materials for *La Prensa*; the CAD provided media specialists to actually prepare electoral reports in Spanish.

One of the most important tasks assigned to the CAD was the preparatory work for the creation of Via Cívica. In May and June 1989, the CAD held meetings with the leaders of the soon-to-be-formed civic group. The CAD brought them to San José; drew up blueprints, statutes, and by-laws; and mediated Nicaraguan squabbles. In June, a CAD representative in Costa Rica, Sylvia Escalante, faxed a message to Adelina Reyes Gavilán at NED head-quarters in Washington: The board of directors for the new civic group had finally been organized, said the message, which included the name of the twelve members.[29] Throughout June and July, CAD organizers pulled together the Via Cívica structures. The CAD's executive director, Sergio Cambronero, and his assistant, Víctor Hugo Rojas, arrived personally in early July for an all-day meeting with opposition leaders.[30] With all the initial groundwork laid by the CAD operatives, Henry Quintero of the IFES could fly in to Managua in August for the final touches and then oversee the press conference, held on August 11, announcing the creation of Via Cívica as an "independent, non-partisan association."

Given the CAD's pivotal contact with the entire civic opposition front through the macro-structure, another adjunct function of CAD teams in Nicaragua was to distribute NED-funded payrolls and per diems to thousands of Nicaraguans. In fact, each CAD representative was supplied by the NED with a $120 per diem while in Nicaragua.[31]

And there was more use to which this multipurpose NED outlet was put. In a letter dated September 29, 1989, for instance, Cambronero explained that, as per the NED's instructions, several vehicles were purchased in San José for the UNO but that when the CAD team crossed the Costa Rican–Nicaraguan border, it would claim the vehicles as personal property "so as to avoid paying customs taxes" and to avoid the need for the UNO to declare this electoral donation to the SEC.[32] This mechanism worked well. A week later Cambro-nero's personal assistant, Sylvia Escalante, sent another letter to the NED: "We would like to know if it is possible for the agency to drop off automobiles at the border with Nicaragua, paying just one percent tax here in Costa Rica. Also, we found out, as you asked, that for the moment all of the vehicles that we would need can be obtained in Nicaragua" (see Appendix A, document 9).[33]

PARTISANSHIP IN COSTA RICA
BUT BIPARTISANSHIP IN NICARAGUA

Another connection, the right-wing Association for the Defense of Freedom and Democracy in Costa Rica, was set up by the NRI in 1986 and given

$500,000 in NED funds over the next two years.[34] The association was created as a center for political training and financial support for the United Social Christian Party (PUSC), the conservative political alliance in Costa Rican politics. (Its liberal counterpart is the social democratic National Liberation Party [PLN], which governed for much of the 1980s under the tenures of Luis Alberto Monge and Oscar Arias.) The NED-NRI funding for the association, described as the PUSC's "alter ego," produced a scandal in Costa Rica in 1989 as that country readied for new presidential elections. The PLN charged that the NED was funding and advising the PUSC's presidential candidate, Rafael Angel Calderón, through the association and was therefore directly and illegally interfering in Costa Rica's internal political system. The PLN charged that support for the association was part of the U.S. government's attempts to "punish" Oscar Arias and oppose the Central American peace process via the Costa Rican right wing. Costa Rican documentation indicates that the association did play a major role in designing the PUSC's strategy of opposition to the peace process and of support for U.S. policy in the final years of the Reagan administration.[35] Calderón and the PUSC did go on to win the 1990 presidential elections.

Sensitive to Costa Rica's concerns, the NED decided to pull back on PUSC support and redirect that same support toward the Nicaraguan opposition. Costa Rica, after all, was complaining that the United States should not intervene in the Costa Rican electoral process but was all in favor of U.S. intervention in Nicaragua's elections. In May 1989, the NED canceled the support program for the association, and the NRI instead redirected the funds toward Nicaragua. Instead of disbanding, the association began to establish contacts with the UNO, moving from an internal Costa Rican group to a San José–based support group for the Nicaraguan opposition, along the lines of the CAD. NRI director Keith Schuette wrote to Carl Gershman, "We have agreed with the leadership of the Association that its work will no longer have any domestic focus after 1 July 1989. This means that all domestic training programs, research projects, and educational activities will cease. The Association will re-focus its work on an international foundation directing its activities toward Nicaragua and other areas. I will travel to Costa Rica next week to begin the restructuring of the Association" (see Appendix A, document 10).[36]

On July 6, the newly reorganized association sent its first team into Managua, which met with Miriam Arguello and other Nicaraguan Conservative Party leaders in the UNO. The purpose of this first trip was to discuss association funding and supplies for the UNO headquarters, which was about to be opened in Managua's El Carmen neighborhood. The association proposed a "rapid-sequence" work methodology in which teams would enter and leave Nicaragua in twelve-hour periods, taking advantage of proximity with the Costa Rican border. These teams could establish liaisons with the opposition for material assistance, funding, political support, or whatever tasks were necessary. Two days later, Arguello traveled to San José to "communicate with Washington [NRI headquarters] and inform you of the situation in Nicaragua."[37]

The association also arranged for regular trips to Costa Rica by UNO representatives and assisted in their political training. In October, the NRI, operating through the association, organized the visit of candidate Violeta Chamorro to a "democratic summit" that brought together heads of state from the Americas, included President Daniel Ortega. U.S. strategists envisioned Chamorro's presence as an opportunity to build her stature to that of a Nicaraguan head of state and to trivialize Ortega's presence as the representative head of state.[38]

Meanwhile, the NRI was busy setting up other regional structures to contribute to the "multisectoral support" for the Nicaraguan opposition. In 1987, the NRI had founded the Central American Training Academy with NED funds.[39] With local training centers in each Central American capital, this network was to give political training to leaders of local conservative parties and civic groups that had developed relations with the U.S. Republican Party. Each party set up a training institute similar to the Association for the Defense of Freedom and Democracy in Costa Rica.[40] In 1988–1989, the NRI received $226,000 to consolidate the regional academy. Given this regional structure, the NRI found it easy to channel support to the UNO. In one of many examples, the NRI opened a bank account in Miami under the name of one of the Central American academy groups, the Centro de Estudios Económicos, Políticos y Sociales. At the same time, it opened up another account for the IPCE and juggled funds between the two accounts throughout the fall of 1989 and early 1990. In this way, the NRI could fill the UNO's coffers with moneys appropriated or raised for the programs in other Central American countries.[41]

CAPEL: PROVIDING "COVER" FOR U.S. INTERVENTION

Another group based in Costa Rica was the Center for Electoral Assistance and Promotion (CAPEL). This organization dates back to 1982, when Under Secretary of State for Latin America Thomas Enders met twice, first in February and then in October, with Central American foreign ministers in San José to form a regional anti-Sandinista diplomatic bloc.[42] Among the agenda items of the meetings was the creation of an outlet that could coordinate "technical assistance" for electoral processes in Central America and the Caribbean. The CAPEL was constituted shortly afterward with a $3.1 million grant from the AID.[43] In 1984, the CAPEL became part of another organization formed at the behest of U.S. policymakers, the Central American Human Rights Institute.[44] Between 1984 and 1988, the CAPEL provided assistance for elections in El Salvador, Guatemala, Haiti, and elsewhere in the region.

U.S. officials presented the CAPEL as an independent Latin American organization, and U.S. electoral programs in those countries where it operated were passed off publicly as Latin American initiatives. AID representatives told journalists that the Central American Human Rights Institute belonged to the Organization of American States. In reality, the institute had nothing to do politically or organizationally with the OAS, which had its own Inter-American Human Rights Commission.[45] In this way, the CAPEL gained prestige, while its connections were kept concealed. The organization's board members were drawn from the same incestuous interlocking directorates and included Bruce McColm of Freedom House; F. Clifton White, from several NED grantees (including the NRI, the CFD, and the International Foundation for Electoral Systems); and Richard Scammon (Freedom House, the IFES, and the CFD). During the 1987 Haitian elections, which ended in bloodshed and were canceled, the U.S. ambassador to Haiti stressed that the different NED groups stay behind the CAPEL "cover" to minimize the appearance of U.S. interference in the voting.[46]

The CAPEL provided similar cover for U.S. interference in the Nicaraguan elections. As the Nicaraguan process opened, the CAPEL offered its services to electoral authorities in Managua and signed a technical assistance agreement with the SEC in June 1989 to help administer $150,000 in Swiss and Canadian assistance.[47] Nicaraguan authorities knew little about the CAPEL-U.S. connection, and the CAPEL did contribute expertise on registration and voter identification methods, among other technical aspects.

Parallel to this public and visible activity, however, the CAPEL also provided a channel for U.S. operatives to become involved in the electoral process. The AID allocated $500,000 for CAPEL activities in Nicaragua.[48] The CAPEL developed its program in close coordination with the IFES, an NED group that had created Via Cívica and organized "voter registration drives" inside Nicaragua.[49] The CAPEL organized its own electoral teams, which helped Via Cívica–IFES in their campaigns and which trained UNO personnel in electoral activities. Among those recruited to make up the CAPEL teams were people working closely with the United States. Among those who became involved in UNO support through the CAPEL cover was Sonia Picaddo, a Costa Rican economics professor and official from CAPEL's Central American Human Rights Institute. At the time of the electoral process, Picaddo was a guest lecturer at the Central American Institute for Business Administration, Managua, a conservative Managua business administration school funded by the Ford Foundation. Picaddo became an adviser to Francisco Mayorga, the UNO's spokesperson for economic issues who became Central Bank president after the elections, and to Antonio Lacayo.

THE EUROPEAN CONNECTION

The United States also worked intensively throughout Europe to mobilize political and financial support for the UNO. As in the case of Venezuela, this support often flowed from a convergence of U.S. and European projects and policies. Nevertheless, in this convergence, as in the prior ten years of warfare, the United States applied heavy pressures to force European programs and policies into conformity with U.S. objectives. In several instances, operations were simply transferred from the United States to Europe. Secretary of State James Baker approached political parties in Japan, Western Europe, and elsewhere requesting that they channel money to the UNO.[50] Similarly, the administration lobbied heavily in Europe to obstruct economic support for the Nicaraguan economy (see Chapter 7).

Of particular importance was West Germany, whose political parties set up international wings in the 1970s to support affiliated parties abroad. The West German idea of "international political aid" had in fact helped inspire the founding of the NED.[51] As the electoral project unfolded, the NED asked West German foundations to cooperate with the electoral intervention project. The vice president of the Nicaragua-Gesellschaft foundation, Gotz Frhr. v. Houwald, for instance, promised that his foundation, as it had done since 1983, would continue to develop a favorable image of the opposition and "counter sympathy for the Sandinistas among German public opinion." These activities, he promised, would continue during the electoral campaign, for which purpose "we have already established close contacts" in Managua (see Appendix A, document 11).[52]

Similarly, U.S. agencies coordinated activities with the Christian Democratic Konrad Adenauer Foundation, whose links with the CIA had been exposed several years earlier in the 1984 elections held in El Salvador.[53] According to congressional sources, the Konrad Adenauer Foundation gave $3.1 million to Christian Democratic factions in the UNO. Another West German Foundation, Friedrich Naumann, pitched in $200,000 for several Liberal Party factions in the UNO.[54]

The NED core groups and right-wing private organizations also pulled their strings in Europe. For example, Henry Quintero from the IFES worked with Carl Gershman in arranging for UNO's vice-presidential candidate Virgilio Godoy to meet in Paris, in the course of an October 1989 visit to Europe, with representatives of the Italian Republican Party (PRI). "We need to arrange funding for Godoy through PRI/USA," Quintero said to Gershman.[55] The Italian contact was Vittorio Coco of the PRI.

Godoy, who handled large amounts of foreign contributions, could not produce receipts for some of the donations and halfway through the campaign was accused by members of his own Liberal Party of embezzling funds donated by the Friedrich Naumann Foundation and other sources. Godoy's accusers said he deposited the money in private Panamanian bank accounts. The scandal, dubbed "Godoy-gate" in Managua, prompted officials from the Friedrich Naumann Foundation to send to Managua a team, which after several days of investigations decided to postpone the case until after the voting and quietly departed from Nicaragua.[56]

In another instance, a group called the Jefferson Educational Foundation organized a series of public and private conferences in Paris on December 13–14 on the Nicaraguan elections.[57] The foundation played an important role in the Reagan administration's policy toward Central America. During the 1980s, the Jefferson Educational Foundation ran a "Central America awareness program" that coordinated the anti-Sandinista "public diplomacy" programs. The goal of the Paris meetings was to "gain crucial European commitments" to "build international support for President Bush's emphasis on truly free elections in Nicaragua."[58] Follow-up letters from the foundation to contributors who had helped finance the conferences stated, "Thanks to your continued support, we were able to deliver this much needed support to President Bush and the Freedom Fighters."

The Paris conferences were organized by Robert R. Reilly, a member of the foundation who had worked with the Heritage Foundation in the late 1970s before being named by Reagan as director of the Office for Private Sector Programs of the USIA. Despite its innocuous name, this office was responsible for channeling U.S. government moneys into private organizations participating in Reagan's foreign policy and for building a trans-Atlantic network of right-wing groups in Europe and the United States to coordinate the conservative agenda. Reilly was later appointed to the White House Office of Public Liaison, where he oversaw propaganda about alleged "Sandinista persecution of the Church in Nicaragua."[59]

Among those invited to participate in the Paris program as special guests was Lino Hernandez, a UNO leader and executive director of the NED-funded Nicaraguan Human Rights Commission. The anti-Sandinista bishop Pablo Antonio Vega and Pedro Joaquin Chamorro, Jr., were also invited. Jefferson also brought Jaime Daremblum, a Costa Rican columnist and professor who had achieved prominence in the 1980s on the basis of his anti-Sandinista editorials in that country's newspapers. Daremblum was a major Costa Rican recipient of NED funds and sat of the board or advisory councils of several of the anti-Sandinista propaganda programs set up in Costa Rica by the NED.[60] In Paris, the conference coordinator was the right-wing ideologue Jean-Francois Revel, a close European associate of Freedom House.

THE DIPLOMATS NETWORK IN MANAGUA

The U.S. Embassy under Ambassador Richard Melton's supervision had become a beehive of on-the-ground logistical and political planning between U.S. officials and opposition leaders. The expulsion of Melton and seven of his staff members from Nicaragua in July 1988, after the Nandaime incident, deprived the opposition of important channels of direct U.S. support. The embassy was left in the hands of Chargé d'Affairs Jack Leonard and a skeletal staff. It was not until after the elections, nearly two years later, that full ambassadorial relations were reestablished.

With the loss of an experienced team in Managua, the United States turned to extensive "networking" with other diplomatic personnel in Managua to take up the slack, particularly the Costa Rican and Venezuelan embassies as well as the ambassadors from Japan and Brazil, Jozishu Komishi and Sergio D'Queiros Duarte, respectively. Although each embassy carried through the political agendas of its own government, these four developed particularly close working relations with U.S. officials. Venezuelan ambassador Humberto Rumbos provided backup to the team Carlos Andrés Pérez sent to Nicaragua, headed by Beatriz Rangél, and in turn met regularly with Leonard. Brazil's ambassador participated in this "diplomats network" but was reluctant, according to diplomatic sources in Managua, to take an active role in support of the anti-Sandinista opposition.

Ambassador Komishi assumed a surprisingly visible profile, meeting regularly with UNO leaders in the initial months of the electoral campaign, particularly with Social Christian factions in the opposition coalition. He lobbied in Tokyo for a favorable Japanese response to Washington's request that Japan provide support for the UNO and was accused of having provided funds to Social Christian leader Humberto Guzmán. In November 1989, the Nicaraguan Foreign Ministry lodged a formal protest with Komishi, warning him that his behavior was in violation of international protocols that prohibit diplomats from involvement in the internal affairs of their host countries. From that time on, the Japanese ambassador assumed a more low-key position.

By far the most flamboyant and controversial of the diplomats was Costa Rican ambassador Farid Ayales.[61] A university lecturer on international law and top adviser to Oscar Arias, Ayales had also developed close relations, and business partnerships in Costa Rica, with key opposition figures, among them Alfonso Robelo, who went on after the election to become Nicaraguan ambassador to Costa Rica, and William French, who became a member of Chamorro's economic cabinet. Ayales was appointed to Nicaragua in May 1987, on the eve of the signing of the Esquipulas Accords, with the job of improving communications with Nicaraguan authorities and with the opposition.

Before long, Ayales had become a familiar face in Managua. He mediated negotiations between Violeta Chamorro and Daniel Ortega on the reopening of La Prensa in September 1987 and then facilitated an influx of Costa Rican funds and equipment for the newspaper. In behavior highly unusual for a diplomat, Ayales published several commentaries under his own name in La Prensa on Nicaragua's political situation and on the steps the Sandinistas should take to comply with the Esquipulas Accords. According to one La Prensa editor, during the electoral campaign Ayales wrote regular unsigned editorials for La Prensa and consulted on a daily basis with Cristiana Chamorro. "There was total coordination between Ayales and our editorial staff. The Ambassador would often preview the galleys, and phone in with suggestions before we went to press."[62]

Ayales developed broad contacts with all opposition sectors, including the businesspeople from the COSEP, the political parties, Cardinal Obando y Bravo, and the contra political leaders abroad. His rented house in the fashionable Los Robles neighborhood became the scene of almost nightly dinner parties with Nicaraguan politicans and invited diplomats. Ayales became the talk of the diplomatic circle in Managua. At the time, according to one Costa Rican diplomat, San José had alloted a $5,000 monthly budget for all embassy expenses in Managua. "The money for his wild parties, to which we [Costa Rican] Embassy staff were rarely invited, was coming from elsewhere."[63] Ayales is credited with having convinced Oscar Arias and Carlos Andrés Pérez that the UNO stood a good chance of winning the election, although he was not as successful in persuading a skeptical Jack Leonard. The two, however, worked closely together and agreed on the key goals: achieving opposition unity, selecting Violeta Chamorro as the UNO candidate, and so on. During the tense days of negotiations among the UNO parties over the selection of a candidate, Ayales was present nearly round the clock as a broker.

The Sandinistas became increasingly irritated with Ayales's transgression of diplomatic norms and in March 1989 asked Arias to replace him. The Costa Rican president instead promised to put the leash on his ambassador. Nevertheless, Ayales continued his activities with the opposition, and again in November 1989 the Nicaraguans asked Arias to replace him. Although this time Arias promised he would recall his controversial ambassador, Ayales stayed on until after the elections.[64]

On January 17, 1990, about six weeks before the vote, the Brazilian ambassador invited his colleagues from the fourteen Latin American Embassies that made up the Grupo Latinoamericano, an informal grouping of Latin American diplomats, to a dinner at his residence. "Will the UNO win, or will the FSLN?" D'Quieros Duarte asked the ambassadors. Thirteen of them said the FSLN would win. Ayales was the lone dissenter and on the spot placed a $100 bet on the UNO with the other diplomats. On February 26, Ayales made his rounds in Managua to collect.

MANIPULATING THE ROLE OF
INTERNATIONAL OBSERVATION

The Nicaraguan elections were probably the most closely scrutinized by international observers in world history. The Esquipulas Accords called for electoral observation in each Central American country by the United Nations and the Organization of American States. In addition, Nicaraguan authorities extended observer invitations to the Council of Freely Elected Heads of Government, the European Parliament, and dozens of other human rights, political, and religious groups from around the globe. Many of the groups had a presence in Nicaragua for the duration of the campaign period, and by election day more than three thousand observers representing dozens of groups were in the country.

Washington saw problems and opportunities in this flood of observers. Should the Sandinistas win under the watchful eyes of the international community, the United States would find it difficult to discredit the voting or to deny legitimacy to the Sandinistas. At the same time, the window of international observation provided U.S. operatives with numerous opportunities for manipulating the electoral process. The United States would therefore have to develop means to influence observer views and conduct.[65]

The new political intervention has turned international observation into an instrument for penetrating foreign electoral processes and manipulating them in accordance with U.S. policy objectives. In this, the distinction between neutral or impartial observation and partisan intervention is obscured. The function of the U.S. electoral "observers" in the new environment is both operational and propagandistic. Operatives sent to target countries under the guise of "observation" become deeply involved in the activities of the groups and candidates being promoted by the United States. They attempt to establish public perceptions favorable to U.S. objectives and set the focus and agendas of genuine observer groups.

The Sandinistas realized that opening up the electoral process to observers from around the world carried the risk of heightening U.S. opportunities for interference. But there was little choice in the matter, which involved the perennial catch–22s. Any attempt to restrict intervention under the guise of observation would be condemned by Washington as an impediment to free elections. Moreover, Nicaragua simply did not have the knowledge or resources to be able to distinguish between legitimate observers and premeditated anti-Sandinista activists. Therefore, applying a discriminatory policy against U.S. operatives, although fully justified, ran the risk of hindering genuine neutral observation from the international community.

THE CENTER FOR DEMOCRACY

How "observer group" operations are carried out was seen in Nicaragua in the case of Allen Weinstein's Center for Democracy. Weinstein was one of the original organizers of Project Democracy, which led to the formation of the NED. He was the endowment's first president, a post from which he resigned after setting up the CFD in 1984. The center's board of directors was drawn largely from the boards of the NED and its core groups. Weinstein was a key anti-Sandinista activist throughout the 1980s. He made regular trips to Nicaragua starting in 1982. "At that time I first made contact with the civic opposition," said Weinstein, which was made up of "day and night fighters for democracy."[66] In 1987, the CFD gave its annual Sentinel of Freedom award to Violeta Chamorro.[67]

The CFD was commissioned by Congress in 1986 to observe the Philippine elections in conjunction with NED programs in that country. Weinstein, who maintained close relations with the influential Republican senator Richard Lugar, at the time chair of the Senate Foreign Relations Committtee, gained considerable "bipartisan" clout on Capitol Hill after the Philippine program was successful. The Nicaraguan Foreign Ministry thought he could play a positive role and invited the center as an official observer. Some harshly criticized the decision.[68] At the time, Managua considered the invitation a "calculated risk" and believed the benefits of winning support in the United States for the electoral process would be worth the foreseeable costs.

Weinstein spoke with two tongues: one to the Nicaraguan authorities and the other to the U.S. operatives with whom he worked closely. A few days after he was formally invited, he described his mission to a group of these operatives in Washington as "how to get these non-democratic rulers to transform their rule; we have to put the pressure on now, and continue to put the pressure on throughout the campaign."[69] To the Sandinistas, he said his groups would "be delighted to contribute to democratic elections." To a group of students at Georgetown University in Washington, he said Nicaragua could "never be democratic" unless the Sandinistas were out of government.[70]

By July, Weinstein was running a bustling office in Managua headed by his assistant, Caleb McCarry. Weinstein financed this activity with a $75,000 grant from the NED as well as $250,000 from the AID provided from the $9 million congressional appropriation (out of which he paid himself a $53,000 salary).[71] With these funds, the office brought in box-loads of CFD promotional and electoral materials. The CFD's standard logotype is a bright red symbol with black print, which are coincidentally the two colors used by the Sandinista front. For Nicaragua, however, the CFD changed its logotype colors to blue and white, which were also the colors of the UNO logotype as well as of the Nicaraguan flag. The SEC eventually asked Weinstein to change the logotype so as not to cause confusion. Meanwhile, the CFD conducted nationwide get-out-the-vote drives, as if it were a Nicaraguan civic organization, and prepared "press packets" on the elections for distribution to other observer groups in Managua.[72]

In December, Weinstein's group became involved in an incident of electoral violence in Masatepe, south of Managua. Violeta Chamorro had addressed a rally of UNO supporters in the town on the morning of December 10. As she was departing from the town's plaza, clashes broke out between opposition and Sandinista sympathizers. The nearby FSLN campaign headquarters and two vehicles were burnt in the ensuing melee, and a Sandinista activist, Manuel Guevara Calero, was killed. Most of the evidence backed up the Sandinistas' charge that the violence was organized as a provocation similar to the 1988 Nandaime incident.[73]

A UNO militant, Mauro Francisco Cerda, later admitted to killing Guevara. Cerda testified behind closed doors on separate occasions to U.N., OAS, SEC, and police investigators that he and other opposition supporters had gone to the Masatepe demonstration armed with machetes and bayonets under instructions from UNO organizers, who had said that Sandinista mobs were going to cause trouble and had issued death threats against Violeta Chamorro and Virgilio Godoy. Cerda testified that after Chamorro finished her speech, a whistle was blown and someone in the UNO crowd shouted, "Now!" The fighting began seconds later.[74]

Teams of observers from the OAS and the CFD were present during the incident. The two groups released dramatically contrasting eyewitness reports. The OAS witnesses, who had subdued the melee by placing themselves between the two mobs and negotiating a truce, stated in their report that it was "impossible to discern which side actually initiated the violence" and blamed UNO supporters for burning the FSLN campaign office and the vehicles.[75] The OAS also requested that the SEC carry out an official investigation. The SEC complied, reaching conclusions similar to those of the OAS, and was praised by Jimmy Carter for having done "an excellent job." A separate U.N. investigation also reached similar conclusions.

The CFD delegation claimed that the "Sandinistas perpetrated multiple acts of violence. . . . It was clear that Sandinista supporters intended to disrupt the legitimate political right of assembly by UNO party supporters." The report concluded, "Unless the Sandinista authorities take immediate and decisive measures to permit non-violent and non-intimidating campaigning by the opposition, free and fair elections in Nicaragua are improbable if not impossible." The CFD's report was fraught with distortions and omissions; it even claimed that the man killed was really a UNO member! When pressed on why his report contradicted the OAS's, Weinstein said, "We came to a different conclusion because we saw more."[76]

The CFD delegation's movements were revealing. The Masatepe rally, planned for December 17, was brought forward one week to accommodate the CFD delegates, armed with video cameras, who arrived in Managua on December 9. The next day they traveled to Masatepe, filmed the violence, and returned to Managua, where they boarded a plane for San José. Their seats had been booked in advance, according to Nicaraguan immigration and port authority records. In Costa Rica, they announced their findings to the international press, which was gathered in San José on the second day of a regional heads of state summit. From San José, the group returned to Washington on December 14, where Weinstein promptly went into meetings at the White House with President George Bush, Vice President Dan Quayle, and Deputy Secretary of State Lawrence Eagleburger. Then they released the CFD final report at a press conference organized at the USIA's Foreign Press Center.[77]

The Masatepe incident was a masterful operation in "public diplomacy." The State Department released a declaration reproducing the CFD conclusions and condemning the Sandinistas.[78] The New York Times filed a report from San José conveying the CFD version: "Sandinista mobs" deliberately provoked the fighting as part of a campaign to "intimidate and harass its opponents." (The paper did not mention the OAS version, nor did it subsequently cover the conclusions reached by the United Nations and other investigations.)[79] The USIA interviewed several of the CFD delegates, almost all of whom were procontra activists, via satellite transmission to Europe and Latin America.[80] The operation even involved a classic "blowback" (see the next chapter): Weinstein cited an "AP [Associated Press] wire report" to corroborate his version. This supposed wire report mysteriously appeared in the Guatemalan newspaper Prensa Libre and nowhere else. The report, datelined Guatemala City, quoted an unnamed "eyewitness" in Masatepe who corroborated the CFD's argument, which a Prensa Libre correspondent, whose byline was not included with the article and who was described as "also a stringer for AP," had supposedly interviewed by telephone.[81]

Premeditated provocations such as Masatepe were part of the overall intervention agenda. Although incidents of spontaneous electoral violence did occur throughout the campaign, they were usually sparked by hotheads on both sides in a situation of political polarization. The FSLN called on its supporters to refrain from any violence, as did most UNO leaders. With the assistance of the electoral observers, incidents of violence were brought under control. But spontaneous outbursts were constantly defined by Washington as a "climate of intimidation" against the opposition. (The United States manipulated the issue of electoral violence in the 1984 elections to provide a pretext for withdrawing the opposition candidates and later discrediting the voting.)

After the Masatepe incident, the CFD lost credibility among other international observers. Nevertheless, Weinstein persisted. He took it on himself to be a liaison between the government and the contras. The latter were refusing to demobilize, in violation of regional accords, and were involved in a spate of electoral-related attacks (see Chapter 8). Weinstein met with contra commanders in December in Miami and proposed to them that they call a temporary truce until after the elections so as to see if they were "really fair."[82] In this way, Weinstein legitimized the contras and military pressure against Nicaragua and at the same time cast doubts on the integrity of the elections. Weinstein also demanded that the Nicaraguan government suspend the military draft and "demilitarize" as a necessary precondition for fair elections.[83] He also made a series of proposals, such as an internationally televised "presidential debate" between Ortega and Chamorro, that clearly transcended foreign observer neutrality.

FROM CONTRA PROMOTERS TO ELECTORAL OBSERVERS

Secretary General of the United Nations Javier Pérez de Cuellar, an astute diplomat, wanted to make sure that the U.N. observer role could not be discredited by the United States. He pulled the rug out from under any such attempts by appointing a U.S. citizen, Elliot Richardson, to head the U.N. team. Very much the Republican Party patrician, Richardson had an illustrious portfolio that included stints as the secretary of defense, of state, of human services, and of commerce; ambassador to Great Britain; and U.S. attorney general. He held this last post when the Watergate scandal broke and gained a reputation for impeccable honesty when he resigned instead of complying with Richard Nixon's orders to fire independent prosecutor Archibald Cox.

The Sandinistas were surprised by the appointment, but it soon became clear that the Bush administration would be the real loser. The affable Richardson, who had been a critic of the contra policy, made clear publicly that his responsibility was to the U.N. secretary general, not to an outside political agenda. Both the Nicaraguans and the Bush administration "have to accept the fact that I intend to carry out my mandate from the Secretary General with honesty and objectivity," said Richardson, "on the basis of merit and in an effort to make a fair assessment of the electoral process."[84] Although the Bush administration left all of its options open, the presence of observers with such political prestige in mainstream Washington led U.S. strategists to conclude in the fall of 1989 that the electoral process had to be manipulated from within in addition to being discredited from without.

A host of methods were used to get inside the observer apparatus. Back in 1983, the Reagan administration had unilaterally closed Nicaragua's six consulates in the United States. At the time, the Sandinistas had decided to lift the visa requirement so as not to hinder the flow of U.S. visitors to the country, which they believed to be one of the administration's motives for the closings. As the 1990 electoral process opened, Washington was sending into Nicaragua everyone from former contra fund-raisers to U.S. diplomats accredited in neighboring countries who merely had to pay for a $5 tourist card at the border. As a precautionary measure, Nicaraguan authorities decided in July to require U.S. citizens to apply for a visa, as most countries in the world do. (Nicaraguans have always needed visas to enter the United States.) The State Department protested the decision. NED officials were quick to think of ways to circumvent possible visa denials. The NED sent a circular through U.S. embassies in Latin America to heads of NED programs in host countries that had reciprocal immigration agreements with Managua and whose citizens did not therefore need visas to enter Nicaragua, among them Costa Rica, Uruguay, and Argentina. The plan, as the circular and subsequent events suggest, was to have "indigenous" NED operatives and heads of PVOs funded by the United States join international observer groups going to Nicaragua.[85]

There were other plans by U.S. intervention groups to infiltrate observer groups. The Far Right World Freedom Foundation had been denied permission to send an official observer group by Nicaraguan authorities, who felt that the group's history of active support for the contras would make it difficult for them to be impartial observers. New Right activist Brent Bozell, who headed the foundation, wrote to Allen Weinstein and to Keith Schuette. Bozell proposed that the different U.S. groups sprinkle their operatives among one another and among international observer groups.[86] Weinstein agreed and added Bozell to the CFD's observer team.[87] Schuette wrote back to Bozell, "I believe your strategy with regard to visas is a good one. . . . Much as I would like to join you, it is not clear that it would be a wise decision to do so. . . . *For the moment,* it appears that we will be given the access we require to conduct our work. Since our ultimate objective is to help the opposition, I believe that we will need to treat the issue somewhat differently from others who are less directly involved in support for UNO. . . . I believe it makes better sense for us to pursue a lower profile effort for the time being, though we fully support the effort you are organizing" (see Appendix A, document 12).[88]

In November, the Bush administration announced that it had decided to appoint a presidential delegation made up of congressional members to observe the elections. George Bush made the announcement without the administration so much as having informed the Nicaraguan Embassy in Washington, much less formally communicating with Nicaraguan government authorities. How a government that had been waging war against a country for ten years and then was actively backing one side in an electoral campaign could at the same time send an impartial observer mission was not clear. Nevertheless, the Nicaraguan Foreign Ministry proposed that if the United States ended its logistical support for the contras and transferred the AID contra aid program to the appropriate international humanitarian agencies, in fulfillment of the Central American peace accords, then it would authorize the official U.S. government delegation.

The State Department balked, and Speaker of the House Tom Foley, who was to be included in Bush's "bipartisan" delegation, sent an angry letter of protest to President Daniel Ortega.[89] Assistant Secretary of State John Bolton wrote to Elliot Richardson calling on the United Nations to protest the Nicaraguan decision. "We request that you firmly advise the government in Managua that this latest action is yet another in a series which call into question its commitment to the Central American peace process," said Bolton. He added, "There are serious questions as to whether there will be sufficient UN and OAS election monitors."[90]

In the final months of the electoral process, the State Department churned out a slew of reports on supposed campaign "irregularities" and Sandinista "violations" that "demonstrated" that the elections would not be free or fair. A late December 1989 report prepared by the Central America Bureau at State claimed that the army and state security were "harassing UNO supporters"; "Sandinista mobs" were "increasing violent attacks" on the opposition; and the government was "forcing UNO candidates to resign," taking "preventative measures" to "minimize public participation in UNO rallies," "slandering the democratic opposition," and even paying bribes to opposition members.[91] The sources for these reports were the U.S. Embassy in Managua and the private U.S. groups involved in the electoral intervention project, including the CFD, Freedom House, and the Puebla Institute, which were described as "independent human rights and observer groups."[92] These reports were widely distributed to the media, international observer groups, foreign governments, Congress, and Washington political circles.

In January, the State Department prepared a "confidential" memorandum on the "deterioration of the electoral climate in Nicaragua" that reiterated the anti-Sandinista accusations and was faxed to foreign ministries throughout Europe.[93] "We have no secret agenda, we do wish to see honest elections in Nicaragua," said the memo, but "the electoral climate in Nicaragua has deteriorated markedly over the last few weeks" to the point that holding free elections was in jeopardy and that "fraud" was a real possibility. The memorandum stated that "the U.S. [was] not alone in expressing concern about irregularities" and that recent OAS and other international observer missions had "raised similar concerns."

In fact, OAS and U.N. observer reports at that time raised no such concerns, and although they pointed to several persistent problems, their reports praised the progress in the electoral process. "The difficulties which have been manifested during the process have, to a large extent, been overcome," concluded an OAS report covering the precise period in which the State Department was claiming that the voting was in jeopardy. "It is expected that the elections will take place in a favorable climate so that citizens may freely choose their candidates."[94] A U.N. report reached conclusions that were almost entirely contrary to the State Department accusations and that "view[ed] with grave concern the persistent questioning of basic aspects of the electoral process . . . which suggest[ed] an attempt to delegitimate the process [and] indicate[d] subtle forms of discrediting the international observers."[95]

As the voting approached, the dissonance between the United States and the international observer missions increased. The Washington Post reported that the United States had set a "tone of what has been an almost daily drumbeat of accusations" and was "deliberately exaggerating the extent of campaign irregularities." The paper cited a senior U.N. official: "You are seeing an exercise in political manipulation." The United States was doing "everything possible to make it appear that [the UNO] campaign is close to doomed by Sandinista intimidation. . . . But when our observers ask for specifics, they seem very reluctant to back up their charges with specifics."[96] Jimmy Carter's assistant, Robert Pastor, was more blunt: The administration's accusation's were "rhetorical blasts aimed at one side."[97]

Most of the groups from the electoral intervention network sent U.S.-funded "observer" teams. These included the AIFLD, the CAD, and Freedom House, which received $85,000 from the NED to organize its own delegation. The AID also gave the International Democratic Union, an international grouping of conservative parties, $72,000 to send a delegation.[98] Publicly, the Democratic Union was presented as an international initiative convened by a Guatemalan affiliate, the Solidarity Action Movement. Nevertheless, the union was wholly funded by the NED, under the supervision of the State Department, and it was the NRI, not the Guatemalan group, that made most of the arrangements.[99]

For its part, the CAPEL provided the State Department and other U.S. groups with a list of "electoral experts" from Latin America.[100] This list in turn was used to put together "observer groups" from Latin America financed by the AID. Such was the case, for instance, with a "Costa Rican volunteer observer team" that the CFD assembled in early February with $59,846 in AID funds.[101]

Had the Sandinistas won the elections, many of these partisan observer groups would probably have issued reports questioning the electoral results and providing a negative counterweight to the positive reports issued by the United Nations, the OAS, Carter's group, and other genuine observers. In a memorandum sent to members of his group's delegation on the eve of the voting, Weinstein wrote of "serious problems that have disconfigured the electoral campaign to date. . . . The Center's major distinction from these groups [the United Nations, the OAS, and Carter's group] is that the Center for Democracy will not judge the fairness of this election prior to Election Day itself. Messrs. Baena Soares [secretary general of the OAS], Carter and Richardson on behalf of their groups have already been widely quoted as expressing their belief that the electoral process has been substantially 'free and fair.'"[102]

The orchestrated incidents and catch-22s in which the Sandinistas were placed laid the basis for a continued policy of hostility, rather than normalizing relations, with the Nicaraguans in the event of a UNO defeat. They created a climate in which the Sandinistas were ever more vulnerable. U.S. "electoral observers" were a way for Washington to erect itself as sole judge and arbiter of the electoral process. Turning abstention into an opposition vote required showing the Nicaraguan electorate that the United States alone had the power to decide the fate of the electoral process.

SIX

The CIA, Public Relations, Secret Relations, and Multiple Money Pots

It shall be unlawful for a foreign national directly or through any other person to make any contribution of money or other thing of value, or to promise expressly or impliedly to make any such contribution, in connection with an election to any political office or in connection with any primary election, convention, or caucus held to select candidates for any political office, or for any person to solicit, accept, or receive any such contribution from a foreign national.

—U.S. Public Law 94-283, Section 441-E

In the fall of 1989, when the Bush administration submitted a request to Congress for a special $9 million in "electoral assistance" for Nicaragua, much of the attention in Washington focused on a terse affirmation by one White House official that "we are not ruling out covert activities and CIA participation in this program."[1] The administration, said the official, wanted to "preserve its power to conduct secret intelligence operations" aimed at influencing the Nicaraguan elections and was considering providing "secret contributions or political guidance to opposition leaders."[2]

Government officials do not normally make such public comments on covert actions. This was a deliberate "leak" aimed at "perception management," which refers to the use of psychological operations and media manipulation to control the way in which the public perceives an issue.[3] The administration's objective was to define the issue before the public eye as overt versus covert intervention in Nicaragua; to counterpose overt intervention as the benign, and only, alternative to covert intervention; and thus win support for it. In this way, the administration kept the debate narrowly circumscribed.

Much of Congress, the media, and the U.S. public swallowed the bait. Liberal members of Congress condemned CIA intervention, and then went ahead and approved the $9 million for the NED in exchange for a loosely worded agreement that the CIA would refrain from covertly influencing the elections inside Nicaragua. Similarly, a coalition of major human rights groups that lobbied fiercely against secret CIA electoral action tacitly endorsed overt intervention.[4] Lost in this debate was any question as to whether, covert operations aside, the NED's "overt" intervention was any more acceptable ethically or any more legal vis-à-vis international law and the principle of nonintervention in another nation's internal affairs. White House perception management was able to obscure the unitary intentions of U.S. policy in both forms of intervention and to misframe the issue as one of "overt aid" as an alternative to "covert aid."

Moreover, the loosely worded language of the legislation enacted by Congress merely stated that the CIA could not carry out covert activities aimed at influencing the voting inside Nicaragua. The legislation did not prohibit CIA activities mounted from outside Nicaragua's borders to influence the voting. Nor did it prohibit general CIA activities inside Nicaragua's borders. The political haranguing over legislative language clearly involved subterfuge because Congress and the administration allowed the CIA to continue covert operations against Nicaragua "legally."[5] Many lawmakers were opposed to admitted CIA involvement simply because they believed that the covert route would do more damage than good to the opposition in Nicaragua.[6]

Nicaragua also fell into a trap set by the U.S government, perhaps the most serious of the "damned if you do, damned if you don't" situations imposed on it by U.S. intervention. The Sandinistas decided to make this intervention legally permissible, even though such interference is patently prohibited and criminally punishable in the United States and in most other countries in the world. Yet at the same time, the Sandinista government vociferously denounced "overt" NED actions as evidence that the United States was interfering in the electoral process (which it was) and that the opposition had been bought by Washington (which it had been).

There were two aspects to this issue. First, Managua made its decision only after receiving assurances from the Bush administration and from Congress that if Nicaraguan authorities permitted overt intervention, then the United States would refrain from covert intervention in the elections. The $9 million authorization, stated Managua's U.S. legal adviser, Paul Reichler, "[gave] the United States an opportunity to aid the opposition openly, so [the United States did] not have to resort to covert means."[7] Nicaragua's acquiescence to the $9 million was secured in quiet negotiations between Managua and Washington, with Jimmy Carter as a go-between. In a mid-September 1989 visit to Managua, Carter, who himself came out publicly against CIA activities but endorsed "overt" aid to the opposition,[8] transmitted Bush administration assurances to Daniel Ortega that in exchange for acquiescence to the overt NED funding, no covert funding would take place. "I have absolute assurances from U.S. officials at the highest level, both in the Executive and Legislative branches," Carter told Ortega, "that there will be no covert funding from our government for opposition political parties or other purposes that would subvert the integrity of the Nicaraguan elections" (see Appendix A, document 13).[9]

Whether Carter was deceived by Bush officials or deliberately manipulated, or for that matter whether he himself deceived the Nicaraguans, is unclear. In any case, the assurances given to Nicaraguan authorities were meaningless, and it was not an issue of options for Nicaragua. The CIA carried out extensive operations throughout the electoral campaign. The United States never had any intention of renouncing CIA covert activities "in exchange for" congressional approval of, and Nicaraguan acquiescence to, overt NED intervention. The United States was waging war against Nicaragua and operated with the logic of war, which dictated that all effective weapons be brought to bear on the enemy.

Second, Managua's decision placed the government at a tremendous disadvantage in the battle for public opinion. Because the Nicaraguan government had given its permission for foreign interference in the national electoral process, its subsequent denunciations of this intervention, or attempts to place controls on it, lacked coherence and consistency. Adversaries of U.S. intervention around the world were at a loss when they tried to denounce the U.S. electoral interference because Washington simply retorted that its actions had been legally sanctioned by the Nicaraguan authorities. Thus, Nicaragua lost the authority to condemn the United States for transgressing Nicaraguan sovereignty. (This moral authority had been crucial earlier in mobilizing international public opinion against the contra war.) This situation set a dangerous precedent for an open interference of a superpower in a small country's internal political process.

By having boxed Nicaraguan authorities into a corner in which electoral intervention became legitimized, U.S. officials could freely apply pressures on Nicaragua that in any other country would have been considered preposterous. So much so that in January 1990, NED officials publicly threatened to mount an international campaign to discredit the elections if the Nicaraguan Central Bank continued "to delay" NED payments to the opposition.[10] Even more, NED officials asked Jimmy Carter to intercede with Nicaraguan authorities to expedite these payments. Carter obliged. "It is very important that a political decision be made at the top level of your government that funds approved by Congress in the Nicaragua election will be distributed without delay," Carter told Nicaraguan vice president Sergio Ramírez in January 1990. "As you know, I obtained a commitment from highest authorities that there would be no covert funding through CIA or other government channels. In return, I relayed the commitment from you and President Ortega that overt funding would not be impeded."[11]

With the benefit of hindsight, these U.S. manipulations are easy to identify. But at the time, such overt U.S. intervention was novel and its mechanisms unknown. Some Nicaraguan officials ingenuously believed that covert intervention in the elections could be proscribed. "Our position should be to tell Carter that assurances that there will not be CIA covert operations are not enough," recommended a Foreign Ministry official, "that we would like assurances that all U.S. government agencies will refrain from covert activities and that all U.S. financing will be open."[12]

In addition, Nicaragua had little room in which to maneuver. Employing superior resources on the heels of a decade of the war of attrition, the United States put Nicaraguan authorities on the defensive with the threat of delegitimizing the elections and reproducing the 1984 abstentionist experience. Any attempt by Managua to limit U.S. intervention was interpreted by Washington's propaganda machinery as "signs that the Sandinistas did not intend to hold free elections." In the Sandinistas' cost-benefit analysis, the price Washington could impose if Managua decided to prohibit overt intervention was potentially too high. In this way, Washington exercised a certain veto over Nicaraguan government efforts to distinguish between neutral foreign assistance for electoral processes and partisan political interference.[13]

THE CIA INFRASTRUCTURAL PROGRAM AND REGIONAL PROGRAMMING

Meanwhile, the United States simply ignored the assurances it had given Nicaraguan authorities on not carrying out covert CIA operations. No sooner had the Nicaraguan electoral process opened in April 1989 than the CIA undertook its first of at least three covert operations intended to influence the outcome.

The first program involved $5 million and was carried out from April to September. The moneys went to defray what one intelligence official described as UNO "housekeeping" expenses—slush funds for salaries and payoffs to opposition leaders.[14] The administration was able to spend this money "legally" by calling the operation an "infrastructural program." It went, said one intelligence official, for "political infrastructure," not for "campaigning."[15] Maybe because it was "legal," this covert activity caused little commotion in Washington. Yet the slush funds enabled opposition unity around the formation of the UNO and the selection of candidates.

In early October, Congress had approved the legislation that restricted CIA actions *inside* Nicaragua's borders. "Covert activities would undermine the integrity of the upcoming elections," beamed Joe Moakley (D-Mass.), who as chair of the Rules Committee had been instrumental in drafting the restrictions. Moakley said he was pleased with the assurances he had received from the administration that no such activities would be undertaken.[16] Yet days later, President Bush signed a finding authorizing the expenditure of $6 million for the second CIA program. These funds were spent between October 1989 and the February voting. So as to make the second program legal, it was titled "regional programming," and it proposed numerous anti-Sandinista covert actions *outside* of Nicaragua.[17]

Among the aspects of the regional programming were:

• A secret political training program in Costa Rica for UNO leaders. Latin Americans organized into the CAD did most of the actual training.

- Payments to journalists and news outlets in Europe known for their anti-Sandinista sentiments to travel to Nicaragua and write on the elections or to publish articles from Europe that would reinforce the U.S. positions.
- Financing special programs on Radio Impacto, the contra radio station that the CIA had set up years earlier in Costa Rica for the purpose of transmitting anti-Sandinista programming into Nicaragua. In accordance with the language game, Radio Impacto was prohibited from using these funds to directly interview UNO candidates.
- Support programs for the contras in Honduras and Costa Rica, including programs to train contras to carry out armed electoral propaganda inside Nicaragua (see next chapter).

Among the fruits of the CIA's European media operation was a January 1990 article in the West German daily *Frankfurter Allgemeine Zeitung* on alleged corruption in the FSLN and the supposed existence of multimillion-dollar bank accounts in Switzerland handled by Sandinista commanders. The article was written by the bureau chief of the newspaper's Bonn office and cited "foreign intelligence" as the source of the information. In CIA language, these types of psychological operations are called "blowbacks." In a blowback, the CIA leaks "black information," or simple lies, to little-known or third-country news outlets. Therefore, when they publish this information, it is distanced from Washington or from the country being targeted. Once published, the U.S. press, or the press in the target country, often quite unknowingly reproduces the "news," giving it an aura of credibility and influencing, as intended, the target audiences.

In the case of the *Frankfurter Allgemeine Zeitung* article, Violeta Chamorro's *La Prensa* reported the "news from Bonn" on page one the day after it appeared in Germany and then the following day translated and reproduced the article in its entirety. Then for several days straight, *La Prensa* editorialized on the issue, claiming that the periodical was "one of the most respected dailies in West Germany."[18] UNO activists turned "the discovering of high level Sandinista corruption" and "secret Swiss bank accounts" into a major electoral issue. The commotion made by *La Prensa* and the UNO reached such a pitch that in a rare public commentary of such a nature, the West German government released a statement in Bonn stating that in "reference to the *Frankfurter Allgemeine Zeitung* article, the Government of the Federal Republic of Germany has no information on the subject, but it is known that such information has for some time been promoted by sources in the United States, possibly by the same sources [mentioned] in the article."[19]

CONTRAS–CUM–CIVIC LEADERS

In addition to this $11 million, some of the CIA contingency funds going to the contra offices in Miami and Washington were also redirected to civic opposition activities and the cultivation of so-called agents of influence for the electoral process. The return of contra political leaders to Nicaragua had to be financed and loyalties cemented. As part of this effort, the CIA ran a special covert operation, known as the Nicaraguan Exile Relocation Program (NERP), that paid some $600,000 to about one hundred contra political leaders and organizers to return to Nicaragua.[20] At least eleven of the contras funded by the NERP became candidates in the February elections.[21] The State Department played an active role in the return process. The hard-liners there who had resisted the shift in U.S. policy had cleared out together with the departure of Elliot Abrams. State Department officials shifted their contra support from the military diehards to those more politically savvy who would be able to take up the reigns of the civic struggle inside Nicaragua.

In February 1989, the State Department reduced its monthly payments to the contras' U.S. offices from $800,000 to $400,000 and then several months later suspended the stipend altogether.[22] Between February and July, State Department officials held a series of meetings with contra representatives from the Miami and Washington offices to work out the restructuring. The attenders, among them longtime contra leader Adolfo Calero, and the contras' U.S. spokesperson Bosco Matamoros, were told that the U.S. offices would be permanently closed by the beginning of the electoral campaign and that the politicians should return to Managua.[23] Leadership of contra troops, which had an important role to play in the elections, would be passed to the field commanders in Honduras (see Chapter 7). "The State Department has betrayed us," charged a furious Calero.

In the first half of 1989, dozens of high-level contras returned to Managua to assume positions of leadership in the UNO campaign, including the industrialist Alfonso Robelo, who had spent many years as a director of different contra groups. Robelo had close political and business ties to Costa Rican governing circles, including Oscar Arias. After the UNO victory, Robelo was appointed ambassador to Costa Rica. Social Christian leader Azucena Ferrey and Pedro Chamorro, Jr., both former contra Directorate members, also returned.

The closure of the offices sparked fierce infighting over control of remaining assets. In August, Ernesto Palazio, who worked as spokesperson with the Washington office of the Nicaraguan Resistance, was "fired" by Matamoros and stripped of his $36,000 annual salary. Matamoros accused Palazio, who controlled the Washington bank accounts, of embezzling thousands of dollars. Matamoros presented canceled checks showing that Palazio had been using a bank account set up to provide medical treatment for injured contras for his own personal expenses, including a $700 reimbursement for tickets to President Bush's inauguration and life insurance premiums.[24]

Palazio was one of the more moderate and astute of the contras. He had allied himself with the pragmatists in the Inter-American Bureau at State. "Palazio is operating under the assumption that his good relations with State Department officials made him 'untouchable,'" said Matamoros. "Palazio is an asset of State." Matamoros was gradually eclipsed by Palazio. At 2:00 A.M. one morning in September, before closing the doors for the last time to the Nicaraguan Resistance office in Washington, Palazio brought in a moving crew to remove the archives, office furniture, and other items and changed the locks to the offices.[25]

A few days later, Palazio was named *La Prensa* correspondent in Washington; he was later appointed UNO representative when the electoral campaign itself began.[26] Palazio's job had previously been to facilitate contra-administration relations in Washington; now it was to facilitate internal opposition–administration relations. After the UNO triumphed in the February 1990 voting, Palazio remained in Washington; he was appointed by the Chamorro government as ambassador to the United States.

The most important of the contras–cum–civic opposition leaders was Alfredo César. He and a handful of associates founded the Social Democratic Party in Nicaragua a few days after the Sandinista triumph. In 1980, he was also appointed president of the Central Bank but resigned in 1981 and went into self-exile in Costa Rica. There he worked for a while with the Democratic Revolutionary Alliance contra group. In 1985, he formed the Southern Opposition Bloc (BOS) together with his brother, Octaviano César.[27] The BOS lobbied for support in Costa Rica and among social democratic groups in South America. César developed a personal relationship with influential Venezuelan leader Carlos Andrés Pérez.

César had an uncanny skill for forming and then breaking alliances with almost anyone, from the Sandinistas to the ruthless contra military commander Enrique Bermúdez and Latin American Social Democratic leaders. He was known in Managua as Siete Cuchillos (Seven Knives, which means the backstabber). "He was capable of a rainbow of alliances; he could juggle a multitude of opposition viewpoints while never appearing to hold more than one at a time," said one close associate of his. But the one alliance that César sustained was with the CIA. "The Césars were being funded for their political activities by the CIA. The CIA was happy to be doing business with Alfredo César."[28] César worked with the CIA station chief in San José, Tomas Castillo, whose real name, Joe Fernandez, became well known after his activities in the Contragate scandal were exposed in congressional investigations.[29]

Castillo was replaced in San José by Valentino Martínez, who became César's case officer and CIA-BOS liaison. In early 1989, Martínez was posted to the U.S. Embassy in Managua, shortly before the opening of the electoral process. As the contra political leaders began filtering back to Nicaragua, Martínez worked at integrating them into the opposition political structures and at mitigating, with money and political pressures, the resentment that opposition leaders who had never left Managua felt against the returning contras.[30]

In its eternal search for a "moderate" contra who could win public and congressional support for Nicaragua policy, the State Department discovered César in 1987. With his command of English, impeccable dress, and understanding of the U.S. political system, the Stanford-educated César became a master at charming the Washington crowd. "He alone of the country's politicians was conversant with the new language, the new vocabulary, of the 1980s," said his associate. "César also sought out Oscar Arias and Speaker of the House Jim Wright. His aim was to become the most attractive contra, the one genuinely interested in negotiation and compromise,"³¹ and to build bridges with both the Democratic Party and the Republican White House.

In 1987, César became a member of the Directorate of the Nicaraguan Resistance. This gave him a platform from which to negotiate the conditions for his return to Nicaragua. During the contra-Sandinista cease-fire negotiations of 1988, César entered into secret, unilateral negotiations with Nicaraguan authorities over his return to Managua to participate in elections.³² As César prepared for his return to Nicaragua, he began shuttling back and forth among Guatemala, Caracas, Miami, San José, and Washington, sometimes alone, sometimes in the company of other opposition leaders, and sometimes with CIA officers. He became the bag man for much of the CIA slush funds and played an important role in setting up secret structures. The CIA gave César at least $100,000 of the NERP funds "to distribute to his people."³³ According to one opposition leader, César met individually with UNO leaders on one of his visits to Managua accompanied by Guillermo Potoy of the Social Democratic Party. To each one César offered a monthly stipend of $5,000 in cash from CIA slush funds in exchange for discipline around the UNO formation and program.³⁴ One source explained that the CIA was particularly pleased with César's close relationship with Chamorro. This would assure easy manipulation of the presidential candidate. "We invested a lot of money in César. We put him on the payroll. We turned him into a kind of 'Rasputin.'"³⁵

César developed a following of loyalists. In addition to Potoy, there were Danilo Lacayo, former manager of Exxon's refinery in Managua, who later became the Chamorro government's minister of information; and Carlos Hurtado, who went on to become minister of government. César returned to Managua in June 1989 and became UNO campaign manager. Leaders who had never left the country to join the contras resented the influence of César, whose ever-changing alliances had left him many an enemy. In November, while Chamorro was traveling abroad, a majority in the UNO Political Council voted to remove him from the campaign. On Chamorro's return, however, she immediately appointed him as her personal campaign manager.

One of those who accompanied César in his regional travels was Antonio Ibarra. Although born in Nicaragua, Ibarra was a U.S. citizen. He had worked in the anti-Sandinista cause with such far-flung rightist groups as the World Anti-Communist League and the Moonies. Ibarra was particularly active in the Institute for Religion and Democracy (IRD), a group set up by conservative leader Michael Novak in 1981 to counteract progressive religious tendencies in the United States and Latin America. The IRD helped the Reagan administration design a propaganda campaign around "religious persecution" under the Sandinistas and funneled moneys to Archbishop Miguel Obando y Bravo.³⁶

In 1989, Ibarra presented a study to the Army–Air Force Center for Low-Intensity Conflict in Langley, Virginia, on the threat of liberation theology and Marxism in Latin America. The study condemned the movement in Latin America known as liberation theology, or the "church of the poor," as "an adoption of the Marxist interpretation of Christianity," which in Nicaragua had meant being "an accomplice of the torture and genocide" practiced by the "Sandinista communist regime."[37]

In early March, the director of the State Department's Nicaraguan Coordination Office, Alfred Barr, provided Ibarra with a letter of introduction for the Honduran Consulate describing Ibarra as "an Adviser to the Nicaraguan Resistance." Ibarra "wishes to travel to Honduras on official Resistance business," it stated. "We would appreciate your efforts to facilitate his travel."[38] Ibarra also advised Freedom House in its anti-Sandinista projects.

In June 1989, Ibarra entered Nicaragua from Costa Rica on a U.S. passport and presented press credentials issued by Freedom House. He was given a visa and accredited as a foreign correspondent. In the following weeks, he began organizing an electoral survey for *La Prensa*.[39] One of the documents he distributed to *La Prensa* editors was a pamphlet he had prepared in Spanish for Freedom House titled "Nicaragua: Model for Short-Term Agitation and Propaganda."[40] The pamphlet recommended a "large-scale program for social agitation" aimed at "modifying the conduct of the Nicaraguan people toward the electoral process." The document provided basic data on Nicaragua's economic crisis; "these dismal figures underscore that the population is acutely suffering." The program would therefore involve opposition leaders from each sector—labor, political parties, and social groups. It spelled out slogans and strategies for each of these sectors to "multiply daily conflicts among the most volatile sectors" and promote actions that "square off the urban population with the state machinery."[41]

In early July, Ibarra showed up at the offices of the SEC to register as an electoral observer from Freedom House. Nicaraguan immigration authorities decided at that point to cancel his visa. The State Department condemned the cancellation as evidence that the Sandinistas were "harassing the press, the opposition, and international observers."[42] After the UNO won the election, Ibarra returned to Nicaragua, his Nicaraguan citizenship was restored, and the new government named him deputy minister of the presidency.

MANAGING THE OPPOSITION CAMPAIGN IN THE UNITED STATES

CIA funds can be channeled through any number of institutions in Europe, Latin America and the United States—through foundations, kindred institutional groups, etc. There are millions of ways to get money into Nicaragua.

—Philip Agee[43]

Although the electoral intervention project was a transnational undertaking, Washington became the veritable command center. The city of Miami, the gateway to Latin America from U.S. territory, became the staging point for the operatives, finances, and materials involved in the electoral intervention project. And as in Central America, the task in Miami was not to create new structures but to transform what was already a key contra political and logistical rearguard into a functioning support system for the electoral effort.

In their August 1988 planning meeting at the State Department, U.S. officials examined the options for mounting operations out of Miami. The participants discussed forming a "committee for free elections and democracy in Nicaragua." The objective of this committee would be to act as one of several liaisons between Washington and Managua.

As U.S. agents set about to form such an organization in Miami, they ran up against problems in the changeover from contra to internal opposition rearguard. The contras did not want to demobilize or to lose their U.S. sources of funding and power. Miami had been invaded in 1979 by *Somocista* businesspeople, politicians, and National Guardsmen fleeing the revolutionary triumph. These groups and the CIA agents who ran the contra program gained great influence within the community of several hundred thousand Nicaraguans who came to settle in the city. Many Nicaraguan power brokers in Miami panicked at the realization that the piñata of the contra war was nearly empty. Groups such as the Nicaraguan American National Foundation, run by longtime contra leader and CIA agent Adolfo Calero, Bosco Matamoros, and Alvaro Rizo, complained bitterly and refused to cooperate with the efforts to reorient structures. Hard-line *Somocistas*, such as former National Guardsman Cristobal Mendoza, who had allegedly headed Somoza's Mano Blanca (White Hand) death squad, formed different Nicaraguan "exile committees" and even organized demonstrations against the electoral process, taking out ads on local radio stations condemning opposition participation as "traitorous."[44]

The Bush administration eventually found the ideal candidate, José Antonio Alvarado. Alvarado, a one-time Somoza diplomat and business associate of Alfredo César, ran an investment operation in Miami called AIBC Financial Corporation. His outfit had been used by the CIA in earlier years to launder contra funds. As a Hispanic securities broker, Alvarado had also been awarded several contracts under federal quota programs for minority businesses that were allegedly also used to send money secretly to the contras.[45] In the stormy months of late 1988 and early 1989, when the contra program was being shut down, Alvarado formed the Nicaraguan Civic Task Force under the guidance of the CIA to regroup the Miami community around the internal political campaign and to stifle renegades resisting the change.[46]

The Miami operation moved into high gear with the opening of the electoral process in April 1989. In that month, NED officials met with Chargé d'Affaires Leonard at the U.S. Embassy in Managua to discuss on-site strategy. "What role for a Committee for Free Elections in Miami?" was one of the items on the agenda. "Who will administer it? How will it function?" Shortly afterward, the Nicaraguan Civic Task Force was selected as the nucleus for the Miami liaison work and was renamed the Committee for Free Elections and Democracy in Nicaragua. The committee was given office space in a building owned by Jeb Bush who became an "honorary member" of its board.[47] (Jeb Bush purchased the building with loans from a savings and loan bank that went insolvent. As part of its bailout of the savings and loan industry, the federal government paid more than $4 million to make good on Bush's loan.) Alvarado gathered together a board of directors that included Nadia Palláis, a member by marriage of the Somoza family; Carlos García, former Nicaraguan National Guard officer and business partner of Somoza; and Nicolás López, the former director of the Somoza family newspaper, *Novedades*.

Publicly, this committee was presented as a group of "professionals from the Nicaraguan exile community" who, together with UNO leaders in Managua, had taken the initiative to organize support among exiles for the opposition.[48] As part of the deception, during her September 1989 visit to Miami, Violeta Chamorro announced the official formation of the committee as an initiative she herself had undertaken.[49] "I have decided to set up the committee. . . . because we need your help," stated the press release she read. "The Sandinista campaign is completely computerized, and we have nothing but our heart and our courage. We need to unite our forces against these Marxist-Leninists who preach war and destroy the family." Chamorro announced that she had opened an account at the Miami office of Merrill Lynch and Company for the Miami committee and that the group would help the UNO with public relations in the United States and with fund-raising among the exiles. In fact, Chamorro knew absolutely nothing about the committee until she was handed the press release in Miami. This strategy of presenting the UNO as the promoter of the Miami committee allowed the U.S. role to remain undisclosed.

This press release was actually prepared by a Washington public relations firm, the Carmen Group, which was founded in 1982 by David Carmen; his father, Gerald Carmen; and Max Hugel.[50] The firm brought together several former intelligence officials and conservative figures who became prominent during the Reagan administration. Hugel, one of Ronald Reagan's top campaign managers,[51] served briefly as director of operations of the CIA after Reagan's victory.[52] Both the Carmens were senior Reagan associates, and Gerald Carmen was also a senior adviser to the Bush transition team in 1988. Another top Carmen Group official, Carol Boyd Hallett, a former ambassador to the Bahamas, was appointed commissioner of the U.S. Customs Service by Bush in November 1989.[53]

The Carmen Group was a prime promoter of the contra war.[54] The Carmens and Hugel were founding members of Citizens for America, which was set up at a White House ceremony in 1983. Citizens for America, a quasi-governmental organization, played a key role in mobilizing congressional and public support for military aid to the contras and in promoting Reagan's foreign policy agenda in general.[55] After the Iran-contra scandal, Citizens for America became inoperative, and most of its staff moved to the Carmen Group. Operating out of their public relations firm, the Carmens and their staff made an easy transition from the contra to the electoral intervention project.

The Carmen Group took on responsibility for supervising the work of the Committee for Free Elections and Democracy in Nicaragua and for assuring that the committee's functions would be synchronized with the overall electoral intervention project. The Carmen Group would direct the committee-UNO public relations and fund-raising in the United States. But this activity would be presented as the work of the Nicaraguan exiles. A working document circulated internally by the Carmen Group in September 1989 explained that "a sizable co-ordinating office, the Committee for Free Elections and Democracy in Nicaragua, will have to be developed and funded in Miami and funded for 5 months. . . . A small support staff that will deal on a day-to-day basis will be needed to co-ordinate press outreach and response, distribution of aid, donors relations and supervise budgetary implementation. This office will have a full time staff of 4, plus a director and outside professional services. Expected costs [will be] $275,000" (see Appendix A, document 18).[56]

The Carmen Group also coordinated its work with several members of Congress who had taken a keen interest in the Nicaraguan campaign, among them Senator Bob Graham (D-Fla.), who had put his staff to the task of shipping materials to the UNO in Nicaragua, and Representative Dante Fascell. These people organized an "honorary steering committee of prominent Americans" for the Miami committee. Among those on the steering committee were about two dozen members of Congress; Sofia Casey, the wife of the late CIA director; Jeb Bush; and Governor Bob Martinez of Florida. The Carmens registered the Miami committee with the U.S. Department of Justice as the "only organization sanctioned by the UNO to receive campaign contributions in the United States" (see Appendix A, document 14).[57]

In October 1989, Carmen officials met with the NED's deputy director of programs, Barbara Haig, to discuss coordination of the Nicaragua project with the NED. "We are excited about the opportunities that lie ahead," stated David Carmen in a follow-up letter to Haig. "I am positive that together we'll bring about real change for democracy in Nicaragua" (see Appendix A, document 19).[58]

The Carmen Group's fund-raising among wealthy conservatives differed little from the "private" fund-raising efforts led by Oliver North and company in the mid-1980s. The main difference was that the funds were not for the "freedom fighters" but for the "democratic opposition." The same names, faces, and private network of right-wing activists who came to power during the Reagan years and put into motion the Nicaraguan counterrevolution cropped up again and again during the electoral intervention project. The Iran-contra crowd had not disappeared. It made the passage, in consonance with the Reagan to Bush transition, from the military to the internal political terrain in the campaign against the Sandinistas.

One of the Carmen Group's projects involved organizing a U.S. tour for Violeta Chamorro, for which Republican millionaire Fred Sacher donated $145,000. In 1985, Sacher had made a $305,000 donation to the National Endowment for the Preservation of Liberty, one of Oliver North's front groups set up by Contragate accomplice Carl "Spitz" Channel. Sacher's donation was deposited in one of the secret Swiss bank accounts used to purchase black-market arms for the contras.[59] Now, Sacher's donation to the Carmen Group was to finance the Chamorro U.S. tour, which David Carmen baptized the Sacher Project.[60]

The one-week tour was scheduled for mid-January and involved daytime meetings with all of the major print and television media on the East Coast, followed by nightly $1,000-per-plate fund-raising dinners in Boston, New York, Washington, and Miami.[61] The tour was canceled at the last minute after Chamorro broke her knee. Nevertheless, the Carmen Group's post-tour budget report indicated that despite the cancellation, $95,000 of Sacher's donation were in fact spent, including $15,000 paid to Gerald Carmen as "tour manager."[62] Upset that much of his donation was spent even though Chamorro never came, Sacher called David Carmen to complain. Carmen responded, "I was deeply disturbed by your clear disappointment. I know that everything we are doing for you is valuable and tremendously worthwhile. . . . As for your project, I was so taken by your extraordinary commitment, I bent over backwards to make sure you were not ripped off."[63]

In mid-January, David Carmen and several of his staff met with Violeta Chamorro and Antonio Lacayo in Houston during the UNO candidate's hospitalization in that city for knee treatment. Time was short, said Lacayo, telling Carmen that another $500,000 in cash would be needed for the final phase of the campaign. Among the projects they discussed for this final phase was "an aggressive public relations campaign" run out of UNO headquarters in Managua. The purpose of the campaign, drawn up by Carmen, was to target the foreign correspondents in Managua. The Carmen Group and the Miami committee had earlier assisted in running a "press center" attached to UNO headquarters, which was upgraded for this final public relations effort. Despite his annoyance with the Carmen Group's budgeting, Sacher donated another $53,000 for this project, which was forwarded on to the UNO in Managua.[64]

And although Violeta Chamorro could not be present, the Carmen Group organized a dinner in New York City on February 7 for twenty wealthy Republican couples, at $5,000 per couple. The dinner, held at the home of Seymour and Evie Holtzman, featured Jeane Kirkpatrick as the guest of honor. The invitations sent by David Carmen explained that "these elections can be the turning point in restoring that part of Central America to Democracy and, in my opinion, will set in motion the cure for Cuba and finally end the threat that we face down there. . . . Please join us for an interesting evening with Jeane."[65] The "press is not invited, nor welcome," assured David Carmen to Kirkpatrick and the other guests.[66] Among the invitees were former Reagan chief of staff Donald T. Regan, and Faith Whittlesey, former co-director of the White House Liaison Office set up to run the Reagan administration's "public diplomacy" projects for Central American policy.[67] Other guests were Sofia Casey; Holly Coors of the Coors family, which had earlier donated millions of dollars to the contras; and Bill Simon, whose curriculum included positions with PRODEMCA, the Nicaraguan Freedom Fund, and other right-wing groups that had provided assistance to the contras (see Appendix A, documents 15 and 16).

Nine days after the dinner, Kirkpatrick appeared as the keynote speaker at a Capitol Hill conference titled "Elections in Nicaragua: Democracy or Deception?" and convened by the Far Right American Defense Institute. In her presentation, Kirkpatrick described the elections as a "farce orchestrated by the communists." During the conference, an eight-minute UNO public relations video was shown that painted Chamorro as the Cory Aquino of Nicaragua fighting "communism and totalitarianism." J. R. Black produced the video, for which he was paid $12,000 by the Carmen Group.[68] Black, who ran a shadowy operation called International Media Associates, had been introduced to Carl Gershman by William Geimer, the president of the Jamestown Foundation. (Geimer and his foundation have been linked to U.S. covert activities.)[69] In an introductory letter to Gershman, Geimer explained that "Black proposes to produce a videotape [which will] speak about the evils of communism, and to disseminate the tapes in Nicaragua prior to the February election. . . . We will of course provide him with access to Jamestown clients."[70] After evaluating the project, however, the NED decided to send Black over to the Carmen Group for sponsorship.

In addition to financing the video, the Carmen Group also assigned Black to assist the Miami committee in preparing press communiqués. Black worked together with the Nicaraguan radio journalist Alan Téfel, a UNO militant who ran a news program at the NED-funded station Radio Corporación. One document explained, "Any significant operation in Nicaragua needs a strategic bridge to American and European public opinion."[71] The Black–Téfel–Carmen–Miami committee circle also helped disseminate the CIA's blowback operation in the West German newspaper *Frankfurter Allegemeine Zeitung*.[72]

MONEY LAUNDERING OR MONEY POCKETING?

Not all went smoothly with the semiclandestine U.S. "private" fund-raising for the UNO in the United States. Rivalries among the different factions within the Nicaraguan opposition and lingering fears from the still-smoldering Iran-contra scandal hampered the effort. In Managua, Chamorro's campaign advisers Alfredo César and Antonio Lacayo had proposed to Ernesto Palazio, the UNO's official representative in Washington, that he participate in the fund-raising efforts. They asked Palazio to take advantage of the broad contacts he had developed among wealthy conservative Americans during his tenure as contra spokesperson, and of his close ties to the State Department, to coordinate efforts with the Carmen Group and the Miami committee. The Carmen Group resented the prominence given to Palazio, who, they complained, had been accused earlier of embezzling funds raised privately for the Washington contra office. In late December 1989, David Carmen wrote to UNO campaign chief Antonio Lacayo in Managua:

> In our fundraising efforts on behalf of Mrs. Violeta Chamorro and the UNO, we have encountered a very disturbing and disruptive situation which we feel we must bring to your attention. On several occasions, we have called potential donors and introduced ourselves as the official fundraiser committee for the UNO and Mrs. Chamorro. These people have then claimed that when they were in Managua and asked you how they could be helpful to the party and Mrs. Chamorro, you have referred them to Mr. Ernesto Palacios [sic] in Washington.

I know that we have discussed this problem in the past, but this referral has caused a direct loss of contributors among those people who vividly remember the Iran-Contra problem and have no desire to give to a cause represented by someone who they see as intimately connected to the Contras—probably due to a great deal of unfair publicity surrounding Ernesto.

Also, this confusion causes a loss of credibility and effectiveness on our part as the UNO's official fundraising committee. . . .

What we suggest is some direction from you that Ernesto work directly with Ambassador [Gerald] Carmen in a less upfront fashion, so that we can all present a unified front.[73]

On the same day as this letter was sent, David Carmen's personal assistant, Cynthia Lebrun, faxed a copy of it to José Antonio Alvarado in Miami, together with a cover letter in Spanish:

I am sending you a copy of the fax we sent to Tonio Lacayo today regarding the Ernesto affair, which you and I spoke of yesterday. As you can see, David used a moderate tone in his letter, but I want to warn you that we are very annoyed by the situation.

What David did not say to Tonio is that we fear that Ernesto's reputation could prove detrimental to us. . . . With Iran-contra and all the other problems that have come up, we certainly don't need this additional problem of Ernesto. We would like you and Tonio to tell us how this affair will be resolved. I also want to mention to you that Ernesto has told several people that he has already raised $50,000 for the campaign. I hope that money has been forwarded to Managua. [See Appendix A, document 17.][74]

Whether Palazio sent the $50,000 to UNO coffers in Managua is not known. But even if these funds were sent down, they were never reported to the SEC, as Nicaraguan law required. For that matter, *none* of the funds coming from the United States, private or public, were reported to the SEC, except for the official NED funds that came from the congressional $9 million appropriation.

There were also problems in the efforts to enlist the support of Democrats in the private campaign fund-raising. As part of its preparations for Chamorro's January 1990 tour of the United States, the Carmen Group requested that the Democratic National Committee and the Republican National Committee jointly circulate a letter of support for the UNO candidate calling for campaign donations from the U.S. public. Staffers at the Republican National Committee drafted the letter: "Mrs. Chamorro will face Marxist-Leninist dictator Daniel Ortega in the first-ever free election to be held in Nicaragua. We are asking you to join with a diverse group of Americans, Republicans, Democrats, Liberals, Conservatives, Business Owners and Labor Union Leaders to make an investment in Nicaraguan Democracy. We are asking you to give a minimum contribution of $1,000, but you can give MORE!" The letter was signed by several members of the Miami committee's "honorary board," including Jeb Bush and Donald Trump, and by Ron Brown and Lee Atwater, chairs of the Democratic National Committee and the Republican National Committee, respectively (see Appendix A, document 20).[75]

After the letter had circulated, Brown denied that he had endorsed the Chamorro candidacy and had his attorney release a statement asserting that "Brown does not participate in foreign elections."[76] According to David Carmen, aides from the Democratic National Committee had approved the letter without Brown's authorization.[77]

DESIGNING THE UNO's
ELECTORAL CAMPAIGN

The Carmen Group handled a curious combination of public and secret relations. In a working document to the State Department, the NED, and other offices in Washington circulated in September 1989, the group provided strategic guidelines for the UNO electoral campaign, detailing a comprehensive strategy of political and psychological operations and financial expenditures:

> In order to counter what will most certainly be intense and well financed activity on the part of the Sandinistas, the opposition's campaign must and will take advantage of every hour between now and February 25th, election day. . . .
> The population must first be provided with incentives for wanting to attend the rallies. They are therefore fed at these events and given souvenirs of the rally which, in addition to giving them something to take home, also provides a feeling of well being in contrast to the stark poverty in which they have been living under the existing regime. This has the added advantage of keeping the opposition ever present in their minds. Further, these people must be transported to and from the rallies.
> Population mobilization and motivation requires resources for a full time organized activity by many campaign workers in the 16 geographic departments into which Nicaragua is divided. It also requires transportation for the population and campaign staff in each district. Equipment, food and souvenirs must also be purchased. [See Appendix A, document 18.][78]

The document also detailed two phases of the opposition campaign. Phase one was to consist of "raising the consciousness of the Nicaraguans" and was to bring up the following themes among the population: "Hunger, Misery, Obligatory Draft, i.e., the status quo versus Change, Liberty and Employment." Phase two was to "consist of the mechanics and reasons for voting for the opposition and [was to] occur between December 1 and February 26." This phase was to "emphasize the following themes: The Candidates' values and personalities, Full employment for the country, Freedom of expression, Prosperity and improvement of quality of life."[79] These strategy guidelines also spoke of the importance of designing and producing the opposition's campaign materials, a task that was assumed in part by the CAD and in part by other groups.

A careful study of the UNO's electoral campaign from September 1989 to February 25, 1990, reveals that this strategy was fully implemented. The themes it outlined were precisely those on which the UNO campaign was based (see Chapter 7). Although it was not clear who actually authored the document (whether it was drafted by Carmen Group officials or was merely circulated by this group), a cursory reading left no doubt that it was prepared by professionals in intelligence and in political warfare and psychological operations. The language of the document was the same as that found in CIA and Pentagon manuals on political and psychological warfare. The CIA's *Psychological Operations in Guerrilla Warfare* stressed the importance of "unarmed propaganda" and defined it as the use of themes sensitive to the target population.

The document also presented a detailed budget, including funding for these two phases, overall electoral spending, moneys for the Miami office, and other items. It budgeted $709,500 in "souvenirs" for phase one, including UNO caps, T-shirts, plastic glasses, flags, and bumper stickers. Phase two called for an additional $1 million for more "souvenirs" and $1.7 million for "salaries and equipment." Other budget categories were $168,000 in travel for UNO members to Miami and other cities (among them, Houston, San Francisco, Los Angeles, New Orleans, and Washington, D.C.) and $320,000 for trips to Nicaragua by North American, Latin American, and European "observers." The total UNO budget drawn up in the document was $4.3 million. Just days before this document was circulated, a group from the UNO had been brought up to Washington by the NED to lobby for public U.S. assistance. The budget they presented to Congress was for $4,453,732.

The Carmen document allocated $75,000 in salaries for ten thousand "junior campaign workers" and $90,000 in "salaries for senior campaign staff." UNO headquarters did in fact prepare an internal payroll spreadsheet for month-to-month salaries during the electoral campaign. The payroll included hundreds of local and national UNO activists with monthly salaries ranging from $500 to $50: $500 for the UNO's "national electoral control chief," $250 for regional and zonal campaign heads, $150 for district campaign chiefs, $60 for municipal heads, and $50–$60 for UNO workers. Considering that this money was paid every month beginning as early as September and October 1989, the UNO paid out hundreds of thousands of dollars in salaries.[80] And these figures were only for UNO employees; they did not include thousands of other individuals who were paid by the youth, women's, civic, and trade union groups of the national civic front.[81]

The $9 million congressional appropriation for the NED included thousands of dollars in salaries for a nationwide staff from the Institute for Electoral Promotion and Training. Paid IPCE staff was to include 72 "deputy directors" around the country, 108 "supervisors," 432 "department heads," 540 "coordinators," and 15,300 "verifiers."[82] The people from this latter category alone were to be paid a daily stipend of $4 day for their work, amounting to $60,000 for each day that the verifiers were employed.

Exactly how much of the Carmen budget categories were actually fulfilled, or what percentage of these categories was handled by Carmen and what percentage passed through other channels, is not known. It is clear, however, that the specific spending called for in the document was actually carried out: UNO campaign workers did receive their salaries; the plastic cups, flags, bumper stickers, and so on, did arrive in Nicaragua; top-level UNO representatives did shuttle back and forth from Managua to different U.S. cities for "fund-raising events"; and the United States did pay for several foreign observer delegations, among other Carmen categories that were fulfilled. The details of the Carmen Group budget overlapped heavily with details of NED budgets and UNO budgets.

Within a complex division of labor throughout the U.S. electoral intervention project, it appears that the NED assumed overall guidance of certain categories of spending, Carmen assumed others, and the CIA or the AID assumed still others. Many of the Carmen budget categories were distinct from the $12.5 million that Congress appropriated, which is traceable. The NED's charter prohibited it from giving direct campaign aid to the UNO and from carrying out projects within the United States. Thus, while the NED took charge of public and overt funding to the UNO and its auxiliary organizations in Nicaragua, the Carmen Group and the Miami committee ran the public relations work in the United States and direct fund-raising for the UNO. The moneys and supplies raised for the UNO by Carmen, in distinction to the NED funds, were sent secretly to Nicaragua and never reported to the SEC.

David Carmen admitted that his group raised at least $600,000 for UNO campaign materials.[83] Other Carmen documents indicated that close to $1 million passed through the firm's hands. Alvarado explained that the Miami committee raised additional tens of thousands of dollars through local fund-raising.[84] Using local media outlets, the political infrastructure set up during the years of the contra war, and the assistance of Carmen, the NRI, and other entities based in Washington, the Miami committee carried out dozens of fund-raising events. Throughout the electoral campaign, the flow of UNO leaders to and from Miami was constant. For instance, on February 14 the Miami committee brought UNO leader Francisco Mayorga, who would go on after the elections to become president of the Central Bank, to give a talk to "Nicaraguan American Businessmen and Bankers" in Miami. Afterward, the businesspeople presented him with $8,000 for the purchase of two hundred thousand UNO stickers to take back to Managua. Events such as these were near daily occurrences. For instance, in November, Guillermo Potoy was interviewed on Miami's Channel 23, the local UNIVISION station where Carlos Briceño had worked. As part of the program, hosts from the Miami committee launched an appeal for funding that Alvarado described as a "fund-raising marathon" that raised $20,000.[85]

In late January, the Bush administration made the highly unusual decision to publicly request that the Democratic and the Republican parties make direct, cash donations to the UNO electoral campaign. In a letter signed personally by George Bush and addressed to Lee Atwater and Ronald Brown, the White House stated, "In the crucial last weeks of the campaign, UNO is desperately short of funds needed for campaign rallies, distributing campaign literature, and media time. While Congress has made money available for UNO through the NED, that money is limited by NED's charter to institution-building expenses and cannot be used to defray campaign costs. . . . I am asking your help to give UNO a chance. . . . A joint contribution by both Parties to the UNO campaign would make an immediate difference at this critical moment, as would individual contributions by your Party's members."[86]

Lee Atwater participated in fund-raising events for the UNO. Ron Brown, however, declined formal endorsement. "Democrats do not believe that it is appropriate, proper or wise for our political parties to attempt to influence the outcome of elections in a foreign country," wrote Brown in a letter of response to Bush's request.[87] Brown's response clearly had more to do with tactical differences with the Republicans than with neutrality vis-à-vis the Nicaraguan elections, considering that his party had only months earlier approved the $9 million NED package, $5 million of which went directly to strengthen the opposition. Individual Democrats lent wholehearted support to the fund-raising efforts.

Other congressmen and congresswomen took up the fund-raising drive as if Nicaragua were their home district. Representative Amorty Houghton (R-N.Y.) raised some $45,000 in cash for Chamorro. Representative Cass Ballenger (R-N.C.) donated some $10,000 worth of plastic bags, cups, and banners to UNO as campaign "souvenirs."[88]

SECRET SHIPMENTS

Another activity in which the Carmen Group and the Miami committee became involved was secret shipments of electoral resources to the opposition in Nicaragua. In early October 1989, Carmen official Carol Boyd Hallett met with the NED's Barbara Haig to discuss this. Afterward, she wrote to Haig thanking the NED for resolving the Carmen Group's "shipping dilemma"—the problem of how to clandestinely send supplies to the UNO so as to avoid Nicaraguan taxes and keep this funding secret. "Through your insight, it seems we have solved our problem," stated the letter. "I am currently working with Senator Bob Graham. His office has assured me they will see that the cargo arrives in Nicaragua."[89]

Bob Graham's office was but one of numerous clandestine channels for the UNO shipments to Nicaragua. Other freight was shipped in crates from Miami freight companies to Costa Rica and from there sent secretly overland into Nicaragua for unloading. Receipts and internal letters documenting these shipping transactions indicated, for instance, that the Faith Freight Forwarding Corporation of Miami sent out a twenty-foot crate to Puerto Limón, Costa Rica's Caribbean coast port, on December 19, under the name of Pedro Joaquin Chamorro, Jr. According to the receipts, the crate contained, among other items, a 162-pound box sent by Creative Marketing Ideas and 5,426 pounds of UNO campaign posters and other materials produced by American Photo in Miami, including 12,500 plastic glasses, 200,000 plastic bags, and 100,000 plastic UNO flags—precisely the campaign materials detailed in the Carmen Group strategy document. Roberto Faith, a Costa Rican citizen residing in Miami who at the time was also working with another organization funded by the NED as well as running Faith Freight,[90] sent a fax to UNO headquarters in Managua on December 20 addressed to Pedro Chamorro, Jr. The fax stated, "I'm sending you a copy of 'Loading Guide No. 003944' which describes the contents of the load that left on December 19 and should arrive at Puerto Limón on December 24. From there it will be taken to San José and sent overland to Managua. I have also sent a FAX copy of this project to Mr. Richard Beck of Atlas Electricas in Costa Rica, who will help in shipment from San José to Managua. My office in San José, which has a lot of experience, will also cooperate in this endeavor."

Another Carmen Group "consultant" hired for the Nicaragua project was former Republican congressman George Wortley (R-N.Y.), who had sat on the Banking and Finance Committees. Wortley was paid $6,500 by the Miami committee for "services rendered," which sources from the committee defined as "confidential services." At the same time as he provided these undisclosed services to the Miami group, Wortley was also a consultant for Financial Institution Services Corporation of Washington, D.C., an outlet that served as an intermediary for the financial transactions of Alvarado's security firm, AIBC Financial.[91]

Meanwhile, the NRI was coordinating activities with the Miami committee. Keith Schuette personally oversaw the production in Miami of UNO campaign propaganda, even though the NED charter expressly prohibited such activity. Schuette contracted the Miami printing company Creative Marketing Ideas to print up UNO T-shirts, bumper stickers, and other electoral paraphernalia. Creative Marketing Ideas was run by Luis Arguello, a *Somocista* businessman who left Nicaragua before the revolution. "Thank you for your quick response on the printing of the T-shirts of our Nicaragua program," stated a letter from Schuette to Arguello. The letter specified that the order was for $17,632 worth of T-shirts, with the UNO campaign slogans "UNO por la Democracia" (UNO for Democracy) and "UNO Somos Todos" (UNO Is Everyone). It also stated, "Please advise if this price includes tax, as we are a tax-exempt organization."[92] Thus, in this operation the NED not only secretly violated the prohibitions on providing direct campaign paraphernalia to the UNO but also violated the regulations guiding its tax-exempt status (see Appendix A, document 21).

In the UNO's relations with these U.S. patrons, there was never any question about who was in control. Just as Lacayo was bawled out for having unilaterally authorized Palazio to raise funds, so, too, he was often informed post facto of decisions taken for the UNO by U.S. agents. For instance, on December 22, 1989, the U.S. daily *USA Today* ran a column on its editorial page that quoted Violeta Chamorro affirming that "the Americas are unified in the spirit and desire for democracy, freedom, and entrepreneurship." On the same day, David Carmen's office faxed a copy of the article to Lacayo. *USA Today* had "wanted to get a quote from Doña Violeta with her feelings on the subject," Cynthia Lebrun explained in the fax. "You were unavailable so David and I made up the quote."[93]

The U.S. strategists decided to make the spending of the $9 million highly visible and separate from other U.S. funding. Among other objectives, this would deflect attention away from clandestine and semiclandestine spending through other channels. An internal NRI memorandum recounted a meeting at the State Department on January 12, 1990, of representatives from several of the NED groups—including the NDI and the NRI, David Jessup from AIFLD, and Valentino Martínez from the U.S. Embassy in Managua—and most of the State Department's Nicaragua team. The meeting was called to discuss the funding operations. During the meeting, Roger Noriega, who did the AID's public relations work for the $9 million, proposed "getting out in front of the press and circumventing sending money to IPCE through the Nicaraguan Central Bank [as Nicaraguan laws required], and instead send it through Florida." "We told him to keep the press at bay and forget about any Florida alternatives," recounted the NRI memo.[94]

Meanwhile, the NRI drew up a list of six "possible options" for sending money to UNO:

- Send "through the existing IPCE account in Miami;
- Send direct cash payments by courier;
- Seek Nicaraguan nationals with major holdings in United States who could offer cordobas in exchange for deposits to their U.S. accounts;
- Attempt to free up BCN (Nicaraguan Central Bank) dollar holdings in Panama, or arrange for other BCN access to dollars;
- Apply political and public pressure to Nicaragua to comply with their commitments to UNO and NDI/NRIIA." [See Appendix A, document 22.][95]

FOR WHOM WAS THE PLAYING FIELD NOT LEVEL?

As noted in Chapter 3, U.S. financing for the UNO was justified as a nonpartisan effort to level the playing field. As this and previous chapters have shown, U.S. support for the anti-Sandinista forces went well beyond official NED funding. Yet part of U.S. tactics was precisely to paint the UNO internationally as the destitute David against the Sandinista Goliath. This notion not only helped inculcate an imagined reversal of reality—the Nicaraguan David against the U.S. Goliath—but also justified to the public this unprecedented U.S. involvement in a sovereign nation's electoral process. The UNO's "lack of resources," as projected by the Bush administration and by U.S. press reports, was an integral part of a public relations campaign for consumption in the United States and abroad, with little or no correspondence to reality in Nicaragua.[96]

An apparently more austere campaign on the part of the UNO had little to do with less resources or an uneven playing field. Rather, it was a reflection of the Sandinistas' ability to organize and project a mass base in stark contrast to the UNO's lack of a nationwide base and inability to mobilize the population.[97] In late 1989, for instance, the NDI contracted the consulting firm Interworld Consultants to assess the UNO campaign. After a trip to Managua, Interworld's president, Curtis Cutter, reported in an internal memo, "The FSLN has a well-organized campaign [in contrast to] UNO's lacksidaisical [sic] performance. If this situation continues much longer an impression will be created that UNO does not represent a significant force. . . . The impact of this on the elections could be significant."[98]

Even if the issue is reduced to one of dollar-for-dollar spending, it is not at all clear that the FSLN actually received more external support than its opposition did. As noted, $7.7 million of the $9 million NED package went to the UNO and its affiliated civic, labor, and press groups. In addition, the CIA spent at least $11 million directly and indirectly for the UNO campaign. To this $18.7 million must be added all of those funds that flowed through the clandestine channels analyzed in this chapter into the coffers of the UNO or the pockets of its leaders, which could well number millions of dollars (the actual amounts will probably never be known). For its part, the FSLN reported to the SEC that it received a total of $3,017,085 in contributions of material aid and slightly more than $400,000 in cash contributions from abroad. The material contributions, according to SEC records, included more than 100,000 T-shirts from Mexican, Colombian, and Spanish solidarity organizations; 190,000 posters from French political groups; and 200,000 baseball caps from Vietnam.[99] Fifty percent of the FSLN's cash contributions were recorded as passing to the Fund for Democracy in accordance with the electoral law. "Thus," concluded the U.S.-based Latin American Studies Association, "although the FSLN campaign appeared to cost as much as UNO's, it received considerably less cash than UNO."[100]

The crux of the issue, however, is not the quantity of external support one or another political group received but the external intervention in the electoral process. Neither the solidarity groups in Latin America, Europe, and elsewhere that send cash contributions or electoral paraphernalia to the FSLN nor the socialist countries that, apart from the electoral process, continued to supply economic assistance to Nicaragua as they had done since the early 1980s intervened in the process, imposing their will on the Nicaraguan electorate.

This was a contest between the Nicaraguan Revolution and the United States, not a contest between the FSLN and the UNO. The electoral "playing field" had been created and shaped by the United States during ten years of warfare and then further molded through electoral intervention. Between 1979 and 1990, the United States mobilized and employed against Nicaragua vastly superior technical, material, political, and ideological resources in which the UNO and the resources supplied to it were but the latest anti-Sandinista instrument. Indeed, this was not a very level playing field; the United States enjoyed the overwhelming advantage on it. How U.S. strategists brought together, on a playing field in which they enjoyed overwhelming advantage, the diverse elements of a ten-year war, is shown in the next chapter.

SEVEN

The Contras and the Economy: The Making of a Faustian Bargain

Psychological warfare and violence [are employed] to induce unbearable tension in the target population. At the appropriate time, the terrorist offers, and the victim accepts, a Faustian bargain. To obtain relief from the tension of daily life in an atmosphere of constant and apparently random violence, the victim surrenders his birthright of freedom in exchange for peace—literally, at any price.

—Fred Iklé[1]

Nothing is more misleading than the notion that politics is one aspect of conflict among others—military, economic, etc. In fact, politics is not one part of conflict but the organizing principle of the whole, that which makes sense of all one does in a fight. Any government that marshals human energies through tools of political warfare must also make sure that its military and economic activities are reasonably calculated to achieve the same ends it seeks through obviously political tools. Success in political warfare means that foreigners come to understand what a protagonist is about in ways that lead them to associate their own lives, fortunes and honor with it.

—Angelo M. Codevilla[2]

At their fourth summit meeting, held in February 1989 in Costa del Sol, El Salvador, the Central American presidents called for the definitive demobilization of the contras. The contras' disarming and reintegration into civilian life had been on the agenda since the Esquipulas Accords were signed. In Costa del Sol, President Daniel Ortega proposed moving the 1990 national elections up from November to February to enable the contras to substitute political for military struggle and to reintegrate into civilian life.[3] With the Costa del Sol Accords, there was no longer any justification for postponing demobilization. The disbanding of the contras became the core of the regional peace effort. The Costa del Sol Accords also called on "all regional and

133

extraregional governments" to suspend all assistance to the contras, except that destined to finance demobilization.[4]

At their next summit six months later, the Central American presidents reiterated the call for the demobilization of the contras. At this meeting, in Tela, Honduras, the heads of state set up a timetable and instruments to carry through this demobilization—U.N. and OAS peacekeeping and verification commissions. They attached a special protocol to the Tela Agreement that provided step-by-step procedures for demobilization and also set a deadline of December 5. They called again on the United States to end its funding for the contras, stating that any such assistance should be reprogrammed under the aegis of the U.N. and OAS demobilization commissions.[5]

Managua's peace initiatives, including continued commitment to elections despite any demobilization from the contras, were taken with the implicit understanding that the United States would forsake the contras as a policy instrument, choosing instead to challenge Nicaragua on the political terrain. "We understood the logic of Tela to be that as we advanced in these elections, the contras would begin to be demobilized," said Deputy Foreign Minister Víctor Hugo Tinoco. Although the United States was not a signatory to the Costa del Sol or Tela Accords, said Tinoco, "it had established a political commitment to the process."[6]

The Nicaraguan government believed that giving Washington the space to wage political counterrevolution would increase collateral pressures on the United States to dismantle the military counterrevolution. The Sandinistas' belief in the effectiveness of such pressures turned out to be a serious miscalculation. Just as U.S. policymakers never had any intention of forsaking covert for overt intervention, they had no intention of renouncing contra military aggression for a political system open to nonmilitary intervention. The Nicaraguans opened the electoral process with the expectation that it would be allowed to unfold under relatively normal, peaceful conditions. An initial deescalation of the war following the 1988 Sapoá cease-fire agreement (see Chapter 2) heightened expectations on the part of the Nicaraguans. But once the electoral process was initiated, the Sandinista government was forced to go through with it even though the United States took calculated steps throughout the process to revive and escalate the military war.

The relation between the contra military pressure and the electoral process was calculated; the contras had an active role to play.[7] The strategists of the new political intervention stressed operations at the political level and believed that military pressure was an essential ingredient in overall policy. "The use and disposition of the military also must be the constant background, and occasional foreground, of the effort."[8] The military activity, according to Washington, would be calibrated to its "effect on the political-strategic climate."[9]

A LEASE ON LIFE FOR THE CONTRAS

After the Esquipulas IV Accords, the United States sought at all costs to postpone demobilization until after the elections. In March, the administration and Congress forged a new working consensus around Nicaragua policy with the signing of the Bipartisan Accord on Central America. The agreement paid lip service to the Esquipulas peace process, saying U.S. policy should be "consistent" with it. In practice, the Bipartisan Accord laid the groundwork for U.S. actions diametrically opposed, in letter and spirit, to the peace process. The accord was signed just before an existing contra aid package of $27 million was to run out. Before the ink was even dry on the accord, the administration and Congress set about to negotiate new aid for the contras. At the time, liberal Democrats said they went along so as to phase out the contras gracefully, without unduly embarrassing Bush and the right wing of his party.

Baker, however, in lobbying for the new aid, spelled out in no uncertain terms its purpose: to "keep the contras alive, intact and in existence throughout the electoral process." Baker stated that by keeping the contras intact, the United States would have "an insurance policy until after the February elections are certified as free and fair" so that the contras would be available "for their possible or potential use further down the road."[10] The Bush administration introduced a "humanitarian" aid package of nearly $67 million, and Secretary Baker personally spent two days on the Hill lobbying for its approval.[11] Liberals eventually agreed to endorse the package with the stipulation that four special committees would take up the issue again in November and would suspend further disbursements if the contras had engaged in offensive military actions. On November 30, just six days before the deadline set by the Central American presidents in the Tela Accords for the contras to have been fully demobilized, Congress quietly approved the continuation of the package through to the elections.

The term *humanitarian aid* is deceitful, a euphemism for what is essentially nonlethal military aid.[12] The contras had arms stockpiles and military aid lines, both of which were used in tandem with humanitarian aid from Washington. The U.S. aid package allowed the whole contra network to remain intact. Moreover, the package included several million dollars for "standard military attire," including fatigues, boots, ponchos, field packs, canteens, and mess kits, procured and airlifted in from the Department of Defense.[13] Six hundred midlevel contra officers were given a course in Honduras between April and June to help them strengthen their military structure.[14] Tens of thousands of dollars were also spent on communications equipment, which permitted coordinated actions among contra patrols, brigades, and entire battalions.[15] The package also provided for the continuation of a "cash for food" program handled by the CIA whereby cash was sent from Honduras to contras inside Nicaragua to purchase supplies in local markets.[16] This program allowed contras inside Nicaragua to remain there.

The Pentagon also complemented the humanitarian aid package with the deployment of its own forces in the region, including military exercises, electronic surveillance of Nicaraguan territory, and engineering operations along Nicaragua's land borders.[17] In the first quarter of 1989, Sandinista military intelligence reported more than sixty flights over Nicaragua of different U.S. aircraft, including the famous AWACS, involving everything from electronic radio exploration to strategic aerial photography flights. U.S. naval forces continued to patrol Nicaragua's maritime frontiers, including the permanent stationing of the ARL 24 spy ship. This encirclement of Nicaragua, which had been in place since the early 1980s, provided a vast logistical and intelligence rearguard network for the contra forces. Sustaining it throughout the electoral process meant providing the contras with the capacity to continue operations.[18]

The United States responded to the Tela Accords (signed in August) by upping the ante in its resistance to demobilizing the contras. On the eve of the meeting, the United States sent letters to the four Central American allies proposing that they adopt the slogan "Democratization Before Demobilization." President Bush followed the letter up with personal phone calls to the Central American leaders. And he received a personal visit from Enrique Bermúdez, the former Somoza Guard colonel who was supreme commander of the contra forces, and told him that the United States "continues to support you." The meeting was well publicized, especially in the Central American media. James Baker even kept Oscar Arias on the phone for an hour, in a direct line from Washington to Tela, trying to convince him to prevent contra demobilization.[19]

Back in March 1988, the Sandinista army had flushed most of the contras out of Nicaragua in Operation Danto. After the Tela Accords, the contra command announced that it would send forces from Honduras into Nicaragua to avoid demobilization. Mass reinfiltration began in August and peaked at several hundred per week by October. Bermúdez boasted that he had sent in six thousand troops in just a few weeks.[20] The August–October contra invasion nearly cleaned out the Honduran camps. It was one of the largest land invasions in the history of the contra war, although it was not so widely reported by the international press. The U.S. aid program had permitted a quick deployment. "The impact of these programs has been significant," said an internal State Department report released shortly after the Tela Accords were signed. "Morale remains high, and the Resistance has maintained itself as a viable organization in support of the diplomatic initiatives for irreversible democratic reforms."[21]

According to the Nicaraguan Defense Ministry, contra actions, which averaged about fifty per month during 1988, jumped in the first half of 1989 to about one hundred. Between August and October, these actions averaged three hundred per month, a rate sustained right through to the voting. The contras took up the task of armed propaganda and intimidation in favor of the opposition, becoming in effect the armed wing of the UNO. Starting in February, the contras began sending in armed propaganda teams and reestablishing a presence in rural areas they had been pushed out of in the preceding year. One State Department official described this contra activity as encouraging "their supporters to register for the election and to vote."[22] In October 1989, the Nicaraguan Resistance issued a communiqué, signed by Bermúdez, that said, "We want to express all our backing and unconditional support for the UNO candidates. . . . We are not going to put down our arms, we are not going to accept demobilization. . . . We will carry on in the mountains with our weapons loaded against Sandinismo. So as to avoid fraud, we are going to prevent Sandinista accomplices and collaborators from registering. We are going to assure the triumph of UNO."[23]

Among the contra actions were threats of reprisals following the election against those voting for the FSLN. These threats were made in the context of the imposition of a general climate of intimidation in the zones where the contras regained a presence. In some instances, intimidation was very crude. In one village the victims of a contra attack recalled, "They told us they have a little machine that detects who we're going to vote for . . . and that they'll come back and kill us if we vote for the Front."[24] They also distributed huge quantities of pro-UNO propaganda leaflets. CIA contingency funds were distributed to contras inside Nicaragua "to encourage voters."[25] "Our infiltration into Nicaragua has nothing to do with combat," explained one contra commander of a twenty-person "electoral unit" that went by the nom de guerre Vladimir. "Our only goal is to maintain a presence in our fatherland and alert the people about the elections and who they can vote for."[26]

One objective was to establish a general military-electoral presence, particularly in the more remote zones where UNO politicians could not so easily canvas. The strategists of political intervention usually recommend NED and AID programs aimed at the peasantry in target countries.[27] The Nicaraguan case was unique, however, in that the counterrevolution was rural warfare. The only two significant political forces in much of the countryside were the Sandinistas and the contras. The NED and other U.S private groups did not therefore become deeply involved with the peasants. The contras had already been designed to target the peasantry, and there was no room in the war zones for alternative political strategies separate from the military conflict. In this division of labor, U.S. strategists singled out the contras to bring the peasantry into the electoral intervention project.

For this purpose, the contras were given rudimentary propaganda training. At least $4.5 million was spent on training these forces in "courses in civic action, in basic democratic processes, forms of government and Nicaraguan history and geography," said one State Department report.[28] So-called training in human rights was also included. Some of these funds went to set up the contra "human rights" school in San José, which was then used for "civic education" of contra leaders and unit commanders during the electoral process. One contra defector, a June graduate from the contra human rights propaganda school, said the courses taught the virtues of the UNO and how contra electoral campaign activities in the rural areas could contribute to the "civic defeat" of the Sandinistas.

The contras also carried out a highly selective campaign of terror against Sandinista campaign workers. No fewer than fifty FSLN rural campaign activists were assassinated in operations that clearly required prior intelligence information and substantial planning. Similarly, officials from the local electoral councils were singled out for harassment.[29]

An attack in January against the farming community of Las Tijeras in Jinotega was typical. Armed troops had infiltrated and kidnapped a young girl at gunpoint. They marched her from house to house, warning that the girl would be shot if doors were not opened. At each house, the contras repeated the same message: "If you don't vote for UNO, we are going to shoot you after February 25." The contras then singled out the known Sandinista supporters in the village as well as the electoral workers. The president of the local voting station recounted, "They told us that if we were going to be stupid and make propaganda for the Front, then they were going to return and kill us."

After two hours of such rampaging, the contras flagged down a pickup truck as it drove into the village. The driver had spent the day distributing voting materials from the SEC to local voting stations in the area. At gunpoint, the driver was ordered to drive four of the contras into Jinotega. Once there, he was told to drive quickly through the center of town, at which point the contras tossed anti-Sandinista and pro-UNO propaganda out into the streets.[30]

These incidents were repeated hundreds of times throughout the Nicaraguan countryside. They underscored that the electoral process unfolded in the midst of war. Voting was under the gun. Some 42 percent of the electorate resided in rural areas, and of these, more than 50 percent lived in the zones of military conflict. In other words, approximately 25 percent of the electorate was directly affected by contra military activity.[31] Nevertheless, the contra redeployment did not have as its main objective the intimidation of isolated peasant communities. Rather, the redeployment was the cornerstone of a sophisticated psychological warfare operation aimed at sending a powerful message to the entire electorate: The Sandinistas are not capable of ending the war; thus if the Sandinistas win the elections, the war will continue. The use and the threat of the use of military aggression were thus employed in the electoral intervention project as a political trump card.

By 1989, the peace process, government-contra negotiations, and a cease-fire that the Sandinista army had been renewing on a unilateral basis since May 1988 had brought relative peace to many of the communities that had been the scene of several years of traumatic warfare. And although the military draft remained in effect, conscription levels had been significantly reduced, and fewer draftees were actually being sent off to the zones of conflict. In sum, there was a general mood throughout much of the country that real peace was not too far off. The FSLN, having led the nation in defeating the Reagan strategy and bringing the armed conflict to a close, anticipated that with contra demobilization an achieved fact, the front would enter the electoral campaign as the "party of peace." In this context, the contras' 1989 redeployment into Nicaragua became an ideal method for U.S. strategists to try reversing this Sandinista advantage. "Backed up by military action when it becomes necessary, POLWAR and PSYOPS, within the realm of their competence, can turn situations of disadvantage into victory," pointed out one of these strategists.[32]

By reinfiltrating the contras and having them engage in enough visible activity so as to make their presence an issue in the media, and thus in the entire population, the United States caused the Sandinistas' claim of having defeated the contras to lose credibility. This forced the FSLN to demote the peace issue in its electoral campaign to a promise, at best, for the postelectoral period. In the countryside itself, the escalation of contra activity sent the message to the peasant population that the contras were able to reestablish themselves in Nicaraguan territory and thereby initiate a long-term reescalation of the war. Therefore, Nicaraguans in general, and those in the war zones in particular, had to contemplate the consequences of their vote in relation to the contras. "When we examine coercive diplomacy and limited military actions as forms of psychological warfare," said one U.S. strategist, "we should bear in mind that [their] effectiveness depends on our enemy's perception of what will happen to him if he fails to do as we wish."[33]

In late October, after several weeks of escalating attacks, a contra unit ambushed nineteen young reservists traveling in a flatbed truck en route to their hometown to register to vote. The contras had to carry out such spectacular attacks to make the threat of continuing the war credible. For the government, the ambush of the reservists was the last straw. A week later at the democracy summit meeting of heads of state from the hemisphere in San José, President Ortega announced the end of the government's unilateral cease-fire. The U.S. media and Congress reacted by condemning the Sandinista revocation of the cease-fire, *not* the killing of the reservists.[34] In this way, the Sandinistas were forced to take steps that underscored to the electorate that the FSLN had *not* been able to end the war.

International pressures on the United States to demobilize were enormous and grew as the electoral campaign proceeded. The Central American presidents met on December 12 for their sixth summit, in San Isidro de Coronado, Costa Rica. They issued yet another call for the disbanding of the contras and summoned the United States explicitly to transfer its contra aid program to the U.N. and OAS commissions set up to disarm and repatriate the contras.[35] All the United States had to do was hold out until after the voting.[36]

The flip side of snatching the "peace banner" from the Sandinistas was attaching it to the UNO. The message was simple: Because the contras support the UNO, and because the United States sponsors both the UNO and the contras, an electoral victory for the UNO will mean an end to the military war with the contras. The UNO, by virtue of its relation to the superpower waging war against Nicaragua, will be able to achieve peace. A vote for the UNO is a vote for peace.

In synchronization with the contras' armed propaganda and military violence, a central plank of the UNO campaign platform was the abolition of the military draft. This was another of the no-win options that the U.S. war imposed on the Sandinistas. The need to defend the nation inevitably bore a high political cost in the elections for the party responsible for organizing national defense—the FSLN. Opposition to the draft was widespread and could only grow to the extent that the war was prolonged. But the draft had also made a critical contribution to the defensive capacity of the nation and had helped accomplish the strategic defeat of the contras. So long as the United States could maintain the existence of war fronts, the Sandinista government would have to chose between sustaining an unpopular and politically damaging draft or making the country more vulnerable to foreign military aggression. And holding the threat of prolongation of the war over the heads of the electorate gave voters the clear perception that a vote for the FSLN could mean an open-ended continuation of the draft. A vote against the military draft, independent of political preferences, was a chief motivation for many a ballot cast on February 25.

The Sandinistas gauged correctly that most Nicaraguans rejected the contras and resented U.S. interference in their internal affairs. Their electoral strategy was therefore to expose to the public the numerous organic links between the UNO and the counterrevolution, to demonstrate that the contras and the UNO had grown out of the same U.S. interventionist project.[37] But the dynamic was not so simple; there was no such vertical relation between rejection of the contras and rejection of the UNO. To the contrary, the United States was able to incorporate anticontra sentiment into the electoral strategy against the Sandinistas. The more the FSLN exposed the connection between the UNO and the contras, the more the population became convinced that only a UNO victory could put an end to the war.

A similar dynamic was at work when the Sandinistas denounced U.S. intervention elsewhere in the region, or when they attempted to articulate a committed anti-interventionist position. For example, when the United States invaded Panama in December 1989, most Nicaraguans were genuinely repulsed. The UNO's image was even further tarnished as an apologist of U.S. intervention, especially after the coalition waffled on condemning the invasion for several days and then only did so timidly when it became clear that Nicaraguan public sentiment was overwhelmingly against the aggression. Conventional logic would suggest that the UNO's identification with U.S. intervention would therefore have damaged the coalition electorally in the wake of the invasion. But the invasion showed that the United States was ready and willing to invade Central America, to unleash its bombs and cannons on the Nicaraguans just as it was doing in neighboring Panama. The invasion reinforced the message to the electorate that the U.S.-backed candidates could avoid such a repeat in Nicaragua. Over ten years Washington had been putting out the message to Nicaraguans that they could not challenge the United States and get away with it. The invasion of Panama made this threat more real in people's minds. And in this construct, keeping the Sandinistas in office meant continued confrontation with the United States. This message was magnified in the electoral campaign by the advantageous position the United States enjoyed in the wake of the events in Eastern Europe just months before the voting in Managua.

ECONOMIC BLACKMAIL

The economic crisis will be key in generating popular discontent. Responsibility must be given to the Sandinistas.

—an NED official[38]

Phase I will raise the following themes among the population: Hunger, Misery, Obligatory Draft, i.e., the status quo versus Change, Liberty and Employment. . . . Phase II will consist of telling the population why they should vote for the particular candidates fielded by the UNO. This will emphasize the following themes: The Candidates' values and personalities, Full employment for the country, Freedom of expression, Prosperity and improvement of quality of life.

—UNO campaign strategy document[39]

Sustaining the contra threat was a calculated element in the economic dimensions of U.S. strategy. As long as the contra forces remained intact, the Nicaraguan government was forced to keep up the nation's defenses, thus limiting what it could do to resolve the worsening economic situation. Preventing any shift from defense to social spending became a top U.S. priority. "The economic situation in Nicaragua is very bad, and the resistance forces remain an element in the equation," said Luigi Einaudi, the U.S. ambassador to the OAS. "So there are reasons for which to believe that the Sandinistas [can be removed]. That is our operating assumption. That is the situation we are trying to induce."[40]

Bush renewed the trade embargo twice during the electoral process, first in May 1989 and then again on October 25, at the height of the campaign.[41] In November, Chamorro was brought to the White House for a well-publicized photo session with Bush, after which he released a statement declaring that if Chamorro were elected, the United States would lift the embargo. "The President looks forward to the day when, with a democratic government, Nicaraguans will have good political and economic relations with the United States and the rest of the free world, and will be able to begin rebuilding after decades of dictatorship," said the statement. In their meeting, Bush "received a letter from Mrs. Chamorro stressing that a Chamorro administration would be committed to reconciliation of the Nicaraguan people and reconstruction of the economy in peace and democracy," the statement affirmed. "Should this occur, the President [of] the United States would be ready to lift the trade embargo and assist in Nicaragua's reconstruction."[42]

The blackmail could not have been more explicit. Bush seemed to have been sending a message to the Nicaraguan electorate: "Never mind that the International Court of Justice had ruled that the embargo was illegal and had ordered the United States to lift it. It was not the rule of law or the scales of justice that the Nicaraguans could appeal to for Washington to lift its economic sanctions. Their only effective recourse was the U.S.-backed candidates." Violeta Chamorro was billed as a savior who could alleviate the suffering of Nicaraguans by mending things with the United States and attracting millions of dollars in reconstruction moneys. And this message went out with the Nicaraguan electorate very carefully in mind. The White House statement received minor attention in the U.S. press. In Nicaragua, however, *La Prensa* ran splashy headlines on the end of the embargo if Chamorro were to win. The pro-UNO radios all blared the same message.

As noted earlier, ten years of U.S. war had shattered the fragile Nicaraguan economy, identified early on by U.S. strategists as the "soft underbelly" of the revolution. Overall direct and indirect losses related to the war exceeded $12,000 billion, or 4,400 percent of annual export earnings and 600 percent of GNP. The war forced Nicaragua to transfer huge outlays of material, financial, and human resources from production to defense.[43] The grueling economic crisis was the price Nicaragua had to pay to defend itself. The challenge for U.S. war strategists as the country moved toward elections was how to incorporate the campaign of socioeconomic attrition into the specifics of the electoral intervention project.

On coming to power, the Sandinistas had reoriented social priorities toward the poor majority. The government introduced subsidies on essential consumption (food, bus transportation, etc.) and greatly expanded health and education, housing projects, and social spending. The Nicaraguan Revolution won international awards for its literacy campaign and broad praise for its great strides in improving the basic health of the people. But the war gradually eroded the government's capacity to finance these programs—exactly what the attrition process was intended to do.

The Sandinista leadership held heated discussions for several years on how to deal with the macroeconomic distortions unleashed by the war.[44] With hyperinflation reaching an incredible 33,000 percent in 1988, the GNP falling for the fifth year in a row, and the fiscal deficit surpassing 20 percent of GNP, the Sandinistas made the very painful decision in early 1988 to introduce a stabilization program. It included sharp currency devaluations, the layoff of thirty thousand public employees, the lifting of most subsidies and price controls that kept basic consumption items at low prices, greater credit restrictions, and significant reductions in health and education.[45] The austerity measures were deepened in January 1989 and then again in April after the electoral process had opened.

The program proved controversial. Many friends of the Nicaraguan Revolution criticized it as unacceptably hard on the poor and as similar to antiworker austerity programs traditionally implemented by conservative governments.[46] Nonetheless, few disputed the reality that the Sandinistas faced objective constraints, had little room to maneuver, and had few real alternatives open to them. Although the government sought social consensus beforehand as well as a relatively equitable distribution among social sectors of the sacrifices that austerity involved, the stabilization measures ultimately had a high political price tag for the FSLN.

The two prerequisites for success in the austerity program were peace, which would allow a drastic reduction in defense spending, and an inflow of international aid. Putting in place the austerity program with high defense spending would be like placing a Band-Aid on an arterial hemorrhage. And to do so without international assistance would be like performing surgery without anesthesia. Yet this was precisely what the United States sought to assure—that the austerity program would fail or that at the least there would be no tangible improvement in the economy during the electoral campaign. In addition to keeping the contras "alive and intact," this tactic required blocking international assistance.

According to one source, NSC official Roger Robinson was in charge of designing the economic aspects of the electoral intervention strategy. Robinson reasoned that no government in the world that presides over sustained hyperinflation is ever reelected.[47] His plan was to turn the election into "a simple pocketbook vote" through international economic isolation and internal political operations. Not only would contra demobilization have to be postponed, so as to force the country to keep concentrating its internal resources in defense, but also U.S. actions would help sustain hyperinflation by blocking external financing for the recovery program.

In designing its economic program, the Sandinista government received help from the Swedish International Development Authority. The Swedes had commissioned a study of the Nicaraguan economy and international aid requirements in preparation for an international donors' conference. A report was prepared by a team of economists from Sweden, Latin America, and the United States, headed by economist Lance Taylor from the Massachusetts Institute of Technology. The Taylor Report was presented to the Managua government confidentially in April 1989, although it was later leaked to U.S. newspapers.[48]

There were three "extremely difficult" stabilization and adjustment problems, observed the report. One was hyperinflation. Another was external trade. A third was the need for external assistance. The government program addressed the first two areas. But "to help alleviate the hyperinflation and break bottlenecks to renewed export flows, the economy will require liquid foreign resources," the report said. It continued:

> The mission's general appreciation is that the Nicaraguan authorities have put a serious program in place. This package is feasible and coherent. However, its prospects for success are far from certain unless external circumstances improve. The possibilities for stopping inflation and renewed growth will be enhanced if additional, untied foreign resources become available within the next few months. . . . The new [austerity] measures would almost certainly call forth an IMF standby loan plus additional international support, under normal political circumstances. Given the trade embargo and effective blockage of multilateral loans imposed in the past several years on their country by the United States, Nicaraguan authorities bear an unusual burden in their attempt to raise liquid external funds.[49]

The Bush administration did not want to see any such international relief for Nicaragua during the electoral period. Policymakers in Washington reasoned that the blockage of external financing would render the government unable to implement stabilization without a regressive redistribution of income.[50] Macroeconomic correctives would enhance productive conditions for exporters and property owners, but the absence of liquid foreign resources would force inflation and deficits to be contained by sharp contractions in consumption without sustaining social safety nets. The alternative was renewed hyperinflation, which was in itself a form of regressive redistribution.[51]

The United States blocked financing from the World Bank. In 1988, Nicaraguan authorities had requested that the bank send a team to explore renewed lending to Managua (lending had been cut off in 1982). The bank had agreed. But Baker had sent a letter to bank president Barber Conable voicing U.S. opposition to any attempt to mend relations with Managua.[52] Bank authorities had eventually succumbed to the pressure and had reversed their March 1989 decision to send the team, an action that was "due definitely to very strong pressure" from the United States, according to a senior bank official.[53]

In May 1989, President Daniel Ortega made a three-week tour of Western Europe in search of emergency liquid assistance for the austerity program. The tour culminated in an international donors' conference in Stockholm that the Swedish government sponsored to explore ways to secure international aid. The Bush administration pressured the World Bank, the International Monetary Fund, and the Inter-American Development Bank to not send delegates to the meeting.[54] Great Britain went along with the boycott, and the West German government downgraded its representative to observer status.

At the time of the conference, Baker was in Europe making phone calls to European government officials in last-minute attempts to dissuade them from participating or from providing Nicaragua with assistance. Assistant Secretary of State Bernard Aronson admitted after the elections that Baker dedicated "a fair amount of personal intervention" to block Western European aid.[55] "The telexes and telefaxes in foreign ministries all over Europe were clogged up with anti-Sandinista messages" from Washington, said one European official.[56]

Another plank of the Nicaraguan government's program was *concertación*, or negotiations with the private sector to reach agreement on economic measures. The Taylor Report highlighted this *concertación* as a critical component of recovery. The Nicaraguan government invited private producers from across the political spectrum to join the delegation to the Stockholm conference, proposing that any aid obtained would benefit the private sectors. The COSEP announced it would boycott the meeting because the Sandinista government was "illegitimate." When one of its members, dairy farmer Juan Diego López, declared that he would travel to Stockholm, the COSEP denounced him as persona non grata and accused him of breaking organizational discipline.

In fact, the COSEP had received a $100,000 grant from the NED channeled through the Center for International Private Enterprise, the international branch of the U.S. Chamber of Commerce and an NED core group, specifically to oppose the government's economic policies during the electoral campaign.[57] "The objective of this program is to present strong arguments against the Sandinista government's economic program, influence the economic policies of the opposition . . . and maintain the issue [of the economy] in the public eye during the electoral process," stated the CIPE.[58]

Ortega returned from Europe with $49 million. This was more assistance than Washington wanted to see, but it was also far less than the target of $250 million. A follow-up conference was scheduled for the last quarter of 1989 in Rome to consider a range of actions, including restructuring existing debts and extending new credits. But the United States successfully pressured for the meeting to be postponed until after the elections.[59]

As with the contra military activity, the undermining of the recovery program sent a clear psychological message to the electorate: A vote for the FSLN means the United States will continue economic destabilization. Thus, a vote for the Front is a self-punishing vote for continued economic hardship. A vote cast for the UNO will lift the economic sanctions, open the spigot of international aid, and bring economic respite.[60]

ELECTORAL COUP D'ETAT

The conduct of War is the formation and conduct of the fighting. If this fighting was a single act, there would be no necessity for any further subdivision, but the fight is composed of a greater or less number of single acts, complete in themselves, which we call combats, and which form new units. From this arises the totally different activities, that of the formation *and* conduct *of these single combats in themselves, and the* combination *of them with one another, with a view to the ultimate object of the War.*

—Karl von Clausewitz[61]

Political war [seeks] to penetrate the political entity itself: the "political animal" that Aristotle defined.

—CIA[62]

In the U.S. electoral strategy, playing the contra trump card and applying economic blackmail went together like hand and glove. In synchronization, these two tactics made effective Washington's funding and political guidance of the opposition. While the contra and economic dimensions would convince the population that voting for the Sandinistas would mean more war and hardship, the U.S. material and political support for the opposition would see to it that this same population, once it decided not to cast a ballot for the FSLN, would indeed know for whom to cast the ballot. U.S. strategists had to assure that a population traumatized into not voting for the FSLN would not squander the vote on twenty-one different opposition parties and that an amalgamated opposition would have the means—nationwide organization, media outlets, trucks and transportation, communications systems, money—to actually reach the soul of the entire population, to penetrate Aristotle's "political animal."

U.S. material assistance for the opposition was not intended to have the UNO actually outspend the FSLN dollar for dollar (although the UNO probably did). Rather, this support was to operate in careful synchronization with the entire gamut of U.S. intervention at every level and in the context of ten years of the war of attrition. All the UNO needed was sufficient resources and conditions in which to disseminate the overall psychological message analyzed in this chapter. U.S. assistance enabled the UNO to do this quite effectively.

Essential to the U.S. strategy was converting the vote into a referendum.[63] Every U.S. program and operative stressed turning the vote from a multiparty election into a simple plebiscite-type decision by the people: "War—yes" or "War—no." The United States made sure that the Sandinistas could not give the people what survival required and at the same time presented the UNO as the people's benefactor. As Alfredo César candidly affirmed, the UNO did not need to persuade Nicaraguans to support Chamorro or become enthusiastic for the UNO program. All the opposition needed to do was "convince them that their vote can change the country."[64] Hence, the UNO's main campaign slogan was "UNO can change things."

At the heart of U.S. warfare was a simple dichotomous message that hung over the head of each and every Nicaraguan: A vote for the Sandinistas meant a continuation of hostility from the United States, and thus continued poverty, hardship, war, and isolation. A vote for the UNO would mean an immediate end to the U.S. aggression, a definitive cessation of military hostilities, and millions of dollars in U.S. economic aid. Nicaraguans voted on February 25 with this gun placed at their heads. U.S. involvement turned the vote into an electoral coup d'état.

The U.S. electoral intervention project can be understood only when seen in its entirety—as a skillful combining of military aggression, economic blackmail, CIA propaganda, NED political interference, coercive diplomacy, and international pressures into a coherent and unitary strategy. The whole was much more than the sum of the parts. And the project can be appreciated only as the culmination of ten years of war, as the climax of Washington's number one foreign policy program in the 1980s. The entire population had become exhausted from war and economic crisis. The Bush strategy was to harvest this exhaustion through the elections.

EIGHT

The Future: "Low-Intensity" Democracies?

Washington believes that Nicaragua must serve as a warning to the rest of Central America to never again challenge U.S. hegemony, because of the enormous economic and political costs. It's too bad that the [Nicaraguan] poor must suffer, but historically the poor have always suffered. Nicaragua must be a lesson to others.

—Richard John Neuhaus[1]

We have 50 percent of the world's wealth, but only 6.3 percent of its population. . . . In this situation, we cannot fail to be the object of envy and resentment. Our real task in the coming period is to devise a pattern of relationships which will allow us to maintain this position of disparity. We should cease to talk about the raising of the living standards and democratization. The day is not far off when we are going to have to deal in straight power concepts.

—George Kennan[2]

In a world of advanced communication and exploding technology, it is no longer possible to rely solely on force to promote stability and defend the national security. Persuasion is increasingly important, and the United States must enhance its capacity to persuade by developing techniques for reaching people at many different levels.

—Carl Gershman[3]

The day after the elections, the streets in Managua were deserted. There were no UNO victory celebrations, no mass outpouring. The somber mood contrasted sharply with the joy in Washington, which certainly suggests something about who won and who lost.[4] The electoral results represented a triumph for U.S.-sponsored low-intensity warfare against Nicaragua. Not surprisingly, they were recognized as such in Latin America and around the

147

world. In Washington, the electoral results were called a "victory for democracy."[5]

Although indeed a surprising outcome, the electoral coup hardly represented a departure in the history of U.S.-Nicaraguan relations. From the demise of Spanish colonial rule at the beginning of the nineteenth century until the present, Central America has been viewed by Washington as its "strategic backyard." The popular insurrection that overthrew the Somoza dictatorship and brought the FSLN to power was a mass movement that pursued social justice and the recovery of national sovereignty. This rupture of U.S. hegemony set in motion the gears of counterrevolution among the Nicaraguan elite and the United States.

In mid-1979, as the war raged in Nicaragua, a distraught Carter administration debated how to prevent a Sandinista victory. Secretary of State Cyrus Vance proposed a strategy based on the "preservation of existing institutions, especially the National Guard." National security adviser Zbigniew Brzezinski insisted that "we have to demonstrate that we are still the decisive force in determining the political outcomes in Central America."[6] In 1979, Brzezinski's edict went unfulfilled. Eleven years later, however, the United States once again made its point.

FREE AND FAIR ELECTIONS?

In terms of procedure, the elections were free and fair.[7] But these were not normal elections under normal circumstances. They can perhaps best be described as "transnational elections" in which the will and material resources of a foreign power with deep vested interests in the outcome were superimposed on the internal political system of a sovereign nation.

For Washington, the stated yardstick of democracy is the degree to which a given population can make a free electoral choice among competing alternatives. Even if we limit the concept of democracy to this narrow definition, the Nicaraguan people's right to freely express themselves electorally was undermined by U.S. intervention. Instead, the Nicaraguan people were left with no alternative but to choose between war and peace, between starvation and economic relief. As noted in Chapter 1, the aim of the war of attrition was to isolate, delegitimize, and suffocate the revolution and its program of popular social transformation to the point where it was no longer considered a viable political option in the eyes of the population. By making it unequivocally clear to the electorate that the continuation of this program meant prolonged warfare, the United States succeeded in this objective. The vast majority of Nicaraguan voters did not choose on the basis of political convictions or differing visions of how society should be organized but rather out of a gut need to survive. Indeed, the U.S. intervention project was quite successful in reducing the vote to a referendum on survival.[8]

The Bush administration won an unexpected victory with the electoral coup. Washington's operational assumption was that through intervention in the electoral process, the U.S. objective of attrition and eventual destruction of the Sandinista Revolution would be advanced. It was a no-lose proposition. As noted in Chapter 2, policymakers in and out of the administration did not fully agree on what the goal of the electoral intervention project should be. Although all desired an opposition victory, many in Washington assumed a probable Sandinista triumph. Following an FSLN victory, there would be two alternative courses of action. One was to claim post-facto fraud. The other was to accept the results and take advantage of the political and institutional space expanded for pro-U.S. forces through the elections for continuing the anti-Sandinista campaign under new and more favorable circumstances. For many, this consisted of a major opposition bloc in the National Assembly plus a network of U.S. guided civic, political, and labor organizations and communications media. As one U.S. observer put it, "Even if the opposition does not win—and defeat is probable—the effort opens the way [for new U.S. actions in the attrition process]. . . . In the long run, [the] best chance [the United States has] of countering the Sandinistas is by building national support step by step [for the opposition]. Sustained internal opposition can eventually pay off."[9]

Given polls that were misread, the lack of real political support in Nicaragua for the opposition, and the perceived ineptness of the Chamorro candidacy, the Bush administration and most other anti-Sandinista groups in the United States concluded several weeks before the voting that the UNO was headed for defeat. By late January 1990, administration officials and other Washington power brokers were already mapping out new tactics and policies for the postelectoral period on the premise that the FSLN would win. The Carmen Group had even drafted press releases in advance for a Sandinista victory, comparing the would-be FSLN electoral triumph to the Chinese massacre at Tiananmen Square.[10] In the State Department, officials began to think up exactly how anti-Sandinista attrition would continue in the postelectoral period.

On the afternoon of February 24, just hours before the Nicaraguan polls were to open, I spoke on background with a high-level official from the State Department's Inter-America Desk. "The electoral process was neither fair nor honest," he said. "The Sandinistas' strategy was to steal the elections during the campaign in order not to have to resort to massive fraud on voting day, when the international observers could discover it." The official continued, "There are no fixed positions yet. We have prepared a series of options for the President, but the situation is fluid and everything depends on what happens tomorrow—on the results, the verdict of the observers, and the posture the losers assume toward the winners." He concluded, "If the Sandinistas win and the observers say that it was an honest triumph, then President Bush will formulate a critical assessment of the electoral process, without condemning the vote out of hand. In this case, the United States would follow the scheme laid out by Baker."

Baker's "scheme" was predicated on a Sandinista victory. The secretary of state had declared just two days before the Nicaraguan vote that regardless of what the international observers concluded, the United States was "reserving for itself the right to decide if the Nicaraguan elections of February 25 [were] fair and free." Baker said recognition of Sandinista legitimacy would be tied to "a sustained period of good behavior" and "an open political spectrum in Nicaragua."[11]

Senator Richard Lugar had earlier spelled out what the United States meant by "good behavior" and "an open political spectrum." The United States should prepare a set of "benchmarks" for judging "democratic progress" in Nicaragua, he said. Any improvement in relations would depend on Sandinista progress in these benchmarks, among them "demobilization of the huge Sandinista army" parallel to the demobilization of the contras, the dismantling of Sandinista security forces, the dismantling of the Nicaraguan judicial system, and "the drafting and adoption of a new constitution."[12]

Lugar's benchmarks made clear that even if the Sandinistas had won elections certified by the world community as free and fair, the United States would simply have moved to a new phase in a never-ending campaign of attrition, *never* acknowledging the legitimacy of the Sandinistas so long as they remained in power. The only way for the Sandinistas to have achieved legitimacy before the eyes of the aggressor power, and to therefore have brought an end to hostilities, was to have stepped down from power. In other words, the United States had every intention of following up with its threat to continue the war of attrition and the economic quarantine of the country had the Sandinistas won.[13]

The Nicaraguan electorate, after ten years of U.S. warfare, was well aware that the U.S. threat was not idle. In some ways, Nicaraguans made a wise decision in electing U.S.-backed candidates. Between February and June 1990, some twenty thousand contras were disarmed and demobilized, effectively bringing the war to an end. The United States also lifted the embargo and normalized relations. Although the Sandinistas clearly expected to win the contest, the electoral process itself was conceived less as an exercise to ratify Sandinista power than as a means to assure survival for the Nicaraguan nation by achieving peace. For the Sandinistas, losing power had become the price that U.S. intervention had placed on peace, and they made clear they were willing to pay that price. Even though they clearly regretted having lost the vote, the Sandinistas could leave office rightly proud of having achieved that peace and having set the country on the path of democratization. "We Sandinistas have never sought to cling to power," declared Daniel Ortega in an emotional concession speech at dawn, February 26. "We were born poor and we will be satisfied to die poor."

Holding truly free elections implies the risk of losing, and the FSLN accepted the consequences beforehand. What makes the Nicaraguan experience important for other countries and peoples is not that the FSLN lost elections but that massive foreign interference completely distorted an endogenous political process and undermined the ability of the elections to be a free choice regarding the destiny of the country. U.S. intervention undercut the Nicaraguan people's right to exercise self-determination.

Substituting the fanatical national security argument with the rhetoric of democracy allowed the U.S. government to deceive much of the U.S. public as well as parts of the international community, concealing a travesty of international (and U.S.) law as a benevolent undertaking in "democracy promotion." This places those who oppose U.S. interference, or those who defend other people's right to self-determination, in a difficult and seemingly contradictory position: How does one point out that behind a free and secret ballot, which gives the appearance of popular will through elections, stands a new and more sophisticated form of intervention?

This new face of U.S. intervention—hijacking movements for democratic change—was given a tremendous psychological and political boost by the "victory" in Nicaragua. It is little wonder that the NED is now spending millions of dollars in Eastern Europe and the Soviet Union to build up groups similar to those it promoted in Nicaragua—conservative, anticommunist, elitist, fanatical advocates of free markets and U.S.-style "democracy."[14] As in Latin America, the idea is not to create movements for democratic change—which are endogenous developments—but to gain control over them. This is the sophistication of the new intervention—it accurately identifies mass sentiments and aspirations and then channels them in ways the United States perceives to be in its interests. It is incumbent on the world community and particularly on U.S. citizens to prevent the United States from making such a mockery of democracy. This is particularly so in an age in which mass social movements for democratic change are burgeoning in Latin America, Africa, Eastern Europe, and elsewhere.

DEMOCRACY IN NICARAGUA, U.S. INTERVENTION, AND THE ELECTORAL OUTCOME

By way of conclusion, it is worth reiterating the obvious: U.S. intervention in Nicaragua *subverted* real democracy. The proposition that Nicaragua under the Sandinistas was undemocratic provided a convenient ideological prop for U.S. policy. Yet far from "enlightening" Nicaragua to democracy, the United States has historically impeded democracy in that country, suppressing and negating the Nicaraguan people's most fundamental national and human rights. The United States sustained the Somoza dictatorship and then launched a policy in the 1980s aimed at stifling the democratization process initiated with the Sandinista Revolution.

Democracy means the rule, or power (*cratos*), of the people (*demo*). Democracy means people's control over their vital affairs. It means people's control over the collective material and cultural resources of their society. It means, ultimately, people's control over their destiny—self-determination. By imposing its will on a people, in this case the Nicaraguans, the United States inverted the very meaning of democracy.

From Nicaragua's independence in 1821 until 1979, Nicaragua's traditional elite went about the business of government through back-room deals and interelite pacts aimed at dividing up spoils and perpetuating a repressive and corrupt status quo. The country's legal system was designed to protect the interests of the economically powerful and their right to exploit the majority. Throughout Nicaraguan history, there was a conspicuous absence among the broader population of participation in any type of democratic institution. Nicaraguans had come to view government as of the few, by the few, and, above all, for the few.

It was the Sandinista Revolution in 1979 that first placed Nicaragua on the path to authentic democratization.[15] The Sandinista government pursued a concept of democracy that combined formal with participatory democracy. Nicaraguans for the first time began to gain some real control over their lives and their destiny. Perhaps the most important change to take place with the demise of the dictatorship was a fundamental reorientation of social priorities in Nicaraguan society toward the poor and the dispossessed, which brought new values and a redistribution of political power.

The Sandinista program was based on political pluralism, a mixed economy, and international nonalignment. It stressed pluralism according to the "logic of the poor majority," transformation of society, and democratization of the economy along lines that addressed historic social injustice and inequalities. The program put into practice in the ten years of Sandinista rule set out to achieve sovereignty and national independence; the restoration of political, civil, and human rights; a more equitable distribution of wealth; the development of institutions and channels for popular participation in vital affairs; land reform; health; education; the rights of the Atlantic coast minorities; and women's emancipation. This program was legitimate, necessary, and profoundly democratic in character.

The constitution that was drafted in the mid-1980s provided a blueprint for the type of society promoted by the Sandinistas. The Law of Laws provided for all of the traditional Western political rights and civil liberties, such as freedom of speech, assembly, and movement and the right to due process. It legally proscribed racial, ethnic, religious, and sexual discrimination. It established the traditional separation of powers in a presidential system and mandated national elections every six years, thus establishing the alterability of power. But it also included economic, social, and cultural rights—for example, health care, education, agrarian reform, social security, a decent wage, decent housing, women's emancipation, a healthy environment—as constitutional rights in themselves, restricted only by the material limits of society.[16] It enshrined the structures of participatory democracy alongside representative democracy, mandating that the population had the right, and the duty, to participate in decisionmaking at all levels of society.

The real problem, in the eyes of the United States, was not that Nicaragua lacked democracy but that it was *too* democratic. The revolution empowered dispossessed majorities that in neighboring countries closely allied with the United States were locked out of political power. This empowerment was seen by the United States as a threat, a dangerously attractive model for other peoples.

If U.S. policy in the 1980s failed in its attempt to destroy the Sandinistas, it is also true that, against the constraints imposed by prolonged U.S. aggressions and other objective limitations, the Sandinistas failed to achieve stability as well as ratification of their political hegemony on the heels of their strategic victory over the contras. The Sandinistas ultimately paid a high political cost for what was a skillful victory over the U.S. contra project. By the time that victory was achieved, the Sandinistas simply did not have the material resources or the political-ideological reserves with which to alleviate the exhaustion among Nicaraguans and to depolarize society, much less to harness a majority of votes.

U.S. intervention radically altered the political system in Nicaragua and was crucial in determining the conditions as well as the constraints under which the electoral process unfolded. Nevertheless, two questions remain: What factors internal to Nicaragua and to the Sandinista Revolution contributed to the electoral outcome? How determinant was U.S. intervention relative to these factors? Clearly, a whole host of factors that cannot be simply reduced to, or explained by, U.S. intervention also contributed to the unique circumstances of the 1990 Nicaraguan elections. But to ask if U.S. intervention was *the determining* factor in the outcome—that is, if the Sandinistas would have won had the United States not intervened in the vote—is to pose the question in the wrong terms. The elections were inseparable from the ten years of conflict that preceded them. This conflict framed the electoral process, and the U.S. electoral intervention was predicated on the conditions created by that conflict.[17]

A critical, yet largely unexplored counterpart to the "untold story" of U.S. involvement in the electoral process revealed in this book is an analysis of the Sandinistas' own strategy, counterstrategy, and response to U.S. intervention. Efforts to evaluate this are being made in Nicaragua and elsewhere and are more appropriately the subject of another book.[18] The magnitude and complexity of the U.S. electoral intervention project as well as the fact that much of it has been shrouded in secrecy make imperative a more immediate study with clearly defined parameters.

Nevertheless, there are several observations to be made here. First, many aspects of the U.S. intervention were unanticipated in Nicaragua, and the influence or importance of others was simply underestimated. Even though the electoral intervention project was the continuation of an anti-Sandinista campaign that had begun a decade earlier, it was also considerably more sophisticated. U.S. electoral interventionism in Nicaragua was more intelligent, coordinated, and multidimensional than earlier phases in the anti-Sandinista campaign had been and, indeed, than earlier U.S. interventionist undertakings in other countries had been. In some senses, this returned the initiative to the United States and caught the Sandinistas off balance, leaving them in a reactive and defensive position.

Second, the Sandinistas designed their own electoral strategy on the basis of a completely mistaken assessment that a majority of Nicaraguan people still stood behind them, ready to endure more hardship and sacrifice for hopes and ideals that, given constraints imposed by the outside power and other international factors, simply could not be realized. The FSLN seriously underestimated the extent to which the attrition process had succeeded in eroding their broad social base and in exhausting the population.[19] The Sandinista campaign slogan, "Everything Will Be Better," argued that an electoral victory for the FSLN would deprive the United States of any reason to continue hostilities and would free up international aid. Although the slogan itself was an acknowledgment of just how miserable things had become, it did little to convince the population that the FSLN would be in a better position than the U.S.-backed candidates to achieve these goals. In contrast, the opposition slogan, "UNO Can Change Things," was credible. This misreading of the electorate and gross overestimation of the FSLN's internal political strength and popularity led the FSLN to an almost surrealistic triumphalism, a conviction that victory was a foregone conclusion. On the basis of this triumphalism, the electoral campaign was aimed at maximizing the number of winning votes through low-key themes and high-tech rallies rather than through serious competition with the contender to more directly counter what was a U.S. campaign of political warfare and psychological operations.[20]

Third, beyond the specifics of their electoral strategy, the Sandinistas faced problems common to most parties once in government—the development of bureaucracy, opportunism, and the arrogance that comes with the use (or abuse) of power. Operating on the assumption that power would be ratified through the vote and having lost touch, from lofty halls of government and levers of power, with significant portions of the population, the FSLN was unable to accurately gauge the mood of the electorate and the precepts under which the United States was operating. "In ten years, the Sandinista Front adopted the psychology of a party in power," commented Ortega's campaign manager, Dionisio Marenco, after the vote. "We were drunk with this idea that everything was OK. We lost our capacity to converse, to listen, to criticize ourselves, the capacity to measure, and the people punished us for that."[21] Moreover, decisionmaking had become concentrated in the top echelons of the FSLN. Many Sandinistas have concluded in retrospect that the lack of internal party democracy was another factor in reducing the capacity to face the consequences that the sustained external aggression had on the erosion of the revolution's social base.

Fourth, there were real existing problems regarding limitations in political democratization that should not be confused with the rhetorical accusations of the United States. The tragedy of the 1980s was that political antagonisms, both within Nicaragua and between Nicaragua and the United States, became military conflict. War inevitably leads to the militarization of politics and civil society and to polarization, which inhibit the development of democracy. The FSLN opened enormous democratic space in Nicaragua. But as conflict became militarized, the Sandinistas turned to methods of mobilizing the population for defense that involved occupying the democratic space within civil society that the revolution itself had opened. The national defense effort created a political verticalism, and the Sandinistas relied too readily on control over the state apparatus, rather than on appeal to civil society, to defend the nation and assure survival. This in turn had serious consequences for the Sandinistas' ability to arrest the attrition of its social base. Similarly, militarization and "vertical politics" made it difficult for the rule of law to regulate political relations and encouraged arbitrary government decisionmaking. In these conditions, the Sandinistas sometimes had a hard time distinguishing between those who were engaged in destabilization activities and those who were merely withholding support for the national defense effort. There were, therefore, legitimate grievances regarding limitations on democratic development.[22]

Yet U.S. intervention acted as catalyst and fertilizer for these and other deficiencies. It created conditions in which neither the Sandinistas nor the population at large could productively address mistakes. In other words, U.S intervention inhibited the revolution's capacity for democratic development. The United States was not out to help democratize Nicaragua; it was out to destabilize and destroy the democratic experiment itself.

In contrast to other revolutionary parties that came to power through arms, the FSLN, since the approval of the constitution in 1987, had institutionalized the election of national authorities in multiparty, periodic, secret elections every six years and the alterability of power. It was the holding of elections organized by the FSLN, in the framework of a popular democracy and constitutional order developed under the Sandinista Revolution, that enabled the opposition to participate in the electoral process, to win those elections, and then to assume the reins of government. The Sandinista Revolution represented a democratic rupture with four hundred years of history. To the extent that this rupture has become institutionalized, and to the extent that the democratization process can now move forward in the postelectoral situation, Nicaraguans will have gained from the elections despite U.S. intervention.

U.S. INTERVENTION,
AUTHENTIC DEMOCRATIZATION, AND
LOW-INTENSITY DEMOCRACY

A democratic society is one that is in constant motion toward greater political participation, economic equality and well-being, social justice, and cultural development. Electoral democracy is but one component of a democratic society. Truly free elections can be an exercise in the process of the democratization of social, cultural, and economic life. Elections through which national leadership and programs are selected are essential for democracy but do not assure it. "Free" elections can also take place in very undemocratic societies and do not necessarily contribute to democratization.

Authentic democratization is a profound aspiration in Latin America, an aspiration highlighted but far from realized by the transition in the 1980s from dictatorships to elected regimes. During the 1960s and 1970s, repressive military regimes took over in Brazil, Argentina, Chile, Uruguay, and elsewhere, while in countries such as Guatemala, Paraguay, El Salvador, and Nicaragua military dictatorships or military-civilian regimes remained in nearly permanent control of society. With rare exception, these regimes were either placed in power by the United States or seized power through events and situations engendered by earlier U.S. interventions or by U.S. political, economic, and military support programs. It was the age of the disappeared, "dirty wars" against "subversion," torture chambers, and police states.

Then in the 1980s, most of these naked military regimes gave way to nominal civilian governments through so-called democratic transitions. The format in these democratization processes was routine: Dictatorships crushed popular movements demanding basic reform, social justice, and democracy; terrorized society; and then returned power to civilian elites through controlled electoral processes. Once the dream of a better future was abandoned and "the masses" understood that their only hope was to accept the inevitable impossibility of achieving real social justice and real historic redress, it made good sense to allow a "democratic process." U.S. government officials suddenly began proclaiming the "rising tide of democracy" in Latin America (Nicaragua and Cuba were the exceptions).

Chapter 1 analyzed the emergence of the NED and other instruments of U.S. foreign policy to intervene in the political processes of other countries and, in particular, to penetrate civil society and to control electoral processes. By way of conclusion, it is worth summarizing this "promotion of democracy" as it relates to Latin America and to U.S. engagement in the Western Hemisphere in the last quarter-century.

The Cuban Revolution of 1959 constituted for U.S. policymakers a dangerous rupture in traditional inter-American relations and a hemispheric threat to U.S. hegemony. The Kennedy administration's Alliance for Progress aimed to prevent repeats through a combination of U.S.-led counterinsurgency and reform efforts.[23] The breakdown of that effort led the Nixon administration to commission the Rockefeller Report of 1969.[24] This blueprint for Nixon-Ford policy for Latin America claimed that the "new militaries"—armed forces and security apparatuses that had been "modernized" through U.S. military and security assistance and training programs—were the "last best choice" for preserving social order and traditional inter-American relations. This policy also coincided with the turn to military dictatorship in many Latin American countries. The Rockefeller Report was followed by the Trilateral Commission's well-known report, *The Crisis of Democracy*.[25] This report argued that "democracy" had to be reconstituted to assure that it did not generate its own instability, both within states and in the international system. A year later, the Linowitz Report, which provided guidelines for Carter administration policies, highlighted the conclusions of the Trilateral Commission and stressed that military dictatorship and human rights violations threatened to destabilize capitalism itself and undermine U.S. interests.[26] The report thus recommended a U.S. policy thrust of redemocratization in order to avoid crises and preserve the hemispheric order. The triumph of the Nicaraguan Revolution demonstrated to U.S. policymakers the need for such an undertaking. The 1984 Kissinger Commission Report stated that promotion of civilian regimes was an essential requisite of U.S. policy and should be coupled with greater linkage of the Latin American economies to the U.S. economy as well as with a political, military, and ideological offensive against leftist forces in the region.[27]

The Kissinger Commission, several of whose members were also involved in Project Democracy and the formation of the NED (including Carl Gershman), represented the beginnings of consensus in Washington over a new hemispheric policy and its attendant NED-style intervention. In light of the Trilateral Commission report, the formation of the NED, the Kissinger Commission recommendations, and the introduction of broad new foreign policy initiatives to "promote democracy" abroad, U.S. academia turned its interest to this subject. The U.S. government, through the NED, the AID and other agencies, began funding conferences and studies on "transitions to democracy," and "democratization" literature began to flow out of U.S. universities and government agencies as a major new focus of "scholarly" and policy analysis.[28]

It was in this context that the "last best option" for the United States of supporting military dictatorships such as the Pinochet regime in Chile or the generals of Brazil, Argentina, and Guatemala gave way to promoting transitions to democracy. Yet the civilians who took over from the dictatorships of the 1970s were, with few exceptions, conservative politicians who challenged neither their military predecessors nor the systems of institutionalized social injustice and economic inequalities. Military institutions were not dismantled; in many of the "new democracies," the military was not even subordinate to civilian authorities. Meanwhile, international human rights groups continued throughout the 1980s to document the systematic and gross violations of human rights throughout the continent. In El Salvador, Guatemala, Brazil, Chile, Panama, and elsewhere throughout the Americas, the banner of "democracy" flown by the United States and local groups provided political legitimacy while concealing systematic human rights violations, loss of sovereignty, deepening economic inequalities, and diminishing possibilities for popular political participation.

These were the kind of "democracies" the United States was promoting. As the Kissinger Commission made clear, diverse forms of low-intensity warfare and political intervention were intended to bring about stable "low-intensity democracies." The precepts and parameters of low-intensity democracy are clear. The structures of formal representative democracy are restituted. Constitutional legitimacy and most traditional civil liberties and political rights are restored, although violations of human rights and abuses by authoritarian states continue at a lower intensity than under dictatorship. Social justice, economic equality, and mass, participatory democracy are not on the agenda in Latin America. National sovereignty is subordinated to hemispheric relations under the hegemony of the United States, and free-market "liberalization" of national economies is undertaken under the tutelage of international economic agencies controlled by the United States.[29]

As NED-style programs got under way, funds began flowing to build up political parties, trade unions, and economic and social associations. The point was to control transitions, promote stable foundations for these low-intensity democracies under U.S. hegemony, and at the same time undermine or preempt popular alternatives or movements for more profound democratization. This political intervention contained democratization within parameters compatible with elite status quos and U.S. interests. After the end of the cold war, the most effective way for the United States to maintain exclusive hegemony over the Western Hemisphere (first claimed early in the nineteenth century with the Monroe Doctrine) was by orchestrating low-intensity democracy.

In accordance with U.S. precepts, the two components that constitute democracy are "free" elections and "free" markets. Although elections may not be fraudulent, they are neither free nor fair if they are driven by U.S. intervention, which circumscribes and disempowers the effective participation of the masses. Although they may be procedurally impeccable, elections are neither free nor fair if electoral resources are controlled by small economic and social elites, which use them to achieve the internal and international legitimacy necessary to proceed with antipopular social and economic programs. And "free markets" mean economic systems that are fundamentally antidemocratic and that are integrated into, and dependent on, the U.S. political economy.

Democracy requires sovereignty, which in such countries as El Salvador has long since been forfeited to Washington and in others is highly restricted by debt bondage and U.S. economic hegemony. Democracy means bringing a better life to people. Yet the 1980s was the "lost decade" for social welfare and living standards. In every country in Latin America, per capita income dropped as wealth was concentrated among ever smaller minorities and as huge surpluses were syphoned from Latin America into U.S. banks.[30] In Brazil, a "new democracy," one thousand children die every day from starvation or disease.[31] In Mexico, according to a 1990 report by that country's National Nutrition Institute, nearly half the rural population "is likely suffering from physical or mental deficiencies caused or exacerbated by malnutrition."[32] In Peru, the Education Ministry reported in 1990 that 40 percent of schoolchildren were leaving public schools to assist in their families' survival efforts.[33] In Argentina, another country that turned to the fold of "democracy" in the 1980s, the number of families living in "abject poverty" increased 50 percent. The United Nations attributed this increase to Argentina's debt bondage to U.S. banks.[34]

Democracy requires human rights. Although Colombia, Venezuela, Peru, and other South American countries are now "democratic," human rights groups continue to document widespread systematic abuses. In Chile during the military dictatorship of 1973–1990, tens of thousands were executed, jailed, or exiled for their political beliefs. The generals then turned over government to civilians under a constitution that provided for their immunity from prosecution, gave them significant control over the judicial system and the legislature, and left hundreds of political prisoners languishing in jail.[35] In Guatemala, as many as a quarter million people died in counterinsurgency operations and government-sponsored repression in the 1980s. Midway through the decade, the generals returned the government to civilians under a constitution that guaranteed immunity to human rights violators.[36] Between 1986 and 1990—five years of "democratic, civilian" government—more than three thousand citizens were executed or disappeared by death squads and government security forces.[37] During this "transition to democracy" in Guatemala in the 1980s, the number of families living in abject poverty went from one in every three to nine in every ten.

Here were the "democratic miracles" that the United States marveled over, miracles from which Nicaragua stood apart . . . until the United States "promoted democracy" there. What is taking place is a struggle over conflicting and diametrically opposed definitions of democracy. Claiming that the people have made their "democratic choice" through elections that international observers certify as fair makes it more difficult to point out that the death of one thousand Brazilian children each day is not really democracy. The ideological framework of democratization makes it more difficult to communicate and condemn the injustice and antidemocratic character of repressive systems founded on deepening social and economic inequalities and the effective monopolization of political power by elite minorities. Electoral processes should not be left to the United States to promote and define. To the contrary, they should be political exercises that allow each society to elect leadership and to choose among contending programs. They can and should be an integral element of an ongoing democratization that involves opening up political systems to greater popular participation, achieving economic and social justice, and developing new international relations so that people can gain control over and improve their lives materially, culturally, and spiritually. The challenge for popular and revolutionary movements, for real democrats, is to make sure that elections as an exercise in political democracy are not hijacked by the United States or other foreign powers and that they are not controlled by local elites in which popular leaders, poor majorities, and the Left are shut out. Instead of the traditional vice-ridden electoral culture, the challenge is to convert electoral democracy into a process for achieving the authentic democratization of society.

Despite U.S. intervention, the Nicaraguan elections were an important precedent precisely because a leftist, revolutionary movement situated its struggle for authentic democratization and social change in the legal, electoral arena—an arena often seen as illegitimate by revolutionary movements. The Sandinistas opened up space in Nicaragua for the Right, closed off all other options for the Right and for the United States other than to occupy that democratic space, provided all the guarantees needed to renounce military struggle, and then peacefully and voluntarily turned over power to the Right.

The test for the international community is to assure that the United States and the right-wing regimes it backs now open up such democratic political space for the Left, provide all the guarantees to the Left that the FSLN provided to the Right, allow the Left to participate in authentic electoral processes in which it has a real chance to put forward its program to society, and to be prepared to turn over power to the Left should society so choose.

Observers have pointed out that, except for the Nicaraguan precedent, never before has a leftist revolutionary regime handed over power in elections. The opposite is also true: Never has a popularly elected leftist government in Latin America been allowed by the United States to undertake social reforms without being cut short by a coup, an invasion, an assassination, or a decade-long war of attrition. The September 1991 coup d'état in Haiti once again underscored this point.[38]

In 1990, the same year as the Sandinistas' electoral defeat, the Workers Party in Brazil almost won national elections on a revolutionary platform. In Uruguay, the Broad Front, a leftist coalition, made a major sweep in municipal elections. In Colombia, the guerrilla movement M-19 disarmed and participated in elections for a constituent assembly to draw up a new constitution, winning the most seats of any party. The peace accord signed on New Year's Eve 1991 between the Salvadoran government and the Farabundo Martí National Liberation Front (FMLN) of El Salvador opens up a new period in that country's history and enormous prospects for democratization. These events demonstrate that elections do have the potential to be a mechanism for the democratic participation of all sectors of society (and for the transfer of social and political struggles from violent arenas to political, civic arenas). Nevertheless, the experience to date suggests that the U.S. objective is not to promote the expansion of pluralism and democratization through electoral processes but to gain control over electoral processes precisely to avoid popular or leftist outcomes.

If the FMLN in El Salvador, the Workers Party in Brazil, or revolutionary groups in Colombia were to win free elections, would they be subjected by the United States to economic embargoes, low-intensity warfare, CIA destabilization campaigns, and political and ideological attacks aimed at delegitimizing and isolating them? Or would NED-style electoral intervention assure that these forces never got the chance through the ballot box to put their program before society?

The end of the cold war opens up enormous possibilities for the attainment of democracy in the Third World. For decades, the East-West prism was imposed on every attempt by peoples and nations to define new paths for independence, development, and democracy. Any independently minded government that sought to "diversify" dependence by developing relations with the "other bloc" was seen by Washington as a national security threat in the zero-sum game of the cold war. Independent nations had to choose between blocs; nonalignment (pursuing national interests by trying to take maximum advantage of a bipolar world) inevitably pitted countries such as Sandinista Nicaragua against the United States.

The end of the cold war generated great hope among those caught in this East-West prism that Washington would no longer view popular and nationalist efforts at self-determination and social justice as a threat. The Soviet Union pulled back from Eastern Europe and allowed those countries to determine their own fate under the new doctrine of *perestroika*. U.S. aggressions against Nicaragua, however, suggested that the United States had yet to adopt a "Yanquistroika" in Central America. It would seem that the collapse of the Soviet system, rather than leading from a bipolar to a more multipolar world offering diversity of systems, opinions, and opportunities, is opening the way to a monopolar world in which the United States faces no obstacles whatsoever in shaping the globe to its liking and in imposing its will on those who dare to differ.

A new face of U.S. intervention, sold to the U.S. public and the world community as the promotion of democracy, has been boosted by the victory in Nicaragua. Electoral intervention in Nicaragua sets a dangerous precedent in international relations and provides the United States with a blueprint for such schemes in other countries. "This is definitely going right in the textbooks," said one Pentagon official after the Nicaraguan vote.[39] So long as the United States continues to plan interventions in the affairs of other peoples, the Nicaraguan experience will remain vital.

Behind the Nicaraguan experience is the very issue of the possibility of democratic social change in the Third World in the post–Cold War world. As the North-South divide becomes the principal global cleavage in the "new world order," the North must guide democratic processes in the South (and now in the East, which is fast becoming part of the South) if the North wants to maintain its privileges. Low-intensity democracy will be a structural, rather than a momentary or transitional, feature of the new world order that the United States is striving to shape.

However, there has always been an enormous gap between *intent* and *ability* in U.S. foreign policy. If the experience of *perestroika* has taught anything, it is that economic and social development cannot take place without political democratization. The same also holds true, in reverse, for U.S. foreign policy. Whether the new policy of promoting "low-intensity" democracy is considered an altruistic undertaking, as U.S. policymakers claim, or intervention aimed at maintaining, or renovating, U.S. hegemony in the post–Cold War world, as I argue, it will not succeed if it does not also involve social justice, economic democracy, national sovereignty, and the democratization of international relations, including the international economic order.

In addition to the gap between intent and ability, there has also been a historic divide in U.S. foreign policy between *intent* and *outcome*. U.S. involvement overseas is a sorry history of unforgotten tragedies imposed on other peoples and nations as a consequence of outcomes unforeseen by policymakers. Irrespective of intent, the outcome of the new political intervention is already taking its toll in spiraling civil conflict in postelectoral Nicaragua, coups d'état in Haiti, the preemption of popular democratic reforms in Chile and the Philippines, and so on. If history is anything to judge by, grim is the outlook for the new world order that novel forms of U.S. political intervention are helping to shape.

Fortunately, however, the new world order is still being defined. And it is *not* the "end of history."

• POSTSCRIPT •

Postelectoral
U.S. Intervention

It became clear in the months following the elections that U.S. intervention was far from over. Rather, this intervention entered a new stage.[1] Although the message from Capitol Hill and U.S. news media reports seemed to be that attention to events in Central America had been downgraded, lack of public focus on Nicaragua did not mean an absence or a deprioritization of policy by the Bush administration toward Nicaragua and the Sandinistas.

Events suggested that U.S. objectives in the postelectoral period were to root out any vestige of Sandinista influence in state and society and to fully reestablish U.S. hegemony over Nicaragua. Having identified during the electoral campaign the key constituencies necessary for countering the Sandinistas, the Bush administration set about to consolidate these constituencies and to continue developing the network of civic and political groups it built up before and during the electoral process. Not surprisingly, most of those opposition leaders who were cultivated by U.S. electoral intervention went on to assume prominent positions in the Chamorro government.[2] Political and economic aid programs have been carefully calculated to reconstitute the traditional Nicaraguan elite that resumed power with the UNO victory.

In the days following the vote, the NED, the AID, and other U.S. government agencies set about to influence the transition from the Sandinista to the Chamorro government. This new anti-Sandinista campaign was described by the NED as an effort to "counter anti-democratic elements that could jeopardize the prospects for a peaceful democratic transition." Some $700,000 in funds allocated as part of the $9 million NED elections program but not spent during the campaign were redirected for use in converting the UNO Managua headquarters into a "Chamorro transition team" office and in sending international legal advisers to the Chamorro transition team, at the specific request of Alfredo César.[3] The AID provided the CFD with funds to set up a permanent office in Managua to advise and train UNO legislators.[4]

163

The flip side of the postelectoral U.S. strategy of neutralizing the influence of Sandinistas at every level was the reversal of the social and economic transformations carried out under the revolution, such as agrarian reform, subsidies for the poor, and health and educational opportunities. Much of the economic assistance provided to the new Chamorro government was made contingent on stringent conditions with regard to its social and economic policies.[5]

Clearly, the Bush administration opted for a multitrack, multiagency approach to slowly undermining the Sandinistas and to remodeling Nicaraguan society to U.S. liking. In this undertaking, preponderant influence over policy was placed in the U.S. Embassy in Managua, which during the Sandinista years had been reduced to the role of implementation and "listening post." The AID program in Nicaragua became the largest in the world, and the embassy became the most heavily staffed in Central America. Personnel increased from seventy-eight accredited diplomats in 1989 to more than three hundred by mid-1990.[6]

The United States sent Harry Shlauderman as the new ambassador. Shlauderman, a veteran State Department diplomat, has a history of involvement in U.S.-guided interventionist efforts in Latin America.[7] As deputy chief of the U.S. Mission in Chile both before and after the 1973 military coup, he was the in-country counterpart to Kissinger's Committee of Forty at the National Security Council and thus played a pivotal role in the CIA covert operations against the Allende government.[8] Shlauderman also occupied several State Department posts, including a stint as ambassador, that involved policy toward the Dominican Republic in the early 1960s. The policy that he played a role in designing culminated with the 1965 U.S. invasion that ousted a democratically elected government there.[9] Shlauderman later served on the Kissinger Commission and then headed the U.S. delegation to the 1984–1985 talks between the United States and the Nicaraguan governments in Manzanillo, Mexico. In 1988, the State Department brought Shlauderman out of retirement to serve as "adviser" to the contras during the contra-government cease-fire negotiations. The appointment of Shlauderman as ambassador indicates not only the continued high priority given Nicaragua by the U.S. government, despite less public attention on this policy and new foreign policy priorities such as Eastern Europe, but also the importance placed by the Bush administration on postelectoral intervention under the rubric of "consolidating democracy."

Meanwhile, there emerged an acrimonious debate, carried out in private, between the NED and the AID over which agency would have control over the democratization process in the postelectoral period. In March 1990, the Bush administration requested from Congress $300 million in economic assistance for Nicaragua, including $5 million for the AID's "Democratic Initiatives" office: "After a long hiatus, democracy has returned to Nicaragua," stated an AID document regarding these funds. "The institutions and processes of democracy are weak and require significant strengthening. This will be addressed through assistance to democratic institutions, a free-press and democratic labor organizations."[10] The NED had been the primary entity for managing the electoral intervention project and resented the intrusion of the AID's Democratic Initiatives office. The AID instructed the NED to postpone postelectoral involvement in Nicaragua until the endowment's June 1990 board meeting. But the NED defied the AID and sent its own delegation down to Managua in March to bypass the AID and work directly with Chargés d'Affaires Jack Leonard, who "feels strongly that NED assistance cannot be postponed until June."[11] "The Endowment *must* have some input" on the ground in Nicaragua in the immediate postelectoral transition, stated an internal NED memorandum drafted two weeks after the vote in response to the AID's directives.[12] The angrily worded memorandum continued:

> Norma [Parker—head of the Democratic Initiatives office] assumes that any future supplementals for Nicaragua will go through the Democratic Initiatives office of AID, and that the Endowment will have to compete with other organizations for those funds. A concerted effort must be made on the Hill—through our Board, the institutes et al.—to have any future funds come directly through the Endowment, not through AID. As Barbara [Haig] has said, what makes the Endowment unique is its flexibility, responsiveness and independence, and we should under no circumstances be subsumed under AID. The Endowment is not a subsidiary of AID, and our funding decisions should not be contingent on their needs assessment. [See Appendix A, document 24.][13]

This was as much a turf fight involving interagency rivalries as a haggle over strategies for consolidating the anti-Sandinista electoral victory. The substantive issue behind this tussle was whether the highly sophisticated political intervention that the NED had so aptly managed in the electoral intervention process would be given continuity in the postelectoral period.

The NED did not wait until June to introduce new, postelectoral programs. "In order to ensure the general prospects for the advance of democracy in all areas of Nicaraguan life, assistance is now required for additional programs to build and strengthen democratic institutions at the grass roots level that will lay the foundation for continued democratic development in Nicaragua," stated a report submitted to the NED March 1990 board meeting.[14] The document listed a series of new programs the endowment was preparing, including

- An additional $107,000 for the UNO trade unions "aimed at countering antidemocratic trade union destabilization during the transition period. . . . After having suppressed strikes for years, some Sandinista trade unionists now threaten mass political strikes to 'protect the gains of the revolution.' A successful organizing drive by independent trade unions, aimed at creating a visible democratic presence in communities and industries throughout Nicaragua, is crucial to maintaining a stable transition period. Just as voters had to be convinced that the election gave them an opportunity to vote without undue intimidation, so now must citizens be convinced they have freedom of association to protect the gains won in the election."[15]

- An additional $75,000 for "the continuation of CAD's training and civic education program during the transition period among youth, women, teachers, professionals, cooperatives and community development organizations. . . . Programs will be designed [to] promote further unity of action [and] citizen understanding of newly rising expectations regarding the prospects for a better life will inevitably come up against the grim realities of Nicaragua's economic situation."

- $175,000 in new funds for *La Prensa* and for the right-wing radio station Radio Corporación. "The Sandinista controlled media has contributed to a generalized atmosphere of uncertainty and anxiety by constantly emphasizing the problems which lie ahead, and fomenting distrust of the new government's future economic, political and social policies among the peasants, government employees, and the general public," stated the program summary. "If the independent media is to meet the difficult challenge of providing timely and informative coverage throughout the delicate transition period, additional resources will be required."

The NED also maintained the "Venezuelan connection" of third-party conduits in Caracas. After the elections, the NED commissioned the Solidarity and Democracy Foundation, a Caracas group set up earlier in 1990 and headed by several of the Venezuelan "consultants" whom the NED had contracted for work in Nicaragua. This new foundation was to implement the Project for the Identification of Obstacles for the Democratic Transition in Nicaragua.[16] The program involved facilitating "a non-traumatic transition from a Marxist to a democratic regime" and the development of "presidential relations with other branches of power and groups within organized society." The objective was to "broaden the circle of political interlocutors with the Presidency in Nicaragua" by taking advantage of Chamorro's close relations with the Venezuelans.

The clear purpose of these postelectoral NED programs was to deepen and extend U.S. penetration of Nicaraguan civil and political society and particularly to consolidate influence over the organs of the new Nicaraguan government. The United States was working hard at restoring its hegemony over Nicaragua.

Elections, Intervention, and Revolution: A Sandinista Perspective

Alejandro Bendaña

Former Secretary General of the Nicaraguan Foreign Ministry;
Member of the FSLN National Campaign Committee for
the 1990 Elections; and Director of
the Center for International Studies, Managua

For most of the Third World, and perhaps for part of the First, the attainment of integral democracy entails revolution. Any attempt to implement transformation requires the breaking of old structures—political, economic, social, and ideological—that constitute barriers to the full development of the individual in his or her relationship to the community. And in much of the Third World the clash between the old and the new, between those who refuse to give up historical privileges and those who demand change, has been marked by violence.

The Sandinista National Liberation Front (founded in 1961) waged a battle, first as an insurgency and then as a government, against national and international structures that in its view stood as barriers to the attainment of full democracy and independence for Nicaragua. That battle continued after the electoral defeat of February 1990. The FSLN began a new phase in its history, entering the unchartered terrain of fighting as a legal, civic opposition force for its vision of Nicaraguan society. In this new stage, unlike the previous one, the pursuit of democratic ideals might not be marked with violence.

With the overthrow of the hated Somoza family dynasty a decade earlier in July 1979, a generation of Nicaraguans had been presented with the opportunity to build the new democratic, revolutionary Nicaragua they had dreamed of, fought for, and sacrificed for. Although the Sandinistas felt a historical obligation to test that ideal, they did not believe it would be exempted from the historical rule that there could be no revolution without a counterrevolution and that in the history of Latin America there had never been a counterrevolution without the support of the Central Intelligence Agency.

In its drive to topple the Sandinistas militarily, the Reagan administration for years remained unwilling to challenge the Sandinistas on the political-civic terrain. Indeed, by insisting on quick results, the administration not only condemned thousands of Nicaraguans to death but also undermined internal civic-political forces within and outside the FSLN that favored achieving greater internal consensus for social transformation with political and economic pluralism. Internal and international political developments had the effect of strengthening Sandinista acceptance of a nonauthoritarian path to revolutionary transformation in a context of multiparty electoral competition and guarantees for the private sector. U.S. aggression, however, led to a tightening of controls and limitations on political expression, making compromise and accommodation all the more difficult.

It was no small achievement, therefore, to have subsequently forced the United States onto the political-electoral battlefield in 1990. By 1987, the Sandinistas had achieved important successes in pushing back the contra military threat, which allowed them to take the initiative in signing the Esquipulas Accords. The strategy called for further isolating the hard-liners in Washington and thereby creating a basis for an eventual diplomatic understanding. The armed struggle was to slowly give way to the political-electoral struggle. But at the time the FSLN recognized that the proposition was risky for two reasons. First, there was no political guarantee that the United States would accept the Esquipulas challenge and agree to substitute electoral for military scenarios. Second, for this "gambit" to work, the entire electoral process had to be as impeccable as possible so as to deny the United States, the contras, and the internal opposition the opportunity to claim fraud and thereby further fuel the military-minded, hard-core contra supporters.

In practical terms, this meant making important concessions to the internal political opposition even at the expense of placing the FSLN at a relative disadvantage. We were cognizant that the election could prove the last chance to ensure contra dismantlement and end the war, and we were hopeful that the process could force modifications in U.S. policy. We made every effort to keep the opposition from pulling out of the campaign in 1984 style. This meant providing the opposition with extraordinary campaign and electoral facilities unprecedented by Latin American standards, including access to foreign funding. Furthermore, thousands of electoral observers were invited, including Jimmy Carter, whose publicized reports on the development of the campaign provided the government with a clean bill of health but at the price of settling differences over facilities consistently to the benefit of the opposition. For the first time in history, a sovereign country requested the United Nations to monitor its election, much to the amazement of international legal specialists. Some Sandinistas insisted that Sandino was rolling over in his grave, but a majority held that conceding on the formality of sovereignty was the only way left to maintain it in substance.

The "other" side, however, made no such concessions: In violation of the Esquipulas agreements, the United States and Honduras did not dismantle the contras. This could have allowed the Sandinistas to call the entire bargain off and suspend the elections, which in any case were not scheduled until November 1990. Our decision, however, was to continue with the electoral process even at the expense of exhausting every organizational reserve.

Mounting an election was only one of several key tasks that the FSLN had defined for itself as part of its strategy to end the war. In the Sandino to Sandino FSLN policy directive of May 1989, first priority was given, not to the Sandinista campaign or even to the election, but to military questions and the economy. Stepped-up defense measures to further weaken contra presence within the country included mounting a conscription effort to provide fifty thousand additional recruits demanded by the military to safeguard the electoral process. This of course did not win the Sandinistas more votes, but the army felt it was indispensable, more so in the light of the approaching confrontation in Panama and new guerrilla offensives in El Salvador. The Sandino to Sandino directive placed second priority on the need to contain galloping inflation and impending economic collapse by implementing shock austerity measures, however unpopular. This, too, did not win the FSLN any votes, but the economists felt it was indispensable.

On top of the military and economic tasks assumed by government and party activists came the enormous effort entailed in organizing what probably came to be the most observed election ever. Four thousand electoral councils and polling booths had to be created, and two million citizens had to be registered; eighty thousand persons were required for the task, which the Sandinistas, in the absence of participation from other parties, had to assume almost in its entirety.

Exhaustion, both cumulative and immediate, was therefore a factor in explaining not only the electoral defeat but also why the Sandinistas were not able to correctly gauge their political standing. The upbeat tone of the campaign and incorrect reading of the polls unconsciously helped reinforce the notion that once again a majority of Nicaraguans, prodded by a minority of determined Sandinistas, would give their vote to the FSLN. The United States proved adept at exploiting this political misreading and these internal weaknesses to mount the electoral intervention project.

In retrospect, some claimed that by making so many concessions, the FSLN had committed electoral suicide. Clearly, had the FSLN possessed a more realistic perception of its own political standing vis-à-vis the referendum process mounted by the United States, the story would have been different. Had the United States not been able to unify the opposition, the Sandinistas might have won with the same number of votes it received on February 25. Had the FSLN been less zealous in promoting voter registration, particularly in zones where the front did not enjoy much popularity, results might have been different even with the same balance of forces in society.

In short, there was nothing inevitable about the Sandinista electoral defeat, even though majority support had evaporated over the years. Nor were elections imposed on the Sandinistas. The FSLN accepted the unfair social and economic conditions under which the contest was held and freely negotiated the rules of the game with the opposition, with the Central American governments under the Esquipulas plans, and with prominent international observers.

In reality, entering into a political-electoral contest was a no-win *and* a no-lose proposition for both the Sandinistas and the Bush administration. On the Sandinista side, the contest was necessary to complement and reinforce the military routing of the contras and the collapse of the political will in Congress to sustain the war. The point was to provide the Bush administration and the contras with an opportunity to climb off the limb on which Reagan had left them hanging. The election was a constitutional imperative but also a means to end the war, to adjust old strategic ideals to new political realities, and launch a new, more broadly based effort to rebuild the nation and implement democracy. That the election could be lost did not change the reality that the war had basically been won, the contras had been forced to dismantle (which might not have been the case had the FSLN won), peace was being attained, and the Sandinista front still remained the strongest and most influential political organization in Nicaragua.

The FSLN had fought and won the right to come down from the mountains to become a legitimate and undeniable component of Nicaraguan political culture, if not as a government perpetually in power, then certainly as a political organization that had brought about and preserved the greatest social, economic, and political transformation in Nicaraguan history. And the FSLN remained alive to push for even greater transformation. The revolutionary process was simply entering a second phase, again independently of the results of the elections. The attempt to turn society, the economy, and politics back to 1979 failed.

Ironically, the United States and the UNO also benefited from the process of popular empowerment promoted by the revolution. They did so through the newfound democratic belief that individuals did make a difference and through a revolution that provided the people with the capacity to turn out a government. The FSLN was the first party in Nicaraguan history ever to lose an election to an opposition and, having lost it, to turn over office. Nothing could have been more revolutionary and more democratic. Nothing could have been further from the counterrevolutionary ideal that Ronald Reagan and the Far Right in Nicaragua had placed their bets on.

A new government appeared on the scene beholden to the United States for material support. But it was also beholden to the Sandinista constitution for legitimacy, to the Sandinista army and police for the maintenance of national defense and internal order, and to the Sandinista Party for political stability and defense against a vocal right-wing opposition that felt betrayed. The new government, or at least the executive, found it necessary and convenient to work with the Sandinistas for the sake of stability and business.

The FSLN had lost the presidency but in many senses had retained the fundamental instruments to preserve and even broaden the popular empowerment process legitimized by the constitution and backed up by the FSLN's organizational strength. None of this would have been possible had the war been lost and had the contras not been dismantled. In recognition of Sandinista strength and notwithstanding U.S. opposition, the new government proceeded to insist on the full disarmament of the remaining contra groupings and agreed to respect the broad social and economic changes of the previous ten years, to uphold the constitution (which included respect for the integrity and professional character of the armed forces), and to work with the FSLN to attain national reconstruction, full pacification, political stability, and economic recovery.

The new question is, Will the United States allow the Sandinistas to act as an opposition where it has not allowed them to govern the country in peace? Indeed, is the cold war over in Central America? Were the elections free and fair in the light of the ten-year siege? Perhaps a more relevant question is, Are there free and fair conditions in the world for building a true democracy—meaning revolutionary change in most of the region. The answer is clearly no, particularly in the backyard of the United States and after the demise of old socialist-bloc assistance for anticapitalist transformation. That is the characteristic of the world we live in, which is not a world of harmony but of contradiction and struggle. And in the course of that struggle there will be reverses and injustices perpetrated in particular by those who, while insisting on fair play, deny it in practice, as in Chile and Nicaragua.

What are the implications then of the Nicaraguan episode for the democratic Left in the Third World? In the face of a foreign onslaught, must the Left necessarily wage and sustain a battle for democracy by undemocratic means? Must the defense of self-determination impose limits on the openness of an electoral process? Can elections be manipulated by the United States and outside forces to contain true democratic change? Can a democratic revolution be undermined by democratic elections?

Perhaps all of these questions exaggerate the importance of elections and governmental power as levers of social change. In the final analysis, the Nicaraguan Revolution and the U.S. strategy will be judged less on the results of an election and the FSLN loss of state power than on whether ten years in office and eighteen years in the armed struggle before then democratized the character of the Nicaraguan political process in a way that could not be reversed by any future government. In that context, revolutionary movements must learn not only how to win elections but also how to survive electoral losses. The Sandinistas, for the first time in the history of revolutionary movements, have learned half of that lesson.

The postelectoral Nicaraguan political scene cannot be divorced either from the global counterrevolutionary context or from the domestic revolutionary framework in which the elections were held. The tug of these two forces will determine the contest between revolution and counterrevolution. The Sandinistas, with nearly 42 percent of the electoral vote, remained the best-organized political and social force in the nation. There was never any doubt about its core constituency. The same could not be said for the new UNO government, whose only binding force was its anti-Sandinista platform, its presidential symbol, and U.S. support, none of which indicated signs of resiliency. Violeta Chamorro and her principal advisers belonged to no particular party and before too long were setting aside the fragile UNO coalition in favor of a working relationship with the defeated Sandinistas.

The United States shared part of the credit, or part of the blame; the artificial nature of the coalition led to an artificial government deprived of an organized social base of its own able to counter that of the Sandinistas. The Far Right, now led by Vice President Godoy, focused on undermining the president's proclaimed policy of reconciliation and coexistence with the Sandinistas. In the final analysis, Chamorro's decision to adopt a policy of reconciliation and coexistence with the Sandinistas was a response to politics as much as to morality. Nicaragua could not be governed against the will of the principal trade unions and social movements that had grown under the revolution. When Daniel Ortega explained that the Sandinistas would now "govern from below," it was more an acknowledgment of social reality than a political threat. If the Sandinistas had lost the consensus necessary for governing, there still could be no consensus without them, and Nicaragua (most now recognized) could not be governed without a democratically rooted consensus.

Moreover, the new government was legally and socially the product of a revolution; it did not have the capacity to dismantle ten years of revolutionary changes. Even those within the UNO coalition and in the United States most bent on dismantling the revolution could no longer deny the Sandinistas' legitimacy. The election, therefore, established a fragile consensus built on the fact that the Sandinista Party had organized the elections, accepted the results, and held the new government to be constitutionally legitimate but also constitutionally bound.

In this way the Sandinista Revolution, perhaps the last major social revolution of this century, became the first in history to turn over the government to a nonrevolutionary, elected alternative without destroying itself in the process. The inability to sustain state power may be regarded as a failure by twentieth-century standards, but who can say that those standards will endure any more than other political models have? Indeed, are revolutions, are democracies, measured in terms of their grip on state power? And just how sovereign and powerful are governments in the Third World in the post–cold war, unipolar political, military, and economic environment? Can state power prove to be a brake on popular empowerment?

In the face of the emergence of civil society, the demand for greater democratic empowerment, and the collapse of both communism and anticommunism, the Sandinistas today, along with most of the new revolutionary Left in the Third World, are acquiring a new perspective on power. The lesson learned from having governed for ten years is that the test of progressive transformation in the search for social justice is not reduced to an electoral verdict or even to the quality of governmental administration. History may well judge the Nicaraguan Revolution on the basis of the permanence of democratization and on whether all future governments, whatever there particular makeup, will remain bound by the basic juridical, political, and social framework established over the course of the Sandinista administration.

Notwithstanding the array of forces pitted against it, the Nicaraguan Left has now been guaranteed a political space to continue working for change. It has won the right to employ forms of struggle and representation that by now are traditional in Western Europe but that are nothing less than revolutionary in Central America. These include the right of the Left not to be gunned down, the right to exist as a revolutionary party in opposition, the right to contest office, and the right to define its own pluralist path toward socialism. These rights, secure in Nicaragua today, have still not been attained in El Salvador or in Guatemala and have not yet been fully recognized by the United States and extreme right-wing elements.

In this context, the Sandinista loss at the polls may prove to be a temporary reversal that unfolds into a new strategic opportunity. It will be put to the test in the unfolding of Nicaragua's unique postelectoral political scenario where a left-wing army has pledged its allegiance to a conservative government, where the head of the army is the brother of the head of the Sandinista opposition, where the vice president is not loyal to the government but rather heads the right-wing opposition, where the government in office still calls itself the United Nicaraguan Opposition administration, where the most powerful political officials grouped around the presidency are eager to reach understandings with the Sandinistas, where poor ex-contras are joining Sandinista campesinos in demanding land.

How such an intriguing scenario unfolds will be determined by the Nicaraguan people and by the Sandinistas themselves, heroic survivors of the worst historical period lived by the socialist Left since 1917. Will the FSLN be able to make the transition from Old to New Left, from a political-military apparatus to a new political party, without losing its historical anti-imperialist credentials and its commitment to social transformation? Most Sandinistas believe their movement cannot simply become another "typical" electoral party seeking votes from everyone by promising all things to all people.

But then the FSLN is far from being just another typical opposition in Nicaraguan or Latin American fashion. No political opposition party in Latin America has the same tested and militant loyalty from unions and social groups and sympathy from the armed forces. And although shaken by the loss of government and in the middle of defining new relationships between party structures and grass-roots movements, the FSLN's core constituency, indispensable for the forging of revolutionary change, is still there. In short, the FSLN has all the classical instruments in its hands to achieve a seizure of power. Yet it has no intention of doing so. Legitimacy, today more than ever, is attained as the result of electoral processes.

The Sandinistas opened up political-electoral space in Nicaragua by the barrel of the gun—space that was sufficient to hold an election but not to attain an electoral victory. Historical gains aside, however, a party does not wage electoral battles simply to come out second. Increasingly, revolutionary movements that have been forced to fight in the mountains now face the challenge of fighting on the electoral playing field—very much a new, unexplored terrain where the opponent may have the benefit of campaign experience and access to U.S. support. The end of the "Soviet strategic threat" opens up possibilities and circumstances that cannot be ignored. The challenge is being taken up in Central America, as in southern Africa, if for no other reason than to pursue people's dreams of peace with justice.

Herein lies the historical significance of the Nicaraguan elections, perhaps the first of their kind in the post–cold war world, in which the United States successfully tested a new interventionist strategy. The Left, too, must draw its lessons from this experience, which are much more complex than trying to ward off all suspicious-looking U.S. citizens. For the Sandinistas or the Central American armed Left to discard the electoral road to power simply on account of the U.S. capacity to carry out electoral intervention would be the equivalent of throwing out the baby with the bathwater. Rather, we must examine our own weakness and identify strategies for successful electoral participation. Core revolutionary constituencies, no matter how loyal and willing to die, are not enough to win elections, which is to say that, although indispensable, these constituencies are no substitute for policies oriented to reach out to a broader majority. In coming to grips with the collapse of the Eastern European regimes and with the electoral defeat in Nicaragua, the Left is now taking a new hard look at the meaning of competitive multiparty elections, heretofore dismissed as "bourgeois." If the Far Right and the United States also lay down their military weapons and play clean in this post–cold war world—a big *if*—then elections take on a new meaning and potential.

Having been forced up into the mountains and into military battle, the Left in Central America is now harvesting the fruit of years of sacrifice by forcing entrenched rightist regimes, however reluctantly, to engage in negotiations. The question now becomes, Is the Left ready and able to make the transition to electoral politics under new frameworks that assure it physical safety and a minimum of political opportunity? If outright military seizures of power are increasingly out of the question, it behooves the Left to waste no time forging and sharpening political-electoral skills to immediately compete on a terrain from which it has been barred by repression or ideological preference. In this context, the Sandinista electoral model is a revolutionary one that, if fully applied in El Salvador, Guatemala, or South Africa, would indeed threaten the continuation of antipopular right-wing regimes. Nicaraguan-type elections can therefore become a revolutionary and anti-imperialist banner not easily dismissed by those heralding the advent of democracy in Eastern Europe.

True, the elections in Nicaragua show that even where the Left is in government, the injection of foreign support on behalf of the Right can undermine the capacity of the Left's core constituency to bring a majority on board. The situation proves all the more disadvantageous, of course, where the Left is in opposition, as in the case of El Salvador or South Africa, fighting a New Right enjoying governmental support, access to media, extensive financial resources, and public and private U.S. support.

In the final analysis, the United States has always been able to capitalize on the mistakes of its opponents, and the Sandinistas were no exception. Generating conditions that force difficult decisions, or the choice between lesser evils, is an objective of low-intensity warfare. Yet because those mistakes or limitations were more electoral than military, today the Sandinistas have the opportunity lost to much of the Left elsewhere of adjusting their political-organizational model and enjoying new opportunities to do battle with adversaries sustained by the United States. This presumes, for the Sandinistas as well as for much of the Left, a renovation not so much of principles or ideals but of programs and structures that will once again allow us to win the support of majorities and to attain the minimal consensus that is necessary not only to win an election but also to govern effectively.

Old Habits, New Opportunities in Nicaragua

Robert A. Pastor

Professor of Political Science, Emory University;
Fellow at Emory's Carter Center; and author of
*Whirlpool: U.S. Foreign Policy Toward Latin America and
the Caribbean* (Princeton, 1992) and *Condemned to Repetition:
The United States and Nicaragua* (Princeton, 1987)

In the early morning of February 26, 1990, hours after voters had cast their ballots, Nicaraguans witnessed the first sign of a spirit of conciliation and comity. Through trusted intermediaries, President Daniel Ortega, who lost the election, and Violeta Barrios de Chamorro, who won, accepted the people's will to change the government peacefully and seek to heal the nation's wounds.

Prior to that moment, suspicion had dominated Nicaragua's political history. "Peaceful changes between different factions of the ruling classes, which have been rather frequent in other Latin American countries, have not taken place in Nicaragua," wrote Carlos Fonseca Amador, the founding father of the Sandinistas (FSLN). "This traditional experience predisposed the Nicaraguan people against electoral farces and in favor of armed struggle."[1] The government in Nicaragua traditionally viewed the opposition as fragmented and ineffectual and did everything possible to keep it that way. The opposition viewed the government as coercive and corrupt. A few opposition groups would participate in elections; others asked the people to boycott the vote, lest they provide a veneer of respect to an illegitimate regime.

This tragic, repetitive pattern of coercion by government and abstentionism by the opposition, which was so well analyzed by the father of the Sandinista party, reached its conclusion under Sandinista rule. The FSLN accused its opposition of being a disloyal pawn of the United States, while the opposition charged the FSLN as being a repressive, Marxist-Leninist surrogate of Cuba and the Soviet Union. The Reagan administration helped both sides' perceptions of the other come true. The contras—both the means and the end of U.S. policy—justified the militarism of the Sandinistas and rendered the internal opposition impotent.

Costa Rican President Oscar Arias offered Nicaraguans an exit, and to his credit, Daniel Ortega accepted. In Esquipulas, Guatemala, in August 1987, Daniel Ortega and the other Central American presidents accepted Arias's proposal to end conflicts in the region through democracy, national reconciliation, and an end to support for insurgencies. The Central Americans asked the United States to stop providing arms to the contras. Reagan called the plan "fatally flawed" and insisted that the Sandinistas would never accept democracy unless Congress approved military aid to the contras.[2] Congress rejected Reagan's argument and was proven right. With the political space permitted by a suspension of aid to the contras, Ortega called for elections on February 25, 1990. He was convinced that free elections would not only return him to power but would also unlock aid from Europe, lift the U.S. embargo, and end the contra war.

The opposition also was eager for an election. Invigorated by returning exiles, encouraged to participate by the Bush administration, and convinced that the economy's collapse, the Sandinistas' militarism, and the spread of democracy in Latin America were all favorable conditions, the opposition felt it could win if free elections were held.

These favorable conditions, however, still came up against Nicaragua's historical burden of mutual suspicion. What made the 1990 elections different was the invitation by both the Sandinista government and the Nicaraguan opposition (UNO) to international groups to observe the electoral process and the elections. The three most important groups were the OAS, the U.N., and the Council of Freely Elected Heads of Government (the Council). The Council was chaired by former U.S. president Jimmy Carter and was based at the Carter Center of Emory University. It included eighteen former and current heads of governments from throughout the hemisphere. The Council fielded a distinguished thirty-five-person delegation that included Prime Minister George Price (Belize) and seven former presidents, including Rafael Caldera (Venezuela), Raúl Alfonsín (Argentina), and Daniel Oduber (Costa Rica).

The three observer groups helped mediate the rules for the elections, reduce Sandinista coercion, preclude opposition abstentionism, and transform international intervention into support for or, at least, acquiescence to democratic elections. In its invitation to the international community, Nicaragua defined a new model for the international community that offered promise for securing democracy elsewhere.[3]

The subject of William Robinson's book is not the 1990 Nicaraguan elections, but U.S. intervention in the elections. His book is a passionate account of how the United States "robbed" Nicaraguans of their democracy. Testimony to his idealism is that he asked me to write the foreword to this book even though I disagree with its thesis. The elections, in Robinson's view, were a contest between the Sandinista revolution and the United States; I believe they were a contest between Nicaraguans. Before explaining his arguments and my reservations, let me describe some of the background of my own involvement in Nicaragua and the elections.

* * *

I had the privilege of organizing President Carter's observer mission to the elections. That mission began when I first broached the idea with President Daniel Ortega and other Nicaraguan leaders in July 1989, and it continued through the inauguration of President Violeta de Chamorro on April 25, 1990. For me, the elections were the culmination of a twenty-year journey in Nicaragua that began when I worked on a banana boat in 1968 that docked in Bluefields, Nicaragua. A decade later, I was the director of Latin American and Caribbean Affairs on the National Security Council.

Between September 1978 and July 1979, the National Security Council met twenty-five times to develop a strategy for dealing with a country struggling to rid itself of the oppressive Somoza dynasty.[4] The consensus was that if the United States did nothing, Somoza would try to repress the popular movement against him, the country would polarize even further, and the FSLN would eventually win a military victory. Although the Carter administration recognized that the Sandinistas had broadened their base of support, it viewed the key leaders as Marxist, who saw Cuba and the Soviet Union as allies and the United States as an enemy. Caught between a dictator it refused to defend and a guerrilla movement that it would not support, the administration tried to facilitate a democratic transition in Nicaragua, but it failed. On July 17, 1979, Somoza fled Nicaragua for Miami, and the Sandinistas arrived to a joyous welcome two days later.

The United States wanted to avoid in Nicaragua the mutual hostility that had characterized early U.S.-Cuban relations and had led to a break in the relationship. At some political cost, Carter met with three members of the Sandinista junta in the White House and subsequently asked Congress for $75 million in aid for the new government. Because of the growing conservative mood in Congress and the Sandinistas' anti-American rhetoric, the issue of aid to Nicaragua was debated at great length and with considerable heat. After a long delay, Congress approved the funding with many conditions, the most important being that the president would have to end aid if he received conclusive evidence that the Nicaraguan government was assisting a foreign insurgency.

In November 1980, the Salvadoran guerrillas persuaded the Sandinistas to support their final offensive in January. This proved a major error for both. The final offensive was a fiasco, and the evidence of Nicaraguan support for it was conclusive. At a press conference in Managua five years later, Carter was asked to explain his decision to suspend aid: "I had no alternative but to cut off aid to the Sandinistas before I left office, because there was evidence that was clear to me that the Sandinistas were giving assistance to the revolutionaries in El Salvador, and the law required me to stop the aid. I was very eager to give the people of Nicaragua economic aid after the revolution was over, but it was not possible under those circumstances."[5]

In this book, Robinson mentions reports that the CIA under Carter's administration contemplated supporting a counterrevolution against the Sandinistas or trying to overthrow them (Ch. 1, p. 12; Ch. 2, note 6, p. 195). These reports are untrue; Carter himself denied them in a letter to the editor of the *Times of the Americas* on March 11, 1987: "I was aware of, and personally authorized, all covert operations during my Administration, and I can assure him [the author of the mistaken report] that my Administration provided no funding or support of any kind to any contra group fighting against the Sandinista government." Carter also confirmed that his administration, including the CIA, never considered contingency plans for overthrowing the Sandinistas. The report in the *Baltimore Sun* is incorrect.

The Reagan administration, of course, took a different approach, organizing an army of contras that numbered over twenty thousand by the late 1980s and providing them with hundreds of millions of dollars' worth of arms to try to overthrow the Sandinistas. The attempt failed, and the policy backfired to such an extent that it almost brought down President Reagan. The war and the economic embargo had a devastating impact on Nicaragua's society and economy and also led the government to deepen its dependence on the Soviet Union and Cuba, militarize the revolution, and reduce political space. No one won the contra war.

When I left the government in 1981 to return to the world of research and teaching, one of the principal subjects that I sought to understand was why the United States and Nicaragua seemed condemned to keep repeating such a tragic history. In my 1987 book, *Condemned to Repetition: The United States and Nicaragua*, I reached several conclusions: First, fraudulent elections had led the opposition to seek outside assistance from either the United States or its enemy as the only path to attaining power; second, international intervention exacerbated the internal conflict but was not its cause; third, unless the political system gave confidence to the opposition that it had a fair chance of gaining power peacefully, then Nicaragua and the United States would remain condemned to repetition.

I tried to organize the election observation mission to avoid the pitfalls of previous elections in Nicaragua. The experience was the most professionally rewarding of my life because *all Nicaraguans*, including the Sandinista leadership who lost, took pride in the fact that they participated in the first election in their country's history that was judged free and fair by everyone inside and outside of the country. Although some foreigners might describe the international involvement by the observer missions as "paternalistic" or "interventionist," the fact is that all of the Nicaraguan parties invited the groups and expressed appreciation for their efforts.

President Bush and Secretary of State James Baker removed the contra issue from the U.S. foreign policy agenda in 1989 by negotiating a compromise with the Democrats in Congress. That accord permitted Bush to retreat from the contras without abandoning them, and it allowed Nicaragua some political space for elections. But to hold elections that both sides in Nicaragua would view as free required delicate negotiations. During the elections, the Sandinistas and the UNO did not trust each other, and the latter did not trust the process—but both trusted the international observers to ensure that the process would be fair and that the other side would play by the rules.

The development that really offered hope for Nicaragua occurred after the elections: President Chamorro and the Sandinistas demonstrated an interest in embarking on a new path of national reconciliation. The essence of this new development is that each side recognizes that no one has a monopoly on the truth; each has a partial claim on it. Compromise is essential and is the only basis for building a democratic society.

*   *   *

William Robinson's story is told with conviction. Sympathetic to the Sandinistas, he still candidly acknowledges that it was a tragedy that they did not have the time to shed the clandestine habits that they had acquired fighting against Somoza. Such habits did not permit the revolution to be as democratic and inclusive as many Sandinista leaders had envisaged or wished. I agree with him on that point and also when he writes that "Nicaraguans should not be stripped of their own historical and social relevance" and that they "were thirsty for change" in 1990. But the thrust of his book is different from those latter two points. Robinson writes that there is an "untold story" of covert U.S. intervention in the elections in such a "sophisticated and extensive operation" as to "deeply influence the electoral process" and transform it into a contest "between the United States and the Nicaraguan revolution, not between the Sandinistas and the domestic opposition." Indeed, he calls the opposition a "marionette" of U.S. policy. That, of course, demeans Nicaraguans and denies them responsibility for their actions.

The points are also untrue. President Carter played an important role in the negotiations between President Ortega and President Bush on the issue of covert versus overt aid by the United States, and Robinson briefly alludes to it, but let me describe what occurred. In a conversation with Carter in early September, President Ortega said that he was willing to permit the United States to fund the UNO overtly, but he would make the CIA the central campaign issue if the United States supplied covert aid. The Bush administration decided against covert aid but would not say so, believing, erroneously in my view, that it should never confirm or deny such operations.

In an effort to remove the issue of covert funding from the campaign, Carter asked Ortega if he would accept his promise that there would be no covert funding if Carter could get assurances from the Bush administration and the Congressional Intelligence Committees. After discussions with both governments, Carter conveyed assurances in a letter to President Ortega on September 22, 1989, that there would be "no covert funding from our [U.S.] government for opposition political parties or other purposes that would subvert the integrity of the Nicaraguan elections." With that, the issue, which had been an important FSLN negative issue in September and had threatened to poison the campaign and a future relationship with the United States, disappeared.

Two years later, on October 21, 1991, *Newsweek* published an article, "CIA on the Stump," that alleged that the CIA secretly gave $600,000 to the contras to participate in the elections, and this violated the assurances. Robinson writes: "Whether Carter was deceived by Bush officials or deliberately manipulated, or for that matter whether he himself deceived the Nicaraguans, is unclear" (Ch. 6, p. 113). Carter was not informed of that decision, and when he learned about it in *Newsweek*, he was very upset and demanded an explanation. Under no circumstances would he have deceived President Ortega; his word is his bond.

Senator David Boren, chairman of the Senate Intelligence Committee, investigated the operation and reported in a letter to Carter on November 15, 1991, that the program was aimed at relocating individual contra leaders and not at influencing the elections. The amounts allocated to individual leaders were so small that it was improbable that they would have been spent on anything other than personal needs related to closing their offices and apartments in Miami or Honduras and returning to Nicaragua. The program was ill-advised, but Carter and Boren concluded that the administration's assurances had not been violated, and Carter conveyed that in a letter to Daniel Ortega on November 20, 1991.

To read Robinson's book is to envisage the great weight of the northern Colossus manipulating the electoral process by pouring millions of dollars into the UNO's operations. Up close, however, the elections looked very different. Rather than being the recipient of abundant resources, the UNO seemed lacking in everything. Its headquarters was a ramshackle tenement, whereas the Sandinistas' was in an enormous modern office building. The campaigns were similarly skewed. FSLN campaign material was omnipresent; good communications equipment was available for rallies; food was often distributed to families, toys to children. Despite the UNO's reputation as upper and middle class, poorer people seemed to come to its campaign rallies, and communications equipment was quite poor. It is not surprising that the FSLN used its incumbency and the resources of the state to help in its campaign. What few people realized until the elections were over was that incumbency and superior resources were liabilities, not assets.

What happened to the fabled $9 million given to the UNO? First of all, the law passed by Congress insisted that none of the money would be distributed directly to the UNO. Most of it went through the National Endowment for Democracy and the two-party institutes to the UNO, some labor unions, and a civic group, Via Cívica. The NED, NDI, and NRI used some of the money for administrative expenses. Ten percent of the total amount—$855,120—was allocated just for accountants to monitor the flow of funds.[6] After a decade of the Reagan administration's misuse of funding to the contras, Congress was not going to take any chances. Some of the money went to observer missions, including the Council's.

Second, as incredible as it appears, the sole purpose of the funds for the UNO was to "undertake civic and voter education . . . promote the democratic process . . . *not to finance the campaign of candidates for public office.*" The regulations contained a long list of "unallowable activities"; none of the funds, for example, could be used to finance a political campaign, polls, or to purchase any "t-shirts, flags, banners, posters, literature, buttons." The Sandinistas were unaware that the U.S. government had imposed so many restrictions on the use of the funds. The idea of $9 million for the UNO was a difficult one for them to swallow. Although President Ortega had agreed in principle to allow the UNO to receive the funds, at the bureaucratic level, many Sandinistas placed hundreds of obstacles in the path of the funding. In a trip to Nicaragua in late January, Carter raised this issue with Ortega, and on January 28, 1990—less than one month before the elections—President Ortega finally permitted the funds to be released.[7]

U.S. restrictions then proved so absurdly unwieldy that there were hundreds of stories about how ineffective the funding was. For example, vehicles provided to the UNO required that some U.S. accountants ride with them to ensure that they would be used for nonpartisan voter education rather than for partisan political purposes!

There were several ironies wrapped in the enigma of a large amount of money that had little if any impact on the election. First, Sandinista resources dominated the electoral campaign, to such a degree that it probably was counterproductive. People were reminded of the strong hand of the state, and this might have persuaded some to vote for a change. Second, the Sandinistas were convinced that their efforts to tie the UNO to the contras and to the United States played to their advantage because of their own nationalism. The UNO resisted being tied to the contras for the same reason. Both parties were apparently wrong. The Nicaraguan people wanted a good relationship with the United States, and that proved an asset to Chamorro. The tie to the contras was not as much of a liability as many, including myself, had thought, and in two or three regions it might have been an asset.

Still another irony in Robinson's argument is that his point about the unfairness of the elections is the same one made by numerous conservatives in the United States. Elliot Abrams said that the Sandinistas had such complete control over the political process that the UNO did not have an equal chance at the ballot box. Abrams insisted that if they had had a fair chance, Chamorro would have won by a lot more than she did.[8]

Abrams's is the mirror-image of Robinson's thesis. Both argue that the playing field was not level and thus that the election was not fair. They just disagree on which way the field was tipping. Both miss the point and demean Nicaraguans by doing so. The people of Nicaragua had a free and fair chance to hold their leaders accountable. The United States had an impact on the election, but it was hardly a secret or "untold story." It was due to a decade of contra war and five years of economic embargo, both of which I strongly condemned. The people of Nicaragua had a chance to blame their conditions on the United States—as the FSLN urged them to do—or on the Sandinistas.

In the end, the election was a referendum on ten years of Sandinista rule. To his credit, Daniel Ortega accepted that fact.

The election was not perfect, but it was the best that Nicaragua ever had for the very simple reason that it was the first time in the country's history that the parties who started the campaign completed it, all parties agreed to accept the results before the election, and all accepted it after the election. That process helped to transform the parties and country in a way that offers hope for Nicaraguans.

Although I disagree with much of Bill Robinson's book, I believe it reflects an idealism similar to that which motivated many Sandinistas. This book is a serious attempt to come to grips with the election defeat of the Sandinistas. Robinson's voice needs to be heard in Nicaragua and in the United States. By implication, the book confirms the most important lesson of a historically tragic relationship: It is time to look to the future with different lenses than we have used to look at our past.

Robinson Responds: Democracy or Intervention?

I was aware that *A Faustian Bargain* would generate controversy. Anticipating debate on substantive issues and contending interpretations among the readership, I wanted to solicit comments from someone who I knew would hold a different perspective. I invited Dr. Robert Pastor to comment because I respect his scholarly work and because he played an important role in the international observer apparatus to the Nicaraguan elections. I am grateful to Pastor for having taken the time to write the preceding afterword.

In soliciting outside commentary, I was less interested in hearing from those who would justify U.S. foreign policy than in serious academic engagement over the issues of substance raised in this book. Pastor and I discussed, in written correspondence and by phone, our disagreements over several of these substantive issues. Three stand out: (1) the weight of U.S. involvement in the elections relative to other factors; (2) the actions of the Sandinistas as protagonists, regardless of U.S. involvement; and (3) the boundaries of the acceptable and the unacceptable in democratic elections, that is, what role an outside power can legitimately play in a sovereign nation's elections.

In the first instance, Pastor expressed that although the United States might have been involved in the Nicaraguan elections, the process was an eminently Nicaraguan affair. In addition, he expressed the view that U.S. policy during the electoral period was a healthy departure from previous, Reagan-style military intervention. In contrast, I concluded that although the process emanated from the Nicaraguans, U.S. intervention distorted what might have been an authentically endogenous affair. I also maintained that the U.S. role in the elections can only be understood in the context of ten years of U.S. war and its consequences. Therefore the issue is not limited to the impact of U.S. involvement in the elections in its own right, but this involvement in conjunction with conditions generated by U.S. policy throughout the 1980s. Behind this disagreement is a debate over the relative weight of distinct factors in the outcome.

This is closely related to the second issue. Pastor argued that the Sandinistas' electoral defeat is due to their performance during ten years of government. As I make clear in the concluding chapter, the complex reality of the Nicaraguan nation cannot be reduced to U.S. intervention, and the Sandinistas' behavior and policies constituted an independent variable for which they are solely responsible. Another book can, and should, be written about these issues. I felt, however, that U.S. involvement in the elections was a crucial aspect that had remained unexposed and needed special and immediate attention. In addition, I maintain in the book that the Sandinistas' own performance and other internal factors were so thoroughly interwoven with external factors, and with U.S. intervention in particular, that they cannot be separated.

Finally, Pastor raised the point in our correspondence, and indirectly alluded to it in his afterword, that the very terms of free elections imply that a vote is necessarily subject to the influence of events as they unfold in the real world, including the actions taken by governments and the consequences of those actions. By way of example, he pointed to Jimmy Carter's 1980 electoral defeat as a result of the taking of hostages at the U.S. embassy in Iran—an event halfway across the globe and beyond the control of the president. I accept that there are inherent risks involved in free elections, but not that a free vote therefore sanctions any premeditated (not to mention illegal) actions on the part of players calculated to influence electorates. Jimmy Carter might have lost the election even if the hostages were freed before the vote, and no one could claim that the 1980 U.S. elections were unfair simply because the hostage crisis, and its non-resolution before the vote, deeply influenced the U.S. electorate. However, if the allegations prove true that members of the Reagan campaign team intervened to postpone release of the hostages until after the vote, then it would be hard to argue that the 1980 U.S. elections were "clean" and that Carter lost simply as a result of events, the consequences of which candidates in any election are subject to accept.

More to the point, my argument is that U.S. interference in the Nicaraguan elections constituted a premeditated exogenous factor whose intent was the same as the alleged Reagan team's secret negotiations with the Iranians—an effort to influence voters outside of any conceivable boundaries of legitimate electoral competition. Moreover, U.S. politicians and officials have no business attempting to influence voters of other sovereign nations. To accept the logic that U.S. intervention in Nicaraguan elections was acceptable because a free vote means that candidates are subject to events in the real world would be to accept that Nicaragua, or any other country, has the right to send (what would be the per capita equivalent of) billions of dollars to its preferred candidates in U.S. elections, to send tens of thousands of campaign advisors to the United States, to set up media outlets and civic and labor groups at the service of its preferred candidates, and so on. And it would also mean that this foreign power, before proceeding to intervene in U.S. elections, could wage a decade-long armed insurgency from Canadian and Mexican territory and impose an effective economic embargo on the United States. Could any U.S. citizen conceivably accept such a scenario?

Pastor's afterword makes no reference whatsoever to the voluminous documentation in this book of these multifarious forms of U.S. intervention in the Nicaraguan elections. This evidence cannot be ignored, even if one does not agree with the analytical conclusions I reach. This evidence confirms that the United States was so deeply involved in the Nicaraguan elections that U.S. intervention cannot be shrugged off as an incident on the sidelines of an otherwise domestic affair. It also makes clear that establishing whether or not Nicaraguans got to deposit a secret ballot on election day, or whether the electoral process was procedurally correct, is not the real issue.

Pastor's arguments have been used by those who make an apology for U.S. intervention in Nicaragua and, more specifically, by those who justify the new political intervention analyzed in Chapter 1 and in Chapter 8 of this book. In this justification, the United States has corrected earlier, misguided policies and is now "promoting democracy"; this situates the new forms of U.S. intervention snugly and constructively between the extremes of authoritarian or militarist regimes and earlier, erroneous U.S. policies. This U.S. intervention is beneficent, or at least is making a constructive contribution, from the sidelines, to the "free elections" and the "transitions to democracy" sweeping the world. Pastor's own book, *Condemned to Repetition*, refers to the argument made by some that the United States should remove "authoritarian" regimes it formerly supported (such as Somoza's) in order to undercut popular or revolutionary outcomes to antidictatorial struggles. It is precisely this reasoning that led policymakers to develop the new political intervention.

A reply to Pastor's comment regarding the Carter administration and CIA programs in Nicaragua is necessary. I state that the Carter administration *contemplated* plans for overthrowing the Sandinistas. Pastor quotes Jimmy Carter asserting that he never *authorized* any such plan. Yet nowhere do I state that these plans were *authorized* by Jimmy Carter, only that his administration contemplated them. The source I cite is none other than Stansfield Turner, Carter's own CIA director, who told the *Baltimore Sun* in May 1983 that contingency plans were *considered* for the overthrow of the Sandinistas. Besides, whether Jimmy Carter actually contemplated any plan to overthrow the Sandinistas is completely marginal to the central content, thrust, and conclusions of the book. Pastor mentions nothing of the CIA programs authorized by Carter before the July 1979 Sandinista triumph to support the conservative anti-Somoza elements (the same elements that would be organized by the Bush administration into the UNO coalition), nor does he mention reports that CIA programs authorized by Carter after the Sandinista triumph to support the internal civic opposition (as opposed to military contras). These programs are duly cited in my notes and have already been exposed and documented elsewhere.

In the end, what we saw in Nicaragua was an updated version of Woodrow Wilson's "civilizing mission" in Latin America early in the twentieth century. At that time, the United States needed stability in the Caribbean Basin to protect its expanding economic and political interests. Marine expeditions and the establishment of U.S. protectorates became the order of the day. The supercilious Wilson gave the "big stick" and "dollar diplomacy" a new twist: the despatching of U.S. envoys who "offered" their good offices to mediate disputes, arrange truces, forge pacts, and hammer together elite coalitions around U.S.-managed elections. This policy was justified as a missionary effort to teach the Latin Americans how to become "civilized" and "democratic." I view Pastor's portrait of U.S. involvement in Nicaragua as one of a paternalist Uncle Sam who, through U.S. interference in the elections, was able to help bickering, "mutually suspicious" Nicaraguans to finally get their house in order. In Pastor's words, it was "international intervention" in the elections that brought democracy to Nicaragua.

I agree with Pastor's conclusion that it is time to look to the future with different lenses than we have used to look at the past. However, everything indicates that the United States has recast, not renounced, foreign policy spectacles predicated on intervention, hegemony, and the arrogance of empire.

▪ NOTES ▪

INTRODUCTION

1. Electoral defeat concession speech by Daniel Ortega, Managua, February 26, 1990, reproduced in *Barricada*, February 27, 1990.

CHAPTER ONE

1. Cited in Karl Berman, *Under the Big Stick* (Boston: South End Press, 1986), p. 151.
2. *Insight*, May 8, 1989.
3. Speech before joint session of Congress, April 27, 1983.
4. Angelo M. Codevilla, "Political Warfare," in Carnes Lord and Frank R. Barnett (eds.), *Political Warfare and Psychological Operations: Rethinking the U.S. Approach* (Washington, D.C.: National Defense University Press, 1988), pp. 77–79. Codevilla was an adviser to Reagan.
5. See Maxwell O. Johnson, "The Role of Maritime-Based Strategy," *Marine Corps Gazette* (February 1984).
6. Ibid.
7. For more on low-intensity warfare and its doctrinal emergence, see William I. Robinson and Kent Norsworthy, *David and Goliath: The U.S. War Against Nicaragua* (New York: Monthly Review Press, 1987), particularly Chapter 1; Deborah Barry, Jorge Vargas, Raul Leis, et al., *Centroamérica: La guerra de baja intensidad* (Managua: CRIES, 1986); Deborah Barry, Raul Vergara, and Rodolfo Castro, *La guerra total: La nueva ideología contrainsurgente en Centroamérica* (Managua: Cuadernos de Pensamiento Propio, CRIES, 1986); Frank R. Barnett, B. Hugh Tovar, and Richard H. Shultz (eds.), *Special Operations in U.S. Strategy* (Washington, D.C.: National Defense University Press, 1984); Lord and Barnett, *Political Warfare*; and Michael T. Klare and Peter Kornbluh (eds.), *Low Intensity Warfare: Counterinsurgency, Proinsurgency, and Antiterrorism in the Eighties* (New York: Pantheon Books, 1988).
8. Council for Inter-American Security, the Committee of Santa Fe, *A New Inter-American Policy for the Eighties* (Santa Fe: Council for Inter-American Security, 1980), p. 5.
9. John D. Waghelstein, "Post-Vietnam Counterinsurgency Doctrine," *Military Review* (May 1985): 42.
10. The Pentagon phrase came from its location on a spectrum in which conventional battlefield combat is considered midintensity and tactical and strategic nuclear warfare is high intensity. In terms of effect on the target country, this is high-cost, high-intensity warfare. Victim societies are literally shattered—militarily, economically, socially. Waghelstein's phrase *counterrevolutionary warfare*, or "total war at the grassroots level," is certainly more accurate. But if one is to understand how the United States is operating, the language of a policy should not be confused with the actual content of that policy.

11. Lord and Barnett, *Political Warfare*, p. xiii.

12. This included the creation of the National Endowment for Democracy in 1983. It also included the establishment of special "public diplomacy," political aid, and "democratic promotion" offices in the State Department, the White House, the Pentagon, and other branches of government. The Joint Chiefs of Staff formed a special low-intensity conflict division within the Department of Defense and within each military service and also reintroduced political and psychological warfare branches. The Pentagon even drafted a PSYOPS "master plan" at the behest of a presidential directive, and the National Security Council set up a top-level "board for low-intensity conflict." See Richard H. Shultz, Jr., "Low-Intensity Conflict: Future Challenges and Lessons from the Reagan Years," *Survival* (July-August 1989). See also Alfred H. Paddock, Jr., "Military Psychological Operations," in Lord and Barnett, *Political Warfare*, p. 50. Paddock is the former director of psychological operations in the Office of the Secretary of Defense. For a good summary of "public diplomacy," see Peter Kornbluh, *Nicaragua: The Price of Intervention* (Washington, D.C.: Institute for Policy Studies, 1987).

13. Carnes Lord, "The Psychological Dimension in National Strategy," in Lord and Barnett, *Political Warfare*, p. 31. Lord was a top-level NSC official in the first Reagan administration.

14. See Carnes Lord, "The Political Dimension in National Strategy," in Lord and Barnett, *Political Warfare*, p. 18.

15. Paddock, "Military Psychological Operations," p. 45. Paddock is the former director of psychological operations in the Office of the Secretary of Defense.

16. From Karl von Clausewitz, *On War*, as quoted by Harry G. Summers, Jr., *On Strategy: The Vietnam War in Context* (Carlisle, Penn.: U.S. Army War College, Strategic Studies Institute, 1981), p. 67.

17. In addition to the Santa Fe document, see Cleto Di Giovannti, Jr., "U.S. Policy and the Marxist Threat to Central America," *Backgrounder*, no. 128, October 15, 1980. According to di Giovannti, the document, considered the intellectual blueprint for Reagan administration policy toward Nicaragua, advocated "a well-orchestrated program [aimed at] . . . dislodging [the Sandinista government] through a determined, coordinated, targeted effort."

18. Nicaraguan analysts misinterpreted the concept of low-intensity warfare as one that ran counter to the possibility of a U.S. invasion of a target country. This confusion was heightened by Washington's use of deception itself as a calculated policy instrument. But invasion never stopped being one of many available policy instruments for U.S. strategists. This confusion derives from misconstruing the relationship between tactics and strategy in U.S. policy as well as between means and ends. In the type of warfare in which the objective is not to annihilate the enemy's military forces but to politically defeat them, an invasion is a tactical instrument to secure strategic objectives, not the strategy itself. In the U.S. war against Nicaragua, invasion was always an option. The threat of invasion served numerous objectives of the war, while the possibility that it would actually be carried out remained real.

In Grenada, for instance, the United States invaded after the revolution had committed political suicide; the invasion was a "mopping-up" operation. The U.S. strategy against Grenada was not to build toward an invasion; rather, it was to isolate and suffocate the tiny country, a destabilization strategy (1981–1983) that helped create the fissures in the New Jewel Movement. In Panama, the U.S. anti-Noriega destabilization campaign (1986–1989) thoroughly altered all internal and international variables until conditions facilitated the December 1989 invasion. But this invasion was not the strategy. The objective was to annihilate Panamanian nationalism as a political force that might counter U.S. interests in that geopolitically strategic country. (In this context, Manuel

Noriega functioned as the heir, unworthy though he may have been, of the nationalist leader Omar Torrijos.) The strategy comprised an ideological siege of the Noriega regime, economic embargo, coercive diplomacy, and complex internal political intervention operations. The invasion was merely the use of a tactical military instrument to ensure a political victory for the United States, a victory ultimately secured with intervention in the May 1989 elections and subsequent coercive diplomacy.

19. Richard H. Shultz, Jr., "Political Strategies for Revolutionary War," in Lord and Barnett, *Political Warfare*, p. 115.

20. *Psychological Operations in Guerrilla Warfare*, a manual prepared by the CIA for the contras. Vintage Books translated and published the document with the subtitle *The CIA's Nicaragua Manual* (New York: Vintage Books, 1985), pp. 70, 80–90.

21. Régis Debray, *Revolution in the Revolution?* (New York: Monthly Review Press, 1967). How this worked in the preelectoral period is thoroughly analyzed and documented in Robinson and Norsworthy, *David and Goliath*.

22. The precursor to the CIA was the World War II–era Office of Strategic Security.

23. The U.S. Senate's Church Committee estimated that at least nine hundred covert operations were carried out between 1960 and 1975 alone. For a summary of this conclusion, see Jonathan Marshall et al., *The Iran-Contra Connection* (Boston: South End Press, 1987), p. 206. Former CIA officer John Stockwell estimated that since its inception, the CIA has carried out up to twenty thousand covert actions (cited in Robinson and Norsworthy, *David and Goliath*, p. 15). Another former CIA officer, Philip Agee, pointed out that just in Indonesia alone, between 500,000 and 1 million people were killed in the wake of the bloody coup against the Sukarno regime that the CIA orchestrated. See Philip Agee, *Inside the Company: CIA Diary* (London: Bantam Books, 1976), p. ix. For some studies on CIA covert operations and their consequences, see the sources listed in the following footnote.

24. These defectors included Philip Agee, John Stockwell, Ralph McGehee, and David MacMichael. Perhaps the most well known is Agee, who published *Inside the Company*. Another well-known account is by investigators Víctor Marchetti and John D. Marks, *The CIA and the Cult of Intelligence* (New York: Dell, 1974), whose publication the CIA tried to prevent.

25. There are hundreds of books published about CIA covert operations abroad. For an excellent summary of some of the most well-documented operations, see William Blum, *The CIA: A Forgotten History* (London: Zed Press, 1986).

26. Two of the original NED founders noted, "Since the advent of the Cold War, the United States has worked abroad politically, mainly covertly, with direct government action and secret financing of private groups." This U.S. political intervention capacity "is necessary for protecting U.S. security interests," but efforts to date have proven inadequate. "[The] various covert means for filling the political gap in U.S. policy solved some short-term needs, but did not provide effective long-term solutions. Covert political aid provided directly by the U.S. government is limited in its effectiveness by the fact that political movements are uncomfortable with such direct contacts, fearing that their independence would be compromised" (William E. Hunter and Michael Samuels, "Promoting Democracy," *Washington Quarterly* [Summer 1981]:54).

27. The *New York Times*, June 1, 1986, noted that NED is a "combination of Government money, bureaucratic flexibility and anti-Communist commitment . . . which mixes public funds and private interests." The NED's work "resembles the aid given by the Central Intelligence Agency in the 1950s, 60s and 70s to bolster pro-American political groups."

28. Raymond D. Gastil, "Aspects of a U.S. Campaign for Democracy," in Ralph M. Goldman and William A. Douglas (eds.), *Promoting Democracy: Issues and Opportunities* (New York: Praeger, 1988), p. 49; Gastil was an adviser to Project Democracy.

29. GAO, *Events Leading to the Establishment of the National Endowment for Democracy*, GAO/NSIAD-84-121 (Washington, D.C.: GAO, July 6, 1984). See also Ralph M. Goldman, "The Democratic Mission: A Brief History," in Goldman and Douglas, *Promoting Democracy*, pp. 18–22.

30. Goldman, "The Democratic Mission," p. 19.

31. Among those on the APF board were Lane Kirkland of the AFL-CIO, former Republican National Committee chair William Brock, former Democratic National Committee chair Charles Manatt, international vice president for the U.S. Chamber of Commerce Michael Samuels, Frank Fahrenkopf, Representative Dante Fascell, Zbigniew Brzezinski, John Richardson, and Henry Kissinger. The APF was chaired by Allen Weinstein, who would later go on to play a critical role in the program of U.S. intervention in the Nicaraguan elections.

32. See *AIFLD in Central America: Agents as Organizers* (Albuquerque, N.M.: Resource Center, 1987).

33. For the best summary of the creation and modus operandi of the NED, see *National Endowment for Democracy (NED): A Foreign Policy Branch Gone Awry* (Washington, D.C./Albuquerque, N.M.: Council on Hemispheric Affairs/Inter-Hemispheric Education Resource Center, 1990).

34. See ibid.; and Richard Hatch and Sara Diamond, "The World Without War Council," *Covert Action Information Bulletin*, no. 31 (Winter 1989): 58–61.

35. See Robert Parry and Peter Kornbluh, "Iran-Contra's Untold Story," *Foreign Policy* (Fall 1988): 5, 9, for background on Raymond. For his relation with North, see *Report of the Congressional Committees' Investigation of the Iran-Contra Affair* (Washington, D.C.: GPO, 1988), and particularly Raymond's deposition before the congressional committees in Appendix B of the report (vol. 22, pp. 1–520). See John Spicer Nichols, "*La Prensa:* The CIA Connection," *Columbia Journalism Review* (July-August 1988): 13, for mention of Raymond's NSC role as liaison with the NED.

36. Parry and Kornbluh, "Iran-Contra's Untold Story"; and Nichols, "*La Prensa.*"

37. Memorandum from Walter Raymond to William Clark, attached to memorandum from Scott Thompson to Carles Wick, January 25, 1983. Quoted in *National Endowment for Democracy*, pp. 12–13.

38. Ibid.; and Parry and Kornbluh, "Iran-Contra's Untold Story."

39. Goldman, "The Democratic Mission," p. 21; and *National Endowment for Democracy*. Fascell chaired the House Subcommittee on International Operations.

40. Richard F. Staar, *Public Diplomacy: USA versus USSR* (Stanford, Calif.: Hoover Institution Press, 1986), pp. 297–299. Staar published the unclassified three-page directive but did not indicate if this unclassified version was the full text of the original classified version. The directive contained four aspects, but two, an international information committee and an international broadcasting committee, appeared to overlap. Also John Kelly, "National Endowment for Reagan's Democracies," *The National Reporter* (Summer 1986), cited an August 1983 memorandum by one top State Department official classified as "secret-sensitive" that listed four components of the "public diplomacy" program: information, political, covert, and a "quasi-governmental institute." The State Department official was Mark Palmer, who in 1990 was appointed to the NED board of directors.

41. See Kornbluh, *Nicaragua*.

42. Staff members from the House Foreign Affairs Committee recommended a full investigation into the matter, but Fascell refused to act. OPD chief Otto Reich was appointed ambassador to Venezuela.

43. Kelly, "National Endowment."

44. National Endowment for Democracy Act (Public Law [PL] 98–164).

45. From its inception in 1983 to its fiscal year (FY) 1990 allocation by Congress, the NED has received approximately $150 million in public moneys. According to NED's public documentation, the congressional allocations account for some 99 percent of its funding. See NED annual reports. It is clear from the study of its operations in Nicaragua, however, that NED spending is so interlocked with other direct and indirect, secret and public U.S. government spending that talk of fixed budgets is not all that meaningful.

46. For these details, see *National Endowment for Democracy*, pp. 23–39.

47. Gastil, "Aspects of a Campaign," pp. 28–29.

48. The NED was involved in Nicaragua long before the 1989 electoral process. In fact, virtually since the moment of its inception, the NED has been heavily involved in Nicaragua, synchronizing its work there with the Reagan administration's policy, including the contra operation. For example, in 1985 Walter Raymond requested that Carl Gershman facilitate NED funding of a contra political project, given that the Boland amendment prohibited direct U.S. funding for the contras at that time. See *National Endowment for Democracy*. Virtually all of the key Project Democracy participants later became deeply involved in the Nicaraguan electoral process.

49. For a detailed breakdown of the structure of interlocking boards of directors from NDI, the NRI, the NED, and the other "private" groups (Delphi, Freedom House, Center for Democracy, etc.) that intervened in the Nicaraguan elections, see *National Endowment for Democracy*; and *The Democracy Offensive* (Albuquerque, N.M.: Resource Center, 1989). Both these publications provide diagrams and flow charts.

50. This "public-private" fusion in U.S. foreign policy has been deepening since the 1970s. It is in part a functional requirement of engagement in low-intensity conflicts. Former secretary of the army John O. Marsh noted in this respect, "The twilight battlefield of low-intensity conflicts includes not only unconventional warfare in the military sense, but also economic, political and psychological warfare. This is an enormous area in which private-sector resources can be used. We must find a way to incorporate into a grand strategy the total resources of our society, so as to address those needs essential to our security" (John O. Marsh, Jr., "Special Operations in US Strategy," in Barnett, Tovar, and Shultz, *Special Operations*, p. 24).

51. Lord and Barnett, *Political Warfare*, p. xiii.

52. For an excellent account of these types of elections put together in Washington and exported to the target countries as part of war policy, see Edward S. Herman and Frank Brodhead, *Demonstration Elections: U.S.-Staged Elections in the Dominican Republic, Vietnam, and El Salvador* (Boston: South End Press, 1984).

53. These were Argentina, Brazil, and Uruguay. For a good summary, see Ronaldo Munck, *Latin America: The Transition to Democracy* (London: Zed Press, 1989). The Reagan administration's policy toward the South American military dictatorships was one of "quiet diplomacy," or low-key support for these regimes coupled with gentle encouragement of a return to civilian rule. The key distinction between the so-called transitions to democracy in these Southern Cone countries and the U.S.-promoted regime changes later in the decade (the Philippines, Chile, Panama, Paraguay, etc.) is that in the former, U.S. intervention was an external adjunct to endogenous processes, whereas in the latter, endogenous developments were transformed by external intervention.

54. In this intersection, the United States may make trade-offs, but these are concessions to local elites; the fundamental reality of foreign (U.S.) domination of national life is rarely altered.

55. For details, see *U.S. Electoral Assistance and Democratic Development* (Washington, D.C.: Washington Office on Latin America, 1990).

56. It is important to note that the United States is promoting a new international division of labor based on neoliberal free-market schemes. This is occurring particularly in Latin America through the reinsertion of Latin American economies into the world market as export platforms integrated into the U.S. productive process. This process involves the intersection of interests between the United States and a new breed of Latin American elites—the so-called neoconservative New Right, or the modernizing technocrats, epitomized by Presidents Carlos Salinas de Gortari of Mexico and Fernando Collor de Mello of Brazil. Through political and economic aid programs, diplomatic strategies, and electoral intervention, the United States has been cultivating these new elites and helping them gain power and implement neoliberal models. These new technocratic elites swept to power in Central America in 1989 and 1990: Alfredo Cristiani in El Salvador, Rafael Callejas in Honduras, Rafael Calderón in Costa Rica, and Jorge Serrano in Guatemala. All four candidates enjoyed the support of U.S. groups tied to the NED. For discussions, see "La nueva derecha Centroamericana," *Pensamiento Propio* (June 1990): 30–38; and "Special Issue: A Decade of Challenges, Latin America in the 1990s," *Latin American Press*, July 19, 1990; Gabriel Gasper Tapia, "Los procesos electorales y su impacto," *Polémica*, no. 11 (Segunda Época, 1990). The theorists of the new political interventions stress that the 1980s/1990s neoliberal free-market models are the economic component to "democratization." See, for instance, John D. Sullivan, "A Market-Oriented Approach to Democratic Development: The Linkages," in Goldman and Douglas, *Promoting Democracy*.

57. This characterization was made to me by David MacMichael.

58. Ralph M. Goldman, "The Donor-Recipient Relation in Political Aid Programs," in Goldman and Douglas, *Promoting Democracy*, pp. 59, 66–68.

59. See "Democracy's Difficult Birth in Haiti and the Philippines," *Insight*, December 28–January 4, 1987, pp. 26–28.

60. The Philippine Left and sectors of the mass, popular movement made a serious tactical mistake of boycotting the elections, with the reasoning that Ferdinand Marcos would steal them anyway and then legitimize his dictatorship. But the population overwhelmingly wanted to partake in these elections as an act of rejection of Marcos and of desire for democratic change. The Left boycott thus helped concentrate both popular and elite support around Cory Aquino. And because she was the widow of the popular Philippine politician Benigno Aquino, murdered by Marcos henchmen, Corazon Aquino enjoyed a special popularity as an individual.

61. U.S. Senate, Select Committee to Study Governmental Operations with Respect to Intelligence Activities, *Covert Action in Chile, 1963–1973* (Washington, D.C.: GPO, 1975).

62. For an excellent summary of the U.S. policy shift toward Chile between 1985 and 1988 and U.S. actions in that period, see Martha Lyn Doggett, "Washington's Not-So-Quiet Diplomacy," *NACLA Report on the Americas* 22, no. 2 (March-April 1988): 29–38. The article cited Elliot Abrams, who declared in 1986, "The strengthening of the far Left in Chile resulting from [a failure to return to democracy] could have a negative impact on some still fragile democracies elsewhere in the region and jeopardize U.S. interests" (p. 37).

63. For an overview, see Peter Winn, "U.S. Electoral Aid in Chile: Reflections on a Success Story" (paper presented at the Washington Office on Latin America [WOLA] conference, "U.S. Electoral Assistance and Democratic Development," Washington, D.C., January 19, 1990).

64. This was said by Frank Greer, "media consultant" for the NDI, in testimony before the Bipartisan Commission for Free and Fair Elections in Nicaragua, Washington, D.C., May 9, 1989.

65. Winn, "U.S. Electoral Aid in Chile."

66. In simplified terms, the United States came to identify the Panamanian Defense Force as the depository of nationalism in Panama and as a threat to U.S. political interests in the region, particularly given the strategic importance of the Southern Command, the Panama Canal, and the international banking-financial center operating out of Panama City.

67. See "La nueva derecha Centroamericana."

68. See ibid.; *U.S. Electoral Assistance and Democratic Development;* "Panama: Reagan's Last Stand," *NACLA Report on the Americas,* 22, no. 4 (July-August 1988): 12–35.

69. Peter Rodman, special assistant to the president on national security affairs and counselor to the National Security Council, in testimony before the Bipartisan Commission for Free and Fair Elections in Nicaragua, Washington, D.C., May 9, 1989. Also, in an April 21, 1989, press conference in Senate Chambers, Senator Richard Lugar noted that U.S. involvement in the Panamanian elections "will provide credibility to our efforts to design a policy towards the elections in Nicaragua. These situations are indivisible."

· CHAPTER TWO

1. Interview, Washington, D.C., November 1987.

2. NED, Nicaragua "Fact Sheet," distributed to reporters in September 1988 after Congress approved a special $2 million NED supplement for Nicaraguan programs.

3. The United States portrayed the "democratic" opposition as having played a major role in overthrowing the Somoza dictatorship but having later been forced out of the anti-Somoza coalition by an armed minority—the FSLN. Most of the key figures in the internal opposition were members of the traditional elite. They did play a significant role in the anti-Somoza coalition but as a minority. The FSLN was clearly the majority force, which mobilized the Nicaraguan population against the dictatorship and was recognized by much of the population as its leadership. The elite anti-Somoza opposition, which was hoping for a smooth transition to a *"Somocismo* without Somoza," did everything possible to prevent a revolutionary outcome to the overthrow of Somoza.

4. Chamorro made these comments in a recorded talk with U.S. visitors in February 1985; these remarks were published in Agencia Nueva Nicaragua (ANN) dispatches datelined New York and Managua, March 19, 1985. For a deeper discussion on how the internal opposition actually operated during the contra war, see William I. Robinson and Kent Norsworthy, *David and Goliath: The U.S. War Against Nicaragua* (New York: Monthly Review Press, 1987), pp. 193–227.

5. For the most detailed insider's account of this period, as told by a top Carter official on Latin America, see Robert A. Pastor, *Condemned to Repetition: The United States and Nicaragua* (Princeton, N.J.: Princeton University Press, 1987). See also Shirley Christian, *Nicaragua: Revolution in the Family* (New York: Random House, 1985).

6. See Bob Woodward, *Veil: The Secret Wars of the CIA, 1981–1987* (New York: Simon and Schuster, 1987), p. 113, for the secret finding. The figure of at least $1 million was reported in the *Los Angeles Times,* March 3, 1985. The CIA also drew up contingency plans in 1980 for the overthrow of the Sandinistas. This was admitted by Carter's CIA director, Stansfield Turner, in Jay Peterzell, *Reagan's Secret Wars* (Washington, D.C.: Center for National Security Studies, 1984), p. 65. Peterzell cited a May 1983 interview with Turner in the *Baltimore Sun.* See also Christian, *Nicaragua,* for pre-1979 CIA operations.

7. Two months after Reagan took office, the NSC proposed an increase in the aid for "political moderates" and the "private sector" in Nicaragua begun under Carter.

8. These same groups were listed in an October 1980 document considered a platform statement for the Reagan-Bush candidacy: "U.S. Policy and the Marxist Threat to Central America," *Backgrounder*, no. 128, October 15, 1980. The document urged "vigorous support for the democratic sectors: The free trade unions, the church, the private sector, the independent political parties, the free press, and those who truly defend human rights." The CDN was formally established in October 1981 in an act attended by the U.S. ambassador to Managua. For the mentioned citation by the ambassador, see Roger Burbach, "Central America: End of U.S. Hegemony," *Monthly Review* (January 1982).

9. The AID program was announced in a September 30, 1981, U.S. Embassy bulletin in Managua and was signed by AID representative Gerald R. Wein and embassy official Roger Gamble. For further details, see Tom Barry, Beth Wood, and Deb Preusch, *Dollars and Dictators: A Guide to Central America* (Albuquerque, N.M.: Resource Center, 1982), p. 90. In 1982, the AID approved another $5.1 million for the COSEP, other CDN groups, and the Managuan archdiocese. But the Sandinista government prohibited the funds from being distributed because, it said in a letter, the AID's "motivations [were] designed to promote resistance and destabilize the revolutionary government."

10. Department of the Army, *Guide for the Planning of Counterinsurgency* (Washington, D.C.: Department of the Army, 1975), pp. 26–27.

11. U.S. House of Representatives, *Hearings Before a Subcommittee of the Committee on Appropriations, House of Representatives, Foreign Assistance and Related Program Appropriations for 1982*, part 5, p. 83; cited in Robinson and Norsworthy, *David and Goliath*, p. 216.

12. In 1983, press accounts reported on the finding, mentioning the $19 million figure for the contras, but they made no mention of further details. The document was obtained years later, in 1989, among materials released to congressional committees that had investigated the Iran-contra scandal. I obtained the finding in May 1989 from among several documents supplied by congressional sources: "Finding Pursuant to Section 601 of the Foreign Assistance Act of 1947. As Amended, Concerning Operations Undertaken by the Central Intelligence Agency in Foreign Countries, Other Than Those Intended Solely for the Purpose of Intelligence Collection." The document, stamped "secret," was heavily censored. Among the information whited out were names of individuals and organizations in the internal opposition that were recipients of the CIA funds as well as names of neighboring countries that were brought into the CIA program.

13. In *Congressional Record* (Senate), June 23, 1989, Senator Tom Harkin asserted that "the CIA is operating under an earlier finding that took place back in the early 1980s [and] that the CIA continues to operate within Nicaragua" (p. 53-1). Aides in Harkin's office later confirmed to me that the early 1980s finding that the senator made reference to was the 1983 Reagan authorization. See also *Newsweek*, October 26, 1987, which reported that such CIA spending totaled about $10 million a year.

14. When the Senate Select Committee on Secret Military Assistance to Iran and the Nicaraguan Opposition first released Gregg's May 18, 1987, testimony, this portion had been labeled classified by the NSC and had been censored out. On May 11, 1989, the NSC declassified it.

15. It should be noted that some of the internal opposition groups, including the Christian Democrats, as well as the opposition media organs were also benefactors of significant financial and material resources from other international sources outside of the United States. For example, West German Social Democratic and Christian Democratic groups provided significant funding to their Nicaraguan counterparts.

16. A great deal of literature exists on the 1984 elections and on the U.S. strategy toward them. For an overall summary, see William I. Robinson and Kent Norsworthy, "Elections and U.S. Intervention in Nicaragua," *Latin American Perspectives* 12, no. 2 (Spring 1985): 22–34. For a discussion on the 1984 Nicaraguan elections compared to others in Central America, see John A. Booth and Mitchell A. Seligson (eds.), *Elections and Democracy in Central America* (Chapel Hill: University of North Carolina Press, 1989). For basic data on the 1984 elections, see "Las elecciones de 1984: Una historia que vale la pena recontar," *Envío* (January 1990). Among other reports from independent poll watchers, see Latin American Studies Association (LASA), "Report of the LASA Delegation to Observe the Nicaraguan General Election of November 4, 1984" (Pittsburgh: LASA Secretariat, University of Pittsburgh, 1984). For an eye-opening account of intrigues and positions regarding U.S. policymakers, see Roy Gutman, *Banana Diplomacy* (New York: Simon and Schuster, 1988), especially pp. 232–257.

17. Cruz admitted this several years later in an interview with the *New York Times*, January 8, 1988.

18. See Gutman, *Banana Diplomacy*, p. 241. Cruz's real intentions remain controversial. Although he declared before arriving in Managua that he had no intention of actually running, and although it is clear that the opposition as a whole did not intend to seriously participate in the electoral process, Cruz might have later reconsidered running after entering into negotiations with the Sandinistas in Managua. Gutman described a critical meeting in October between Cruz and Sandinista leader Bayardo Arce at a Socialist International conference in Rio de Janeiro, mediated by Willy Brandt and Carlos Andrés Pérez. According to this account, after much acrimonious and on-again, off-again negotiation, Cruz and Arce finally reached agreement over the opposition's participation, but Cruz was unable to secure the approval of the other opposition leaders in Managua and was unwilling to proceed unilaterally with the agreement (pp. 246–253).

19. *Washington Post*, July 30, 1984.

20. The CDN itself almost split on the issue of whether to boycott. Several parties were resentful of U.S. pressures, particularly the Social Christian Party (PSC), which at the time was the most influential of the opposition parties (really, the only one with any significant influence in 1984). The PSC had fielded its own candidates, which were withdrawn in favor of Cruz's candidacy.

21. This was alleged by the party's treasurer Gustavo Mendoza. See *The Nation*, May 10, 1986, p. 639.

22. *New York Times*, November 11, 1984.

23. Gutman, *Banana Diplomacy*, pp. 253–254.

24. International groups reaching this conclusion included the British Labor Party, the European Economic Community, the Washington-based International Human Rights Law Group, the Canadian Roman Catholic church, and LASA.

25. For an excellent analysis of how the United States has staged "demonstration elections" as a component of overall U.S. policy in specifically targeted countries, see Edward S. Herman and Frank Brodhead, *Demonstration Elections: U.S.-Staged Elections in the Dominican Republic, Vietnam, and El Salvador* (Boston: South End Press, 1984).

26. Quoted in Peter Kornbluh, *Nicaragua: The Price of Intervention* (Washington, D.C.: Institute for Policy Studies, 1987), p. 176.

27. For statistical summaries of the 1984 elections, see "Las elecciones de 1984"; *Monográfico: Cuenta regresiva en proceso electoral, analisis de resultados electorales* (Managua: Instituto Histórico Centroamericano, 1985).

28. For an analysis of the 1984 elections from this point of view, see Edwin Saballos, "Nicaragua: Amargo despertar," *Pensamiento propio* (March 1990): 11–15.

29. The other 35–40 percent might have been non-Sandinista votes but were not organized behind Cruz. Votes against the Sandinistas did not necessarily imply votes for the U.S.-backed candidates. The character of the 1984 elections was broadly pluralistic and multiparty. In the next elections, the United States stepped in to polarize the process and formulate the elections as a plebicite, organizing the electorate around Violeta Chamorro.

30. In his book *Banana Diplomacy*, Roy Gutman argued that before the abstentionist line was consolidated, two positions were discussed in Washington: a "hard-line" boycott-and-discredit line and a "moderate" participate-and-put-the-Sandinistas-to-the-test line. Before the abstentionist option won out, the State Department attempted to assess possible electoral results. "The Sandinistas would have won free elections in their first three years in office, but with triple-digit inflation, lowered living standards, the draft, and increasing state control of the economy, an overwhelming victory was no longer assured in 1984," said one insider in describing the reasoning of those in the State Department who argued in favor of having the opposition participate in the 1984 elections (p. 233).

31. It should be remembered that abstention in the 1984 U.S. elections was more than 50 percent and that Reagan received a slim majority of votes. Thus, Reagan was elected by about 25 percent of U.S. citizens eligible to vote. Daniel Ortega was elected by more than 50 percent of eligible Nicaraguan voters.

32. Gutman, *Banana Diplomacy*, p. 255.

33. Interview, Managua, April 26, 1986; Ramírez was vice president of Nicaragua.

34. For a detailed summary of Nicaragua's global defense strategy and development in the military, political, diplomatic, ideological, and economic realms, see Robinson and Norsworthy, *David and Goliath*, Chapters 9–12.

35. For an account of Sandinista efforts to secure military assistance, first from the United States, and then from other Western countries, see Robert Armstrong, Robert Matthews, and Marc Edelman, "Sandinista Foreign Policy: Strategies for Survival," *NACLA Report on the Americas* 14, no. 3 (May-June 1985): 15–53.

36. For instance, Managua proposed repeatedly that it sign agreements proscribing foreign military bases and advisers in Nicaragua in exchange for a nonaggression commitment from Washington. Nicaragua even proposed that its land borders be collectively patrolled to guarantee that its territory was not being used to send arms to neighboring countries. In June 1984, the two governments opened talks in Manzanillo, Mexico, but Washington broke them off unilaterally in early 1985. Within the Contadora process, Nicaragua at first insisted that the agenda of regional negotiations be limited to security issues. The United States and its Central American allies replied that the problem was a lack of democracy in Nicaragua. Contadora tried to bridge the gap by introducing both security and domestic considerations at the negotiating table. Managua accepted this. In a classic diplomatic act, the Nicaraguans accepted three separate peace treaties that the Contadora Group drafted and presented to the Central Americans—including one that addressed electoral issues. One or another of the other four countries rejected these treaties, with the result that an accord was never signed under the auspices of the Contadora process.

37. U.N. Economic Commission for Latin America, *Nicaragua 1988* (México, D.F.: ECLA, 1988). For additional information on this report, see Kent Norsworthy, *Nicaragua: A Country Guide* (Albuquerque, N.M.: Inter-American Hemispheric Resource Center, 1990), pp. 66–68.

38. For summaries on the damage caused by the U.S. war, see Norsworthy, *Nicaragua*, pp. 59, 66–67; Robinson and Norsworthy, *David and Goliath*, pp. 145–155; Fallo del Caso, "Nicaragua vs. Estados Unidos: Acciones militares y paramilitares dentro y contra

Nicaragua," International Court of Justice, 1986; Paul Oquist, "Dinámica socio-política de las elecciones Nicaraguenses de 1990" (Managua: Instituto de Estudios Nicaraguenses, 1990); Richard Stahler-Sholk, "Stabilization, Destabilization, and the Popular Classes in Nicaragua, 1979–1988," *Latin American Research Review* 25, no. 3 (Fall 1990).

39. The Esquipulas Agreement is often referred to as the Arias plan, in reference to President Oscar Arias, who prepared one draft of a regional accord. In reality, the agreement grew out of five years of negotiations among the Central Americans sponsored by the Contadora Group of Latin American mediators. Shortly after taking office in 1986, Arias drafted a document together with Senator Christopher Dodd. The document, referred to by some commentators at the time as the Dodd plan, was then presented to the three other U.S. allies in Central America—Honduras, El Salvador, and Guatemala—in a February 1987 meeting in San José that excluded Nicaragua. The Dodd document was rejected by Guatemala, while Managua protested its exclusion from the meeting. Six months later, at the behest of the Contadora nations and as a result of private discussions between the Nicaraguans and the Costa Ricans, among other factors, the five presidents—who had held their first summit a year earlier, also in Esquipulas—met again. On the table were several documents, among them draft Contadora proposals as well as a modified version of the Arias February document. The Esquipulas Agreement was hammered out during forty-eight hours of closed-door negotiations on the basis of these documents and heavy input from Nicaragua and Costa Rica.

40. For summary discussion on this, see Robinson and Norsworthy, *David and Goliath*. For an analysis of the impact of the Iran-contra scandal on U.S. allies in Central America, see William I. Robinson and Kent Norsworthy, "In the Wake of Contragate: Wither the U.S. War," *CENSA's Strategic Report* (June 1987).

41. For a summary of this, William I. Robinson, "Nace un movimiento anti-contra en Honduras," see four-part ANN series datelined Tegucigalpa, March 15–18, 1987.

42. The official was Manuel Acosta Bonilla, a leader of the National Party, as told to me in an interview in Tegucigalpa, March 1987.

43. The best-known case was the revelation that the CIA and former U.S. ambassador to Costa Rica Lewis Tambs had flagrantly manipulated both the Monge and Arias governments between 1982 and 1986 to install a secret airstrip in the border region with Nicaragua. See *The Tower Commission Report* (New York: Random House, February 1987), pp. 468–475.

44. Arias told the Costa Rican newspaper *La nación*, March 1, 1989, that the United States should have patience in the anti-Sandinista struggle. "We must take advantage of this opportunity [the 1990 elections]. In a totalitarian system it is very difficult for a dictator to cede power overnight; we have to remove it from power gradually, step by step."

45. GAO, *Central America: Impact of U.S. Assistance in the 1980s* (Washington, D.C.: GAO, July 1989), p. 1. The report was not actually released in its final, published version until July 1989, but it had been commissioned nearly a year earlier, and several drafts circulated throughout late 1988 and early 1989. The reason for the one-year hiatus was that the GAO submitted drafts to numerous governmental agencies, including the AID, for their comments, before publishing the final report.

46. Despite its stated objective, Esquipulas was not, and could not be, a formula for resolving the civil war in El Salvador or the deep social cleavages in Guatemala and Honduras. This is not to say, of course, that Esquipulas II in general did not have direct bearing on the internal conditions in each country. Esquipulas opened up political spaces in Central American countries for the struggle of popular forces for authentic democratization. But although it was in appearance a regional pact for the resolution

of the conflicts in, and among, all five countries, Esquipulas was in essence a formula for working out an accommodation between Nicaragua and the elite regimes in the other four countries.

47. U.S. foreign policy is often exercised behind the backs of the public by an elite that controls the political and economic strings of society. Nevertheless, it is also a process in which different factions and institutions that make up the U.S. state have influence over varied quotas of decisionmaking at given moments. Tactical and strategic differences as well as personal and institutional rivalries are played out in disputes for control over policy. This "diffusion" of foreign policy making power within an elite (which is tiny in number relative to the population) can make moments of transition and redefinition appear highly contradictory.

48. *New York Times*, August 26, 1987.

49. Ironically, the effort turned out less to be Chileanization modeled after the campaign against Allende than Chileanization modeled after the NED project in the 1988 Chilean plebiscite.

50. This phase involved a greater direct role for the U.S. Embassy in Managua. A few days after the signing of Esquipulas, U.S. Embassy officials in Managua announced they were in the process of strengthening ties to the "democratic opposition" so as to gain increased influence. The Interior Ministry reported that it detected no fewer than 280 contacts between U.S. Embassy officials they identified as CIA agents and opposition figures in 1987. For details, see William I. Robinson, "Special Report: The 'Chileanization' of the Nicaragua Counterrevolution?" *Central America Information Bulletin* year 5, no. 6, February 24, 1988.

51. *New York Times*, August 26, 1987.

52. Robinson, "Special Report."

53. Ibid.; *El nuevo diario*, January 16, 1988; and ANN news dispatch, Managua, January 16, 1988.

54. See United Press International (UPI) news dispatch, datelined Washington, August 1, 1988.

55. UPI, cable, August 7, 1988.

56. Essentially, Bergold had argued for the "civic" opposition strategy well before its time had come. In 1984, he argued that the opposition should participate in the elections instead of boycotting them. Bergold's positions evoked the ire of Abrams, who exercised an inordinate amount of control over Central American policy for an assistant secretary of state. With Bergold's departure, the ambassadorial post remained vacant for months (reflecting the policy transition in Washington) until Melton finally arrived in April 1988. See, among other sources, Gutman, *Banana Diplomacy*, p. 234. Anthony Quainton, Bergold's predecessor, had also had disagreements with Reagan policy and had also embarrassed Washington with such comments as "if by democracy you mean popular participation, then the Sandinista government is very democratic" (p. 234). When the Reagan administration launched its black propaganda about alleged Sandinista "anti-Semitism," Quainton sent a wire to Foggy Bottom asserting that the embassy could find no proof of this. See Gutman, *Banana Diplomacy*, p. 234.

57. For background, see "State Department Hard-Liner, Ousted from Nicaragua, Scheduled to Be Tapped for Brazilian Post," *News and Analysis* (Council on Hemispheric Affairs), June 6, 1989.

58. Documents classified as "secret/sensitive" and reviewed by congressional committees during the Iran-contra investigations revealed Melton's extensive activities in the underground Iran-contra network. Melton's specific role was liaison between Abrams and the network of right-wing groups that worked with the government in illegal procontra operations. These groups were led by the fringe rightist John Singlaub,

head of the World Anti-Communist League. I obtained the memos from congressional sources; the memos were published in part in Robert Cohen, "New U.S. Ambassador Key Figure in Contragate," *Central America Information Bulletin* year 5, no. 16, May 11, 1988, pp. 2, 3.

59. *Washington Post*, August 7, 1988.

60. These were statements made to local and foreign reports in Managua, reproduced in Robert García and William I. Robinson, "Special Report: The Melton Plan, Chronicle of a Destabilization Plot Foretold," in *Central America Information Bulletin* year 5, no. 25, August 10, 1988, pp. 1–6.

61. For instance, on April 27, Melton met with Virgilio Godoy of the Independent Liberal Party and urged him to work toward opposition unity. On June 9, Melton met with Conservative Party leader Fernando Zelaya, urging his party to help organize a strike of doctors, nurses, and teachers that, Melton said, would attract broad international attention. Embassy official John Hope held a series of meetings with Ramiro Gurdían, Enrique Bolaños, and other COSEP leaders to discuss anti-Sandinista programs.

62. The appropriation was approved several weeks after its introduction on May 5 by the House Foreign Operations Subcommittee and was then dispensed at the September 15, 1988, NED board meeting. See NED, "Meeting of the Board of Directors, September 15, 1988, Washington, D.C.," notes on the public portion of the meeting.

63. *Washington Times*, July 13, 1988.

64. Wright made these statements on September 20, 1988. See *New York Times* and *Washington Post*, September 21, 1988.

65. There were several video films of the incident. One was aired abroad, by CNN and several U.S. networks, and did not actually film the police/demonstration clashes as the violence began. Another was filed by Nicaraguan television and aired on national news. This version did show protesters initiating the violence by attacking police with sticks, stones, and even chains. Opposition leaders claimed the film was manipulated by the government. I saw a third filming, done by activists from Virgilio Godoy's PLI who helped organize the demonstration. A copy of the video was sent to the PLI representative in the United States, Enrique Gabuardi, who in December 1989, nearly eighteen months later, provided me with a duplicate. In this version, the marchers' provocations are unmistakable.

66. The manual was published under the title *The CIA's Nicaragua Manual* (New York: Bantam Books, 1985), pp. 80–90. Under the subtitle "Ways to Lead an Uprising at Mass Meetings," the manual described these disturbances as "preconditioning campaigns," to "be aimed at the political parties, professional organizations, students, laborers, the masses of the unemployed, and any other sector of society that is vulnerable. . . . Mass concentrations and meetings are a powerful tool, [and] fusion occurs in tight connection with mass meetings." When conditions are ripe at these meetings the masses will be incited to violently confront the government by political "cadre" in the crowd. "Anti-government hostility must become generalized." Only when the political "cadre" have created "great hostility against the regime" can the government be overthrown (pp. 79–81).

67. Among these reports were Georges A. Fauriol, "The Third Century: U.S. Latin American Policy Choices for the 1990s" (Washington, D.C.: Center for Strategic and International Studies, 1988); L. Francis Bouchey, Roger Fontaine, David C. Jordan, and Gordon Sumner, Jr., "Santa Fe II: A Strategy for Latin America in the Nineties" (Washington, D.C.: Committee of Santa Fe, August 1988); and Richard Stone, "Mexico, Central America and the Caribbean," in *Mandate for Leadership III: Policy Strategies for the 1990s* (Washington, D.C.: Heritage Foundation, 1988), pp. 538–563.

68. *Peace Through Democracy: A Bi-Partisan Initiative for the Central American Crisis* (Freedom House Working Group on Central America, October 1988). Among those on the working group were representatives from the NED and its different grantees, including Penn Kemble and William Doherty (AIFLD, PRODEMCA, etc.); the contra lobbyist Robert Leiken; and Mark Falcoff from the conservative American Enterprise Institute.

69. Quoted in *The Nation*, May 1, 1989, p. 58.

70. The Bipartisan Accord was published on March 25, 1989, by the *New York Times*. The accord also said U.S. goals in Nicaragua, in addition to "democratization," were "an end to subversion and destabilization of its neighbors; and end to Soviet block military ties that threaten U.S. and regional security."

CHAPTER THREE

1. Angelo Codevilla, "Political Warfare," in Carnes Lord and Frank R. Barnett (eds.), *Political Warfare and Psychological Operations: Rethinking the U.S. Approach* (Washington, D.C.: National Defense University Press, 1988), p. 85. Codevilla was a political warfare specialist.

2. Aronson said this to a group of Nicaraguan opposition leaders in an April 1989 meeting in Washington, D.C., as told to me by a participant in the meeting.

3. For a description of such internal bickering, see Tony Jenkins, "The Nicaraguan Opposition: A Lack of Legwork," in *International Policy Report* (Washington, D.C.: Center for International Policy, February 1990).

4. For a deeper discussion on this role, see William I. Robinson and Kent Norsworthy, *David and Goliath: The U.S. War Against Nicaragua* (New York: Monthly Review Press, 1987), pp. 193–227.

5. Cited in Jenkins, "The Nicaraguan Opposition," p. 6.

6. And this did not include the Sandinistas' Far Left opponents, which included at least three groups but which remained outside of and opposed to U.S. policy.

7. Quoted in Lucía Gonzales, "Nicaragua: The Fragmented Internal Opposition," *Central America Information Bulletin* year 5, no. 28, September 21, 1988, p. 5.

8. Both quotes appeared in an October 31, 1988, report by the NDI. The first consultant was David Petts; the second, Analia de Franco.

9. NDI, "Nicaragua: Municipal Elections." This internal report is of an NDI survey mission, October 31, 1987, prepared by Martin Anderson and Willard Dupree. The NDI had argued against the contra strategy as counterproductive to U.S. interests and had maintained contacts with the internal opposition even during the harshest years of the contra war. The original NDI concept was to create a so-called democratic center, or a third way, between the "extremes" of the contras and the Sandinistas. NDI officials argued for a more long-term approach of gradually building up institutions that could confront *Sandinismo* through their own strength rather than through confrontation. The third-way strategy eventually dissipated as U.S. policy moved toward bipartisan consensus and electoral intervention. See my interview with President Brian Atwood and Executive Secretary Ken Atwood of the NDI, Washington, D.C., July 1989, published as an ANN special service, "El partido democrático vuelve a Nicaragua," Managua, August 1989.

10. NDI, "Nicaragua: Municipal Elections."

11. Phone interview, Washington, D.C., November 1987, cited in William Robinson, "The Chileanization of the Nicaraguan Counterrevolution," *Central America Information Bulletin* year 5, no. 6, February 24, 1988, p. 5. See also *New York Times*, August 26, 1987, and October 15, 1987.

12. October 31, 1988, NDI report.

13. NDI program assistant Michael Stoddard in testimony before the Bipartisan Commission for Free and Fair Elections in Nicaragua, Washington, D.C., May 10, 1989. (I attended these hearings.)

14. NED, "Programs of the Endowment and Its Institutions in Nicaragua" (1988; updated, Fall 1989; executive summary).

15. NDI, "Nicaragua: Developing the Organization Capabilities of the Civic Opposition" (August 1987, internal report).

16. NDI, "Nicaragua: Municipal Elections."

17. Eight concrete areas of work for opposition and U.S. organizers were identified: achieving unification, strengthening communications, conducting electoral analysis, developing a message, negotiating with the Nicaraguan government, bringing in campaign specialists, planning polls, and setting up electoral observer teams.

18. Internal August 1988 NED document summarizing State Department/NED strategy meeting, provided to me by a source close to the meeting.

19. Ibid.

20. Chiqui Reyes Gavilán was recommended to Carl Gershman by Max Singer, the New Right activist from PRODEMCA and the Committee for the Free World who had developed contra support programs. For Singer's background, see *New York Times*, April 21, 1985; and Edgar Chamorro, *Packaging the Contras: A Case of CIA Disinformation* (New York: Institute for Media Analysis, 1987), p. 52.

21. Among other polls that backed this interpretation at the time, see "Encuesta de opinión sobre la paz y la democracia en Nicaragua y Centroamérica," *Encuentro*, no. 25 (September–December 1988). It showed a full 60 percent of the electorate was undecided in mid-1988.

22. These positions included special personnel adviser to the director general of the Foreign Service and U.S. coordinator of a special North Atlantic Treaty Organization committee on the challenges of modern society.

23. Delphi was founded in 1976, but it expanded dramatically in the mid-1980s as the practice of NED-style political intervention snowballed. Its annual budget grew from $1.7 million in 1984, the year it began contracting with NED, to $7.3 million 1988. See Delphi annual report for 1988; and my phone interview with Von Ward for his background and for Delphi activities in Nicaragua and elsewhere, July 1989.

24. See Ben Bradlee, Jr., *Guts and Glory: The Rise and the Fall of Oliver North* (New York: Donald I. Fine, 1988), pp. 233–236.

25. For these and other Delphi grants, see NED annual reports, 1987–1989; and NED, "The NED and Its Programs in Nicaragua" (1989, executive summary), provided by NED's public relations office for reporters and the public.

26. Delphi, "National Endowment for Democracy, Grant with Delphi for the Implementation of the Project with Coordinadora Democrática Nicaraguense, Grant No. 88-524-P-039-57.2" (July 20, 1989), Delphi submitted this document to the NED.

27. NED memorandum summarizing notes taken by the April 1989 meeting participants, for circulation among NED officers, provided to me by sources close to the NED.

28. Ibid.

29. NDI, "Nicaragua: Municipal Elections."

30. This was told to me by one top member of the opposition who requested anonymity, April 1988.

31. May 5, 1989, press statement released by the White House Office of the Press Secretary.

32. She was in Managua on May 16, 17, and 18. For details, see *El nuevo diario*, May 19, 1989.

33. "Such an office will provide infrastructure for the 14 members parties so they can carry out normal party functions during the organization and mobilization periods" of the elections, stated the NRI report "National Republican Institute for International Affairs' Quarterly Report" for July 1–September 30, 1989, p. 17. An NRI memorandum dated August 11 stated, under the subheading "UNO General Secretariat," "In Carl [Gershman]'s mind, this program is ready to go. NDI and NRI have been asked to reprogram current funds in order to provide $100,000 each to set up the UNO office and get it going for two months" until a subsequent congressional appropriation was approved. According to the memo, Gershman had met in Costa Rica with the UNO finance committee over the summer: "He told them to send him the number of a bank account in Miami as soon as possible in order to receive $200,000 in start-up costs. Now that he has had time to think this through, he does not know who would be able to sign a grant agreement or even if one is necessary" (see Appendix A, document 6).

34. The memo, printed on NRI stationery, was not dated, but its content indicates that it was drafted in late August 1989.

35. See October 31, 1988, NDI report.

36. For details, see "Setting the Rules of the Game: Nicaragua's Reformed Electoral Law," *Envío* 8, no. 95 (June 1989): 25–34.

37. See "Nicaragua: Four More Years of War?" *Envío* 8, no. 97 (August 1989): 3–9.

38. Richard Lugar, April 21, 1989, press conference in Senate chambers.

39. The quote is from Paul Smith, Jr., who was with the USIA. Quoted in Lord and Barnett, *Political Warfare*, p. 38.

40. See U.S. PL 94-283, Section 441-E.

41. See *Congressional Record* (Senate), March 8, 1963, pp. 1519–1667. Among the extensive documentation officially recorded in the Senate *Congressional Record* on the hearings was a letter from Somoza's U.S. representative, Irving Davidson, to the Nicaraguan president: "I am operating behind the scenes. So far as Nicaragua is concerned, everyone with whom I am dealing knows that I am your registered representative; and everyone knows that much of the money I spend throughout the year is made available to me through your generosity." The hearings snowballed into a veritable scandal. Among other aspects, Somoza paid a bribe to Senator Homer E. Capehart, who in turn sent a letter to President Kennedy in September 1962 recommending that the White House invite the Nicaraguan president to Washington on an official state visit.

42. Fiallos quoted Bentson in testimony before the Subcommittee on Western Hemispheric Affairs of the House Foreign Affairs Committee, April 13, 1989. I was present at the hearings. Fiallos provided me with a copy of his testimony, which was also included in the *Congressional Record* (House), April 13, 1989.

43. The Nicaraguan government agreed to compromise on this demand: 40 percent of public funding was divided up according to the percentage of total votes pooled in the previous elections, and the other 60 percent was divided in equal parts among all participating parties, even those that might have been formed just weeks before the elections and that might have presented just sixty-three members nationwide as the minimum necessary to form a party. The government also agreed to equally partition among all candidates the thirty minutes each day on public television and the forty-five minutes on public radio set aside for the campaign. Parties' purchase of additional time in privately owned radio or periodicals was unlimited, and the law stated that no media outlets could discriminate in selling time slots or space.

44. As it turned out, a little less than 50 percent of the military vote went to the UNO, suggesting that conscription into the military did not necessarily mean political support for the Sandinistas.

45. It was a "damned if you do, damned if you don't" situation that the United States had created for the Sandinistas. The draft was unpopular, and therefore it hurt the FSLN electorally. But as the governing party the FSLN was responsible for organizing national defense and could not do away with the draft so long as the United States maintained its military siege. This is discussed in detail in Chapter 7.

46. Put on the defensive, the government agreed to grant candidates access to army bases to carry out campaign proselytizing. Permitting antidraft electioneering on military bases allowed the United States and its candidates inside Nicaragua to exploit the conditions imposed on the Sandinistas by U.S. military aggression to erode the FSLN electoral base. Yet even this concession did not satisfy the United States.

47. Bolaños admitted this in an interview with the *New York Times*, November 21, 1984.

48. See Jenkins, "The Nicaraguan Opposition," p. 7.

49. ANN dispatch, Managua, September 3, 1989.

50. The accusation was made to the ANN. See "Discrepancias en la UNO," Managua, September 6, 1989.

51. Ralph M. Goldman, "The Donor-Recipient Relation in Political Aid Programs," in Ralph M. Goldman and William A. Douglas, *Promoting Democracy: Opportunities and Issues* (New York: Praeger, 1988), p. 58.

52. "National Endowment for Democracy, Grant with Delphi for the Implementation of the Project with Coordinadora Democrática Nicaragüense, Grant Number 89-58.2," Delphi report submitted on November 30, 1989.

53. *New York Times*, September 4, 1989.

54. For details on the UNO nominations and on candidate Chamorro, see "Navegando el mapa electoral," *Envío* 8, no. 99 (October 1989): 3–15.

55. For summaries on Obando y Bravo's U.S. ties and on his role in the anti-Sandinista campaign, see Irene Selser, *Cardenal Obando* (Managua: Centro de Estudios Ecuménicos, 1989); Ana María Ezcurra, *Agresión ideológica contra la revolución Sandinista* (México, D.F.: Ediciones Nuevomar, 1983); Robinson and Norsworthy, *David and Goliath*, pp. 208–219, 241–248.

56. For the cardinal's role in the elections, see "Whose Side Was God On?" *CEPAD Report* (January-February 1990).

57. *Status Report on the Task Force on Humanitarian Assistance in Central America, Report on Phase III, May 1–August 31, 1989* (Washington, D.C.: AID, September 27, 1989). This money was from a total of $49.75 million appropriated by Congress for contra "humanitarian assistance." Although the funds were supposed to be for "medical assistance to civilian victims of the war" handled by Obando y Bravo's archdiocese, the AID report as well as Obando's office explained that they were used for establishing a national logistical network of communications and transportation for the archdiocese.

58. *La Prensa*, February 24, 1990. Note that *both* sides manipulated the religious issue during the campaign and that the FSLN also tried to present Ortega as a candidate reverent to religious sentiment and capable of working with the church. But the church hierarchy's own sentiment was with the UNO, and the hierarchy could hardly suppress its elation over Chamorro's victory. On February 27, 1990, Obando y Bravo officiated a mass for Chamorro, praising "her excellency" and extolling her as "the president of all Nicaraguans."

59. Daniel Wattenberg, "Opposition That Needs All the Help It Can Get," *Insight*, October 2, 1989, p. 13.

60. *Washington Times*, November 10, 1989.

61. Ibid.

62. This was told to me by a source from the Philippine Embassy in Washington. The breakfast was held on November 10 at Quayle's house.

63. *Washington Times,* November 10, 1989.

64. *Congressional Record* (House), October 4, 1989, p. H6642.

65. See, for instance, a UNO press statement drafted in English and distributed in Washington on September 14.

66. See *Congressional Record* (House), October 4, 12, and 17, 1989; and *Congressional Record* (Senate), October 12, 16 and 17, 1989.

67. *Congressional Record* (Senate), October 17, 1989, p. S13522.

68. David Obey (D-Wisc.), chair of House Subcommittee on Foreign Operations, *Congressional Record* (House), October 4, 1989, p. H6628.

69. Carl Gershman in testimony before the Foreign Operations Subcommittee of the House Foreign Affairs Committee, September 28, 1989. (I attended these hearings.)

70. The bill was approved by Congress on October 17, 1989 (PL 101-119).

71. AID, "Report to Congress (PL 101-119)" (Washington, D.C.: AID, November 1989).

72. The $5 million was broken down as follows: $4.12 million to the NDI and the NRI to support the UNO and the UNO's electoral organ, the Institute for Electoral Training and Promotion; $493,000 for the Free Trade Union Institute to support the UNO-allied opposition unions; $220,000 to the International Foundation for Electoral Systems for Via Cívica, a so-called civic education project run by the opposition. Carter's group got $250,000, and Weinstein's group got $75,000. See AID, "Report to Congress," for the breakdown. See Chapters 4 and 5 for more details on the media, civic groups, and trade unions.

73. Francisco Taboada, cited in Jacqueline Sharkey, "Anatomy of an Election: How U.S. Money Affected the Outcome in Nicaragua," *Common Cause Magazine* (May-June 1990): 24.

74. The Boston-based group Hemispheric Initiatives, which registered with the SEC as an official observer to the Nicaraguan electoral process, estimated that U.S. overt and covert spending on the elections came to $26.5 million (See "Nicaraguan Election Update" [Boston: Hemisphere Initiatives, October 16, 1989]. This estimate, however, does not take into account secret funding through other channels, as discussed in Chapter 6. According to Representative Nancy Pelosi (D-Calif.) (*Congressional Record* [House], October 4, 1989), the congressionally approved funds *alone* were the equivalent of allowing a foreign government to give $800 million to a U.S. candidate's campaign. In contrast, the Federal Election Commission (see *New York Times,* August 27, 1989) reported that the sixteen presidential candidates and aspirants to candidacy in the 1988 U.S. presidential elections spent a *combined* total of $210.7 million, or less than $1 per capita.

75. According to Peter Montgomery, "1980-1990: The Reagan Years," *Common Cause Magazine* (November 1990): 12, Bush spent a total of $70 million in public and private funds.

76. These one-page sheets given to "verifiers" were titled "Unión Nacional Opositora (U.N.O.): Boleta de censo Nicaragua."

77. David Obey, quoted in *Congressional Record* (House), October 4, 1989, p. H6628.

78. See NDI, "Summary Proposal, Nicaragua: Supporting Democratic Process" (December 5, 1989; memorandum to members of Congress), section A. Also see AID, "Report to Congress (PL 101-119)," Appendix III-B, pp. 1-3.

79. Ibid.

80. Quoted in Sharkey, "Anatomy of an Election," p. 27.

81. A copy of the letter, dated August 28, 1989, drafted in Spanish, and signed by Gershman, was provided to me by one of its recipients in the UNO coalition.

82. Letter from the NED to Freedom House program officer Barbara Futterman, dated October 10, 1989. The $10,900 was part of a larger $358,000 grant.

83. NRI, "Third Quarter Activities—Nicaragua Conference FY89 AID." According to this internal NRI report to the AID on activities in the third quarter of FY 1989, these seed moneys, provided before those forthcoming from the $9 million appropriation, "support[ed] the opposition parties during the registration period and . . . [provided] further assistance for infrastructure, organization, training, election monitoring, civic and voter-education."

84. I attended this luncheon.

85. One million dollars did actually go from the congressional appropriation to the council, but this was out of the $2 million provided directly to the UNO. The NDI and the NRI were able to provide $1.5 million to the IPCE without having to legally provide the corresponding quota to the council.

86. It is critically important to note that the particular alliances and disputes that took shape during the electoral campaign were conjunctural to the conditions at that time and quickly gave way to completely new alliances following the elections. Vice President Virgilio Godoy assumed leadership of a right-wing extremist faction, headquartered in the UNO Political Council, that bitterly opposed César, Lacayo, and the inner circle of Chamorro advisers, who were appointed to all of the cabinet positions. And as the Chamorro government began drawing up policies that the United States considered inappropriate or insufficiently belligerent vis-à-vis the Sandinista opposition, the U.S. Embassy began applying pressures on this inner circle and at the same time supporting the Godoy group.

One must remember, however, that individuals such as César and Lacayo are not mere U.S. puppets. Rather, they have their own political project, which converges in different ways with U.S. policy at different moments. Inevitably this convergence produces a senior and a junior partner, and the intensity of U.S. intervention often produces marionette relations, as was the case during the electoral campaign. With the Sandinistas in power, differences that the opposition had with U.S. impositions were subordinated to the anti-Sandinista effort.

87. For details on the coalition-center structure, see Goldman, "The Donor-Recipient Relation," pp. 68–73. Goldman stated, "Under this hypothetical structure, the center could be controlled by an executive committee. The center and the staff would adopt no policy positions; [policies] would be enunciated only by the parent coalition. Funds from foreign donors would go to the center acting strictly as a technical and logistical group. . . . This division of labor would facilitate provision of foreign funding" (pp. 70, 71).

CHAPTER FOUR

1. William A. Douglas and Michael A. Samuels, "Promoting Democracy," *Washington Quarterly* (Summer 1981): 60–61. Douglas was a high-level official from the American Federation of Free Labor Development, and Samuels was from the U.S. Chamber of Commerce. Both were commissioned to help conceptualize and draft programs for NED work in trade unions and private enterprise.

2. Delphi, "National Endowment for Democracy, Grant with Delphi for the Implementation of the Project with Coordinadora Democrática Nicaraguense, Grant No. 88-524-P-039-57.2" (July 20, 1989). This document was submitted to the NED.

3. Internal August 1988 NED document summarizing State Department/NED strategy meeting.

4. Ibid., p. 137.

5. In 1964, it was first revealed that the CIA had set up dummy foundations to launder funds for operations of the AFL-CIO's international affairs department and AFL-CIO–controlled international trade secretariats. New revelations and further details on the CIA links to the AFL-CIO and its organizations snowballed. The FTUI was formed in 1977 when the AFL-CIO resurrected the defunct Free Trade Union Committee. See, among other studies, Winslow Peck, "The AFL-CIA," in Howard Frazier (ed.), *Uncloaking the CIA* (New York: Free Press, 1980), pp. 262–265; Jonathan Kwitny, *Endless Enemies* (New York: Congdon and Weed, 1984), pp. 341–346; Tom Barry and Deb Preusch, *AIFLD in Central America: Agents as Organizers* (Albuquerque, N.M.: Resource Center, 1990). These revelations led the AID to assume a greater U.S. government role in direct financing of trade unions abroad, a role picked up by the NED with its creation in 1983.

6. NED, "Programs of the Endowment and Its Institutions in Nicaragua" (1988; updated, Fall 1989; executive summary). As one of the core-group intermediaries, the FTUI has handled the lion's share of NED funds grants—some $35 million in the first four years of NED operations.

7. NED, "Strengthening Democracy Abroad: The Role of the National Endowment for Democracy" (December 1984), cited in Barry and Preusch, *AIFLD*, p. 54.

8. Roy Godson, "Labor's Role in Building Democracy," in Ralph M. Goldman and William A. Douglas, *Promoting Democracy: Opportunities and Issues* (New York: Praeger, 1988), p. 135.

9. See NED annual reports.

10. See AIFLD 1988 Annual Report, Section D, "Latin America and the Caribbean," p. 23; and FTUI proposal to the NED for appropriations earmarked for Poland and Nicaragua, "Assistance for the Workers and Campesinos of Nicaragua" (December 16, 1989).

11. See FTUI, "Assistance for the Workers and Campesinos of Nicaragua" (December 16, 1988, proposal to the NED). In its January 1989 board meeting, the NED approved another $397,345 to complement these regional efforts.

12. See ibid.

13. Form letter from Lane Kirkland on AFL-CIO stationery, dated December 13, 1988.

14. Ibid. A Venezuelan government source also confirmed to me the CTV role and funding.

15. The Venezuelan unions had been one of the most important recipients of U.S. governmental and AFL-CIO assistance during the 1960s, when the U.S. labor programs for Latin America were getting off the ground. Over the years the CTV had become well trained and professional. (For details of U.S. support for the Venezuelan unions and the role of the unions in that country in the 1960s, see Robert J. Alexander, *The Venezuelan Democratic Revolution* [New Brunswick, N.J.: Rutgers University Press, 1964], pp. 17–18, 239.) In addition, the CTV supported the social democratic government of Carlos Andrés Pérez, who had developed a regional foreign policy in close coordination with the Bush administration and was seeking to play the role of arbiter in the Nicaraguan electoral process. Pérez's government was also supplying covert support to the Chamorro candidacy (see Chapter 5).

16. See William I. Robinson, "Special Report: The Melton Plan—Chronicle of a Destabilization Plot Foretold," *Central America Information Bulletin* year 5, no. 25, August 10, 1988, p. 6.

17. FTUI, "Free Trade Union Institute Proposal Nicaragua Election Supplemental" (August 22, 1989). This proposal was drafted after the NED provided the FTUI with $415,082 out of the June 1989 $2 million congressional appropriation for Nicaragua. After Congress appropriated another $1.5 million in special funds in August, and after discussions began on the $9 million, the NED instructed the FTUI to update and expand the August 22 proposal. The updated version appeared in an October 12, 1989 document, entitled "Free Trade Union Institute Proposal Nicaragua Election Second Supplement."

18. Ibid.

19. Ibid.

20. Ibid.

21. Noriega's role was indicated in internal NED memos supplied to me by sources close to the NED.

22. Form letter from David Jessup to unions, January 22, 1989. Curiously, the letter was sent out, not on AIFLD stationery, but on Jessup's personal letterhead, with his Maryland home address. The letter, however, instructed donators to send checks to "AIFLD-CUS" at AIFLD headquarters.

23. Barmon was not even accredited as a diplomat at the embassy in Managua. She had arrived from Honduras, where the United Federation of Honduran Workers (FUTH) had released a statement demanding that the Honduran government expel Barmon for interfering in internal Honduran trade union affairs and for "fomenting social confrontations in our country from abroad" (FUTH statement, Tegucigalpa, April 17, 1989).

24. "Teachers' Strike: U.S. Fans Flames of Discontent," Envío 8, no. 96 (July 1989): 8.

25. For a summary, see ibid.; and "Nicaragua or the United States—the Electoral Dilemma," Envío 8, no. 96 (July 1989): 3–7. Several opposition members interviewed by reporters affirmed that the U.S. diplomats had offered moral and financial support to strikers. U.S. chargé d'affaires John Leonard, in protesting the expulsions, said the two diplomats "were doing what diplomats normally do: meeting with people and learning about what's going on in Nicaragua. . . . They were meeting with people in Chinandega. It was a chance to get out of Managua, something our officers hadn't had a chance to do recently" (Press conference, Managua, May 25, 1989).

26. In a June 2, 1989, meeting with the teachers, President Ortega asked, "What was a labor attaché of the U.S. Embassy in Honduras doing in Nicaragua? And what was a secretary of economic and commercial relations doing in Nicaragua? What economic relations do we have with the United States? The only economic relationship we have with the Yankees is the relationship of them blockading our country." During the meeting, at the Olof Palme Convention Center in Managua, Ortega stated that the government recognized the teachers' grievances as legitimate and justified. He called on the teachers to assert their grievances with an understanding of the overall situation of war and economic crisis that the country was facing. At the same time, he accused the leaders of the strike movement of being agents of the United States who were exploiting legitimate grievances. The speech was published by Barricada, June 3, 1989. Later these statements were distorted. See, for instance, Carlos Vilas, "What Went Wrong?" NACLA Report on the Americas 24, no. 1 (June 1990): 12, who claimed that Ortega "accused the teachers of being pawns of the United States."

27. La Prensa, May 29, 1989.

28. Letter from Carl Gershman to David Dorn, August 7, 1989. For her efforts, Rivas Zeledón was named deputy minister of education for personnel after the Chamorro government was inaugurated. One of her first projects was to try replacing ANDEN with her federation, which she began promoting from within the Ministry of Education.

In the first four months of the Chamorro government, thousands of "Sandinista" teachers and Ministry of Education workers were fired and replaced by loyal members of Rivas Zeledón's parallel union. See "UNO Goes to School," *Envío* 9, no. 111 (October 1990): 12–15. In justifying this, Education Minister Sofanías Cisneros explained, "We don't want wise teachers; we want loyal ones" (p. 13).

29. Sam Sarkesian, "Low-Intensity Conflict: Concepts, Principles and Policy Guidelines," *Air University Press* (January-February 1985): 2.

30. Michael Stoddard, NDI program officer for Latin America, in testimony before the Bipartisan Commission for Free and Fair Elections in Nicaragua, Washington, D.C., May 10, 1989.

31. For example, see Orlando Nuñez, "La ideología como fuerza material, y la juventud como fuerza ideológica," in *Estado y clases sociales en Nicaragua* (Managua: CIERA, 1982).

32. Delphi, "Youth Voter Education and Training Project in Nicaragua" (May 1989, summary document submitted to the NED).

33. NED, "Programs of the Endowment."

34. Ibid.

35. See NED, "Youth Voter Education Project in Nicaragua" (June 1989, summary of the Delphi programs); Delphi, "CEFOJ Evaluation" (internal evaluation of the first year of the program).

36. Delphi, "CEFOJ Evaluation."

37. NRI, "Status of Nicaragua Conference, FY89—Second Stage" (internal memo).

38. NRI, "NRIIA Program Proposal: Nicaragua FY89."

39. Delphi, "Youth Voter Education."

40. Interview with Hector J. Arroliga, CEFOJ national leader, in the Miami-based newspaper *La prensa Centroamérica*, February 9, 1990.

41. See Delphi, "Delphi International Financial Report, Women Civic Education Projects, Grant No. 88-526-P-039-34.3" (April-June 1989).

42. Delphi, "Women's Voter Education and Training Project in Nicaragua" (May 1989, internal summary sheet on the women's project).

43. Ibid.

44. See, for instance, Department of the Army, *Guide for the Planning of Counterinsurgency* (Washington, D.C.: Department of the Army, 1975); William I. Robinson and Kent Norsworthy, *David and Goliath: The U.S. War Against Nicaragua* (New York: Monthly Review Press, 1987), p. 216. See also *Psychological Operations in Guerrilla Warfare*, the CIA manual prepared for the contras, which was translated and published by Vintage Books (New York: 1985).

45. The internal memo, prepared as a working document for an NED strategy session, was dated June 1989. It was provided to me by sources close to the NED.

46. Ibid.

47. White's involvement in the Reagan administration's Nicaragua programs was cited in a September 7, 1988, staff report of the House Committee on Foreign Affairs, "State Department and Intelligence Community Involvement in Domestic Activities Related to the Iran-Contra Affair." Another board member was Richard Stone, a roving U.S. ambassador to Central America in the early 1980s who was credited with bringing about the military unification of the contras. Stone is also vice president of Capital Bank, a Miami-based financial concern that had been accused of laundering drug funds and that held bank accounts for both the IFES and the NED. See Holly Sklar, "U.S. Wants to Buy Nicaragua's Elections—Again," *Zeta* (November 1989): 49–50.

48. Telephone interview with Richard Soudriette, October 6, 1989.

49. Interview with Henry Quintero, Washington, D.C., January 1990.

50. In 1987, Taboada received $22,000 from the NED to form a mothers of political prisoners group. The group considered all captured contras political prisoners, including the imprisoned former *Somocista* guardsmen. See NED, "Programs of the Endowment," for this funding. For details on Taboada's role and the role of the U.S. Embassy in forming the mothers' group, see William I. Robinson, "Special Report: The 'Chileanization of the Nicaraguan Counterrevolution?" *Central America Information Bulletin* year 5, no. 6, February 24, 1988, pp. 4–7.

51. "Via Cívica has good contacts with the female sector through its relationship with the mostly female federation of primary and secondary school teachers," which Rivas Zeledón headed, stated an IFES memo from Richard Soudriette to Carl Gershman, September 8, 1989.

52. NED internal memo, June 1989.

53. The account that follows is reconstructed from facts gathered by me in direct interviews with Via Cívica and UNO representatives as well as from a two-part report published in *Barricada*, October 10–11, 1989.

54. In an interview, Quintero laughed off this assertion (Washington, D.C., January 1990). Nevertheless, Nicaraguan immigration officials provided me with a copy of the immigration papers all entrants to the country are required to fill out, in which Quintero did in fact list himself as a CYPSA consultant. In addition, Carlos Quiñonez confirmed his meetings with Quintero and Soudriette, saying, "Yes, he [Quintero] could be described as a CYPSA consultant" (interview, Managua, December 1989).

55. See *Barricada*, October 10–11, 1989; and interview with Carlos Quiñonez, who admitted to receiving these funds and justified them as part of Via Cívica's legitimate "civic education activities," despite such irregularities as laundering the funds through CYPSA.

56. NED, "Nicaragua Proposal" (June 1989, document describing Nicaraguan programs funded under special congressional allocations).

57. Interview with Quintero.

58. Following Chamorro's inauguration, the Via Cívica became involved in the formation of right-wing "shock troops," or unofficial "political police." During the general strikes of May and July 1990, Via Cívica published lists of neighborhood and workplace leaders of the strikes. When students took over several high schools in Managua during the month of August to protest arbitrary firings of teachers suspected of sympathizing with the Sandinistas, Via Cívica activists were deployed to try dislodging the occupiers. In other protests, Via Cívica activists were used for crowd control. For these details on postelectoral Via Cívica activity, see "Update on Education," *Envío* 9, no. 111 (October 1990).

59. NED internal memos, including letter from NED financial officer Teresa A. B., January 8, 1990.

60. Raymond D. Gastil, "Aspects of a U.S. Campaign for Democracy," in Goldman and Douglas, *Promoting Democracy*, p. 36. Gastil was a top official at Freedom House, an organization that funneled hundreds of thousands of dollars in NED moneys for Nicaraguan projects, including the publication of anti-Sandinista propaganda.

61. For overall discussions on propaganda and the communications media with regard to U.S. policy toward Nicaragua, see Ana María Ezcurra, *Agresión Ideológica contra la revolución Sandinista* (México, D.F.: Ediciones Nuevomar, 1984); Edgar Chamorro, *Packaging the Contras: A Case of CIA Disinformation* (New York: Institute for Media Analysis, 1987); Peter Kornbluh, *The Price of Intervention* (Washington, D.C.: Institute for Policy Studies, 1987). For a detailed discussion of the content of U.S. media coverage of Nicaragua, see Jack Spence, "The U.S. Media Covering (Over) Nicaragua," in Thomas W. Walker (ed.), *Reagan Versus the Sandinistas: The Undeclared War on*

Nicaragua (Boulder, Colo.: Westview Press, 1987), pp. 182–201. For an analysis of radio warfare against Nicaragua, see Howard Frederick, "Electronic Penetration in Low-Intensity Warfare," in *Reagan Versus the Sandinistas*, pp. 123–142; Robinson and Norsworthy, *David and Goliath*, especially Chapters 1 and 7.

As a specialized communications agency, the USIA played an important technical role. The USIA grew out of a White House project in the early 1950s to develop a propaganda and psychological warfare capacity abroad. It was conceived of in a top-secret National Security Council report and established in 1953 as an agency reporting to the NSC. The report, issued by the president's Committee on International Information Activities, was later declassified and made available by the State Department, *Foreign Relations of the United States, 1952–1954*, vol. 2 (Washington, D.C.: GPO, 1984). For details, see Carnes Lord, "The Psychological Dimension in National Strategy," in Carnes Lord and Frank R. Barnett (eds.), *Political Warfare and Psychological Operations: Rethinking the U.S. Approach* (Washington, D.C.: National Defense University Press, 1989), pp. 13–37.

62. *Miami Herald*, November 20, 1985.

63. For an excellent and detailed analysis of U.S. media coverage of the Nicaraguan electoral process and its relation to U.S. policy toward Nicaragua, see David MacMichael and Edgar Chamorro, "Nicaragua Election Project: Pre-Election Final Report" (New York: Institute for Media Analysis, February 1990).

64. For background on these two radios, see Chamorro, *Packaging the Contras.* Chamorro was a CIA agent in charge of the contras' public relations at the time that these two radio stations were established. For a general discussion of the use of electronic communications by the United States as part of its campaign against Nicaragua, see Frederick, "Electronic Penetration."

65. For more details on the contra radios and communications equipment, see Hugh Stegman, "Tracking Godzilla: The Contra Connection," *Popular Communications* (October 1988): 26–27; and Tom Kneitel, "Nicaraguan Rebels Use Yank Radios" *Popular Communications* (September 1983): 8–9.

66. See Sklar, "Washington Wants to Buy."

67. See NED annual reports, 1984–1989.

68. NED, "Programs of the Endowment and Its Institutions in Nicaragua" (September 1987).

69. NED, "La Prensa" (a four-page project proposal prepared for the January 1989 NED board meeting).

70. See Fred Landis, "C.I.A. Psychological Warfare Operations: Case Studies in Chile, Jamaica, and Nicaragua," *Science for the People* (January-February 1982): 6–37. For the CIA connection, see Bob Woodward, *Veil: The Secret Wars of the CIA, 1981–1987* (New York: Simon and Schuster, 1987), p. 113; John Spicer Nichols, "*La Prensa*: The CIA Connection," *Columbia Journalism Review* (July-August 1988): 34–35. For summaries of how *La Prensa* functioned as an organ of psychological warfare, see Robinson and Norsworthy, *David and Goliath*, pp. 203–208. Also see Michael Massing, "Nicaragua's Free-Fire Journalism," *Columbia Journalism Review* (July-August 1988): 29–36.

71. William I. Robinson and David MacMichael, "NED Overt Action: Intervention in the Nicaraguan Election," *Covert Action Information Bulletin*, no. 33 (Winter 1990): 32–40; Jacqueline Sharkey, "Anatomy of an Election: How U.S. Money Affected the Outcome in Nicaragua," *Common Cause Magazine* (May-June 1990): 22–29.

72. See NED annual reports, 1985–1987. See also NED, "Programs of the Endowment and its Institutions in Nicaragua" (1988; updated version, Fall 1989). The PRO-DEMCA connection caused a scandal after the organization came out in support of military aid for the contras.

73. For a summary of *La Prensa*'s coverage during the spring and summer 1986 debates in the U.S. Congress over approval of the contra aid package, see the special report, María Flóres-Estrada and Eduardo Estrada, "Medios escritos," *Pensamiento propio* (July 1986): 23–44.

74. *La Prensa*, May 13, 1986.

75. See Robinson and Norsworthy, *David and Goliath*, pp. 203–208.

76. For discussions on U.S. manipulation of the issue of press freedoms and censorship in Nicaragua, see Morris Morley and James Petras, *The Reagan Administration and Nicaragua: How Washington Constructs Its Case for Counterrevolution in Central America* (New York: Institute for Media Analysis, 1987); and Spence, "The U.S. Media."

77. Cited in Kent Norsworthy, *Nicaragua: A Country Guide* (Albuquerque, N.M.: Inter-American Hemispheric Resource Center, 1989), pp. 67–68.

78. NED, "Programs of the Endowment."

79. See NED annual reports.

80. A copy of the letter was provided to me in Managua by sources inside *La Prensa*.

81. Further aspects of the Venezuelan connection are mentioned in NED, "La Prensa."

82. *Diario las Américas* is owned by Horacio Aguirre, whose brother Francisco, a former Somoza National Guard colonel, was one of the chief original organizers of the contra movement in 1979–1980. See Chamorro, *Packaging the Contras*, p. 5. The paper stood out as the voice of the Far Right Cuban exile community in Miami, and after the 1979 Sandinista triumph it took on the contras as its second cause, dedicating several pages and columns each day to procontra and anti-Sandinista coverage.

83. This group was headed by Alvaro Corrada, S.J, auxiliary bishop of Washington, who sent out thousands of form letters dated September 20, 1988, to church and lay groups around the United States.

84. See Delphi, "Support for Nicaraguan Independent Radios" (June 1989, internal document) for details. Also see NED, "Programs of the Endowment" (1987, 1988, 1989).

85. Delphi, "Support for Nicaraguan Independent Radios."

86. See, for example, letter from Radio San Cristóbal director José Gutierrez to Paul Von Ward, August 18, 1989. A copy of the letter was given to me by sources close to the radio station.

87. The letter, dated October 19, 1989, was provided to me by a close associate of Roger Guevara.

88. Interview with Pedro Chamorro, Jr., New Mexico, April 1988.

89. The following section on the development of the TV project is from the Briceño-NED correspondence from March to September 1989 provided to me by sources close to the NED; from a direct phone interview with Briceño, Managua, December 30, 1989; and from other NED documentation, including "Programs of the Endowment."

90. Letter from Carlos Briceño to Barbara Haig, March 21, 1989.

91. In the December 30, 1989, phone interview from Managua, Briceño told me that although he used UNIVISION letterhead, the television channel was not involved in the NED project.

92. The five-page proposal was entitled "Independent TV Programming: A Must for the Nicaraguan Opposition."

93. Two-page letter signed by Briceño, Miami, April 30, 1990. As part of the negotiations at electoral freedoms, the electoral law exempted Nicaragua parties participating in the campaign from paying customs taxes on materials for use in the electoral campaign.

94. Letter from Carlos Briceño to Barbara Haig, on UNIVISION stationery, May 2, 1989.

95. The one-page letter was dated June 6, 1989.

96. Letter signed by Jeb Bush, on Bush Klein Realty stationery, May 8, 1989.

97. Letter from Carlos Briceño to Barbara Haig, on UNIVISION stationery, July 13, 1989.

98. This was confirmed by a Venezuelan diplomat posted at the Venezuelan Embassy in Washington who requested anonymity.

99. Letter from Briceño to Haig, July 13, 1989.

100. Letter from Senators Connie Mack, Bob Graham, John McCain, and Charles Robb, on U.S. Senate stationery, to Edward Fritts, July 25, 1989.

101. Letter from Edward Fritts to Stanley S. Hubbard, president of Hubbard Broadcasting, St. Paul, Minnesota, a local affiliate of the NAB, on NAB stationery, July 25, 1989. Similar letters were sent out to other NAB affiliates around the country.

102. Copies of this Gershman-Chamorro correspondence were provided to me by sources close to *La Prensa*. The content of Briceño's August 4 meeting with Gershman was summarized in a letter Briceño sent to the NED president on August 7, 1989.

After the election, Briceño stayed in Nicaragua. He was appointed by the Chamorro government as director of the National Television System.

103. Carnes Lord, "The Political Dimension in National Strategy," in Carnes Lord and Frank R. Barnett (eds.), *Political Warfare and Psychological Operations: Rethinking the U.S. Approach* (Washington, D.C.: National Defense University Press, 1989), p. 17.

104. Sharkey, "Anatomy of an Election."

105. Memo from Richard Soudriette to Carl Gershman, September 8, 1989.

106. For a good overview of the role of the polls in relation to U.S. strategy, see MacMichael and Chamorro, "Nicaraguan Election Project," pp. 19–25.

107. For a postelectoral analysis of polls, see "Report by the Commission on Nicaragua Pre-Election Polls" (Los Angeles: Latin American Studies Institute, California State University at Los Angeles, unpublished ms.). This widely respected commission, formed by a group of professional U.S. pollsters and academicians, studied the methodologies and results of the different pollsters in Nicaragua. Also see "After the Poll Wars—Explaining the Upset," *Envío* (March-April 1990): 30–36; and *Interamerican Public Opinion Report* (January 1990 and Spring 1990).

For the most exhaustive and stimulating analysis of the issue of preelectoral polls, see William A. Barnes, "Rereading the Nicaraguan Pre-election Polls in Light of the Election Results (and What Can Be Learned About the Fate of the Nicaraguan Elections Thereby) (January 1991, unpublished ms.; cited with permission of the author). Barnes was a member of the Commission on Nicaraguan Pre-election Polls, although the views expressed in his manuscript do not necessarily correspond to those of the commission. Copies may be obtained from Barnes, 6542 Dana St., Oakland, CA 94609. I am also indebted to William Bollinger for a critical reading of the first draft of this section on polls.

108. See William Bollinger, "Pollsters Invade Nicaragua," and William A. Barnes, "Overview: Initial Pre-Election Poll Results," *Interamerican Public Opinion Report* (January 1990): 1–4, 5, 14.

109. See *The Nation*, May 17, 1988, pp. 635–638. The USIA often contracted a San José–based polling firm, CID-Gallup, for these polls. Although CID-Gallup holds a franchise from the U.S-based Gallup firm, which allows CID-Gallup to harness the prestige of the U.S. firm, it operates independently. U.S. Gallup has denied any participation in, or responsibility for, CID-Gallup's polling.

110. These distinct objectives in the use of polls explain why some surveys, such as those carried out during the latter stages of the campaign by the Costa Rican consulting firm Borge and Associates, which had worked for Oscar Arias's election, were fairly

accurate in their results, while others, among them several carried out by *La Prensa*, showed the UNO with a huge margin and were clearly propagandistic exercises.

111. Cover letter from Robert Green to Barbara Haig, October 30, 1989, Penn and Schoen Associates, attached to "Proposal on a Strategic Polling Program for the National Endowment for Democracy" (October 30, 1989, submitted to the NED).

112. Penn and Schoen, "Proposal on a Strategic Polling Program." It is not clear if in the end the NED actually approved the Penn and Schoen proposal. NED public records indicate that it did not finance such a polling project, but DOXSA did conduct polling activities during the electoral campaign. Given clandestine and third-party conduits, and the Venezuelan connection, it is entirely possible that the NED was involved with DOXSA or that other U.S. agencies were involved. What is important for the purposes of this study is observing the way in which polls were seen by U.S. strategists as an instrument for gauging the impact and effectiveness of U.S. programs.

CHAPTER FIVE

1. Ralph M. Goldman, "The Donor-Recipient Relationship in Political Aid Programs," in Ralph M. Goldman and William A. Douglas (eds.), *Promoting Democracy: Opportunities and Issues* (New York: Praeger, 1988), pp. 67–68 (emphasis added). Goldman was an original consultant in the formation and definition of the NED and a Project Democracy consultant.

2. The meeting, held on August 12, 1988, was outlined in internal NED documents. The documents did not mention who composed the "ad-hoc group of Latinamericans."

3. For a general overview of Venezuela's regional role, see Terry Karl, "Mexico, Venezuela, and the Contadora Initiative," in Morris J. Blackman et al., *Confronting Revolution: Security Through Diplomacy in Central America* (New York: Pantheon, 1986).

4. This was reported by *Newsweek*, October 9, 1989, p. 47. I also obtained details in interviews with Venezuelan sources and with sources close to U.S. intelligence.

5. As told to me by a Venezuelan source.

6. As told to me by a Nicaraguan participant in the meeting.

7. The internal NED document was provided to me by sources in the NED. It was a one-page sheet entitled "Meeting with CAP" and was used for a planning meeting for the Nicaragua program of top NED officials.

8. Rangél's role was explained to me by Venezuelan diplomats in Managua and by sources close to U.S. intelligence.

9. One of the three, David Zuni, had been an electoral adviser to Alfredo Cristiani in his successful presidential campaign in neighboring El Salvador. Zuni worked closely with Carlos Hurtado, a right-hand man to Alfredo César, who became the minister of government after the elections.

10. As told to me by a source at the Venezuelan Embassy in Managua.

11. See Edgar Chamorro, *Packaging the Contras: A Case of CIA Disinformation* (New York: Institute for Media Analysis, 1987), pp. 18–19. Interview with Edgar Chamorro, Managua, December 1989.

12. The U.S. liaison for the CAD operations was the America's Development Foundation (ADF), an organization founded in 1980 in Alexandria, Virginia. Its director is Michael Miller, who was formerly vice president of the Council on the Americas, an organization that received millions of dollars in the 1980s for NED projects in Latin America. Until 1987, ADF was a major recipient of AID funds for rural development projects in Latin America and elsewhere. After Esquipulas, however, ADF began receiving substantial NED funds for political projects for the "promotion of democracy."

For background on ADF, see *Groupwatch: Profiles of U.S. Private Organizations and Churches* (Albuquerque, N.M.: Resource Center, 1989).

13. NED executive summaries on Nicaragua programs; NED annual reports, 1986–1989. The CAD first began in 1984 under the name Asociación Pro-Democrática.

14. NED-State Department planning session, Washington, August 4, 1988 (see Chapter 3). A record of the meeting was provided to me by sources close to the NED.

15. See NED executive summaries and annual reports.

16. The board of directors included, among others, Emilio López Calderón, the director of the prestigious international management school in San José, INCAE; Ernesto Alwood Lagos, former Salvadoran planning minister; Francisco Lima, a representative of the Salvadoran business chambers; Roberto Brenes, a leader of Panamanian business and of the Civic Crusade (which was also being heavily funded by NED); and Rodolfo Piza Escanalente, of the Inter-American Human Rights Court. See NED, "America's Development Foundation (ADF)/Centro de Asesoria para la Democracia (CAD)" (September 1989, internal document circulated to plan spending of the $9 million approved by Congress).

17. ADF, "Modified Programmatic Structure and Contents for NED Grant 89-08.0 (Election Nicaragua—90)" (July 1990).

18. See NED, "Grants Awarded from Funds Appropriated Under P.L. 100-461 and 101-45" (November 1989).

19. ADF, "Modified Programmatic Structure." The document was submitted along with a letter from Michael D. Miller to Adelina Reyes Gavilán of the NED, on ADF stationery, July 28, 1989.

20. In April 1989, Allen Weinstein and the ADF's Michael Miller met to discuss "collaborating in areas of mutual interest." From this sprung a working relationship between Weinstein's people and the CAD (as told to me by ADF sources).

21. Ibid.

22. Record of NED/State Department meeting, August 4, 1988, provided to me by sources close to the NED.

23. ADF, "Modified Programmatic Structure."

24. Ibid. (emphasis added).

25. See CAD, "CAD Centroamerica—Participation Through Media and Civic Organizations" (November 2, 1989, internal summary of activities and budget). This was faxed to the NED by CAD official Jorge Poveda. A copy of the document was provided to me by sources close to the NED. Another internal NED document, submitted to the AID in March 1990 and requesting permission to spend the portion of the $9 million that was not used during the electoral process, praised the "success" of the CAD's activities in support of *La Prensa* and the radios and requested another $75,000 to continue the program.

26. This was affirmed in a faxed letter from Sérgio Cambronero to the NED, September 29, 1989, and was supplied to me by sources close to *La Prensa*.

27. See CAD, "CAD Centroamerica."

28. Ibid.

29. Faxed message from the CAD to the NED, June 3, 1989. A copy of the fax was given to me by sources close to Via Cívica. See also NED's internal document submitted to the AID to request allocation of unused electoral funds.

30. See *Barricada*, July 6, 1989.

31. Phone interview with Michael Miller, February 1990.

32. Letter from Cambronero to the NED, September 29, 1989.

33. Faxed letter from Sylvia Escalante to the NED, October 5, 1989. This was provided to me by sources inside the UNO.

34. See NED annual reports and association financial reports.

35. Calderón was director of the association until he resigned to enter the presidential race, and even then his inner circle of advisers stayed on at the NED-funded association. For these details, see letter from PLN legislators of the Costa Rican National Assembly to the U.S. Congress, on National Assembly stationery, September 25, 1989. See also "National Endowment for Democracy Interferes in Costa Rica," (a three-page document prepared by the campaign team of PLN's presidential candidate Carlos Manuel Castillo and submitted on September 28, 1989, to the House Foreign Operations Subcommittee of the Western Hemisphere Committee).

36. Letter from Keith Schuette to Carl Gershman, on NRI stationery, June 5, 1989.

37. Fax from the association to the NRI, July 8, 1989.

38. See letter from Keith Schuette to Carl Gershman, on NRI stationery, December 1, 1989.

39. See NRI reports and NED annual reports.

40. These parties included the National Party in Honduras (which won the 1989 elections), the United Social Christian Party in Costa Rica (which won the 1989 elections in that country), the Solidarity Action Movement in Guatemala, and the Nicaraguan Conservative Party. In El Salvador, Keith Schuette suggested supporting the Nationalist Republican Alliance, but the proposal was canceled after U.S. officials concluded that such support would provoke too much controversy. The training institutes set up were the Academy for Liberty and Justice of Guatemala; the Center for Social, Economic, and Political Studies of Honduras; the Association in Defense of Democracy and Freedom in Costa Rica; and the Conservative Institute in Nicaragua.

41. This particular money trail was pieced together by sources from the UNO involved in the coalition's internal accounting and through internal documents supplied by sources close to the NRI.

42. For background on the two San José meetings, see William I. Robinson and Kent Norsworthy, *David and Goliath: The U.S. War Against Nicaragua* (New York: Monthly Review Press, 1987), pp. 105–112.

43. Phone interviews with AID official Norma Parker, from the Office of Public Information; Jim Fox, from the Latin America and Caribbean Program; Ted Morse and Roger Noriega, from the Nicaragua Task Force of the AID, July 1989.

44. Ibid.

45. AID officials regularly told journalists in Washington, for instance, that the institute and the CAPEL were connected to the OAS. This was also told to me (ibid.). But OAS officials reacted angrily to my queries and maintained that there was no relation whatsoever. Sources from the OAS Secretariat General complained bitterly that the United States had been misleading journalists and public opinion. They said individual Latin American diplomats posted at the OAS or working in one of its entities had developed relations with the CAPEL and the Human Rights Institute but that these were not OAS relations with the CAPEL and the institute.

46. Council on Hemispheric Affairs and Inter-American Hemispheric Education Resource Center, *National Endowment for Democracy (NED): A Foreign Policy Branch Gone Awry* (Washington, D.C./Albuquerque, N.M.: Council on Hemispheric Affairs/Inter-American Hemispheric Education Resource Center, 1990), p. 38.

47. SEC, "Brief Description of International Cooperation for the Nicaraguan Supreme Electoral Council" (December 1989, document provided to journalists).

48. This was reported by Representative Robert Torricelli (D-N.J.) on June 28, 1989, in discussions on U.S. electoral aid to Nicaragua. See *Congressional Record* (House), June 28, 1989, p. H3340.

49. Phone interview with Richard Soudriette, October 1989.

50. *Boston Globe,* September 27, 1989.

51. For a summary discussion on West German political aid programs and foundations, see Michael A. Samuels and William A. Douglas, "Promoting Democracy," *Washington Quarterly* (Summer 1981): 52–65.

52. Letter from Gotz Frhr. v. Houwald to Carl Gershman, August 22, 1989.

53. See *Miami Herald,* May 12, 1984; and *Washington Post,* May 4, 1984.

54. Senator Tom Harkin mentioned this financing in comments before the Senate plenary on October 17, 1989, during debates on the $9 million. See *Congressional Record* (Senate), October 17, 1989, p. S13527. Harkin's staff assistants confirmed the details in a phone interview in late October.

55. Internal memorandum from Henry Quintero to Carl Gershman, October 3, 1989. This was supplied to me by sources in the NED.

56. For details, see reports in *El nuevo diario,* November 7 and November 15, 1989.

57. Among its board members are John Singlaub, Lieutenant Colonel Gordon Sumner, Barry Goldwater, John Lehman, Christopher Middleton, and Jeremiah Denton, Alfonso D'Amato (R-N.Y.), Orrin Hatch (R-Utah), Connie Mack (R-Fla.), and Strom Thurmond (R-S.C.). One of Jefferson Education Foundation's most important programs in the 1980s was pro–South African lobbying in Washington; it was a major force behind the efforts to block economic sanctions against Pretoria.

58. See conference documents prepared by Jefferson Education Foundation, including press release, December 12, 1989; and memorandum from Robert Reilly to Jaime Daremblum, on Jefferson Educational Foundation stationery, November 30, 1989. Both documents were provided to me by the public relations section at the foundation.

59. For background on Reilly and on the Jefferson Education Foundation, see S. Diamond, (Boston: South End Press, *Spiritual Warfare* 1989), p. 155; "The Jefferson Foundation," *Covert Action Information Bulletin,* no. 34 (Summer 1990): 36.

60. These are Libro Libre, which published several of his books and pamphlets, the CAD, and Pensamiento Centroamericano. See NED annual reports, 1984–1989; Freedom House reports on Libro Libre; and the reports of the Costa Rican–based groups. See also memorandum from Reilly to Daremblum, November 30, 1989.

61. This section on Ayales is pieced together from interviews carried out both before and after the elections with Costa Rican diplomats in Managua, officials from the Nicaraguan Foreign Ministry, and members of the anti-Sandinista opposition.

62. This was told to me in an interview with a member of the *La Prensa* editorial staff who requested anonymity. Ayales's writings for *La Prensa* were also confirmed in an interview with a diplomat at the Costa Rican Embassy in Managua.

63. Interview with the Costa Rican diplomat, who requested anonymity.

64. This was told to me by high-level officials at the Nicaraguan Foreign Ministry.

65. For a good summary of the U.S. relation to international observation of the elections, see David MacMichael and Edgar Chamorro, "Nicaragua Election Project: Pre-Election Final Report" (New York: Institute for Media Analysis, February 1990), pp. 25–34.

66. Testimony given by Allen Weinstein before the Bipartisan Commission for Free and Fair Elections in Nicaragua, Washington, D.C., May 9, 1989. Weinstein's testimony is contained in the commission's published report, *Proceedings of the Bipartisan Commission for Free and Fair Elections in Nicaragua* (Washington, D.C.: World Freedom Foundation, May 9–11, 1989).

67. See CFD, "The Center for Democracy," a promotional brochure that lists its activities and also contains a biographical sketch of Weinstein.

68. See, for instance, Guillermo Cortes Dominguez, *Reves electoral Sandinista: La lucha por el poder* (Managua: Editorial Vanguardia, 1990), p. 144.

69. Ibid.

70. "Profiles of U.S. Private Organizations and Churches: National Endowment for Democracy," *Groupwatch* (Albuquerque, N.M.: Resource Center, 1989).

71. AID, "Report to Congress (P.L. 101-119)" (Washington, D.C.: AID, November 1989). For the NED grant, see NED annual report, 1989; and CFD, "Nicaraguan Election Monitoring Project."

72. CFD, "CFD—Nicaraguan Election Monitoring—Fact Sheet" (June 1989). This was distributed through the CFD's Managua office and through its Washington office to journalists and the public.

73. For a summary of this incident, see Abid Aslam, "Election Violence in Nicaragua," *Lies of Our Times* 1, no. 2 (February 1990): 4.

74. After his closed-door testimony, Cerda repeated his testimony at a press conference in Managua on December 18. For a summary, see ibid.

75. OAS, "Grupo de observadores del Secretario General de la OEA, proceso electoral de Nicaragua: Apreciación de los hechos en Masatepe" (emphasis added). This was made available to reporters in Managua on December 11 and at OAS headquarters in Washington on December 12, 1989.

76. The CFD put out an initial one-page press release on December 11 and three days later released its final fifteen-page report, "Violence at Masatepe: An Eyewitness Report by a Center for Democracy Observer Delegation to the Nicaraguan Elections." I attended a press conference that Weinstein offered at a USIA press center in Washington, D.C., in which he made the "we saw more" comment. The United Nations' report was titled "UN Observers' Report Summary."

77. The delegates movements, including the meetings with Bush and Quayle, were detailed by Weinstein at the December 14, 1989, press conference that the USIA sponsored. These movements were also detailed in CFD press package prepared for the press conference and given to all reporters in attendance, including me. The press package handouts included a step-by-step chronology of the activities of the delegation, from its arrival in Nicaragua to its return to Washington.

78. State Department briefing by spokesperson Richard Boucher, December 11, 1989.

79. See Mark Uhlig, *New York Times*, "Honduran Leader Walks Out on Talks," December 11, 1989.

80. The delegation included the director of the archconservative World Freedom Foundation, Brent Bozell, Jr., who weeks earlier had visited contra camps in Honduras to urge the contras not to demobilize; Peter Flaherty of the Conservative Campaign Fund, which had raised moneys for the contras; Peter Kelly of the firm Black, Manafort, Stone, and Kelly, which was contracted to help run Ronald Reagan's presidential campaigns in 1980 and 1984 and also represented Angolan contra leader Jonas Savimbi in Washington; and Mary J. Matalin, chief of staff of the Republican National Committee.

81. *Prensa libre*, December 11, 1989; and Weinstein's December 14, 1989, press conference.

82. See CFD press release, December 30, 1989. The meeting took place on December 29 in Miami.

83. Phone interview with Allen Weinstein, Washington, D.C., October 3, 1989; and *Washington Times* interview with Weinstein, October 2, 1989.

84. Interview with Elliot Richardson, Washington, D.C., September 14, 1989.

85. NED internal memorandum, November 1989, provided to me by a source in the NED.

86. Letter from Brent Bozell to Keith Schuette, on World Freedom Foundation stationery, October 26, 1989.

87. Bozell was part of the official CFD observer team that went to Masatepe on December 10, 1989. Although he had been denied a visa to go down as leader of the World Freedom Foundation, he was granted a visa to participate in the CFD group. He was also included by Weinstein on the CFD's official list of observers for voting day itself, but this time authorities denied him a visa.

88. Letter from Keith Schuette to Brent Bozell, on NRI letterhead, October 30, 1989.

89. Letter from Tom Foley to Daniel Ortega, January 30, 1990.

90. Letter from John Bolton to Elliot Richardson, December 1, 1989.

91. State Department, "Sandinista Harassment of the Opposition" (December 27, 1989, prepared by the Nicaragua Desk of the Central American Bureau).

92. Together with these State Department reports, the right-wing U.S. groups such as Freedom House and Puebla Institute issued their own reports in the final months of the campaign, duplicating almost word for word the U.S. government position. See, for instance, Puebla Institute, "Report on Nicaraguan Electoral Process" (January 25, 1990). The report was translated into Spanish and distributed in Managua by the U.S. Embassy.

93. The memorandum was dated January 23, 1990, and was faxed in the last week of January. I obtained it from the Nicaraguan Embassy in London, which was presented with a copy by a group of British Members of Parliament, who met with Nicaraguan diplomats in London to discuss the issues raised in the memorandum.

94. OAS, "Fourth Report by the Secretary General of the Organization of American States on the Observation of the Nicaraguan Electoral Process (January 1–February 15, 1990)" (February 20, 1990).

95. United Nations Observer Mission, "Third ONUVEN Report," for period covering December 1989 to January 1990, released on February 1, 1990.

96. *Washington Post*, January 25, 1990. In its third report on the process (released in December 1989), the U.N. team denounced the persistence of attempts "to disqualify the electoral authorities, to anticipate electoral fraud, and to reiterate the argument that the only explanation for a defeat at the voting booths would be fraud." The report also criticized the Sandinistas' "identification, not of individual opposition leaders, but of the opposition alliance as a whole as, with Somoza's National Guard, with the counterrevolution, with war, with death, all of which tends to disconfigure an adversary whose coming to power would therefore be inadmissible."

97. Ibid.

98. See "AID Nicaragua" (March 30, 1990). Apparently, moneys from the "reserve fund" set aside out of the $9 million in PL 101-119 were used for some of these observer groups.

99. See, among other documents, several reports from Jorge Serrano of the Guatemalan group to the NRI and the NED as well as budget reports from the NRI to the AID. See, in particular, letter and report from Keith Schuette to Barbara Haig on the observer mission, January 24, 1990.

100. Author's interviews with AID officials.

101. See letter from Comptroller Avis Worrell to Sharon Isralow of AID's Office of Democratic Initiatives, February 9, 1990. A budget breakdown was included with the letter.

102. Internal memorandum from Allen Weinstein and Peter Kelly to CFD observer delegation members, February 9, 1990. This was provided to me by a member of the delegation.

CHAPTER SIX

1. *New York Times*, June 11, 1989.

2. Ibid.

3. This term was first used by the Pentagon in a secret document, drafted in 1983 and later leaked to the press, that discussed the existence of a "program of perception management" for Central America. See William I. Robinson and Kent Norsworthy, *David and Goliath: The U.S. War Against Nicaragua* (New York: Monthly Review Press, 1987), p. 36.

4. See letter from leaders of Americas' Watch, the International Human Rights Law Group, the Washington Office on Latin America, and others to Tom Foley, September 6, 1989. The signatories made strong and quite laudable arguments against covert intervention. The problem was that they adopted the terms of debate set by the U.S. government and thus lost sight of the unitary intentions of covert and overt intervention.

5. The stipulations restricting CIA activities were contained in the FY 1990 Intelligence Authorization Bill, which was legislation separate from that authorizing the $9 million. For details, see "DSG Legislative Report" on H.R. 2748 (October 5, 1989); and "Colloquy Between Chairman Beilenson and Chairman Moakley," which was provided by the Rules and the Intelligence committees of the House as a description of the specific terms of the CIA restrictions.

"Legally" by this definition merely means in accordance with congressional stipulations. There is an enormous gap between what is "legal" in accordance with legislation set by the Congress and what is legal in accordance with international law. There is also little correlation between what is "legal" and what is moral. Congress passed $100 million in contra military aid in June 1986, so the killing of thousands of Nicaraguans with those funds was, by the perverted logic of U.S. lawmakers, "legal." But when the contras killed Nicaraguans with funds supplied secretly by Oliver North, these killings were "illegal."

6. See, for example, Arms Control and Foreign Policy Caucus, "U.S. Efforts to Promote Democracy in Nicaragua: Choices for Congress on Covert and Overt Aid," *Issue Preview*, August 3, 1989.

7. *New York Times*, April 25, 1989.

8. Carter made this endorsement in comments to reporters after meeting with George Bush in the White House on September 21, 1989. On another occasion, Carter said he personally believed that the $9 million amount was "excessive." He stated this in private meetings at a symposium organized by the Carter Center at Emory University in Atlanta on November 14, 1989, titled "The Nicaraguan Elections: A Turning Point?"

9. Stated in a letter from Jimmy Carter to Daniel Ortega, September 22, 1989, as a follow-up to their mid-September meetings in Managua. The letter was provided to me by aides to Ortega.

10. Brian Atwood and Keith Schuette sent a letter to Nicaragua's deputy foreign minister, Víctor Hugo Tinoco, January 16, 1990, warning that "despite the assurances given to us . . . we are seriously concerned that [there is] a pattern of delay" in NED payments to the opposition through the Nicaraguan Central Bank. "This will seriously undermine Nicaraguan and international confidence in the electoral system." I attended the public portion of the January 15 NED board meeting in Washington D.C., where NED officials discussed the letter and a possible international campaign.

11. Letter from Jimmy Carter to Sergio Ramírez, January 22, 1990.

The late 1970s "Koreagate" scandal in the United States was sparked when it was discovered that several U.S. congressional electoral campaigns had received donations from South Korean interests. Imagine if instead of reacting as it did to such foreign interference, the U.S. government had made the foolish decision to permit South Korean financing of U.S. elections. Then imagine that the South Koreans sent a public threat to the State Department that its funds—destined for blatant interference in U.S. elections— had better not be blocked or there would be retribution!

12. Nicaraguan Foreign Ministry, "Ayuda memoria, 22 September 1989" (internal evaluation submitted to Ortega's office on Carter's mid-September visit and his September 22 letter).

13. There was a third aspect: The Sandinistas' reasoning was that instead of blocking U.S. interference, they would be wisest to document and denounce before the electorate blatant U.S. tutelage of the opposition. But as I analyze in Chapter 7, the issue was more complex, and the effort backfired.

14. *Newsweek*, September 24, 1989, first reported on the $5 million CIA program and then gave additional details in the October 9, 1989, edition. I obtained further information from a source close to U.S. intelligence as well as from several UNO leaders. Also see COHA, "News and Analysis" (March 1990).

15. *Newsweek*, September 24, 1989.

16. *New York Times*, October 4, 1989.

17. *Newsweek* reported on this program in its March 12, 1990, edition. I obtained further details in interviews with sources close to U.S. intelligence and with UNO leaders.

18. See, for instance, *La Prensa*, January 7, 1990.

19. The statement was distributed as a press communiqué on January 11 by the West German Embassy in Managua.

20. This was told to me by sources close to U.S. intelligence in September 1989. More than two years later, *Newsweek* reported the existence of this program (October 21, 1991, pp. 46–47). For further details, see William I. Robinson, "Nicaragua: The Inside Story of the 'César Scandal'" (Albuquerque: Latin America Data Base, Latin American Institute, University of New Mexico, October 25, 1991).

21. *Newsweek*, October 21, 1991, p. 47.

22. This was reported by contra (and later opposition) leader Alfredo César; see "Nicaragua's Electoral Process—the New Name for the War, *Envío* 8, no. 95 (June 1989): 7. Also see *Washington Post*, August 4, 1989.

23. These meeting and related events regarding the closing of the contra offices, contra rivalries, and contra–State Department disputes were widely reported in the U.S. media. Among other reports, see *Washington Post*, July 18 and 28, 1989; *New York Times*, July 18, 1989; *Washington Times*, July 17, 1989; *Miami Herald*, June 6 and July 18, 1989; *Wall Street Journal*, July 17, 1989; and *Los Angeles Times*, June 8, 1989. Some $200,000 in State Department political subsidies for the U.S. offices was redirected toward getting contra leaders back into Managua.

24. For details, see *Washington Post*, September 2, 1989, and September 7, 1989.

25. Ibid.

26. Interview with Ernesto Palazio, Washington, D.C., December 1989.

27. Octaviano was later implicated in drug trafficking out of Costa Rica to generate funds for use in the contra war. He was publicly questioned on this by Senator John Kerry (D-Mass.), who chaired the subcommission that investigated the contra-drugs connection. For one inside account by an associate of César, see Arturo Cruz, Jr., *Memoirs of a Counterrevolutionary* (New York: Doubleday, 1989), pp. 203–207.

28. Ibid., p. 203. Cruz had been recruited by the CIA in the early 1980s to work with the contras.

29. Ibid.

30. Martínez was expelled from Nicaragua in early January 1990, along with some twenty other U.S. diplomats, after U.S soldiers illegally entered and ransacked the residence of the Nicaraguan ambassador in Panama City in the days following the U.S. invasion of Panama.

31. Cruz, *Memoirs*, pp. 192, 247.

32. See *New York Times* and *Washington Post*, June 11, 1988.

33. *Newsweek*, October 21, 1991, pp. 46–47.

34. This was told to me by one top-level opposition leader, who said that he decided not to accept the payment and then later withdrew from UNO.

35. As told to me by a source close to U.S. intelligence.

36. For details, see Ana María Ezcurra, *Agresión ideológica contra la revolución Sandinista* (México, D.F.: Ediciones Nuevomar, 1984), pp. 89–92; and "Archbishop Obando y Bravo and the Institute for Religion and Democracy," *Covert Action Information Bulletin*, no. 18 (1983): 6. See also Irene Selser, *Cardenal Obando* (México, D.F.: Centro de Estudios Ecuménicos, 1989).

37. Antonio Ibarra Rojas, "Liberation Theology and the Marxist Sociology of Religion" (Langley, Va.: Army–Air Force Center for Low-Intensity Conflict, June 1989), pp. 31, 32.

38. Letter from Alfred Barr to consular officer, Embassy of Honduras, on U.S. Department of State stationery, March 20, 1989. This was provided to me by Honduran Embassy sources.

39. This was reported by *La Prensa*, July 6, 1989.

40. The pamphlet was reproduced in *Barricada*, July 12, 1989.

41. Ibid. For instance, the trade unions should "multiply crises in public and private production and service units," promote the demand for "automatic wage hikes in accordance with inflation," and work for the "demobilization of the Sandinista army."

42. State Department declaration read by spokesperson Richard Boucher at State's daily press briefing, July 11, 1989. "Professor Tony Ybarra [*sic*]," said the declaration, was "a representative of Freedom House, a respected independent human rights organization. Mr. Ybarra had been in Nicaragua observing the electoral process."

43. Interview with Philip Agee, Washington, D.C., November 1987.

44. PLI representative in Miami Enrique Gabuardi gave me a detailed description of this Miami infighting in the 1988–1989 period in an interview, Miami, January 4, 1990.

45. The background on Alvarado, the AIBC Financial Corporation, and its role in contra money laundering was provided by several sources, among them Alberto Suir (a former contra money launderer in Honduras who had a falling-out with the contras in 1987 and moved to Miami) and confidential legal and journalist sources in Miami.

46. The NED and the State Department would later set up a "Nicaragua task force" to coordinate interagency activity in Washington around the NED programs (see Chapter 3).

47. The office building was at 1390 Brickwell Avenue. In 1990, Jeb and his Miami building would become embroiled in a savings and loan scandal. See AP, October 15, 1990; and *New York Times*, October 15, 1990.

48. See "Fact Sheet" on the committee distributed to journalists in Miami, September 15, 1989.

49. Chamorro press conference at Bayfront Park, Miami, September 15, 1989. See also stories in *Miami Herald* and *Diario las Américas*, September 16, 1989; and *New York Times*, September 19, 1989.

50. The firm was founded under the name Carmen, Carmen and Hugel.

51. Together with William Casey, Hugel had reportedly directed an illicit, covert intelligence operation against the presidential campaign of Jimmy Carter in 1980. As part of this operation, Hugel infiltrated a "mole" into Carter's campaign staff who stole confidential campaign papers. See Bob Woodward, *Veil: The Secret Wars of the CIA, 1981-1987* (New York: Simon and Schuster, 1987), pp. 277, 278.

52. Hugel was forced to resign after the press revealed that he had been engaged in illegal stock market dealings.

53. In 1986, Hallet had been named ambassador to the Bahamas, a post traditionally related to U.S. intelligence activities in the Caribbean basin and to clandestine financial transactions, including the kind of money laundering through the Bahamas that was revealed during the Iran-contra investigations.

54. Shortly after William Casey's death, Hugel worked with Sofia Casey in organizing a fund-raising dinner in which 50 percent of the moneys went to cancer research and the other 50 percent to the "freedom fighters fund" set up by Sofia to continue "private" support to contra groups around the world. David Carmen was a senior staff adviser to the Reagan presidential campaign. Gerald Carmen was one of the Reagan administration's top one hundred officials, serving under Reagan as U.S. permanent representative to the United Nations in Geneva and chief executive officer of the Federal Asset Disposition Association. For a summary, see "The Carmen Group," *Covert Action Information Bulletin*, no. 34 (Summer 1990): 32.

55. Among the Carmen Group clients was the National Right to Work Committee. On the day of the Grenada invasion, the Reagan administration contracted the Carmen Group for proinvasion public diplomacy in the United States. Interestingly, Gerald Carmen led the Reagan transition team in 1981 at the Department of Housing and Urban Development, just before the multibillion dollar scandal got under way in the department. David was an official at the Republican National Committee. See Carmen Group promotional brochures for these details.

56. The five-page document, titled "Budgetary Needs for the Committee for Free Elections and Democracy in Nicaragua" (September 15, 1989), was obtained from sources in Miami connected to the UNO. Although the Carmen Group circulated the document, it is not clear who actually drafted it.

57. For these details, see Miami committee one-page "Fact Sheet." The committee's letterheads displayed a logotype of the UNO on the left-hand corner and Alvarado's name and address on the right-hand corner.

58. Letter from David Carmen to Barbara Haig, on Carmen Group stationery, October 2, 1989. In different interviews in October, November, and December 1989, both NED and Carmen Group officials denied the meeting had taken place and that any coordination was going on between the two. In subsequent interviews in January 1989, after the Carmen Group's role became public, NED officials acceded that the October meeting had taken place but said it was just a discussion and that the NED was not involved in the Carmen Group project. This assertion contradicted information from David Carmen, however, who admitted the two groups were working together.

59. *Secret Military Assistance to Iran and the Contras* (Washington, D.C.: National Security Archive, 1987), p. 226. Also, on the National Endowment for the Preservation of Liberty, see Robert Parry and Peter Kornbluh, "Iran-Contra's Untold Story," *Foreign Policy* (Fall 1988): 14, 21–22.

60. See Carmen Group's Chamorro-tour documents, including the tour budget.

61. Ibid.

62. Ibid. The senior Carmen staff, in addition to helping get Violeta Chamorro elected, profited from the deal. George Wortley was paid $12,000 for several weeks of lobbying at the State Department and in Congress. Carol Boyd Hallett, in her few

weeks of work before being appointed by the Bush administration, got $12,500 for Washington fund-raising.

63. Letter from David Carmen to Fred Sacher, on Carmen Group stationery, February 16, 1990.

64. For these details, see Carmen Group documentation, including budget reports and an internal memorandum from David Carmen to Gerald Carmen, January 18, 1990. Another millionaire, Harry Lucas, gave $10,000 for the UNO press project, according to Carmen Group fax to Miami committee, January 18, 1990.

65. One of the invitees provided a copy of the invitation to me.

66. Letter from David Carmen to Jeane Kirkpatrick, January 30, 1990.

67. After Whittlesey left the Office of Public Diplomacy, she was appointed ambassador to Switzerland—the very same year the secret accounts were set up in that country to funnel money to the contras and other of North's "enterprise" ventures.

68. Carmen Group budget documents.

69. See D. Wise, *The Spy Who Got Away* (New York: Random House, 1988), p. 237.

70. Letter from William Geimer to Carl Gershman, December 4, 1990.

71. International Media Associates, "A Future for Nicaragua" (November 28, 1989). This was provided to me by sources close to the Carmen Group.

72. Phone interviews with J. R. Black, José Antonio Alvarado, and David Carmen, January 1990.

73. Letter from David Carmen to Antonio Lacayo, on Carmen Group stationery, December 22, 1989. In a subsequent phone interview David Carmen admitted to these differences with Palazio and his role but said that they were all working together.

74. Letter from Cynthia Lebrun to José Antonio Lacayo, on Carmen Group stationery, December 22, 1989.

75. The letter was dated January 9, 1990, and was made available to journalists by the Republican National Committee.

76. See letter from Christine A. Varney, legal counsel, to David Carmen, on Democratic National Committee stationery, January 9, 1990.

77. Phone interview with David Carmen, January 29, 1990. Carmen said that DNC official Barbara Drake had authorized Brown's signature but that after the letter went out, another DNC official, Lyn Cutler, decided to withdraw Democratic support and convinced Brown to cancel his endorsement.

78. "Budgetary Needs for the Committee." In a phone interview, January 29, 1990, David Carmen refused to discuss the document.

79. Ibid.

80. *El nuevo diario*, January 9, 1990, published one of the payroll spreadsheets given to it by a member of the UNO. The publication caused a small scandal in Managua. The newspaper interviewed several UNO leaders, none of whom denied the spreadsheet's authenticity. Rather, they defended this expenditure as necessary and acceptable.

81. For other U.S.-funded budgets that included tens of thousands of dollars in salaries to UNO personnel, see "Nicaraguan Budget," faxed by Antonio Lacayo to Keith Schuette, November 6, 1989; and "UNO Budget, 8/25/89–02/25/90," circulated by UNO representatives in Managua and in Washington in their September 1989 visit to Washington.

82. NDI, "Summary Proposal, Nicaragua: Supporting Democratic Process" (December 5, 1989). This document on the program was provided to Congress.

83. Phone interview with David Carmen, January 1990.

84. Phone interview with José Antonio Alvarado, January 30, 1990.

85. Francisco Mayorga's talk was on January 14, 1990, at the Sheraton Brickwell, and the UNIVISION program was on Sunday, November 12, 1989, according to phone interviews with José Antonio Alvarado, December 1989, January 1990.

86. The letter was dated January 24, 1990, and was signed personally by George Bush. The White House Office of the Press Secretary made a copy available to journalists.

87. Letter from Ronald H. Brown to George Bush, on Democratic National Committee letterhead, January 29, 1990.

88. Cited in Jacqueline Sharkey, "Anatomy of an Election: How U.S. Money Affected the Outcome in Nicaragua," *Common Cause Magazine* (May-June 1990): 28.

89. Letter from Carol Hallet to Barbara Haig, on Carmen Group stationery, October 4, 1989. This was supplied to me by sources close to the NED. Senator Bob Graham's office confirmed to me that staffers were involved in shipping supplies to Nicaragua but refused to go into details.

90. The fax explains that Roberto Faith was the chair of the Calderón Committee in Miami. Rafael Angel Calderón of Costa Rica's United Social Christian Party won the February elections in Costa Rica. During 1988 and 1989, his party's political foundation—the Association for the Defense of Freedom and Democracy in Costa Rica—received nearly $500,000 from the NED. The National Liberation Party of Oscar Arias claimed that the funds constituted a campaign contribution to Calderón as part of the effort to punish Arias for his role in the Central American peace process.

91. The services payment to Wortley was confirmed in a phone interview with José Antonio Alvarado, January 1990. AIBC's transactions with Financial Institution Services Corporation were confirmed by sources close to the Miami committee who also provided me with receipts. Although Alvarado gave no clue as to why Wortley was paid so much for his services to the committee, one wonders whether it had anything to do with money laundering for the UNO, given Wortley's experience in banking and the earlier relation between AIBC and Financial Institution Services Corporation.

92. Letter from Keith Schuette to Luis Arguello, October 6, 1989.

93. A copy of the fax, December 22, 1989, was provided to me by sources close to the Miami committee.

94. Internal NRI memorandum provided to me by sources close to the NED.

95. NRI, "Options for Financial Transfers" (December 22, 1989, internal memorandum).

96. One example of how U.S. media reports distorted the issue was depicted in the *Washington Post*, November 13, 1989, which ran a front-page story, sent by its Nicaragua correspondent Lee Hockstadter, titled "Nicaraguan Opposition Operating on a Shoestring." The Institute for Media Analysis, which sponsored a "Nicaragua election project," noted, "This [budget] was exemplified, according to the story, by the report that UNO's Managua headquarters only had a telephone by grace of tapping into a friendly neighbor's home. Not only poverty was a factor, of course, but, the article said, clearly the Sandinistas were denying the opposition even access to the telephone system. Diligent readers who went past the lurid first paragraphs could learn that, in fact, the government telephone company had just installed three new lines especially for UNO." (See David MacMichael and Edgar Chamorro, "Nicaragua Election Project: Pre-Election Final Report" (New York: Institute for Media Analysis, February 1990), p. 22. The "no telephones for UNO" argument was also sent out by the AP wire service, November 12, 1989, and other U.S. media. On November 12, Jeane Kirkpatrick gave a speech in Blacksburg, Virginia, in which she repeated the argument and claimed that the "refusal" of the Sandinistas to supply the UNO offices with phones showed that the Sandinistas did not intend to "allow a fair election." In addition to the fact that three phone lines were already being installed just for the UNO, this propaganda argument ignored the fact that the UNO was a coalition of fourteen parties and that each party had its own offices in Managua, all with phone lines. It also ignored that

the UNO's office had only been opened in October—just weeks before U.S. press reports claimed the Sandinistas were denying the opposition phone lines. In fact, the waiting list for a phone line in Managua is usually several years' long. Thus, not only were the U.S. reports distorted but also the UNO actually received special treatment in getting three phone lines within a matter of weeks.

97. The FSLN was, and still is, the largest and best-organized political force in Nicaragua and the only one with a national presence and a mass social base. This meant not only tens of thousands of members and supporters organizing campaign activities around the country but also contributions in domestic currency from a mass base of support.

98. Memorandum from Curtis Cutter, president of Interworld Consultants, to Ken Wallock, vice president of the NDI, January 9, 1990.

99. For these statistics, see Latin America Studies Association, "Electoral Democracy Under International Pressure" (Pittsburgh: LASA, University of Pittsburgh, March 15, 1990), p. 26.

100. Ibid.

CHAPTER SEVEN

1. Fred C. Iklé, "The Modern Context," in Carnes Lord and Frank R. Barnett (eds.), *Political Warfare and Psychological Operations: Rethinking the U.S. Approach* (Washington, D.C.: National Defense University Press, 1988). Iklé was an architect of U.S. policy toward Nicaragua.

2. Angelo M. Codevilla, "Political Warfare," in Lord and Barnett, *Political Warfare*, pp. 77–79.

3. As part of the accords, Nicaraguan authorities also made the commitment to reform electoral legislation and media laws so as to "assure free and fair elections," release remaining prisoners held for war-related crimes, and invite the United Nations and the OAS so that the elections would be "verified by international observers."

4. The text said, "except that humanitarian assistance which contributes to the goals of Esquipulas IV" (i.e., to the disbanding and civilian reintegration of the contras). The text was signed on February 15 in the Costa Rican town of Costa del Sol and was reprinted textually, among other places, in "Esquipulas IV," *Envío* 8, no. 92 (March 1989): 3–4. A few days after the agreement was signed, the State Department sent two emissaries to Central America, Assistant Secretary of State for Political Affairs Robert Kimmitt and Special Envoy for Central America Morris Busby, to lobby against contra demobilization. Kimmitt met with Honduran president José Azcona to request that the contras be allowed to remain in Honduras for another year. For details, see *Barricada internacional*, March 25, 1989.

5. The protocol was titled "Joint Plan for the Demobilization and Voluntary Repatriation or Relocation in Nicaragua and Third Countries of the Members of the Nicaraguan Resistance and Their Families." The accord and the protocol were published textually in *Envío* 8, no. 98 (September 1989): 46–48.

6. Press briefing given by Víctor Hugo Tinoco at the Nicaraguan Embassy in Washington, D.C., November 15, 1989.

7. For an excellent overview of this role, see David MacMichael, "The U.S. Plays the Contra Card," *The Nation*, February 5, 1990. See also William Robinson and David MacMichael, "NED Overt Action: Intervention in the Nicaraguan Election," *Covert Action Information Bulletin*, no. 33 (Winter 1990).

8. Raymond D. Gastil, "Aspects of a U.S. Campaign for Democracy," in Ralph M. Goldman and William A. Douglas (eds.), *Promoting Democracy: Opportunities and Issues* (New York: Praeger, 1988), p. 29. Gastil was a top official at Freedom House.

9. Ibid.

10. James Baker in testimony before the House leadership, April 12, 1989.

11. The package was for $66.6 million, including $49.75 million for "humanitarian aid"; $7.7 million for "transportation"; $4.16 million for "medical assistance for victims of the civil war," which was to be channeled through Cardinal Obando y Bravo's archdiocese; and $5 million in administrative costs. PL 101-14 was approved by Congress on April 13, 1989, and was signed by Bush on April 18, 1989.

Several liberal Democrats proposed that the bill stipulate that funds be specifically earmarked for the demobilization of the contras, in accordance with the Central American peace accords. But Deputy Secretary of State Lawrence Eagleburger made clear the administration's position: "Any explicit reference [to the dismantling of the contras] is unacceptable." According to Eagleburger's reasoning, the existence of the contras would not hinder free elections because they could "convert offensive military action into defensive military action" (Eagleburger made these statements in testimony before select House committees on April 11, 1989).

12. General Paul Gorman, commander of the U.S. Southern Command in the Panama Canal Zone, which was the command headquarters for U.S.-coordinated contra operations, explained in 1984 with regard to "humanitarian assistance" in Central America: "Humanitarian assistance [is] a fundamental Department of Defense mission in low intensity warfare. [It is] an integral part of military operations" (*New York Times*, July 1, 1984).

13. AID, "Status Report on the Task Force on Humanitarian Assistance in Central America," *Report on Phase III, May 1–August 31, 1989* (Washington, D.C.: AID, September 27, 1989).

14. Interview with Nicaraguan army chief of military intelligence, Lieutenant Colonel Ricardo Wheelock, ANN, June 1989.

15. Ibid.

16. AID, "Status Report," p. 8.

17. During the electoral process, the Pentagon held continuing "Paths of Peace" military construction activities in Costa Rican and "Ahaus Tara [Big Pine] 89" and "Terencio Sierra" military maneuvers in Honduras, among others, which had been conducted with little interruption since 1981. For a summary on these maneuvers, and on the whole U.S. forward deployment and military activities around Nicaragua, see William I. Robinson and Kent Norsworthy, *David and Goliath: The U.S. War Against Nicaragua* (New York: Monthly Review Press, 1987), especially Chapter 6.

18. It also meant that Nicaragua could not let its guard down; the electoral process would unfold under the ever-hovering threat of direct U.S. aggression.

19. The U.S. pressures, including those mentioned here, are summarized in "After Esquipulas II and Sapoá: What Happens Next," *Envío* 8, no. 98 (September 1989): 3–11. Also see the *New York Times*, August 7 and 8, 1989; and *Washington Post*, August 7 and August 8, 1989. The August 7 *New York Times* reported, "Diplomats who took part in the meeting said that [U.S. pressure] was overshadowed by fear that the armed rebels would disperse inside Honduras or otherwise pose new risks to regional security."

20. For a summary of the August–October contra redeployment in Nicaragua, see William I. Robinson, "Nicaragua to U.S.: Either UNO or the Contras—But Not Both," ANN special news service, November 1989. The article was republished in the U.S. news magazine *Frontline*, November 27, 1989.

21. AID, "Status Report," p. 6.

22. Doug Boucher, cited in Jacqueline Sharkey, "Anatomy of an Election: How U.S. Money Affected the Outcome in Nicaragua," *Common Cause Magazine* (May-June 1990): 29.

23. The letter was reprinted in *Barricada*, November 2, 1989. In November 1989, *Barricada* published a letter from Alfredo César to Enrique Bermúdez that had appeared in *El tiempo*, November 12, 1989, the independent newspaper of San Pedro Sula, Honduras. In it César asked Bermúdez not to demobilize because the existence of the contras was necessary for a UNO victory. Asked by a journalist at the rally to clarify the contra-UNO relation, Virgilio Godoy, known for his loose tongue, put the issue to rest a few days later: "We are working together jointly in this electoral process with the Nicaraguan Resistance" (said at a UNO rally in Managua, December 1, 1989).

24. Quoted in *Barricada internacional*, October 28, 1989.

25. This was reported by *Newsweek*, September 25, 1989.

26. Quoted in *Christian Science Monitor*, September 20, 1990.

27. See, for instance, Richard L. Hough, "Peasant Organizations in Democratic Development," and Red Weihe, "Cooperatives as Agents of Democracy," both in Goldman and Douglas, *Promoting Democracy*, pp. 185–206, 207–226. Hough was a Foreign Service officer with the State Department, and Weihe was an adviser for the AID.

28. AID, "Status Report," pp. 11–12.

29. *Barricada*, March 8, 1990, provided a good summary of these contra activities during the electoral campaign.

30. This particular attack on Las Tijeras was described in detail by eyewitnesses to investigators from the U.S. religious organization Witness for Peace. It was detailed in "Nicaragua Hotline," no. 29, February 1, 1990; and in reports appearing in *Barricada* and *El nuevo diario*, January 22, 1990. Throughout the electoral campaign Witness for Peace published such firsthand chronicles from its witnesses and investigators stationed around Nicaragua.

31. For these statistics and for an overall analysis of the rural aspects of the electoral process, see Vanessa Castro, *Resultados electorales en el sector rural* (Managua: Instituto para el Desarrollo de la Democracia, October 1990).

32. Iklé, "The Modern Context," p. 9. Interestingly, Iklé continued, "Victory is the restoration of democracy, as we did in Grenada, or helping in Nicaragua to do the same" (pp. 10–11).

33. Alvin H. Bernstein, "Political Strategies in Coercive Diplomacy and Limited War," in Lord and Barnett, *Political War*, p. 146. Bernstein is chair of the Department of Strategy at the Naval War College.

34. A sampling of editorial headlines from major U.S. newspapers: *New York Times*—"Mr. Ortega's War"; *Washington Post*—"The Sandinistas' War"; *Baltimore Sun*—"Ortega's Provocation"; *Miami Herald*—"Peace Plan Imperiled. If Ortega Reneges"; etc. Both houses of Congress approved resolutions condemning the "Sandinistas' war moves." In attendance at the summit in San José, President George Bush, using uncharacteristic invectives, said Ortega was that "little man" and "that unwanted animal at a garden party." A Nicaraguan government communiqué stated that the measure was intended to protect the security of Nicaraguan citizens and international observers precisely so that the electoral process could proceed as programmed. In fact, sixty-seven registration centers in twenty rural towns were forced to close during voter registration because of contra activity, and three thousand people had already been killed or wounded in contra actions.

35. Such was the pressure that the administration decided in December to lift its opposition to a U.N. Security Council resolution authorizing the formation of the U.N.

peacekeeping force that would oversee contra demobilization. The process of demobilization, however, would not actually begin until after the voting. And by December, the electoral die had already been cast.

36. The administration had already drawn up contingency plans for the contras' demobilization, but these were not public. All the United States had to do was hold out until after the voting. It did not matter that the Nicaraguan government became aware of these plans; it was the Nicaraguan electorate that was the target of the threat to continue the war. Thus, when several U.S. newspapers reported one month before the voting that the administration had met with contra commanders to discuss postelectoral disarming, Under Secretary of State Bernard Aronson immediately issued a public denial: "The United States considers that it has a moral commitment to the contras, we won't walk away from them," and renewing military aid was "not being ruled out." This postelectoral "U.S. commitment" to the contras made headlines in *La Prensa* and was the top news story in the U.S.-funded radios. See *La Prensa*, January 13, 1990.

37. In this effort, the Sandinistas did not have to make anything up. Local UNO slates around the country, for instance, ran known *Somocistas* politicians and former National Guardsmen as candidates. Many of the most prominent UNO leaders, among them Alfredo César, Azucena Ferrey, Alfonso Robelo, and Roberto Ferrey, were former directors of the Nicaraguan Resistance, as was Pedro Joaquin Chamorro, Jr. And these people had already publicly stated their alliance with the contras.

38. This was stated by an NED official in an internal NED document that summarized a State Department/NED Nicaragua strategy session (August 1988, emphasis added). This was provided to me by sources close to the NED.

39. "Budgetary Needs for the Committee for Free Elections and Democracy in Nicaragua" (September 15, 1989), circulated by the Carmen Group.

40. Testimony before the Bipartisan Commission for Free and Fair Elections in Nicaragua, Washington, D.C., May 11, 1989.

· 41. On May 1, 1985, Reagan issued Executive Order No. 13513, which declared a national emergency and allowed the executive to apply the embargo. Each extension of the embargo, at six-month intervals, required the president to renew this "national emergency." See, for example, "White House Notice," April 21, 1989, signed by George Bush.

42. White House statement, November 8, 1989, released by the Office of the Press Secretary.

43. Between 1979 and 1981, defense accounted for 15 percent of the national budget. In 1982, the aggressions began in earnest, forcing the beginning of a transfer of resources. By 1985, the defense effort was consuming 60 percent of the budget, 40 percent of material output, 25 percent of GNP, and 20 percent of the economically active population. See Kent Norsworthy, *Nicaragua: A Country Guide* (Albuquerque, N.M.: Inter-American Hemispheric Resource Center, 1990), p. 67.

44. It should be stressed that in addition to the war, Nicaraguans faced the same adverse international economic conditions as all of Latin America in the 1980s and on top of that had a legacy of extreme underdevelopment and backwardness.

45. For a summary of Nicaraguan economic indicators at this time, and an outline of the austerity measures, see ECLA, annual reports, Nicaragua country section, 1988, 1989, and 1990.

46. For one simplistic critique, see Carlos M. Vilas, "Nicaragua: Critique of Sandinista Economic Policy," *Crítica* (July-August 1990): 11–14. For an analysis with more perspicacity, see Richard Stahler-Sholk, "Stabilization, Destabilization, and the Popular Classes in Nicaragua, 1979–1988," *Latin American Research Review*, 25, no. 3 (Fall 1990): 55–88.

47. This was told to me by the director of the Washington-based Council on Hemispheric Affairs (COHA), Larry Birns, who cited intelligence sources.

48. The report was presented to the Nicaragua government in April 1989. It was reported in U.S. newspapers in July. *New York Times*, July 6, 1989 and July 12, 1989.

49. "Report of the Findings of an Economic Mission Coordinated by the Secretaría de Planificación y Presupuesto" (internal report, Managua, 1989), Introduction, p. 6; Chapter 1, pp. 2–3.

50. See Stahler-Sholk, "Stabilization," especially p. 71.

51. Under the conditions, the UNO and its trade union counterpart, the Permanent Congress of Workers, raised legitimate demands that workers put forward anywhere in the world. But in the environment imposed by prolonged war and crisis, the FSLN was helpless to meet these demands. The legitimate economic grievances of the people became electoral demagogy for the United States.

52. For a summary of these pressures, including those on the World Bank, see "Bush Administration Tries to Block International Efforts to Provide Economic and Humanitarian Aid to Nicaragua," *News and Analysis* (COHA), May 11, 1989. COHA cited World Bank officials who requested anonymity.

53. Ibid. Sending such blackmail letters had already been routinized by the Reagan administration as part of its economic strangulation policies. In 1984, Secretary of State George Shultz conveyed a letter to European Economic Community foreign ministers who were scheduled to meeting in Costa Rica in an unsuccessful attempt to prevent them from providing economic assistance to Nicaragua. He similarly sent a letter in 1985 to the president of the Inter-American Development Bank as well as to all Latin American foreign ministers. Shultz warned them not to give final authorization to a loan already approved on technical grounds for Nicaragua's private agricultural sector, threatening to cancel recapitalization of the bank if the loan went ahead.

54. Deputy Assistant Secretary of State for Inter-American Affairs Crecencio Arcos, whom President Bush later named as ambassador to Honduras, admitted to these pressures at a February 28 breakfast meeting with reporters in Washington. Arcos said the United States would encourage Western European and multilateral banks not to attend or, if they did attend, to condition any new aid on "democratization" in Nicaragua, a condition the State Department had never proposed in dealings with Chile or other Latin American right-wing allies. The Inter-American Development Bank resisted U.S. pressures and sent its representatives to Stockholm, but the other two succumbed.

55. State Department background briefing given by Aronson, February 27, 1990.

56. *Los Angeles Times*, May 24, 1989.

57. See NED, "Reprogramming Request: Superior Council of Private Enterprise" (October 1989, internal document summarizing the COSEP-CIPE program). Also see letter from CIPE program coordinator John D. Sullivan to Carl Gershman, October 24, 1989.

58. NED, "Reprogramming Request."

59. "Economy," *Envío* 9, no. 102 (January 1990).

60. There was a flip side to this message: The population had to actually "sensualize" U.S. dollars. This was "a strategy of the gringo dollars," said one observer. Tens of thousands of people became paid employees of the United States through the NED and other funding. It need not be important that overall the UNO might have been austere when compared to the incumbent—as U.S. press reports were quick to point out. All the UNO needed to do was demonstrate to the population its connection to the U.S. largess. The UNO campaign strategy drafted by the Carmen Group specified, "The population must first be provided with incentives for wanting to attend the rallies.

They are therefore fed at these events and given souvenirs of the rally which, in addition to giving them something to take home, also provides a feeling of well being in contrast to the stark poverty in which they have been living under the existing regime. This has the added advantage of keeping the opposition ever present in their minds" (see Appendix A, document 18).

61. Karl von Clausewitz, *On War* (London: Pelican, 1968), p. 172. This was originally published in 1832 in German as *Von Kriege*.

62. CIA, *Psychological Operations in Guerrilla Warfare* (New York: Vintage Books, 1985), p. 33.

63. In a letter to the U.S. Senate encouraging it to approve the $9 million NED package, Violeta Chamorro wrote, "My colleagues and I believe the voting in February is more than an election. It is a referendum, a chance for the Nicaraguan people to choose between democracy and dictatorship." Letter from Violeta Chamorro to Robert Dole, *Congressional Record* (Senate), October 17, 1989, p. S13523.

64. Quoted in Julia Preston, "The Defeat of the Sandinistas," *New York Review of Books*, April 12, 1990, pp. 25–26.

CHAPTER EIGHT

1. Cited in Penny Lernoux, "The Struggle for Nicaragua's Soul: A Church in Revolution and War," *Sojourners*, May 14, 1989, p. 23. Neuhaus was a founding member of the IRD, which helped promote U.S. policy toward Nicaragua in the 1980s.

2. *FRUS* 1 (part 2), February 24, 1948, p. 23. Kennan, one of the most important icons of the post–World War II international system, was at the time of this quote (1948) the director of policy planning at the State Department.

3. Carl Gershman, "Fostering Democracy Abroad: The Role of the National Endowment for Democracy" (speech delivered to the American Political Science Association Convention, August 29, 1988), p. 13. Copies of the speech were provided to journalists and the public by the NED's public relations office.

4. *Who* achieved victory was further illustrated a few days after the vote when the NED circulated a "list of unsung heroes" of the Nicaraguan elections to the network of "core groups." Among these "heroes" were Keith Schuette, Janine Perfit, and Martin Krauze from the National Republican Institute; Ken Wollock, Brian Atwood, Donna Huffman, and Mark Feierstein from the National Democratic Institute; Barbara Haig, Tresa Bass, and Chiqui Reyes Gavilán from the NED staff; and Hank Quintero and Richard Soudriette from the IFES. See two-page circular on NED stationery. This was provided to me by a source close to the NED.

5. See Noam Chomsky, "The Decline of the Democratic Ideal," *Z Magazine* (May 1990): 15–27. The article surveyed the reactions to the elections in several Latin American capitals and around the world in comparison to the reactions in Washington.

6. Quoted in Robert A. Pastor, *Condemned to Repetition: The United States and Nicaragua* (Princeton, N.J.: Princeton University Press, 1987), p. 162.

7. In addition to the final reports released by U.N., OAS, and Carter group observers, see LASA, "Electoral Democracy Under International Pressure: The Report of the Latin American Studies Association Commission to Observe the 1990 Nicaraguan Election" (Pittsburgh: LASA, University of Pittsburgh, March 15, 1990). It was not only with irony but also with extreme hypocrisy that Bush, who throughout the entire electoral process had not ceased questioning the integrity of the elections and lambasting the Sandinistas for all kinds of alleged "irregularities" and "stacked decks," actually sent a message to Ortega the day after the vote "congratulating him on the conduct of the

NOTES TO CHAPTER EIGHT ■ 233

election." See statement by George Bush, February 26, 1990, released by the White House Office of the Press Secretary.

8. Several postelectoral polls are revealing in this regard. In one of these, 75.6 percent of those surveyed, and 91.8 percent of those surveyed who voted for the UNO, when asked if they agreed or disagreed with the assertion that "the war would never have ended if the Sandinistas had won" said they agreed. Similarly, when UNO voters were asked what most motivated them to vote for the UNO, 66 percent said the promise to immediately end the military service and to end the war, and 20 percent stated the promise of immediate economic improvement. These postelectoral surveys were carried out by the Institute for Nicaraguan Studies (IEN) and are contained in a paper by IEN director Paul Oquist, "Dinámica socio-política de las elecciones Nicaraguenses 1990" (Managua: Instituto de Estudios Nicaraguenses, October 1990). For other quantitative and statistical information that corroborates the argument, see "After the Poll Wars— Explaining the Upset," *Envío* 9, no. 104 (March-April 1990): 30–36.

U.S. intervention also distorted the political pluralism that had been developing in Nicaragua. Parties that traditionally had a social base, such as the Social Christians or the Conservative and Liberal groupings that remained outside of the U.S. fold, lost influence, while parties that had only small followings and little organizational strength gained disproportional influence because of their access to U.S. funds and support, which then became the key to political leadership in Nicaragua. By polarizing the political process and by linking political fortune, not to popular appeal or to internal strength, but to outside support, U.S. intervention completely distorted the internal balance of forces.

9. Abraham Lowenthal, "Even Loss in Nicaragua Vote Can Be Gain," *Los Angeles Times*, September 20, 1989, Op/Ed page commentary.

10. An advance copy of the release was provided to me by the Miami committee, which specified that the release was embargoed until after the vote count was known. The statement was, of course, never released.

11. Baker said this in testimony on February 23, 1990, to the House Committee of Foreign Relations. He also claimed in his testimony that Nicaragua was "still sending arms to the El Salvadoran insurgents," among other accusations, and said that such activities should be the focus of U.S. attention.

12. Speech by Richard Lugar before an international conference on promoting democracy, San José, Costa Rica, January 12, 1990. *Christian Science Monitor,* January 17, 1990, published excerpts of the speech. Lugar demonstrated his complete ignorance of Nicaragua in the speech. He said, for instance, that a new constitution would have to be drafted because the current one did not recognize "freedom of the press, property rights, and the normal freedoms which similar documents in our hemisphere have enumerated." In fact, the Nicaraguan constitution recognized directly and *explicitly* all of the traditional political and civil rights of the constitutions in the Western Hemisphere, including each and every right enumerated in the U.S. Bill of Rights.

13. Probably, the contras would eventually have been demobilized, given that their continued existence, independent of the electoral outcome, was not a viable option for the United States regionally or internationally. The U.S. strategy would have been continued economic and political attrition in the framework of aggressive containment.

14. In November 1989, the NED was given $6.7 million for a special program, "Support for Eastern European Democracy." See NED, "National Endowment for Democracy: Proposal for Program to Support East European Democracy" (January 1990). See "Contra Funders Aid Soviet Right," *The Guardian*, September 26, 1990, for a summary of NED interference in Eastern Europe and the Soviet Union. For more detailed information and analysis, see *Covert Action Information Bulletin*, no. 35 (Fall

1990), Special Issue, "Friendly Enemies: The CIA in Eastern Europe," which discusses not just NED intervention in that part of the world but also CIA and other U.S. covert activities.

15. For a succinct summary of the development of the structures and institutions of formal and participatory democracy in Nicaragua between 1979 and 1990, see Susanne Jonas and Nancy Stein, "Democracy in Nicaragua," in Susanne Jonas and Nancy Stein (eds.), *Democracy in Latin America: Visions and Realities* (New York: Bergin and Garvey, 1990), pp. 13–51. Also see José Luis Coraggio, *Nicaragua: Revolución y democracia* (México, D.F.: Editorial Línea, 1985).

16. The document stated that "the basic needs of the poor have a prior claim on scarce resources in relation to the wants of those whose basic needs are already satisfied."

17. One analyst of democratization processes has noted, "The objective factors constitute at most constraints to that which is possible under a concrete historical situation but do not determine the outcome of such situations" (Adam Przeworski, "Some Problems in the Study of Transition to Democracy," in Guillermo O'Donnell et al. [eds.], *Transitions from Authoritarian Rule* [Baltimore, Md.: John Hopkins University Press, 1988] vol. 2, p. 48). The "concrete historic situation" that made up the Nicaraguan electoral process was the intersection of a series of internal and external factors, both long term and conjunctural, at the unique moment in which the elections took place. There were two external and closely intertwined factors: ten years of U.S. low-intensity warfare and the collapse of socialism, which meant that the international forces most strongly opposing and containing U.S. aggressions disappeared, as did an alternative economic lifeline for Nicaragua. The internal factors, among others, were the FSLN's own tactics and strategies as well as limitations and weaknesses in the revolutionary process that the Sandinistas led. Nevertheless, this distinction between "internal" and "external" factors, made here for methodological purposes, is artificial. Every step of the way, internal factors were modified by external changes; the relation between internal and external was dialectic. More importantly, the nuts and bolts of electoral intervention allowed the United States to secure the outcome it sought on the foundations of the "concrete historical situation."

18. In early June 1990, several hundred Sandinista militants met in a special assembly to analyze the reasons behind, and implications for Nicaragua of, the electoral outcome. The concluding document, "Resoluciones de la Asemblea Nacional de Militantes del FSLN en El Crucero, Departamento de Managua, 17 June 1990," said, "The policy of aggression practiced by successive U.S. governments against Nicaragua is the principal factor in the erosion and attrition of our revolutionary project. At the same time, the socialist countries entered a deep economic, technical and social crisis that gave way to political crisis, which had serious consequences worldwide and diminished the possibilities we had to deal with the effects of the war. . . . The results of the recent elections constitute a success for imperialist policy, which was able to divide our people." The document then went on to analyze numerous other factors, including strong self-criticism of the Sandinistas' own policies and strategies, as contributors to the electoral outcome. The electoral defeat unleashed an onslaught of self-critical reflection among Sandinistas and independent observers, reflected in hundreds of articles, commentaries, and essays published in different Nicaragua media in the wake of the elections.

19. In early July 1989, the FSLN mapped out its campaign strategy in an internal document circulated to party militants. A reading of this document, juxtaposed to the contours and objectives of U.S. electoral intervention, makes clear that the FSLN designed its electoral strategy with a limited understanding of how the United States was operating at the level of political operations and psychological warfare. The

Sandinistas would stress to the population that "only the FSLN can guarantee peace, stability and the security of the country," stated the fourteen-page document. See "Líneas rectoras para la estrategia de la campaña electoral" (July 1, 1989). This was provided to me by members of the FSLN campaign committee.

20. Moreover, the method chosen to maximize votes was a slick, high-profile campaign. Ortega cavorted on platforms throughout the country, dancing, kissing babies, handing out thousands of Sandinista T-shirts, hats, stickers, and cigarette lighters. He resembled a rock star more than an incumbent executive burdened down by a dismal economy and an implacable empire as enemy. The lavish campaign, an ill-conceived adaption of Madison Avenue electoral techniques, was in arrogant contrast to the country's reality of war and poverty.

21. Quoted in William A. Barnes, "Polling Failure in Nicaragua Assessed," *Interamerican Public Opinion Report* (Spring 1990): 2.

22. Similarly, some economic, social, and political measures engendered legitimate grievances and had negative consequences for the Sandinistas' social base. For example, there were emergency wartime economic measures such as state confiscation and redistribution of foodstuffs, the suppression of speculative practices among merchants, fixed prices for peasant-produced foodstuffs, and rationing cards. These steps, portrayed abroad as "totalitarian," were done with the intention of assuring an equitable distribution of limited foodstuffs and guaranteeing minimal dietary needs for everyone. But these measures alienated market vendors as well as those affected peasants and, in the context of wartime macroeconomic distortions, ironically actually aggravated economic conditions for the very poor majority they were aimed at helping. Much has been written on this theme. See, among the many works, Carlos M. Vilas, *Perfiles de la revolución Sandinista*, (Madrid: Editorial Legasa, 1984); Richard Harris and Carlos M. Vilas (eds.), *La revolución en Nicaragua: Liberación nacional, democracia popular, y transformación económica* (México, D.F.: Ediciones Era, 1985); Rose J. Spalding (ed.), *The Political Economy of Revolutionary Nicaragua* (Boston: Allen and Unwin, 1987). For a general study on the complex dilemmas that nationalist revolutions in the Third World face, see Richard R. Fagen, Carmen Diane Deere, and José Luis Coraggio (eds.), *Transition and Development: Problems of Third World Socialism* (New York: Monthly Review Press, 1986).

23. See David Horowitz, "The Alliance for Progress," in Robert I. Rhodes (ed.), *Imperialism and Underdevelopment: A Reader* (New York: Monthly Review Press, 1970).

24. Nelson Rockefeller, *The Rockefeller Report of a United States Presidential Mission for the Western Hemisphere* (Chicago: Quadrangle Books, 1969).

25. Michael Crozier, Samuel Huntington, and Jiji Watuanuki, *The Crisis of Democracy* (New York: New York University Press, 1975).

26. Commission on United States–Latin American Relations, *The Americas in a Changing World* (New York: Quadrangle Books, 1973).

27. National Bipartisan Commission, *The Report of the National Bipartisan Commission on Central America* (New York: Macmillan, 1984). See also U.S. Department of State, *The U.S. and Central America: Implementing the National Bipartisan Commission Report* (Washington, D.C.: Bureau of Public Affairs, July 1986). The report specifically referred to Central America but was seen by policymakers and analysts as a general policy statement for Latin America.

28. For instance, the NED funded a massive, four-volume study, with one five-hundred-page volume dedicated to Latin America (Larry Diamond, Juan J. Linz, and Seymour Martin Lipset [eds.], *Democracy in Developing Countries* [Boulder, Colo.: Lynne Rienner, 1989]) that has become one the standard classroom textbooks in U.S. universities for "democratization in Latin America" courses. Similarly, another standard text

is Guiseppe Dipalma and Laurence Whitehead (eds.), *The Central American Impasse* (New York: St. Martin's Press, 1986), which was funded by the AID through the Inter-American Institute for Human Rights. For a critical survey of this literature, see William I. Robinson, "Democratization in Latin America: Discourse on the Issues" (Albuquerque: Latin American Institute, University of New Mexico, 1991, unpublished ms.).

29. For deeper discussions on "low-intensity democracy," see Robinson, "Democratization in Latin America"; Bob Carty, and "Central America in Perspective," *Central America Update* 12, no. 1 (August-September 1990): 1–8.

30. During the "lost decade," GNP per capita in Latin America dropped by 9.6 percent, a trend that continued in 1990 with a further 2.6 percent drop, according to the 1990 annual report of the ECLA. According to a special commission report on poverty published in 1990, cited in *Latin America Debt Chronicle*, September 5, 1990, in many countries in Latin America, including Mexico, Colombia, and Brazil, per capita income increased even as absolute poverty levels increased, "an indication of the role of unequal income distribution in the spread of poverty."

31. Cited in Carty, "Central America." One year after "free elections" returned that country to "democracy," the Brazilian Bishops' Conference called for popular mobilization against "a system of perverse and destructive relations between capital and labor which translates into abject poverty for millions of Brazilians, and in which a huge portion of the wealth produced by Brazilian workers is captured by foreign companies and banks." The Brazilian economic model "is directed at the uncontrolled accumulation of profits by capital, without minimal guarantees of a dignified life for workers," concluded the Roman Catholic bishops (*Correio Braziliense*, February 14, 1991).

32. Mexican National Nutrition Institute 1990 report; cited in *Notimex*, September 7, 1990.

33. EFE, September 10, 1990.

34. U.N. Commission for Latin America and the Caribbean, *Preliminary Overview of the Economy of Latin America and the Caribbean, 1990* (Santiago, Chile: ECLAC, 1991).

35. See Thomas Klubock, "And Justice When?" *NACLA Report on the Americas* 24, no. 5 (February 1991); Maureen Meehan, "Chile: Military Rejects Human Rights Report," *Latinamerica Press*, April 4, 1991.

36. For a summary of the Guatemalan "transition to democracy," see William I. Robinson, "Guatemala into the 1990s," *Central America Update, Latin America Data Base* (Albuquerque: Latin American Institute, University of New Mexico, March 1990).

37. See Guatemalan Human Rights Committee, 1990 Report, *Latin America Data Base*, (Albuquerque: Latin American Institute, University of New Mexico, 1990).

38. In Haiti, the United States intervened massively, along the same lines as in the Nicaraguan electoral intervention project, in favor of a conservative candidate, Mark Bazin. Despite this intervention, Bazin lost in a landslide to the liberation theologist Father Jean-Bertrand Aristide in the December 1990 elections. Although immensely popular in Haiti, Aristide was viewed with hostility and suspicion in Washington. Nine months later he was overthrown by a repressive military, which the United States had sustained through security programs and subtle political support since the collapse of the Duvalier dictatorship in 1986. For background, see Fritz Longchamp and Worth Cooley-Prost, "Breaking with Dependency and Dictatorship: Hope for Haiti," *Covert Action Information Bulletin*, no. 36 (Spring 1991): 54–60; "Toward a New Future: Emerging Democracy in Haiti," *Haiti Backgrounder* 4, no. 1 (Cambridge: Third World Reports, February 1991); and William I. Robinson, "The Haitian Coup: Ominous Harbinger for the New Latin American Left," and "The Tragic History of the Haitian Republic," Notisur, January 8 and January 22, 1992, *Latin America Data Base*, Latin American Institute, University of New Mexico.

39. Quoted in Jacqueline Sharkey, "Anatomy of an Election: How U.S. Money Affected the Outcome in Nicaragua," *Common Cause Magazine* (May-June 1990): 23.

POSTSCRIPT

1. For an overall summary and analysis of postelectoral U.S. activities in Nicaragua, see "Chamorro's Nicaragua: The U.S. Team Moves In," *Resource Center Bulletin*, no. 21 (Fall 1990). See also William I. Robinson and Kent Norsworthy "The Nicaraguan Revolution Since the Elections," in *CrossRoads*, no. 6 (January 1991): 21–27.

2. This list is quite extensive and includes Carlos Briceño (see Chapter 4), who became director of the state television channels; Alfredo César, who became president of the National Assembly (the U.S. equivalent of this position is Speaker of the House); Miriam Arguello, who became vice president of the National Assembly; Antonio Lacayo, who became minister of the presidency; Virgilio Godoy, who became vice president of the republic; Alfonso Robelo, who became ambassador to Costa Rica; Ernesto Palazio, who became ambassador to Washington; Silviano Matamoros, who became minister of social welfare; Humberto Belli, who became deputy minister and then minister of education; Carlos Hurtado, who became minister of government; Antonio Ibarra, who became deputy minister of labor and then deputy minister of the presidency; Luis Sánchez, who became the presidential spokesperson.

3. See memorandum from Adelina Reyes Gavilán to Carl Gershman, dated March 6, 1990. This was supplied to me by sources in the NED.

4. See "Chamorro's Nicaragua."

5. This included, among other categories, $30 million for agricultural inputs, whose disbursal was conditioned on "agricultural reforms"; $73 million in private-sector production imports to "support the development of a policy reform agenda and the initiation of reform activities"; $50 million for payment of Nicaraguan arrears to international financial agencies, to be "linked to a sound policy framework" approved by the United States. See AID, "Nicaragua: A Commitment to Democracy, Reconciliation, and Reconstruction," (March 1990, "Fact Sheet" prepared for reporters and the public). For a more detailed analysis of the $300 million program, see William I. Robinson, "Nicaragua: When AID Is Not Aid," *Latin America Data Base* (Albuquerque: Latin American Institute, University of New Mexico, October 1990); William I. Robinson, "AID to Nicaragua: Some Things Just Aren't What They Seem," *In These Times*, October 24–30, 1990. Also see "Chamorro's Nicaragua."

6. See "Chamorro's Nicaragua."

7. For a summary, see Grant Fisher, "U.S. Ambassador Shlauderman: Front Man for Counter-Revolution," *NICCA Bulletin* (July-August 1990): 8–9. See also "Chamorro's Nicaragua."

8. Fisher, "U.S. Ambassador Shlauderman."

9. Ibid.

10. AID, "Nicaragua."

11. See internal memorandum from Chiqui Reyes Gavilán to Carl Gershman, March 8, 1990 and marked *"for internal use only, NOT FOR THE FILES,"* provided to me by sources close to the NED.

12. Ibid.

13. Ibid.

14. NED, "Nicaragua" (March 1990, internal document), prepared for submission to the AID. This was provided to me by sources close to the NED.

15. According to the report, these new, postelectoral funds would go to "hire 40 additional organizers and launch membership drives. . . . Efforts will continue to

coordinate post-electoral activities among all democratic trade unions." The funds would also go to opening a new central office in Managua and five regional offices for the right-wing unions.

16. See Solidarity and Democracy Foundation, "Project for the Identification of Obstacles for the Democratic Transition in Nicaragua" (August 1990, submitted to the NED). This was provided to me by sources close to the NED.

AFTERWORD, R. A. PASTOR

1. Carlos Fonseca Amador, *Nicaragua: Hora Cero*, first published in *Tricontinental*, no. 14 (1969); excerpts reprinted in Tomas Borge, et al., *Sandinistas Speak* (New York: Pathfinders Press, 1982), p. 29.

2. Neil A. Lewis, "Reagan Sees Fatal Flaws in Central American Pact," *New York Times*, September 13, 1987, p. A24. In an address to the American people, Reagan said that if aid were cut to the contras, "the Sandinista Communists [would] continue the consolidation of their dictatorial regime and the subversion of Central America." (Excerpts were reprinted in the *New York Times*, February 3, 1988, p. A10.)

3. See Robert A. Pastor, *Whirlpool: U.S. Foreign Policy Toward Latin America and the Caribbean* (Princeton: Princeton University Press, 1992), Chapter 12, "Redrawing the Political Boundaries of Sovereignty: The Nicaraguan Model."

4. See Robert A. Pastor, *Condemned to Repetition: The United States and Nicaragua* (Princeton: Princeton University Press, 1987), and Anthony Lake, *Somoza Falling* (Boston: Houghton, Mifflin, 1989).

5. Transcript of press conference by Hon. Jimmy Carter, February 9, 1986, Managua, Nicaragua.

6. U.S. Agency for International Development, *Report to Congress on P.L. 101-119*, December 1989.

7. The specific agreement is included in the Council's final report. Council of Freely Elected Heads of Government, *Observing Nicaragua's Elections, 1989-1990* (Atlanta: Carter Center of Emory University, 1990), p. 92.

8. Elliot Abrams made this argument in a debate that I had with him at Princeton University on May 4, 1990.

· APPENDIX A ·

Documents

UNIVISION

TO: MS. BARBARA HAIG
FROM: CARLOS A. BRICENO
RE: TV FOR NICA OPPOSITION
DATE: JULY 13, 1989

I'm back from Nicaragua, but dissapointed
of the lack of coverage I received from
Barricada. I guess they were busy trailing
Mark Feirstein around.

Things are starting to heat up way
ahead of the Aug. 25 deadline. I was
really impressed with the march in Leon,
for which UNO only had a day to promote.
We shot great video that I'll send you
soon, once I finish the series that runs
all next week. *(scenes that have not been seen*
totally ignored the — the Sandinista network by the Nicaraguan public)
I met with UNO leaders and its communication's
committee, and they are counting on me
to get the equipment and funds for the
television project. They have no other
TV plan other than the one I've presented
to them. Luis Sanchez was to meet with
the CSE to negotiate UNO's airtime and
to present them with my project for approval.

According to Luis I won't have any trouble
introducing the equipment. In the worst
case I would have to pay a 15 percent
import duty on it, which would not be
substantial since purchase receipts could
be fudged down.

I've enclose and interview with the notable
on the CSE, Rodolfo Sandino, in which
the 50/50 requirement was circumvented
in a shipment on in-kind goods shipped
by the Germans to the PLC.

2103 Coral Way, Miami, FL 33145   305 285 9588

UNIVISION

I spoke to Bill Haratunian who told me
about NABs intention to help in the project.
He asked me about the possibility of
having the equipment loaned to us; however,
that would be the least desireable alternative
because the idea is for the equipment
to become the basis for the first independt
TV in the country if things change.
If they don't I plan to take the equipment
outside the country and beam a TV signal
from a neighboring country.

Please call me and let me know what
there are or any suggestions you
might have.

Sincerely,

Carlos A. Briceno

2103 Coral Way, Miami, FL 33145   305 285 9588

BUSH KLEIN REALTY

Bush Klein Realty inc
Museum Tower
150 W Flagler Street, Suite 1500
Miami, Florida 33130
(305) 536-3722

May 8, 1989

Mr. Carlos Briceno
Univision
2103 Coral Way
Miami, FL 33145

Dear Carlos:

It was a pleasure meeting with you last week to discuss your exciting
project to build an independent production facility in Managua.

As we discussed, the Sandinista government continues to deny television
licenses in Nicaragua. However, it does appear the opposition political
organizations will have access to the government controlled television
stations. Thus, your idea to provide the production capability for the
opposition is very important.

Your professionalism in the television field and knowledge of Nicaragua will
be of value should the production facility go on stream. I wish you every
success in generating political and financial support.

Sincerely,

Jeb Bush

JB/ad

P.S. This should be a project which is supported by people who believe in
democracy from the right and left. I hope it works out that way.

President & CEO
1771 N Street, N.W.
Washington, D.C. 20036
(202) 429-5444
Telex: 360-088

Edward O. Fritts

July 25, 1989

Mr. Stanley S. Hubbard
President & CEO
Hubbard Broadcasting, Inc.
3415 University Avenue
St. Paul, MN 55114

Dear Stan:

Recently a number of U. S. Senators have asked NAB to assist in an effort toward furthering Democracy in Central America. Specifically, we are being asked to donate certain broadcast equipment which would be used to establish a facility to produce TV programming on behalf of groups opposing the Sandinistas in the national elections to be held on February 25, 1990. As part of a recent agreement, the Sandinistas will permit the opposition candidates "equal air time on state-owned TV and radio stations."

This will be the first time in ten years that the opposition to the regime will be permitted to have broadcast media access to the electorate. Opposition parties can broadcast their messages up to 30 minutes daily. But there is a serious problem - the need to produce political programs and campaign commercials independent from Sandinista-controlled TV facilities.

It is with this in mind that I am writing to you. I have enclosed a list of equipment needed for an independent production facility in Nicaragua. I ask you to see if you can donate any portion of these items from your equipment inventory for this worthy cause. If you can make a donation of equipment we ask that its title be transferred to "The National Endowment for Democracy", a tax-exempt, 501(c)(3) foundation with whom we are cooperating. They will then tranship it to the proper recipients in Nicaragua.

One other matter. Time is of utmost importance. The election campaign will begin on August 25, 1989 and air time will be available to the Democratic opposition parties on that date.

I have asked Bill Haratunian, NAB's International Consultant, to call you next week to see if you can participate in this project.

Sincerely,

Eddie

Stan - Hope you
can help. Thanks

CONNIE MACK
FLORIDA

United States Senate
WASHINGTON, DC 20510

July 25, 1989

The Honorable Edward O. Fritts
President
National Association of Broadcasters
1771 N Street, NW
Washington, DC 20036

Dear Mr. Fritts:

As you know, the Sandinista government in Nicaragua has promised to hold elections on February 25, 1990. They have also promised to allow the opposition access to their television stations to broadcast political advertisements.

We believe that the Nicaraguan opposition must be given the fullest opportunity to utilize the television time alloted to them under Nicaragua's electoral law. The free flow of information is critical to the holding a free and fair election in Nicaragua, and therefore to the promotion of human rights and U.S. national security interests in the region.

We are encouraged that the NAB has taken an interest in supporting an effort to equip a production facility for the Nicaraguan opposition in Nicaragua. This effort is in NAB's tradition of support for democracy-building efforts around the world.

Thank you again for your interest in this important matter.

Sincerely,

Connie Mack
United States Senate

Bob Graham
United States Senate

John McCain
United States Senate

Charles Robb
United States Senate

LA PRENSA

TELEFONOS:
DIRECCION 41140-41240
REDACCION 40319-43160
ANUNCIOS 42790

KM. 41/2 PISTA PEDRO JOAQUIN CHAMORRO C.
APARTADO POSTAL No. 192
TELEX No. 375 2051
MANAGUA, NICARAGUA

TELEFONOS:
P. y VENTA 42890
CIRCULACION 42051-42590
CONTABILIDAD 42690

HOJA CUBIERTA DE FAX

MANAGUA, NICARAGUA

NUMERO DE FAX: (5052) 43569   TELEFONO 41051

PARA: SR. CARL GRESHMAN   Y BARBARA HAIG

DE: CRISTIANA CHAMORRO B.

FECHA: 9-2-89

FAX No.: (202) 223002

CIUDAD: WASHINGTON

TOTAL DE PAGINAS: _____2_____   INCLUYENDO HOJA CUBIERTA

OBSERVACIONES:

Queridos Carl y Bárbara:

MI MAMA Y YO REGRESAMOS EL LUNES DE CARACAS DONDE FUIMOS A LA TOMA DE CARLOS ANDRES PEREZ Y TUVIMOS UNA REUNION CON LA GENTE A QUIEN CARLOS ANDRES, DESIGNO MANEJAR LA FUNDACION.

LA INFORMACION QUE LES PUEDO SUMINISTRAR ES LA SIGUIENTE:
- Siempre existen unos estatutos para que ésta sea legal en Venezuela. Los estatutos me aseguraron me los mandarían esta semana.

- La fundación va a estar manejada por personalidades del sector privado venezolano, relacionadas con los medios de comunicación. Por lo que pude apreciar, no están involucrados los partidos políticos de ninguna tendencia.

* El hombre que nos contactó en Venezuela se llama Dr. Eladio Larez y es Presidente de Radio Caracas y Televisión RCTV y se identificó como un miembro del sector privado y periodista, que conoce los problemas de libertad de expresión en estos países y las necesidades y dificultades de los medios hablados y escritos.

- Sobre la mecánica para que funcione esta fundación en conjunto con la National Endowment y las compras que se hacen para LA PRENSA, el Dr. Larez dijo que estaban de acuerdo con dejar todo lo que ya está establecido. Es decir, que López Oña siga comprando y que el se encargue de enviar los materiales vía Miami-Costa Rica o vía Venezuela y que en el caso que se vea complicada vía Venezuela, éllos buscarían que una compañía venezolana radicada en Miami, sea la que aparezca como que es la que está mandando las cosas.

2.-

- Ellos al igual que nosotros y ustedes, están de acuerdo en que todo esto sea público y que se sepa que ustedes envían la ayuda a esta fundación.

- Le pedí al Dr. Larios que se pusiera en contacto con ustedes. Sus teléfonos en Caracas son 351737 y el 2565761. Télex 21340 POBOX 70734.

- Ellos me dijeron que los llamarían tanto a ustedes como a López Oña. Entiendo que para hoy ya se comunicaron con López Oña.

- Ayer recibí una llamada de Caracas en la que me dicen que la Sra. Yoly Muñoz, es la que va a ser encargada de la oficina que éllos abrirán en Caracas para esta fundación. Yoly todavia no tiene teléfono, pero dijo que cualquier cosa llamáramos al Dr. Larez.

- Me gustaría escuchar los comentarios de ustedesa como va este proyecto. En Caracas yo sentí que Carlos Andrés lo tiene muy en cuenta. Beatrice me dijo que está segura que tiene que funcionar porque el Presidente tiene gran interés.

- Por otro lado en Nicaragua se están dando cosas muy interesantes, que creo que nos pueden cambiar el panorama despmés de San Salvador.

Muchos besos y espero oír pronto de ustedes,

Cristiana Chamorro .

TELEFONOS:

DIRECCION   41140-41240
REDACCION   40319-43160
ANUNCIOS   42790

EDITORIAL LA PRENSA, S. A.

KM. 41/2 PISTA PEDRO JOAQUIN CHAMORRO C.
APARTADO POSTAL No. 192
TELEX No. 375 2051
MANAGUA. NICARAGUA

TELEFONOS:

P. y VENTA   42890
CIRCULACION   41051-42590
CONTABILIDAD   42690

Managua, Nicaragua
11 de Agosto de 1989

Señor
Carl Greshman
y/o Barbara Haig
y/o Adelina Reyes
National Endowment Democracy
1101 Fifteenth Street. N. W.
Suite 203. Washington. D. C.   20005

Querido Carl:

A como quedamos en Costa Rica, les estoy enviando el análisis de las encuestas que creo que todavía puede tener alguna validez.

Referente a la solicitud que presenté para poderle introducir color a LA PRENSA a la hora de campaña, nuestro departamento de producción estima que con esos 120 mil dólares que creemos nos costaría el proyecto podríamos cubrir seis (6) meses.

Hoy viernes 11 de agosto, salió a luz vía cívica. Vamos a ver como lo enfocan mañana sábado los periódicos. Les envío el último Nuevo Diario que habla sobre las aventuras de la NED y su Reina en Nicaragua. Sobre la pregunta que ustedes me hicieron de Briceño, he podido conocer que él podría ser excelente en cuanto a asuntos técnicos, pero necesitaría mucha ayuda para el enfoque político, es decir dirección.

Bueno creo que eso es todo, lo que teníamos pendiente.

Mil besos y saludos.

Cristiana.

11 August 1989

TO: KES

FROM: JTP *GP*

SUBJECT: NICARAGUA

While the month of August has been a relatively slow one, the Nicaraguans have been thinking and working at a steady pace. The following is a status report of sorts on where we stand with our various projects and ideas and where we need to be in one month's time.

1. PNC representatives to Tokyo:
After a rather divisive battle between Mario and Diablo/Silviano over PNC representation in Tokyo, I have two faxes signed by Silviano which designate both Mario and Diablo to attend. During the battle I was asked to provide some assistance to the PNC for this trip and ultimately decided on $4,000.00 for two passages. The question now is: is it worthwhile to spend this much money to send the Nicos? Is their presence necessary? If we don't pay they won't go.

2. Carlos Briceno:
In Carl's proposal before the NED Board, he is prepared to request about $400,000.00 for the T.V. project. I have spoken with Carlos a number of times and he would like to know what his next steps need to be. We need to find out from Carl if Carl is planning on putting us in charge this program or if NED wants it. Then we must learn how to set up and agreement with Briceno. Does he need to form a non-profit institution with a committee of notables to oversee it? (This was Carl's idea.) Who will sign the grant agreement? Carl would like this too to be bipartisan, but Ken knows nothing about it.

Along with these questions, there are others about ownership of the equipment, FSLN approval of Carlos' program as the UNO T.V. time, fees to be charged to buy T.V. time, etc.

I have told Carlos that he will probably have to wait until September before he sees any of this assistance. I have not told him that it may be as late as September 30. He also knows that the Germans are interested but that they are out of touch until the end of August. As you know, he would like to move on this beginning 25 August. He even has ideas to start producing spots and interviews in Miami

Nicaragua Memo
Page 2

and sending the tapes to be aired in Nicaragua as soon as
T.V. access becomes available on 25 August. He will call
again Monday in search of some concrete guidance on how
much he should do prior to NED approval.

3.   UNO General Secretariat:
      In Carl's mind, this program is ready to go.   NDI and
NRI have been asked to reprogram current funds in order to
provide $100,000.00 each to set up the UNO office and get
it going for two months.   Then the Institutes would be
expected to keep the secretariat going for four more months
at $50,000. per month.   In Carl's proposal to the NED Board
he is prepared to ask for $400,000. for the Institutes to
run this program.

      Carl's meeting in San Jose was with the UNO finance
committee.   They are the ones who prepared this budget and
made the request.   Carl assumes they will be the ones to
manage the funds.   He told them to send him the number of a
bank account in Miami as soon as possible in order to
receive the $200,000. in start-up costs.   Now that he has
had time to think this through, he does not know who would
be able to sign a grant agreement or even if one is
necessary.   He sees that NED will need one more round of
consultation before this process is completed and is
suggesting a meeting with UNO representatives on 11
September either in D.C. or San Jose.   See attached budget.

      And all this talk of UNO, parties, candidates, and
campaigns makes NDI very nervous.

      (Of course this idea goes against that which we
discussed with Mario about each godfather helping its own.
I dread telling him that a decision was made about UNO
without consulting him.)   (And won't Myriam be pleased that
we have decided to do this without her help?)

4.   Other NED Nico programs:
      For your information, Carl has the following plans for
the remainder of the $1.5 million:
      FTUI and union training   — $467,000
      La Prensa (16 pages and color,
      with a wider distribution   250,000
      Radios   50,000
  ·   Via civica   probably nothing
      Center for Democracy   75,000
That's more than $1.5 million, so he will have to trim
somewhere.

5.   Also attached please find a translation of the
UNO/FSLN accord form last week.   Lastly there is a brief
analysis of the accord from Diablo.   Who shall we share it
with?

Nicaragua memo
Page three

6. Mario is still pressing on IDU activities in Nicaragua. Would like to know when the monitoring group will come. Wants to know about election observers as the hotels are filling up for the 25 of February. We must remember to write Willoch's letter about this.

7. Current NRIIA Nico budget status:

As of 31 July, our Nico Conference budget had $85,000. remaining. See Dan's memo attached on the status of his youth program plans. We also owe Bill Harris $2,500. and will spend $4,000. more if we send the Nicos to Tokyo.

The second Nicaragua account has not yet been opened but will be in the total of $120,000. which contemplated $80,000. for the Institutes and $40,000. for NRI.

As you can see, that's not so much left for the UNO secretariat. We will need to get a substantial increase from the September Board meeting.

8. Next plans: NDI may go to Managua at the end of August with some of their consultants. I have told our folks that I may drop by also at the end of August to discuss all the answers to all these questions.

<u>Budget</u>
UNO General Secretariat

<u>Investment</u>

1 Pick-up truck	$ 16,000
1 Micro bus	20,000
2 Motorcycles	6,000
1 IBM PC-2 computer	14,000
1 Mimeograph machine	3,000
2 Xerox copiers	10,000
6 IBM typewriters	6,000
10 Executive desks	5,000
10 Chairs	2,000
10 Chairs (Visitors)	1,500
2 Sofas	500
10 Metal Filing cabinets	3,000
4 Calculators/Adding machines	1,000
1 Telephone console & 12 extensions	4,000
2 Fax machines	5,000
1 24" television	500
1 VHS VCR	500
1 Amplifier with radio/cassette recording capability, microphone and speakers	1,000
2 Cameras	1,000
TOTAL INVESTMENT	$100,000

<u>Monthly Administrative Costs</u>

Rent, telephone, fax line, electricity, water	$ 6,000
Salaries for 5 division heads ($500 each)	2,500
Salaries for 80 department activists ($150 each)	12,000
Salaries for 6 secretary/ receptionists ($250/month)	1,500
Salaries for 2 handymen, 2 cleaning people, 1 messenger ($100/month)	500
Salaries for 5 drivers ($200/month)	1,000
Per diem costs/travel *	9,000
Operator costs for vehicles/ motorcycles	2,500
Paper/office supplies	2,000
Printed materials (not propaganda)	3,000
Travel and international per diem	10,000

TOTAL ADMINISTRATIVE COSTS $50,000 x 6=$300,000

TOTAL BUDGET UNO SECRETARIAT $400,000

Meeting with CAP:

— CAP believes freedom of the press is a precondition for democracy and is anxious to do what he can to help La Prensa.

— A representative of the GON attended the Venezuelan elections in December. CAP told him that he objected to the new law and if it is not lifted, he would work with his friends in the U.S. who have paper and supplies to insure La Prensa would get what it needs. He strongly protested a law which would punish receipt of outside aid and said that La Prensa needs outside aid for its very survival.

— He believes that everything possible should be done to exploit the "cracks" which exist in the system. He believes that the time is right for the international community to do so and that there is hope that the combination of internal and external pressure can force the Sandinistas to compromise.

— Since La Prensa's situation is urgent, CAP wanted to do something immediately which would allow La Prensa to receive US assistance and also pledged to try and come up with some Venezuelan support.

— He specifically proposed using a Venezuelan institute, which would be comprised of representaives from the media, business, labor and the parties, as a pass-through for NED support. This organization would probably not actually have to serve as a pass- through other than on paper.

— He will continue to press the Sandinistas to lift the ban for La Prensa as well as the rest of the civic opposition.

AMERICA'S DEVELOPMENT FOUNDATION
600 SOUTH LEE STREET, OLD TOWN, ALEXANDRIA, VIRGINIA 22314, TELEPHONE (703) 836-2717

July 28, 1989

Ms. Adelina Reyes-Gavilan
National Endowment for Democracy
1101 - 15th Street, N. W., Suite 203
Washington, D. C. 20005

Dear Chiqui:

     As discussed, enclosed is the revised narrative and budget for the CAD program in Nicaragua which has been presented to us by CAD. I am now seeking additional budget details from CAD and some clarifications on the program design. You may also wish to consult with CAD on this as well as other topics during your upcoming visit with them. After you agree on the revisions to reflect the current work, we will seek to conclude an amendment to the present grant.

Sincerely,

Michael D. Miller
President

MDM/lm

WASHINGTON, D C • ALEXANDRIA, VA.

MODIFIED PROGRAMATIC STRUCTURE AND CONTENTS FOR
NED GRANT # 89 - 08.0 (ELECCIONES NICARAGUA - 90)

BACKGROUND:

Once the conditions of the Nicaraguan Political context changed with the programming of presidential elections to be held on February 25, 1990, "ENCUENTROS DEMOCRATICOS" had to give way to a new program which could adapt itself to this specific circumstance in order to provide international support to the Nicaraguan Civic Opposition.

The idea is to re-design the original proposal of "ENCUENTROS DEMOCRATICOS" to offer on a short-term basis, substantive contributions to the recently initiated process in Nicaragua.

Besides attempting to create a democratic and participative attitude in Nicaraguan society, an immediate goal is also the promotion of concrete actions to prepare the democratic organizations for the upcoming electoral process. The latter will be done by providing the Civic Opposition with the necessary technical instruments to attain political balance.

CAD-centroamerica must become:

A service unit: to maximize strengths and diminish weaknesses in concrete electoral tasks such as organization, communication, promotion, image and the development of technical electoral assistance.

A logistic unit: to channel Centralamerican and international support and to facilitate coordinating procedures among several of the International Organizations with programs in Managua.

OBJECTIVES:

CAD seeks to balance the political forces in Nicaragua by helping to modernize the democratic civic and political organizations so they may become effective political alternatives.

CAD will assist the civic groups and organizations within the civic opposition as to organize the population to actively participate and verify the electoral process.

CAD will enable the political and civic organizations participating in the electoral process to plan, guide, and evaluate their own actions by assimilating new technical skills, and putting them into practice.

CAD will assist the political and civic organizations participating in the electoral process in developing means of communication and coordinating ties in order to form a macro-structure for the 1990 elections.
This objectives will be accomplished through workshops and specialized work sessions on planning, electoral training, motivation, campaign logistics communications, and leadership:

CAD will carry out seminars for the training of technical groups in charge of developing organizational skills and image enhancement within each group or organization.
CAD will further develop and technically support the new structural and individual capabilities originating from the above mentioned training activities. These activities will seek to motivate participants to organize themselves in order to favor unity on election day, and use other national and international events and initiatives to increase the proposed structure's effectiveness and support.

ACTIVITIES:

1-SISTEMAS: This component will become the main recipient of all information gathering efforts such as, opinion surveys, small scale polling and voting trends analysis. With this information (and the processing of the electoral data available), SISTEMAS will be able to evaluate the promotional and campaing achievements of the Nicaraguan opposition.

• SISTEMAS will also offer assistance on design and production of specific documents and promotional - educational materials for other programs (ie. YOUTH, WOMEN, VIA CIVICA).

• SISTEMAS will process the existing information on: total population, population by sex, density by regions, employment, unemployment, delimitations and characterization of the electoral areas, and others. On election day, SISTEMAS will attempt to monitor any effort made for the quick count of votes, make periodic estimates to measure the porcentage of voter turnout, and process whatever final results may be available to obtain the outcome of the elections.

• SISTEMAS may also provide a structured support for exit polling efforts.

2- ELECTORAL TRAINING: Through a series of workshops, this component will procure the general electoral training for the members of the voter reception committees.
CAD will also attempt to establish a "HOT LINE" mechanism to provide updated electoral information. During election day CAD will provide pertinent and newsworthy information for the international media.

3

3- **YOUTH**: The youth vote represents over 44% * of the total voter population, therefore the program must develop specific actions to promote democratic values among this important segment of the Nicaraguan society.

CAD will assist the CENTRO DE FORMACION JUVENIL (CEFOJ), and other democratic youth organizations, to carry out activities to promote voter turnout, recruit and train guides and receptionists on logistics for election day, train youth to carry out small scale opinion surveys (SISTEMAS), and provide technical support to carry out national meetings for youth. These will serve as forums for the discussion of electoral issues.

4- **WOMEN**: The women in Nicaragua represent 50.8 % * of the total population, therefore it is important to address their needs in terms of the electoral process.

CAD will assist the MOVIMIENTO DE MUJERES NICARAGUENSE (MMN), and other democratic women organizations to carry out a series of activities to promote voter turnout, recruit and train guides and receptionists on logistics for election day, train women to carry out small scale opinion surveys (SISTEMAS), and provide technical support to carry out national meetings for women. These will serve as forums for the discussion of electoral issues.

5- **LABOR**: The democratic labor organizations in Niacragua such as the CENTRAL DE UNIFICACION SINDICAL (CUS) and the CENTRAL DE TRABAJADORES NICARAGUENSES (CTN) will actively participate in the 1990 elections. The labor movements in Nicaragua have a grassroots organization that thoroughly covers the country's territory, and therefore have great incidence and impact on the upcoming electoral process.

CAD will assist the CENTRAL DE UNIFICACION SINDICAL (CUS), the CENTRAL DE TRABAJADORES NICARAGUENSES (CTN), and other democratic labor organizations to carry out a series of activities to promote voter turnout, and recruit and train labor leaders on logistics and procedures for election day.

)

*REF. FUNDACION MANOLO MORALES - SOURCE POLL MARCH 1989.

CAD **Centro de Asesoría para la Democracia**
133-1007 San José Costa Rica- Phone(506) 53-6101 Fax (506)34-6322

TELEFAX TRANSMISSION

To   Adelina Reyes Gavilan
            NED

From: Sylvia Escalante H
            CAD-centroamérica

Date: October 5, 1989

Fax: (202) 223 - 6042

Pages: 2   (Including cover)

NOTES:_____

_____

_____

_____

_____

Jueves 5 de Octubre, 1989

Adelina Reyes Gavilan
NED

Querida Chiqui:
    A petición de Sergio te envio la información sobre la compra de los automoviles para Nicaragua.
    Te informo que si es posible que la agencia nos coloque los automoviles en la frontera de Nicaragua, pagando únicamente un uno % de impuesto aquí en Costa Rica. También te averiguamos que por el momento tienen disponibles todos los tipos de vehículos necesarios en Nicaragua.
    Esperando esta información te sea de alguna utilidad, me despido muy.

                    Atentamente

                    Sylvia Escalante H.
                    CAD-CENTROAMERICA

National Republican Institute for International Affairs

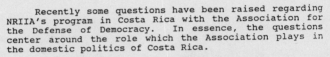

June 5, 1989

Mr. Carl Gershman
President
National Endowment for Democracy
1101 15th St., NW
Washington, D.C. 20005

Dear Carl:

Recently some questions have been raised regarding NRIIA's program in Costa Rica with the Association for the Defense of Democracy. In essence, the questions center around the role which the Association plays in the domestic politics of Costa Rica.

As you know, NRIIA takes great caution to ensure that our grant programs do not become involved in partisan campaign politics. We have been especially cautious in Costa Rica in this regard, as there is a record of unfounded charges by officials of the National Liberation Party that NRIIA has supported campaign activities of the Social Christian Party. While these charges are absolutely untrue, the re-emergence of such questions at this time is obviously cause for concern.

In order to prevent this matter from becoming a serious problem here and in Costa Rica, we have agreed with the leadership of The Association that its work will no longer have any domestic focus after 1 July 1989. This means that all domestic training programs, research projects, and educational activities will cease. The Association will re-focus its work as an international foundation directing its activities toward Nicaragua, Panama, and other areas such as Mexico. I will travel to Costa Rica next week to begin the re-structuring of The Association and I will have a more detailed explanation and plan upon my return. Obviously, we will keep you fully informed on the progress of this exercise in the weeks ahead.

601 Indiana Avenue, N.W., Suite 615, Washington, D.C. 20004. (202) 783-2280. Telex: 5106000161(NRIIA), Fax: 202-783-9480

Nicaragua-Gesellschaft e.V. Bonn

Nicaragua-Gesellschaft e.V. Postfach 120-403 5300 Bonn 12

National Endowment for Democracy
Ms. Adelina Reyes Gavilán
1101 15th Street N.W.
Suite 203
Washington D.C. 20005
U. S. A.

Nicaragua-Gesellschaft e.V. Bonn

Postfach 12 04 03
5300 Bonn 12
Telefon: (02 28 XXXXXXX 38440
XXXXXXXXXXXXXX
Fax: (49/228) XXXXXX 384534

| Ihre Nachricht vom: | Ihr Zeichen: | Unser Zeichen: | Datum: 22.08.1989 |

Dear sirs:

I hereby have the honor of bringing to your attention the activities that for the past six years have been carried out by the NICARAGUA-GESELLSCHAFT e.V. (Nicaragua Society) and the ZENTRALAMERIKA-GESELLSCHAFT e.V. (Central American Society) in support of democratic development in Central America.

The Nicaragua Society was founded in 1983 and since then has been publishing a bi-weekly newsletter entitled "INFORMATIONSDIENST NICARAGUA" (IDN). This publication covers a variety of developments in Nicaragua, having as its main objective bringing to the attention of European public opinion the viewpoints of the democratic and non-violent political and civic opposition groups inside Nicaragua. We believe coverage of such issues is often lacking in the general media.

Over the years, IDN has become a key source of information even among high level opinion/decision makers. We count among our readers members of the German parliament, journalists, etc.

Additionally, the Nicaragua Society has set up special campaigns in support of the victims of human rights violations inside Nicaragua. The best publicized among these was a solidarity campaign in Germany during the time of the closure of the daily "La Prensa" in 1986. The Society also became active on behalf of indian (Sumu) refugees in Honduras, and other Nicaraguan refugees in Costa Rica, El Salvador, Mexico and Spain. The Society has also campaigned for a project of the CTN labor union.

A constant supply of first-hand information to the national and international press as well as the production of a film about the situation in Nicaragua have contributed to changing a hitherto uncritical sympathy for the Sandinista regime in German public opinion.

Of special importance has been the program of assistance to visitors and delegations from Nicaragua. Many prominent members of the internal civic opposition have visited our office in Bonn and have been assisted in making contacts and organizing their political programs in the Federal Republic of Germany. Our office's assistance has been highly appreciated both by our Nicaraguan guests as well as by German parties/organizations and, over the years, became an important task of the society.

In 1985, the ZENTRALAMERIKA-GESELLSCHAFT e.V. (Central American Society) was founded. As it became obvious that it was not sufficient to contain Sandinista ruled Nicaragua's expansionist policies through support for the internal oppo-

- 2 -

sition, it was decided to also promote support for the democratic sectors in
other Central American countries. The Society has recently launched a new information bulletin on the region.

As the leading members of both societies have had the chance to extensively
travel to Central America over the past seven years, close contacts have been
established in all countries of the region. Visitors from Central American
nations other than Nicaragua have also frequently visited our Bonn office
during the past three years.

The Nicaragua and Central America Societies are both legally recognized as
non-profit organizations according to German law. Nevertheless, funds have been
very limited. As we feel that both societies and the NATIONAL ENDOWMENT FOR
DEMOCRACY share the same values and interests, we would be interested in establishing contact with your organization.

Specifically, we would like to know if you are supporting any projects of the
kind we are carrying out in support of democratization in Central America, e.g.
in the field of publications, visitors' assistance and political education. If
so, we would be interested in supplying you with more detailed information on
the work of both societies, including visitors' lists, projects and the like. In
order to provide you some initial information, we are including some of our publications as well as the constitutions and names of the members of the board
of directors of both societies.

Hoping to hear from you, I would like to express our thanks for your interest.

Most sincerely

Dr. Götz Frhr. v. Houwald
vice-president

Enclosure

October 30, 1989

Mr. L. Brent Bozell III
Chairman
World Freedom Foundation
111 South Columbus Street
Alexandria, Virginia 22314

Dear Brent:

Thank you for your 26 October letter regarding the situation in Nicaragua. I share your deep concerns regarding developments in Managua as they relate to both international observers and the civic opposition.

I also believe that your strategy with regard to visas is a good one; it does appear that the Sandinistas are making a clear differentiation between what they consider to be acceptable and non-acceptable international visitors.

Much as I would like to join you, at the moment it is not clear that it would be a wise decision to do so. As you know, NRIIA will be one of the primary vehicles for the special $9 million assistance package for the Nicaraguan civic opposition. For the near-term our primary objective is to get into Nicaragua to organize and execute our assistance program. While members of the NRIIA staff have been denied visas in the past, we were finally given permission to visit Nicaragua, and we did so last week. That visit, and others which we must make in the four months ahead are absolutely essential to our ability to assist opposition groups as they prepare for the February elections. For the moment, it appears that we will be given the access we require to conduct our work. Since our ultimate objective is to help the opposition, I believe that we will need to treat the issue somewhat differently from others who are less directly involved in support for UNO.

You can rest assured however, that if we are denied visas in the coming weeks we will make as much noise as possible. Should we be denied visas, the Sandinistas would not only be making a "left-right" distinction,

601 Indiana Avenue, N.W., Suite 615, Washington, D.C. 20004, (202) 783-2280, Telex: 5106000161(NRIIA), Fax: 202-783-9480

page 2

    For these reasons I believe it makes the best sense for us to pursue a lower profile effort for the time being, though we fully support the effort you are organizing.

Warm Regards,

Keith E. Schuette
President

JIMMY CARTER

September 22, 1989

To President Daniel Ortega

First of all, let me thank you for your assistance in making my weekend visit both enjoyable and productive. My conversations with you and Sergio Ramirez were very helpful.

Your assurance that there will be no more conscriptions into the active military service was welcome, and I hope you will decide that this will also apply to the reserve forces during the next five months. I have reminded the opposition parties that they should present to the Electoral Council a list of political prisoners and send a copy of the list to me, the UN, and the OAS observer teams. Your expeditious handling of this matter will help to remove a constant complaint. As you may have noticed, I made the appropriate statement to the press concerning expropriation of property and your continuing commitment to the land reform laws.

As you requested, I sent to Cardinal Obando y Bravo a request that he call for moderation in rhetoric and actions during the coming months. I have, by the way, read several recent speeches by UNO and the FSLN and have found that those of the FSLN are far more negative. I expressed to you my opinion that this is not an attractive political tactic. It is obvious to me that the Nicaraguan people are eager to look to the future, with hopes for peace, reconciliation, and prosperity.

I spent yesterday in Washington, following up on the issues we discussed. I met with Brooklyn Rivera and his associates, the top officials in the White House and State Department, a bipartisan group of members of both houses of the U.S. Congress, and then the OAS Secretary General and Elliot Richardson. Let me summarize the results:

Brooklyn Rivera signed the agreement that Minister Tomas Borge and I agreed to in Puerto Cabezas, and stated that he plans to return to the East Coast as soon as possible -- probably early next week. Since a clear agreement was reached with you and your government's officials while I was in Nicaragua, no changes should be proposed either by your government or by Indian leaders. I have sent your government a partial list of other Miskito leaders who plan to come home. I understand

Page 2

that you have given your embassies in Costa Rica,
Honduras, and the United States instructions to expedite
this process, providing appropriate papers for those who
do not have passports. Many of the Miskito Indians who
are Contras in Honduras will likely want to join their
leaders as soon as practical.

I have absolute assurances from U.S. officials at
the highest level, both in the Executive and Legislative
branches, that there will be no covert funding from our
government for opposition political parties or other
purposes that would subvert the integrity of the
Nicaraguan elections. They know that I am making this
guarantee to you, and that you will let me have any
evidence you have to the contrary before you make a
public allegation that this agreement is violated. As
we discussed, I expect that the FSLN's campaign will
refrain from any attacks or accusations of CIA funding
of UNO or covert destabilization of the election. In
addition, I would like for you to assure me that the
FSLN will abide by the same restrictions concerning
compliance with your country's election laws: that any
foreign funding to the FSLN be disclosed and distributed
in accordance with Nicaraguan law.

At the present time, plans are to provide a total
of about five million U.S. dollars to help with the
election. These funds will probably not go to any
particular party, but will be channeled through the
National Endowment for Democracy (NED) to support the
democratic process. If this proposal is approved by
Congress, it will be necessary for you to arrange for
visas to be issued to these people so that they can
carry out their duty of monitoring use of the U.S.
funds. Additional funds may be approved for
distribution to political parties, but Congressional
leaders have assured me that these will be spent in
accordance with Nicaraguan laws.

There is little likelihood that additional
financing will be requested for the Contras above that
already approved -- the last portion of which amounts to
about 48 million dollars. The money will be used in
compliance with the Tela agreement, as interpreted by
the United States government. However, as you know, the
emphasis in Washington is on voluntary demobilization.
It may be possible for me to visit the Contras in
Honduras to encourage their repatriation, but this will
not be possible right away. The Reconciliation
Commission headed by Cardinal Obando Y Bravo could be

Page 3

very helpful in assuring the Contras that they will
receive a proper welcome when they return. As part of
the Tela agreement, you will be expected to refrain from
providing arms to the FMLN.

It seems to be too early to initiate an exchange of
ambassadors, but a step-by-step increase in embassy
personnel will be well received. If you desire, this
can be done without embarrassment or friction if handled
properly. Assistant Secretary of State Bernie Aronson
is prepared to work this out.

At OAS headquarters, Baena Soares, Elliot
Richardson, and I agreed to cooperate as election
observers. As I discussed with you and the Electoral
Council, we plan to conduct an independent vote count on
February 25, with observers at about 10 per cent of the
mesas. We will withhold publication of these data until
after the official results have been issued -- or at
least until a previously agreed time on February 26. As
you can see, we are trying in every way to be able to
certify that the election is completely fair and free.

Best wishes to you during the coming months. You can always
contact me directly or through Dr. Pastor if I can be of help.

Sincerely,

Jimmy Carter

His Excellency
Daniel Ortega
President of the Republic
 of Nicaragua
Managua

by fax

Chairman
Jose Antonio Alvarado
1390 Brickell Avenue #401, Miami, FL 33131
(305) 372-8000 Fax (305) 372-5751

COMITÉ PRO ELECCIONES LIBRES Y DEMOCRACIA EN NICARAGUA

COMMITTEE FOR FREE ELECTIONS AND DEMOCRACY IN NICARAGUA

FACT SHEET

COMMITTEE FOR FREE ELECTIONS AND DEMOCRACY IN NICARAGUA

The Committee for Free Elections and Democracy in Nicaragua was organized by the Nicaraguan Civic Task Force to assist the Union Nacional Opositora (UNO) in its campaign.

At the UNO's request, the Committee is raising private funds from the Nicaraguan exiled community and others in the US to purchase a variety of much needed campaign equipment and materials.

The Committee is based in Miami, Florida. Its members, all Nicaraguan professionals, are:

Jose Antonio Alvarado, Chairman
Nicolas Lopez-Maltez
Lucy Reyes
Ramiro Sacasa
Leonidas Solorzano
Carlos J. Garcia

Alvaro Jerez
Nadia Pallais
Leda SanchezdeParrales
Polidecto Correa
Pedro Joaquin Chamorro

An honorary steering committee of prominent Americans has also been formed. Its members are:

Hon. Chester Atkins (MA)
Hon. Cass Ballenger (NC)
Mrs. Sofia Casey
Senator Alfonse D'Amato (NY)
Hon. Chuck Douglas (NH)
Hon. Dante Fascell (FL)
Hon. Amo Houghton (NY)
Hon. Duncan Hunter (CA)
Dr. Tirso del Junco
Hon. Robert Lagomarsino (CA)
Governor Bob Martinez, FLA
Hon. Ron Packard (CA)
Hon. Ilena Ros-Leihtnen (FL)
Hon. E. Clay Shaw, Jr. (FL)
Hon. Denny Smith (OR)
Hon. Charles Wilson (TX)

Hon. William Broomfield (MI)
Jeb Bush
Senator Dan Coats (IN)
Hon. Robert Dornan (CA)
Hon. David Dreir (CA)
Senator Bob Graham (FL)
Peter Huessy
Mr. Henry Hwang
Hon. John Kyl (AZ)
Senator Connie Mack (FL)
Hon. John Miller (WA)
Hon. John Rhodes (AZ)
Hon. Richard T. Schulze (PÀ)
Hon. Norman Shumway (CA)
Hon. Gerald Solomon (NY)
Hon. Frank Wolf (VA)

The Committee for Free Elections and Democracy in Nicaragua is registered with the U. S. Justice Department and is the only organization sanctioned by the UNO to receive campaign contributions in the United States.

UNO

Chairman
Jose Antonio Alvarado
1390 Brickell Avenue #401, Miami, FL 33131
(305) 372-8000 Fax (305) 372-5751

COMITÉ PRO ELECCIONES LIBRES Y DEMOCRACIA EN NICARAGUA

COMMITTEE FOR FREE ELECTIONS AND DEMOCRACY IN NICARAGUA

VIA TELECOPIER

TO: John Stabile

FROM: Gerald P. Carmen

SUBJECT: Fundraiser for Nicaragua Elections

DATE: February 2, 1990

Ambassador Jeane Kirkpatrick has agreed to be with us on Wednesday, February 7, 6:30 pm to 9:00 pm for cocktails and buffet to speak on the campaign in Nicaragua. Seymour and Eva Holtzman have donated their apartment at the River House, 435 E. 52nd Street, and the ensuing cost of the reception and buffet. We now have to find 20 couples or individuals that would contribute $5,000 to raise $100,000 that evening that has been targeted. Please circle that night and see if Nick and Ted can come along.

This election can be the turning point in restoring that part of Central America to Democracy and, in my opinion, will set in motion the cure for Cuba and finally end the threat that we face down there. That's not to minimize the tragedy that has engulfed the people of these countries and will at least give them a chance to be free and prosperous.

THE
CARMEN
GROUP
PUBLIC RELATIONS

January 30, 1990

Honorable Jeane J. Kirkpatrick
American Enterprise Institute
1150 17th Street, NW
Suite 700
Washington, DC 20036

Dear Jeane:

Thanks so much for agreeing to be the honored guest at a New York fundraiser for Violeta Chamorro February 7. THe fundraiser will be at the Holtzman's New York home - River House, 435 East 52nd Street (between 52nd and Sutton) from 6:30 p.m. to 9:00 p.m., cocktails and buffet dinner.

My understanding is that accommodations have been set at the Waldorf for you to change and rest on arrival. We will pick you up by limo and take you to the airport to arrive back at D.C. on the night of the 7th. I do not yet have, but hope to have, a private jet donated.

Attendees will be donating $5,000 per couple to the Committee for Free Elections and Democracy; the registered and official vehicle for funds to Violeta. Press is not invited, nor welcome.

Again, thank you -- I'll keep Winnie posted.

Sincerely,

David Carmen

DC/pc
cc: Winnie Peterson

THE
CARMEN
GROUP

PUBLIC RELATIONS

December 22, 1989

Dr. Jose Antonio Alvarado
Committee for Free Elections
    and Democracy in Nicaragua
1390 Brickell Avenue, Suite 400
Miami, Florida 33131

Querido Jose Antonio:

Adjunto te mando copia de un fax que mandamos hoy a Tonio Lacayo,
sobre el asunto de Ernesto del cual hablamos tu y yo ayer. Como
veras, David uso un tono bastante suave pero quiero advertirte
que estamos muy molestos por la situacion, tal como descrita en
el fax.

Lo que David dejo de decirle a Tonio es que tememos que la
reputacion de Ernesto nos podra perjudicar--porque no deja de
haber gente que piensa que si estamos trabajando por una causa en
la cual Ernesto (que ya tuvo problemas de haber manejado mal la
plata de la contra) anda tan visible, que a lo mejor, a nosotros
tambien se nos debe faltar fe.

Esta situacion de Tonio haciendo parecer que Ernesto es el
"fundraiser" oficial de Dona Violeta en los Estados Unidos, o
aunque solo en Washington, D. C., no puede continuar si esperas
que nosotros funcionemos de la manera mas efectiva en tratar de
recaudar fondos para la campana de Dona Violeta y de la UNO. Con
lo del Iran-Contra y mas problemas que ya se nos han presentado
(que fueron totalmente inesperados), no nos hace falta este
problema adicional de Ernesto.

Deseamos oir algo de Tonio o de ti sobre como se resolvera este
asunto.

Quisiera tambien mencionarte que Ernesto ha dicho a varias
personas que el ya ha recaudado $50 mil para la campana. Espero
que esa plata se haya transmitido a Managua.

Muchos recuerdos y Feliz Navidad.

Cordialmente,

1667 K STREET, N.W. SUITE 700
WASHINGTON, D. C. 20006
(202) 785-0500   FAX: (202) 785-5277

BUDGETARY NEEDS FOR THE COMMITTEE FOR FREE ELECTIONS AND DEMOCRACY IN NICARAGUA

DATE: September 15, 1989

The Union Nacional Opositora, the opposition coalition of 12 political parties, one private sector council and the organization of trade unions whose acronym UNO, significantly means ONE in Spanish, has wisely decided to field only one candidate to oppose the Sandinista regime. This candidate, the widow of a well-known figure in Nicaraguan politics thought to have been killed by the Sandinistas, Violeta Chamorro, is already popular with the Nicaraguan masses. However, in order to counter what will most certainly be intense and well financed activity on the part of the Sandinistas, the opposition's campaign must and will take advantage of every hour between now and February 26th, election day.

Campaigns in less developed countries, particularly in those long repressed by dictatorial governments where elections have been suspended for many years require much more activity and expense than equivalent campaigns in developed nations.

The population, which tends to be skeptical about the opposition's resources and chances of winning, vis a vis the ruling party, and about the honesty with which an election will be conducted, must be enervated and motivated to vote. More importantly, their votes must then be protected to ensure accurate results.

The population must first be provided with incentives for wanting to attend the rallies. They are therefore fed at these events and given souvenirs of the rally which, in addition to giving them something to take home, also provide a feeling of well being in contrast to the stark poverty in which they have been living under the existing regime. This has the added advantage of keeping the opposition ever present in their minds. Further, these people must be transported to and from the rallies.

Population mobilization and motivation requires resources for a full time organized activity by many campaign workers in the 16 geographic departments into which Nicaragua is divided. It also requires transportation for the population and campaign staff in each district. Equipment, food and souvenirs must also be purchased.

It has been decided that the most effective campaign must be one that is divided into two phases: Phase I will consist of raising the consciousness of the Nicaraguans and will be conducted between September 1 and December

- 2 -

1 and Phase II will consist of the mechanics and reasons for voting for the opposition and will occur between December 1 and February 26.

Phase I: Consciousness raising will address the following themes: Hunger, Misery, Obligatory Draft, i.e., the status quo versus Change, Liberty and Employment

In this phase, rallies will be conducted in each of the 16 departments of the country. The UNO will require the following resources for this stage of the campaign:

100,000	caps	$360,000.00
100,000	T-shirts	$200,000.00
100,000	plastic glasses	$ 25,500.00
3,000	medium and large flags	$ 18,000.00
100,000	small plastic flags	$ 35,000.00
50,000	first aid kits	$100,000.00
20,000	bumper stickers	$ 6,000.00
150,000	ball point pens	$ 30,000.00
	wall posters	$ 30,000.00

TOTAL REQUIRED FOR SOUVENIRS FOR PHASE I $709,500.00

Phase II will consist of telling the population why they should vote for the particular candidates fielded by the UNO. This will be conducted from December 1st to election day and will emphasize the following themes:

> The Candidates' values and personalities
> Full employment for the country
> Freedom of expression
> Prosperity and improvement of quality of life

Aside from the rallies, the opposition will try to present its message in a limited fashion, as allowed by the Sandinista government, on radio, TV and in newspapers. Because media access will be tightly constrained by the Sandinistas, campaign posters, billboards and pamphlets will also transmit the opposition's message. The committee will look to other sources to provide the funds necessary for TV, radio and newspaper advertising.

A campaign theme song is presently being composed which will be played on the radio constantly.

- 3 -

For this phase, rallies will be conducted in the following locations:

Managua
Leon
Chinandega
Masaya
Granada
Rivas
Esteli
Matagalpa
Chontales

The month of December will be largely targeted to the children and the giveaways are planned accordingly:

Resources required for Phase II are as follows:

10,000	flags, 3 sizes	$ 20,000
200,000	T-shirts	$ 400,000
100,000	coloring books with UNO logo	$ 40,000
100,000	plastic beach balls with UNO logo	$ 50,000
200,000	caps	$ 100,000
100,000	bumper stickers	$ 30,000
200,000	plastic glasses	$ 51,000
200,000	first aid kits	$ 400,000

TOTAL REQUIRED FOR SOUVENIRS FOR PHASE II $ 1,091,000

In addition to the giveaways, the UNO will need the following resources for the 6 months of the campaign:

10	buses	$ 300,000
20	pick ups	$ 200,000
30	cars	$ 450,000
200	megaphones and batteries	$ 45,000
4	500-watt electric generators	$ 2,000
	Photocopier	$ 2,000
	Salaries for 10,000 campaign workers (junior)	$ 75,000
	Communications equipment	$ 370,000

- 4 -

Training material for campaign $ 50,000
Salaries for senior campaign staff $ 90,000
Gasoline for vehicles $ 150,000

TOTAL IN SALARIES AND EQUIPMENT $ 1,734,000

Travel must also be undertaken both by UNO members as well as for members of the Nicaraguan Civic Task Force and the Committee for Free Elections and Democracy. This travel will consist of the following:

Travel for UNO members to Miami
     and other states $ 70,000
Travel for Task force and Committee
     Members to Nicaragua $ 40,000
Lodging:
     Houston, TX $ 6,000
     San Francisco, Los Angeles, CA $ 21,000
     New York $ 6,000
     Puerto Rico $ 6,000
     New Orleans $ 7,000
     Washington, D.C. $ 12,000

TOTAL TRAVEL EXPENSES REQUIRED $ 168,000

It is absolutely necessary to bring in large numbers of international observers to observe both the campaign process as well as the election process and the vote count. It is planned to bring in 125 observers, 50 each from the U.S. and Latin America and 25 from Europe. The anticipated cost of this element is as follows:

     50 U.S. observers $ 100,000
     50 Latin American observers $ 100,000
     25 European observers $ 120,000

TOTAL TRAVEL EXPENSES FOR OBSERVERS $ 320,000

In addition to the above funds a sizable co-ordinating office, the Committee for Free Elections and Democracy in Nicaragua, will have to be developed and funded in Miami and funded for 5 months. A small support staff that will deal on a day-to-day full time basis will be needed to co-ordinate press outreach and response, distribution of aid, donors relations and supervise budgetary implementation.

- 5 -

This office will have a full time staff of 4, plus a director and outside professional services. Expected costs including office space, equipment, telephone, insurance and payroll will costs in the neighborhood of $275,000.

A budget summary of all of the above follows:

PHASE I Giveaways	$ 709,500.00
PHASE II Giveaways	$1,091,000.00
Salaries and Equipment/Nicaragua	$1,734,000.00
Travel Expenses	$ 168,000.00
Travel Expenses, Observers	$ 320,000.00
Miami Office	$ 275,000.00

TOTAL FUNDING REQUIRED   **$4,297,500.00**

Fundraising expenses to raise these funds will be extensive. The Carmen Group will be retained to co-ordinate all fundraising aspects. The preliminary budget for fundraising costs is detailed below. There will be three major areas of fundraising: major donors, which will be cultivated through one-on-one solicitations; major events; direct mail solicitations.

Materials needed for the activities in addition to cost of events will be printing of an impressive binder on the campaign for hand-out to major donors; a stock brochure; a promotional videotape; travel, Federal Express, out-of-pocket expenses.

Commissions shown are the standard 10% paid to registered solicitors of contributions not otherwise employed by The Carmen Group or the Committee and a standard 5% bonus of the gross paid to The Carmen Group on achieving each $1 million dollar gross raised by the Committee.

THE
CARMEN
GROUP
PUBLIC RELATIONS

RECEIVED
OCT 05 1989

October 2, 1989

Ms. Barbara Haig
Deputy Director of Program
National Endowment for Democracy
1101 15th Street, NW
Washington, DC 20006

Dear Barbara:

Thank you for taking the time to meet with us today. We are excited about the many opportunites that lie ahead. I am positive that together we'll bring about real change for democracy in Nicaragua.

In the mean time, anything that I can do to be of assistance, please let me know.

All the best,

David /ps

David Carmen

1667 K STREET, N.W. SUITE 700
WASHINGTON, D.C. 20006
(202) 785-0500 FAX: (202) 785-5277

Mr. Lee Atwater
Mr. Ron Brown
727 Fifteenth St.,N.W. Suite 1200
Washington, D.C. 20005

January 9, 1990

Democratic Chairman Ron Brown and Republican Chairman
Lee Atwater invite you to join them in supporting Violeta Chamorro.

Mrs. Chamorro is the mother of four children and the widow of Nicaraguan
martyr, Pedro Joaquin Chamorro.

Mrs. Chamorro is owner and publisher of the largest pro-democracy
newspaper in Nicaragua,"La Prensa," which is the most important source
of independent information in the country.

Mrs. Chamorro will face Marxist-Leninist dictator Daniel Ortega in the
first-ever free election to be held in Nicaragua on February 26th.

Conditions in Nicaragua are ripe for change. Since the Sandinistas came
to power, wages have fallen 80 percent. At $300 a year, per capita
income is among the lowest in Latin America. Last year the economy
shrank 11 percent and prices rose 36,000 percent. Now that's inflation;
people don't count bills they weigh them.

Mrs. Chamorro's party, Union Nacional Opositora,(whose acronym UNO means
ONE in Spanish) must face the intense and well financed activity of the
Sandinistas. UNO must not waste a minute between now and the election.

Campaigns in less developed countries, particularly in those represented
by dictatorial governments where no elections have been held, require
more activity and expense than campaigns in more developed nations.

That's where we come in. We are asking you to join with a diverse group
of Americans, Republicans, Democrats, Liberals, Conservatives, Business
Owners and Labor Union Leaders to make an investment in Nicaraguan
Democracy.

Mrs. Chamorro will be in Boston on January 16, at the Copley Plaza Hotel
(Copley Square, Boston) in the Venetian Room for a private reception
from 7:00 - 8:30pm. We invite you to come and meet this courageous
lady. UNO's budget for this election is four million dollars so we ask
you to be as generous as you can be. We are asking you to give a
minimum contribution of $1,000, but you can give MORE! UNO has set up a
U.S. committee, The Committee for Free Elections and Democracy in
Nicaragua. The committee is registered with the U.S. Government and you
can be sure that your donation will go to help bring democracy to
Nicaragua.

Since time is short, please respond to this invitation immediately. For
further information call (202) 347-0044. Thanks for your time and
interest.

Ron Brown	Lee Atwater	Richard Ravitch	Ed Koch
Chairman	Chairman	Former Mayoral	Former Mayor
DNC	RNC	Candidate NYC	New York City
James Daley	Chet Atkins	Ray Shamie	Jeb Bush
	Congressman	Chrm. Mass.	
		Rep. Party	Donald Trump

October 6, 1989

Mr. Luis Arguello
Creative Marketing Ideas
4075 SW 83rd Avenue
Suite 202
Miami, Florida 33155

Dear Mr. Arguello:

Thank you for your quick response on the printing of the t-shirts of our Nicaraguan program.

Per our conversation of 5 October, Creative Marketing Ideas is authorized to begin work on the t-shirts as specified in your 10/5/89 invoice (#189191). NRIIA agrees to pay the invoiced price of $17,632.00. Please advise if this price includes tax, as we are a tax-exempt organization. Please advise us of your bank account number and we will make arrangements to wire the funds upon completion of the printing.

Thank you again for your prompt action and cooperation.

Sincerely,

Keith Schuette

INVENTORY LIST
(LISTA DE CONTENIDOS)

Departure Date From Baton Rouge: October 3, 1989

A (TO):   Mr. Luis Arguello
                 4075 Southwest 83rd Avenue
                 Suite 202
                 Miami, Florida 22155
                 Telefono: (305) 227-9333

INSTRUCTIONES
ESPECIAL: T-Shirts are to be expedited by delivery to Miami, Florida,
                 for distribution to Latin America for the poor and needy there.

DESCRIPCION (DESCRIPTION): T-SHIRTS

CARTON NUMBER	QUANTITY IN DOZENS	STYLE NUMBER	CROSS REFERENCE	SIZE
001NI	20	1714	B-10	L
002NI	36	1714	358	M
003NI	20	1714	B-24	M
004NI	20	1714	B-53	L
005NI	20	1714	B-52	M
006NI	18	1711	11172	L
007NI	20	1714	B-92	L
008NI	20	1711	16707	S, M, L, XL
009NI	18	1711	16179	XL
010NI	20	1714	B-15	L
011NI	20	1714	B-14	L
012NI	20	1714	B-38	M
013NI	20	1714	B-12	L
014NI	20	1714	B-94	L
015NI	20	1714	B-9	L
016NI	20	1714	B-24	L
017NI	20	1714	B-60	L

CREATIVE
MARKETING
IDEAS

4075 S.W. 83 AVENUE, SUITE 202, MIAMI, FLORIDA 33155, 305 227-9333

CREATIVE MARKETING IDEAS
4075 SW 83RD AVENUE   SUITE 202   MIAMI, FLORIDA 33155   (305) 227-9333

FAX MESSAGE

DATE: OCT/5/89

REF. No.:

TOTAL PAGES: (including this page) 1

FROM: LUIS ARGÜELLO
TO: MR. SCHUETTE
ATTN:

CUSTOMER
NATIONAL REI
CONTACT
Mr. Keith Sc
ADDRESS
CITY, STATE, ZIP
CUSTOMER P.O. NO.

QTY.	DESCRIPTION
23,200	T-SHIRTS: Stock: Supplied Ink: Blue & green Imprint: Two sides, Two colors Area of Imprint: Approximate 50 square Text on front reads: "UNO POR LA DEMOCR Text on back reads: "UNO SOMOS TODOS" Price based on ¢0.76 per item.

Terms: _____ Received By: _____

A 2.5% late charge will be added to any past due balance. After 60 days delinquency it will be turned o

282 • DOCUMENT 22

12/22/89
NRIIA

OPTIONS FOR FINANCIAL TRANSFERS

BACKGROUND:

It had been the intention of NDI/NRIIA to wire transfer grant funds to both UNO and IPCE in accordance with what we understand to be Nicaraguan law. After nearly eight working days of effort we were unable to successfully wire grant funds to the Central Bank of Nicaragua (BCN) despite the assurances of several U.S. and Canadian banks that they could accomplish the task.

On Tuesday 12/19/89 NDI/NRIIA decided to send cashier's checks directly to Managua by courier after our grantees and Project Staff had been assured by the Central Bank of Nicaragua that cashier's checks drawn on U.S. banks would be cleared in five working days. The checks totalling $1.2m were sent to Managua and arrived in Nicaragua on 12/21/89.

On Thursday 12/21/89 Project Staff and grantees again met with BCN officials to review the procedures for accepting the cashier's checks. However, the BCN officials noted that the five day clearance was no longer possible, and that the normal time to clear would be 15 working days under normal circumstances. Further, the BCN explained that its dollar reserves (from which it would obtain the dollars required to honor the checks) were held in Panamanian banks, and that the state of war which existed in Panama made it impossible to secure the dollars needed to honor the checks. BCN also explained that any investigations of Panamanian bank funds which might arise from the U.S. action could further delay the delivery of dollars.

We are therefore in a situation in which it seems highly unlikely that our grantees will be able to obtain either dollars or cordobas with the checks currently in hand.

-2-

POSSIBLE OPTIONS

<u>1) SEND IPCE GRANT FUNDS THROUGH THE EXISTING IPCE ACCOUNT IN MIAMI.</u> Will address some of the short-term cash needs for IPCE, probably not sufficient to meet IPCE's cash needs for more than two weeks.

<u>2) SEND DIRECT CASH PAYMENTS BY COURIER TO IPCE/UNO.</u> Not especially practicable, but could address some near-term needs perhaps up to $250k. Could be done with/without cooperation of BCN. If done with cooperation, could conceivably cover more than $250k.

<u>3) SEEK NICARAGUAN NATIONALS WITH MAJOR HOLDINGS IN U.S. WHO COULD OFFER CORDOBAS TO IPCE/UNO IN EXCHANGE FOR DEPOSITS TO THEIR U.S. ACCOUNTS.</u> Relatively easy if donors are willing, but does have financial costs as conversion to cordobas reduces purchasing power.

<u>4) ATTEMPT TO FREE UP BCN DOLLAR HOLDINGS IN PANAMA, OR ARRANGE FOR OTHER BCN ACCESS TO DOLLARS.</u> Has clear policy implications, would require time.

<u>5) APPLY POLITICAL AND PUBLIC PRESSURE TO NICARAGUA TO COMPLY WITH THEIR COMMITMENTS TO UNO AND NDI/NRIIA.</u> Unlikely to succeed, could damage further access.

<u>6) OTHER:</u>

_____

_____

_____

_____

1101 King Street, Suite 601
Alexandria, VA 22314
October 27, 1989

Mr. Carl Gershman
President
National Endowment for Democracy
1101 15th Street, NW, Suite 203
Washington, DC 20005-5003

Dear Carl:

   Per your conversation yesterday with Frank Fahrenkopf, the
Simon Bolivar Fund would like to apply to the National Endowment
for Democracy to assist with the special programs which are being
formulated for the upcoming Nicaraguan elections. We understand
that the Bolivar Fund would provide services which, for one
reason or another, neither of the party institutes, nor the
organizations specifically mentioned in the special legislation,
would perform.

   Consistent with the brief discussions which we have
previously had with you on this matter, and Andres Hernandez'
longer discussion with Barbara Haig, we believe that the Bolivar
Fund can also act as a most appropriate vehicle or conduit of
funds as well as materiels, and services to the united
opposition, providing the requisite oversight, expertise and
credibility.

   We would like very much to meet with you early next week and
present a formal and timely proposal, consistent with your needs.
We will be in touch with your office to arrange a time,
convenient to your schedule. The Bolivar Fund welcomes the
opportunity to assist the NED in this significant and sensitive
project.

   Warmest personal regards.

            Cordially,

Andres R. Hernandez   John P. Loiello

cc: Frank Fahrenkopf, Jr.

The Simón ▮ Bolívar Fund
A Campaign Fund to Promote Democracy Abroad

<u>for internal use only</u>
<u>NOT FOR THE FILES</u>
March 8, 1990

To: Carl
From: Chiqui
Thru: Barbara
Re: Nicaragua/AID Project Update

Welcome back! I hope you had a good trip. I've taken the
liberty of having this messengered to your home in the hopes that you
will read it before Monday and that Barbara and I can have your input
on the issues discussed below as soon as possible. I know that next
week will be extremely hectic.

Roger Noriega has "passed the baton" to Norma Parker (LAC/DI) on
all matters relating to the administration or coordination of the
remaining funds under NED/AID Nicaragua electoral assistance grant.
Norma called Barbara and me on March 5 to request information on the
disposition of funds already allocated, and the NED's plans for use
of the remainder of the funds. Norma also indicated that she
anticipates a large economic aid package for Nicaragua sometime down
the pike (perhaps as a supplemental to the Panama aid package), which
would include funds for democratic development to be channeled
through the Democratic Initiatives office. Therefore, she was also
interested in knowing our thinking on potential democracy-building
programs for the future (e.g., programs focusing on administration
of justice, constitutional reform, etc.).

According to Norma, those programs for which funds have already
been allocated (Via Civica, CUS, IPCE, UNO) will probably be able to
proceed with whatever funds they have left. As for the reserve fund,
Norma said that no funds can be reprogrammed (for other projects not
originally in this package such as radios, youth, women, CAD, La
Prensa, etc.) until after AID sends a 15-member delegation to Managua
for two weeks in May to conduct what she called a "needs
assessment." Apparently, this would enable the Endowment to prepare
new programs for the June Board meeting. However, she indicated that
emergency funds (i.e., partial funding of <u>La Prensa</u>) might be able to
move forward before then. Norma would like someone from the NED to
represent us and the institutes on the delegation, but Barbara and I
plan to conduct our own needs assessment in late April. [In
preliminary discussions with Alfredo Cesar, he indicated that the
greatest need between now and the inauguration on April 25 is for
consultants, primarily lawyers. They need, but do not have the funds
to pay for, Nicaraguan and international lawyers to draft laws,
agreements relating directly to the transition. They have real needs
during the transition period that cannot wait until AID takes its
traveling show to Managua. Preliminary soundings in Managua indicate
that Jack Leonard feels strongly that NED assistance cannot be
postponed until June.] <u>Please note that this is AID's preliminary
position and should not be interpreted as irrevocable.</u> The Endowment
<u>must</u> have some input here. I will describe suggested course of
action later.

Barbara cautioned Norma that we must be very careful not to get out ahead of the Nicaraguans on the issue of future programs: the UNO transition team is engaged in delicate talks with the Sandinistas, and it could prove counterproductive for the U.S. government or the Endowment to take public positions on such issues as the need for constitutional reform, etc. We emphasized that, as usual, we would be responsive to requests from the Nicaraguans rather than initiate programs on our own. Priorities are set by the Nicaraguans. Nonetheless, we described some of the kinds of programs we have supported in other transitional situations (e.g., forums for dialogue, training for legislative assembly leaders, broader civic education programs, etc.).

Regarding the ongoing grant, we reviewed with Norma the status of the IPCE, UNO, Via Civica, and CUS grants as follows:

UNO: Only time will tell whether UNO will remain a united coalition or splinter into its individual party components. Issues such as constitutional reform, land reform, etc., will be debated on the National Assembly floor, and the parties that comprise UNO will in all likelihood take differing positions (it's hard to envision the Communist Party siding with the Conservative Party against the Sandinistas on land reform, for example). NRI and NDI have received requests for continued funding to pay for the rent and salaries of the Consejo Politico house (of the 14 parties), and also what is now the transition team house (formerly campaign headquarters). According to NRI and NDI, UNO has no funds left from the original grant.

IPCE: IPCE was originally envisioned as a long-term institution, as reflected in the $50,000 allocation for post-electoral activities under the current grant. According to Donna Huffman of NDI, IPCE may have as much as $250,000-300,000 left over from the electoral program, but final accounting for this and the UNO program will not be available until late March at the earliest. Issues under current discussion among NRI, NDI, and the IPCE reps pertain to IPCE's post-electoral purpose and configuration; so far, there's an informal consensus that IPCE's activities should probably focus primarily on civic education and training (something along the lines of the CED in Paraguay). At the moment, nonetheless, IPCE was described to us by NRI and NDI as an institute "without a mission." It should be noted that IPCE has enough equipment to staff one central and two regional offices. Janine feels that if they could contract a top-notch executive director and staff, it has a future.

CUS: Mike Donovan claims that CUS has used up most if not all of the original $493,013. As you know, AID has previously indicated that in order to be reimbursed for costs incurred under this grant, CUS must document its good faith efforts to comply with Nicaraguan law or provide justification as to why it could not. AID said that it was 90% certain that the auditors would approve a reimbursement. FTUI/AIFLD have indicated that they need $50,000 in the next two months to assist CPT activities aimed at countering Sandinista trade union (CST) destabilization efforts.

VIA CIVICA: VIA CIVICA will also be reimbursed for costs incurred under this grant once it provides documentation of its good faith efforts to comply with Nicaraguan law. IFES told me that most of VIA CIVICA's activities during the electoral period were undertaken with funds from the $3.5 million, and that only a small portion of the $220,000 out of the $7.+ will have to be reimbursed. This means that VIA CIVICA will have a good portion of the current grant available for its post-electoral activities. Again, the terms and conditions of the current grant must be renegotiated before we can send them any of the funds.

In synthesis, the issues that face us right now are:

1) The status of the reserve funds and any unspent funds: Does the Endowment have the authority, or not, to reprogram the reserve funds for projects/groups not originally in the $7.435 million package? Also, we have received no formal indication at this point (other than Norma's off hand remark) as to whether AID agrees that funds already allocated (IPCE, etc.) can be reprogrammed to support other activities which require immediate support. The Endowment is not a subsidiary of AID, and our funding decisions should not be contingent on their needs assessment. The Endowment and its institutes should set up a meeting with AID no later than March 16 with the objective of ensuring NED control over programming decisions and the use of remaining funds.

2) Formulation of program priorities: This is related to #1 above. As I noted earlier, the Endowment and its institutes have received indications from UNO representatives, CUS, and other groups that the opposition has immediate needs between now and April 25. These pre-transition needs can either be met with the reserve funds or with previously allocated funds to IPCE which may remain unspent. We have also received formal funding requests from La Prensa for immediate needs, and from the radios, CAD, and the women and youth groups for longer term needs; these groups would like their proposals to be considered for funding at the March Board meeting. We have asked our institutes to submit their own ideas, after consultation with their grantees and other Nicaraguans, regarding program priorities, both in the immediate term and in the longer term. Assuming that we obtain authorization from AID to reprogram unspent funds, we will then have to decide on how to proceed. We have to keep in mind that there's a Board meeting in March.

3) Renegotiation of the terms and conditions of the current grant: The Endowment and its institutes, together with AID, must ensure that the terms and conditions imposed by the US Congress on this assistance which modified NED's standard operating procedures (i.e., compliance with Nicaraguan laws: Ministry of External Cooperation, Central Bank, etc.) are renegotiated. Otherwise, we are bound by the terms of the NED/AID grant to abide by the Nicaraguan foreign donations laws, and each foreign grantee will have to have concurrent audits, submit monthly reports, etc. The current agreement also specifies May 31 as the expiration date of the grant and clearly we will want it extended to some later date.

4) <u>Future Funding Mechanisms</u>: Norma assumes that any future
supplementals for Nicaragua will go through the Democratic
Initiatives office of AID, and that the Endowment will have to
compete with other organizations for those funds. A concerted effort
must be made on the Hill -- through our Board, the institutes, et al
-- to have any future funds come directly through the Endowment, not
through AID. As Barbara has said, what makes the Endowment unique is
its flexibility, responsiveness, and independence, and we should
under no circumstances be subsumed under AID. We are not a PVO. AID
should be reminded that we have worked in Nicaragua since 1984; we do
not need, nor do we want, to take our lead from AID. This is a
broader issue which goes beyond Nicaragua and which I understand
Barbara would like to discuss in-depth with you.

I hope that we'll have an opportunity to discuss this further
next week.

cc: Program, TB, DL, MF, MP

• APPENDIX B •

Chronology

This chronology focuses on the 1979–1990 period in Nicaraguan history, but important historical dates beginning with Nicaragua's independence in 1821 are also included in order to place the period under study in context. In the pre-1979 section, emphasis has been given to events relating to U.S.-Nicaraguan relations.

1821–1978

1821   Central America declares its independence from Spain.

1833   U.S. troops intervene briefly in Nicaragua.

1854   In the first major U.S. intervention, the U.S. Navy burns down a Nicaraguan town, San Juan del Norte, following an insult to millionaire Cornelius Vanderbilt.

1855   To secure the rights to a canal for the United States, mercenary William Walker hires an army, invades Nicaragua, and declares himself president. Walker reestablishes slavery in the country, and his regime is subsequently recognized by Washington.

1857   Walker is overthrown, and constitutional rule is reestablished.

1893   Nationalist José Santos Zelaya comes to power. U.S. troops intervene four times in the next five years.

1909   Under intense U.S. pressure, Zelaya is forced to resign.

1910   U.S. troops intervene, beginning twenty-three years of repeated marine occupation.

1911   The United States places Nicaragua under customs receivership, controlling the country's revenues.

1916   Conservative Emiliano Chamorro is elected president in U.S.-staged elections.

1926   U.S. Marines launch what would become Central America's first counter-insurgency war against a peasant army, led by Augusto C. Sandino, the "General of Free Men."

1932   Liberal Juan Bautista Sacasa is elected president.

1933   After failing to defeat Sandino's guerrilla army, the marines withdraw, having established the Nicaraguan National Guard, with Anastasio Somoza García as commander-in-chief.

1934   Sandino is murdered, on Somoza's orders.

1936   Sacasa is removed by Somoza's forces; the presidential election is won by Somoza.

1936–56   Rule of Anastasio Somoza García (Tacho I).

1956–66   Rule of Somoza García's son, Luis Somoza.

1966–79   Rule of Anastasio Somoza Debayle, brother of Luis.

1961   Carlos Fonseca, Tomas Borge, and Silvio Mayorga form the Frente Sandinista de Liberación Nacional (FSLN).

1977   The Group of Twelve (Los Doce), comprising prominent Nicaraguan political figures and intellectuals opposed to Somoza regime, is formed.

A major FSLN offensive is launched.

1978   Pedro Joaquin Chamorro, editor of *La Prensa* and leading opposition figure, is assassinated.

The National Guard is sent in to break a national strike.

The Broad Opposition Front (FAO) is formed.

The CIA begins funding to the conservative opposition to Somoza.

An FSLN commando seizes the National Palace.

An FSLN-led insurrection is launched.

1979–1990

1979   *June:* The FSLN calls for a "final offensive" against the Somoza regime. A nationwide civil war ensues.

July: The FSLN triumphantly enters Managua and installs a revolutionary government.

President Carter signs a top-secret finding authorizing covert CIA assistance to conservative groups in Nicaragua.

1980   *March:* The revolutionary government launches a massive literacy campaign that reduces illiteracy rate from more than 50 percent to 13 percent in five months.

May: The Council of State (legislature) is inaugurated. U.S. Congress approves a $75 million economic aid package for Nicaragua.

1981   *March:* The United States cuts off $9.8 million in food aid to Nicaragua.

April: Washington suspends all bilateral aid to Nicaragua but continues support to the private sector and the Catholic church.

August: The Agrarian Reform Law is promulgated.

September: The AID approves several million dollars in assistance to anti-Sandinista business, labor, religious, and civic groups.

November: The Reagan administration authorizes $19 million to destabilize the Nicaraguan government, giving the CIA a green light to organize ex–National Guardsmen into a counterrevolutionary army based in Honduras.

December: By the end of the year, health-care campaigns have reduced the infant mortality rate 40 percent in relation to pretriumph figures.

1982

March: Following contra destruction of two bridges in the north, the government declares a state of emergency.

June: U.S. Congress approves $5.1 million in economic assistance for the Nicaraguan private sector.

November: U.S. Congress approves $24 million in covert aid to the contras.

1983

January: The Contadora Group, formed by Mexico, Venezuela, Colombia, and Panama, attempts to mediate Central American dispute.

February: More than five thousand U.S. and Honduran troops take part in the Big Pine military maneuvers near the Nicaraguan border.

March: The first large-scale invasion of contras from Honduran territory occurs. In the United Nations, Nicaragua denounces U.S. support for the contras; only El Salvador, Honduras, and the United States vote against the Nicaraguan motion.

May: Washington reduces Nicaragua's sugar importation quota by 90 percent.

June: The U.S. Treasury Department announces an official policy of opposing all multilateral loans to Nicaragua. The Patriotic Military Service (draft) is instituted.

September: The contras launch their Black September offensive, including sea- and air-based attacks against petroleum installations and key economic infrastructure and ground attacks against the principal entry points on the country's northern and southern borders.

President Reagan signs a secret finding authorizing an expansion of the CIA program in Nicaragua, including an expansion of covert funding for the anti-Sandinista internal opposition.

October: The contra offensive deepens with heavy fighting in the north and south, eight aerial attacks, and sabotage actions against the ports of Corinto and Sandino.

The United States invades the republic of Grenada.

1984

January: The NED begins funding for Nicaraguan opposition media, labor unions, civic groups, and political groups.

March: The CIA and Pentagon units assist the contras in the mining of Nicaraguan harbors in gross violation of international law. Seven foreign vessels and several dozen Nicaraguan ships are damaged by the mines.

April: More than thirty-five thousand troops surround Nicaragua as the Pentagon simultaneously stages maneuvers off the Atlantic and Pacific coasts and in Honduras.

May: The International Court of Justice orders the United States to suspend the mining of Nicaraguan ports and support for the contras.

November: Nicaragua holds the first free elections in history. The FSLN's candidate, Daniel Ortega, is elected to a six-year term with 67 percent of the vote against six opposition parties. Reagan denounces the elections as a sham.

1985   *February:* The Nicaraguan government implements the first economic stabilization package.

May: The White House declares a trade embargo against Nicaragua.

June: U.S. Congress approves $27 million in "humanitarian" aid to the contras.

1986   *June:* A $100 million contra aid package is approved by U.S. Congress. The contras escalate military attacks.

The International Court of Justice rules that the United States is in breach of international law on multiple accounts for aggressions against Nicaragua.

October: U.S. mercenary Eugene Hasenfus is shot down and captured during a contra resupply mission.

November: The Iran-contragate scandal breaks in Washington.

1987   *January:* A new constitution is signed.

June: The Nicaraguan government estimates that the U.S. war has inflicted some $12 billion in damages on Nicaragua.

August: The presidents of Costa Rica, El Salvador, Guatemala, Honduras, and Nicaragua sign the Esquipulas Peace Accords. Nicaragua becomes the first signatory to the Esquipulas Accords to form a national reconciliation commission.

September: La Prensa is allowed to resume publication after a one-year suspension; the church hierarchy's Radio Católica is permitted to resume broadcasting. The government announces an end to all prior censorship of the media.

President Ortega announces a unilateral suspension of offensive military operations for the month of October.

Several NED groups send teams to Nicaragua to meet with opposition and design assistance programs. This begins a regular flow of NED officials to Nicaragua and a general expansion of NED programs.

November: Following several meetings with House Speaker Jim Wright, President Ortega announces a new eleven-point proposal for achieving a cease-fire, disarmament, amnesty, and the integration of the contras into civilian life. Nicaragua also agrees to name Cardinal Obando as mediator between the government and the contras. Nicaragua releases 985 political prisoners, 200 of whom are ex–National Guardsmen, and complies with many other provisions of the Esquipulas Accords.

December: U.S. Congress approves an additional $8.1 million for the contras.

1988   *January:* Nicaragua announces its willingness to enter into direct talks with the contras and lifts the five-year state of emergency.

March: A provisional government-contra cease-fire is signed in Sapoá.

Days after the Sapoá Accord is signed, U.S. Congress approves an additional $17.7 million in nonlethal aid for the contras.

May: Contra leader Alfredo César enters into secret negotiations with the government.

July: An opposition demonstration in the town of Nandaime turns violent. Nicaragua expels U.S. ambassador Richard Melton. Washington reciprocates, expelling Nicaraguan ambassador Carlos Tunnerman.

September: Congress approves a special $1 million allocation for NED programs in Nicaragua.

October: With U.S. funding and advice, the anti-Sandinista trade unions unite in the Permanent Congress of Workers. A NED-financed program leads to the founding in Managua of the CEFOJ anti-Sandinista youth organization and the anti-Sandinista Nicaraguan Women's Movement.

1989   *February:* The Costa del Sol summit of Central American presidents calls for the dismantlement of the contra army. Nicaragua agrees to advance the date for elections by eight months, to February 25, 1990.

The Nicaraguan government deepens the economic austerity program.

March: The Nicaraguan government invites the OAS and the United Nations to send observer teams for the electoral process.

April: The Bush administration and the leadership of the U.S. House and the Senate approve the Bipartisan Accord on Nicaragua, which includes the approval of $49.75 million in nonlethal aid to keep the contras intact.

May: The Bush administration renews the economic embargo against Nicaragua.

June: In compliance with the Costa del Sol Accords, Nicaragua's media and electoral laws are modified.

The National Opposition Union is formed by fourteen anti-Sandinista parties.

U.S. Congress approves a special $2 million appropriation for NED programs in Nicaragua.

August: President Ortega and representatives from twenty opposition parties sign an accord that meets most of the electoral demands of the opposition.

The Central American presidents, meeting in Tela, Honduras, approve a plan to have a U.N. force oversee contra demobilization, to be completed by December 5, 1989.

With NED funding and guidance, the anti-Sandinista Via Cívica group is formed in Managua.

September: The UNO selects *La Prensa*'s Violeta Chamorro and the Liberal Party's Virgilio Godoy to lead the opposition ticket in the 1990 presidential elections.

Newsweek reports that the United States has been covertly funneling millions of dollars since April, through the CIA, to help the opposition in the elections.

Up to five thousand contras reinfiltrate Nicaraguan territory from Honduran base camps and renew military hostilities, including "armed electoral propaganda."

October: U.S. Congress approves $9 million in aid for the UNO campaign. In addition, President Bush signs a secret authorization of $6 million for a new CIA program to influence the Nicaraguan vote.

More than 88 percent of Nicaraguans eligible to vote register.

The Bush administration renews the trade embargo against Nicaragua.

November: Following a sharp escalation in contra attacks against civilians, the government suspends its unilateral cease-fire, and the army launches an offensive.

December: A UNO campaign rally in Masatepe degenerates into riot. An FSLN activist is killed.

The United States invades the republic of Panama.

1990

January: A U.S.-based polling firm announces that its latest surveys have increased the FSLN's probable margin of victory for February's elections. The latest poll shows Daniel Ortega with 51 percent of respondents' preference and Violeta Chamorro with 24 percent.

President Bush sends a letter to the chairmen of the Democratic and Republican parties asking that cash donations be made directly to the UNO electoral campaign. Secretary of State James Baker requests that European and Asian governments also provide financial assistance to the UNO.

Jeane Kirkpatrick is the guest of honor at a $5,000-per-couple fundraising dinner in New York for the UNO.

February: The UNO's closing campaign rally draws an estimated sixty thousand people, by far the largest opposition rally since 1979.

Three days later, an estimated four hundred thousand attend the FSLN's closing rally.

The UNO's electoral upset gives Violeta Chamorro 54.7 percent of the vote to Daniel Ortega's 40.8 percent, margins that are closely followed in races for legislative seats.

▪ ACRONYMS ▪

ADF   America's Development Foundation
AFL-CIO   American Federation of Labor and Congress of Industrial
             Organizations
AID   Agency for International Development
AIFLD   American Institute for Free Labor Development
ANDEN   National Association of Nicaraguan Educators (Asociación Nacional
             de Educadores de Nicaragua)
ANN   Nicaragua News Agency (Agencia Nueva Nicaragua)
AP   Associated Press
APF   American Political Foundation
BCN   Central Bank of Nicaragua (Banco Central de Nicaragua)
BOS   Southern Opposition Bloc (Bloque Opositor del Sur)
CAD   Center for Democratic Consultation (Centro para la Asesoria
             Democrática)
CAP   Carlos Andrés Pérez
CAPEL   Center for Electoral Assistance and Promotion (Centro de Asistencia
             y Promoción Electoral)
CDN   Nicaraguan Democratic Coordinating Committee (Coordinadora
             Democrática Nicaragüense)
CEFOJ   Youth Development Center (Centro de Formación Juvenil)
CEI   Center for International Studies (Centro de Estudios Internacionales)
CFD   Center for Democracy
CIA   Central Intelligence Agency
CINCO   Center of Central American Research and Information (Centro de
             Investigaciones e Informaciones Centroamericanas)
CIPE   Center for International Private Enterprise
COHA   Council on Hemispheric Affairs
COSEP   Superior Council of Private Enterprise (Consejo Superior de la
             Empresa Privada)
CPT   Permanent Congress of Workers (Congreso Permanente de
             Trabajadores)
CTCA   Confederation of Central American Workers (Central de Trabajadores
             de Centro Americana)
CTN   Nicaraguan Workers' Confederation (Central de Trabajadores de
             Nicaragua)
CTV   Venezuelan Federation of Workers (Central de Trabajadores de
             Venezuela)
CUS   Confederation of Trade Union Unity (Central de Unidad Sindical)
CYPSA   Construcciones y Proyectos, SA
ECLA   Economic Commission on Latin America

295

EPS	Sandinista People's Army (Ejercito Popular Sandinista)
FDN	Nicaraguan Democratic Force (Fuerza Democrática Nicaragüense)
FMLN	Farabundo Martí National Liberation Front (Frente Farabundo Martí de Liberación Nacional)
FSLN	Sandinista National Liberation Front (Frente Sandinista de Liberación Nacional)
FTUI	Free Trade Union Institute
FUTH	United Federation of Honduran Workers (Federación Unitaria de Trabajadores de Honduras)
FY	fiscal year
GAO	General Accounting Office
GNP	gross national product
ICFTU	International Conference of Free Trade Unions
IEN	Institute for Nicaraguan Studies (Instituto de Estudios Nicaragüenses)
IFES	International Federation of Electoral Systems
IML	Inversiones Martínez López
INSI	Institute for North-South Issues
IPCE	Institute for Electoral Promotion and Training (Instituto para la Promoción y Capacitación Electoral)
IRD	Institute for Religion and Democracy
LASA	Latin American Studies Association
MMN	Nicaraguan Women's Movement (Movimiento de Mujeres Nicaraguenses)
NAB	National Association of Broadcasters
NDI	National Democratic Institute for International Affairs
NED	National Endowment for Democracy
NERP	Nicaraguan Exile Relocation Program
NRI, NRIIA	National Republican Institute for International Affairs
NSC	National Security Council
NSDD	National Security Decision Directive
OAS	Organization of American States
OPD	Office of Public Diplomacy
PL	Public Law
PLI	Independent Liberal Party (Partido Liberal Independiente)
PLN	National Liberation Party (Partido Liberal Nacionalista)
PRI	Italian Republican Party
PRODEMCA	Friends of the Democratic Center in Central America
PSC	Social Christian Party (Partido Social Cristiano)
PSYOPS	psychological operations
PUSC	United Social Christian Party (Partido de Unidad Social Cristiano)
PVO	private voluntary organization
SEC	Supreme Electoral Council (Consejo Supremo Electoral)
UNO	National Opposition Union (Union Nacional Opositora)
UPI	United Press International
USIA	United States Information Agency
WOLA	Washington Office on Latin America

▪ ABOUT THE BOOK AND AUTHOR ▪

A penetrating analysis of the controversial U.S. role in the 1990 Nicaraguan elections—the most closely monitored in history—this book exposes the intervention in the electoral process of a sovereign nation by the Central Intelligence Agency, the Department of State, the National Endowment for Democracy, and private U.S.-based organizations.

Robinson begins by tracing the evolution of U.S. foreign policy in recent decades and reviewing U.S.-Nicaraguan relations since the Carter administration. He then describes specific aspects of the "electoral intervention project," bringing to light the clandestine activities of U.S. officials. Finally, he examines the implications of such an undertaking for U.S. foreign policy and for social change in the Third World in the post–cold war era, arguing that it is a dangerous harbinger of a new interventionism conducted under the pretext of promoting democracy.

Drawing on an extensive array of confidential documents and on interviews with representatives from U.S. and foreign government agencies, private organizations, and anti-Sandinista groups in Nicaragua, the author offers a chilling account of a foreign policy venture that was at the very least duplicitous and quite possibly illegal as well.

William I. Robinson, a former investigative journalist, is a research associate at the Center for International Studies in Managua and a news analyst for the Latin America Data Base at the University of New Mexico. He is a Ph.D. candidate in Latin American studies at the University of New Mexico. Robinson is coauthor, with Kent Norsworthy, of *David and Goliath: The U.S. War Against Nicaragua*, which won the 1987 Gustavus Myers Book Award for outstanding scholarship in the study of human rights and intolerance in the United States.

• INDEX •